THE American Jewish Experience

THE American Jewish Experience

Second Edition

Edited with Introduction and Notes by
JONATHAN D. SARNA

HM
Holmes & Meier
NEW YORK / LONDON

Second edition published in the United States of America 1997 by
Holmes & Meier Publishers, Inc.
160 Broadway
New York, NY 10038

First edition published 1986
by Holmes & Meier

Library of Congress Cataloging in Publication Data

The American Jewish experience.

Bibliography: p.
Includes index.
1. Jews—United States—History. 2. United States—
Ethnic relations. I. Sarna, Jonathan D.—2nd edition
E184.J5A34 1986 973'.04924 86-7579
ISBN 0-8419-1376-5 (pbk.)

Book design by Ellen Foos

Manufactured in the United States of America

CONTENTS

In memory of
Jacob Rader Marcus (1896–1995)
Teacher, mentor, friend

Acknowledgments for the Second Edition

The second edition of this textbook constitutes a substantial revision designed to take advantage of recent scholarship in the field. Nine new pieces have been added, requiring me to delete seven excellent chapters from the earlier edition for which room could no longer be found. I am grateful to numerous friends and colleagues who have used this book over the past decade for making suggestions on how to improve it. Special thanks for specific recommendations are due Penny Schine Gold, Pamela Nadell, Mel Scult, Edward Shapiro, Lance Sussman, Beth Wenger, and Stephen J. Whitfield. I am also indebted to my colleagues and students at Brandeis University for their advice and assistance, and particularly to its President, Jehuda Reinharz, whose support and friendship have made my years at Brandeis as enjoyable as they have been productive.

Professor Jacob R. Marcus, to whom the first edition of this work was dedicated, died on November 14, 1995, just a few months short of his 100th birthday. In his tenth decade of life, he published at least one book a year and maintained an active interest in all aspects of American Jewish history. His legacy is incalculable; all students of the field stand in his debt. May his memory be for an everlasting blessing.

* * *

Acknowledgments for the First Edition

This volume is another in a series of texts issued in conjunction with the Center for the Study of the American Jewish Experience to increase public awareness of American Jewry's past and present, and to enhance the teaching of American Jewish history and life, particularly at the college level. When it began to take shape six years ago, this volume was no more than a collection of photocopied articles prepared for my students at Hebrew Union College–Jewish Institute of Religion in Cincinnati. Several years' worth of student comments and criticisms have improved my selections (not to speak of my ideas), and I am pleased to express my gratitude. I am also grateful to all of my colleagues at the College-Institute, the American Jewish Archives, and the Center for the Study of the American Jewish Experience for their friendship and encouragement, and particularly to Drs. Jacob R. Marcus, Benny Kraut, Alexandra S. Korros, Abraham J. Peck, Murray Friedman, and Rabbi Lance Sussman for specific suggestions and for reading earlier drafts. The late Professor Julius Weinberg generously shared with me his ideas about a reader, and might have been a collaborator on this volume but for his premature death. I am also particularly appreciative to President Alfred Gottschalk of Hebrew Union College–Jewish Institute of Religion for his ongoing support of my research, to Louise Stern whose copyediting of this volume resulted in numerous improvements, to my parents, brother, and sister-in-law for their love, and to Ruth Langer, who came into my life just as this volume was being completed, and who is responsible for the fact that a new chapter in my life is about to begin.

Once again, the Memorial Foundation for Jewish Culture generously underwrote some of the costs connected with this volume. The Foundation's support has done much to further both my personal scholarship and the broader work of the Center for the Study of the American Jewish Experience, and I am pleased to acknowledge its contribution here.

I have dedicated this volume to my teacher, colleague, and friend Dr. Jacob Rader Marcus, now in his ninetieth year. As a rabbi, scholar, teacher, and active participant in American Jewish affairs, Dr. Marcus, the dean of American Jewish historians, has devoted his entire adult life to the American Jewish experience. This dedication represents but a small token of my esteem for all that he has done, and cannot do justice to my deep personal indebtedness to him for favors far too numerous to mention. Happy birthday, Dr. Marcus! May you continue to bless us with your happy returns for a great many years to come.

* * *

Introduction

Jonathan D. Sarna

American Jewish history weds together two great historical traditions: one Jewish, dating back to the Patriarchs, the Prophets, and the rabbis of the Talmud, the other American, dating back to the Indians, Columbus, and the heroes of the Revolution. Bearing the imprint of both, it nevertheless forms a distinctive historical tradition of its own, now more than three centuries old. It is a tradition rooted in ambivalence, for American Jews are sometimes pulled in two different directions at once. Yet it is also unified by a common vision, the quest to be fully a Jew and fully an American, both at the same time. It is closely tied to Jews worldwide, and just as closely tied to Americans of other faiths. It is perpetuated generation after generation by creative men and women, who grapple with the tensions and paradoxes inherent in American Jewish life, and fashion from them what we know as the American Jewish experience—a kaleidoscope of social, religious, cultural, economic, and political elements that makes up the variegated, dynamic world of the American Jew.

In this volume, leading students of American Jewish life explore how the American Jewish experience developed and changed over time, from the colonial period down to the present. Organized chronologically, the selections highlight critical moments and issues in the past that helped to shape the present, as well as broader themes—the central tensions of American Jewish life—that recur like a familiar refrain generation after generation. No effort has been made here to be encyclopedic, to cover every name or every fact. Instead, the articles selectively profile the American Jewish experience, emphasizing essential features and trends, with detailed bibliographies appended for those who wish to fill out the larger picture.

The basic outline of this volume follows the traditional periodization of American Jewish history, and is organized into five parts:

early American Jewry, the "German Period," the era of East European Jewish immigration, the interwar years, and the contemporary period ("the Holocaust and beyond"). This periodization serves to underscore the basic unity of the modern Jewish world, for it shows how currents of American Jewish life have been affected by events taking place far beyond the nation's shores. Within each of the five parts, attention is also paid to the American dimension of American Jewish history. Individual articles make the case both for American influence on American Jewish life and for American Jewish influence on American life, recognizing that American Jews, however strong their links to world Jewry, have still been integrally and intimately involved with the society in which they live.

In dealing with all of these historical periods, events, and influences, it is easy to lose sight of the overarching themes that characterize American Jewish history, distinguishing it both from the historical experience of other Americans, and from that of Jews in other times and places. Generalizations covering the entire American Jewish experience must obviously be approached with caution, and can never be considered definitive. Still, there are four broad characteristic features and five ongoing challenges that seem to me to be critical to any serious effort at understanding what Jewish life in America, especially since the Revolution, has been all about. They are summarized here in brief outline:

Belief in the promise of American life. The promise of American life—freedom, equality, opportunity—was what originally drew most Jews to America's shores, and for many it has proved a continuing inspiration. Jewish immigrants dreamed that in the New World the oppression and poverty that had so often been their lot elsewhere in the Diaspora would disappear. While the more utopian of these expectations were naturally doomed to disappointment, the conviction that America represents the great hope of Jewry, a model for how Jews should be treated all over the world, has remained over the years basically unshaken. Some have looked to America as the anvil upon which a Jewish homeland in Zion should be forged. Others have insisted enthusiastically that America actually is Zion, sharing a common destiny with Jews, and cherishing values that are for all intents and purposes "Judaic."

Faith in pluralism. Cultural pluralism, a model of American society that promotes ethnic diversity as a positive good and rejects calls for Anglo-conformity or "the melting pot" as incompatible with America's democratic ethos, has been widely embraced by American Jews. America's chief exponent of cultural pluralism, Horace Kallen, was himself a conscious Jew, and his experiences as an American Jew helped give rise to his theory. By then, pluralism within the American Jewish community had already been achieved by default; there was no other way that Jews of so many different backgrounds and beliefs could coexist. The realities of American Jewish life—inner diversity on the one hand, minority status on the other—and the community's consistent ideological commitment to pluralism have thus happily reinforced one another. The result has seen this sociological model, born of necessity, transvalued into one of the central axioms of American Jewish life.

Quest for success. Based on a study of Jewish immigrant memoirs, Professor Moses Kligsberg has pointed to the importance of *takhlis*, an orientation toward final outcomes, ends rather than just means, as an important cultural attribute of East European Jewish immigrants. In fact, this orientation, akin to what Max Weber called "The Spirit of Capitalism," is part of a broader success-oriented mentality that has characterized the American Jewish experience as a whole. The quest for success motivated not only Jewish immigrants of every generation, but also their children who struggled to achieve what their parents did not. This goes far to explain American Jews' high rate of geographic and social mobility, their concentration in commercial and financial centers, particularly large, rapidly developing urban areas, and their willingness to venture into new frontiers, whether as peddlers in the West, as scientists in new fields of research, or as entrepreneurs venturing into newly emerging industries. Not that vaulting ambition was ever a Jewish monopoly in America; the "Horatio Alger" mentality extends far more widely. The characteristic, however, has in Jewish circles been particularly pronounced—with results that by any standard of measurement have been utterly remarkable.

Commitment to Jewish survival. As a small minority, never reaching even 4 percent of the total population, Jews in America have always had to work at survival: losses through conversion, assimilation, and intermarriage have been an ever-present threat. Spurred by this challenge, and motivated also by traditional religious values, American Jews from the colonial period onward have labored to create for themselves a self-supporting Jewish community: a network of individuals and institutions working together as a unit for the sake of Jewish fellowship, to provide for Jewish education and culture, to care for Jews in need, and to fulfill other functions as required in an effort to ensure the well-being of its members and the continuity of American Jewish life from one generation to the next. Looking beyond their own community, American Jews have also concerned themselves with world Jewry. Anti-Jewish outbreaks overseas, natural disasters affecting Jews, calls to relieve Jewish communities in need, and most especially appeals from Jews in the Holy Land have traditionally met with sympathetic American Jewish responses, based on the principle that "all Israel is responsible for one another." As Jews have done throughout their long history in the Diaspora, American Jews have linked their own survival as a Jewish community to the survival of Jews elsewhere, and particularly (since 1948) to the State of Israel. This commitment, maintained through the generations, is summed up in a three-word slogan popularized by the United Jewish Appeal—"We Are One!"

If these characteristic features of American Jewish life suggest a certain unwavering continuity over three centuries, the five challenges that have faced American Jews are of a different order. They have been a source of ongoing tension, for they pit basic values against one another, and sometimes demand that excruciatingly difficult choices be made. Fundamentally, all of these challenges are irresolvable, for they spring from dilemmas inherent in the very nature of the American Jewish experience itself. Yet, the existence of these challenges has in the final analysis also proved salutary, for confronting them has enormously enriched the lives of American Jews, and has provided an important stimulus for individual and communal creativity.

1. Assimilation-Identity Probably the foremost challenge of American Jewish life, this tension pits the desire to become American and to conform to American norms against the fear that Jews by conforming too much will cease to be distinctive and soon disappear. The problem is not unique to Jews; themes such as "adaptation vs. retention" and "accommodation vs. resistance" characterize all minority group history in America. In the case of Jews, however, the dilemma has been compounded, for they form at one and the same time both a minority ethnic group ("the Jewish people") and a minority religion ("Judaism")—a fact that explains why, among Jews, assimilation has so often been linked to apostasy. Jewish tradition and history have been trotted out to legitimate a whole range of positions on this issue—everything from massive concessions to American ways, justified by "the law of the land," the "needs of the hour," and the virtues of "peaceful neighborly relations," to utter resistance to any form of accommodation, even with regard to dress, for fear of "following in the ways of the Gentiles." Since American Jewish leaders have been as divided as their followers in deciding what concessions to the majority culture American Jews should and should not make, answers have spanned the spectrum. None has ever proved totally satisfactory.

2. Tradition-Change While related to the problem of assimilation and identity, this historical challenge has been solely confined to the realm of religion. The spectrum here ranges from those who have insisted that tradition unites world Jewry, and that *any* changes are thus divisive and potentially disastrous (where will they end?), to those who have considered changes ("reforms") of one sort or another essential to Jewish survival, particularly given the number of Jews estranged from their religious heritage. All involved in this debate have been able to legitimate their positions on the basis of what they see as best for American Judaism. But the question of where (if at all) the demands of tradition and change must compromise has always defied solution. The challenge has been confronted anew every time another religious reform has been suggested—beginning early on in the nineteenth century with proposals to introduce choral singing and vernacular discourses into the synagogue, and continuing all the way down to contemporary proposals designed to alter the traditional place of women in synagogue life.

3. Unity-Diversity Just as general American life has long been challenged by disputes that pit the interests of the national government against those of the individual states, so too American Jewish life has seen a pervasive tension between the interests of the Jewish community at large and those of various subcommunities, defined by region, socioeconomic background, religious orientation, or political ideology. The problem of the "one" and the "many" has been addressed throughout recorded history by covenants and federative systems, and at an organizational level this has been the tendency in American Jewish life as well. But the basic problem persists. On the one hand, American Jews have appreciated the benefits that unity brings in its wake, and have pledged their firm allegiance to the traditional Jewish value of *ahavat yisrael,* the expression of solidarity with fellow Jews of every sort. On the other hand, the innate diversity of Jewish life, the fact that there are many kinds of Jews and many ways to be Jewish, has encouraged a healthy respect for multiformity.

4. Majority rule-Minority rights. Woven into the fabric of American life, this tension also lies at the heart of American Jewry's historic relationship to the secular polity. On a host of domestic policy questions, especially those affecting church-state relations, American Jews have been forced to choose: should they subordinate American Jewish concerns to the larger will of the Christian majority, or should they demand that the wishes of the majority be cast aside so as to protect the Constitutional rights of the minority? Translated into concrete terms, this issue has, over the years, involved Jews in debates over such things as Sunday blue laws, the place of religion in the nation's schools, and the public observance of Christmas. Foreign policy questions have not generated the same degree of controversy, but have demanded an equally difficult choice: should Jews subordinate themselves to the majority's international affairs agenda, or should they create a minority agenda of their own, highlighting issues like the protection of persecuted Jews around the world, and support for the State of Israel? The challenge has always been to find some means of preserving Jewish rights and interests without unduly offending majority sensitivities—a goal which, historically speaking, has proved much easier said than done.

5. Historical experience-American exceptionalism Is America different? This is, perhaps, the most vexing challenge that American Jews have faced. It pits their faith that America is somehow an exception, not subject to the same turnabouts that have so afflicted Jews elsewhere, against their bitter historical experience everywhere in the Diaspora, even in countries like Spain and Germany where they also felt fully at home—until disaster struck. Evidence can be adduced on both sides. One side points menacingly to instances of vicious anti-Semitism scattered throughout the course of American history, warns that dangerous demagogues stand for election in America and often garner unexpected support, and cautions that prophecy is a very inexact science, the past being by no means a reliable barometer of what the future holds. The other side counters that America nonetheless *is* different, especially when compared to the experience of Jews in Europe. In America, they note, Jews never needed to be emancipated, and have therefore never worried about having their emancipation revoked. The nation's central documents guarantee Jews religious freedom, and its first president conferred upon them his blessing. Jews are only one of many persecuted minorities in America; national hatreds have as a result been varied and diffused. There has been in America a long-standing liberal religious tradition ("the great tradition of the American churches") that includes Judaism among the nation's great faiths, and advocates, just as Jews do, religious freedom and diversity, church-state separation, denominationalism, and voluntarism. Finally, proponents of this view point out that the two-party system, with close elections the rule and power widely diffused, makes anti-Jewish laws difficult to effect. Politicians have learned from experience that broadly based appeals aimed at all major blocs of voters prove far more successful at the polls than appeals to narrow provincialism or bigotry.

Whatever the future course of American Jewry proves to be, whether it goes down as the "great exception" in Jewish history or not, this much at least seems certain: that the future will be fashioned from the remains of the past. The characteristic features and ongoing challenges that have for so long helped to define American Jewish life, the events that have shaped it, the two great historical traditions drawn together within it—all these and more form the collective memory of American Jews, a repository of past experience now more than three hundred years in the making. What will become of that memory? What will American Jews learn from it? What will others derive from it?

Prophecy, Jewish tradition warns, is in our day given over to fools.

THE
American Jewish Experience

PART ONE

THE AMERICAN JEWISH COMMUNITY TAKES SHAPE

In 1654, twenty-three Jews from Recife, Brazil, sailed into the port of New Amsterdam, seeking refuge from the Portuguese. This flight to freedom marks the traditional beginning of American Jewish history. But it took many decades before a viable Jewish community began to take shape. In New York (formerly New Amsterdam), and later in other port cities where Jews congregated, synagogues were gradually established to meet communal needs, particularly in the areas of worship, education, and charity. Jews also fought their first battles for civil and religious rights. For the most part, however, early American Jews concerned themselves with the basics of making a living. As merchants and traders, they played a small but important role in the expanding American economy.

The articles in this section show how the American Jewish community developed and changed during three distinct periods in American history: the Colonial period, the era of the American Revolution, and the early national period. During these roughly 175 years many of the basic dynamics of American Jewish life were set—shaped by the conditions of American life. Three challenges faced by early American Jews particularly stand out: first, how to meld utterly diverse Jews, immigrants from different countries with different traditions, into a cohesive community supported on a voluntary basis alone; second, how to establish and safeguard the right of Jews to differ from the Christian majority without prejudice; third, how to preserve Jewish distinctiveness in an open society where Jews and non-Jews could mix freely. These challenges met with no easy solutions. Instead, they revealed early some of the basic tensions underlying American Jewish life—tensions between unity and diversity, majority rule and minority rights, and, most important of all, between identity preservation and the assimilation of alien ways.

CHAPTER 1

Jews formed only a minute element in Colonial America, not more than one-tenth of 1 percent of the population. Nevertheless, they deserve attention, for as Jacob R. Marcus points out in this essay, a summary of his three-volume work on the same subject, Colonial American Jews established patterns that shaped and characterized the lives of those American Jews who came later. Concentrated in urban centers and in largely mercantile occupations, intensely mobile, eager to better themselves economically, intent on achieving social, political, and religious equality without having to sacrifice Jewish traditions, Colonial American Jews were, from the start, distinctive enough from other Americans to be noticeable, and yet at the same time similar enough to their neighbors to allow for free interaction. Jews did face some restrictions and intolerance in the colonies—hardly surprising in a world that still viewed religious nonconformity of all sorts as a threat to social order. But in retrospect, mistreatment of Jews during this period seems less important than the rights Jews won in law, and the privileges frequently extended to them in fact. Compared with the Jewish situation in most of Europe, or even with the restrictions faced by Catholics, not to speak of the plight of Blacks in the colonies, Jews in the New World had much to be thankful for. Unsurprisingly, their numbers steadily increased.

In explaining Colonial American Jewish History, Marcus, taking his cue from the great American historian Frederick Jackson Turner, stresses the impact of the frontier: "If to be a frontiersman is to be a man who dares to hazard, then the Jews as a whole are America's frontiersmen par excellence." According to this view, Western American pioneers and Colonial American Jews shared many of the same qualities and attributes—"that buoyancy and exuberance which comes with freedom"—for both faced similar conditions. Other historians have pointed to the economic basis of Colonial America as the prime determinant of Jewish life in the period. Since, under the mercantile system, the colonies were supposed primarily to enrich the mother country, it made good economic sense to treat Jews well and encourage them to prosper. Colonies that admitted Jews frequently did so explicitly on these grounds. Yet another factor affecting conditions of Jewish life was the social character of Colonial American cities. Urban centers, filled with heterogeneous immigrant populations—peoples of different backgrounds and different religions—had to encourage a tolerant live-and-let-live attitude to prevent civil strife. This situation proved beneficial indeed to Jews, not only in the Colonial era but later as well.

The American Colonial Jew: A Study in Acculturation

Jacob R. Marcus

"Jews"—people of Jewish origin—had been settling in the Western hemisphere since at least the early 1500s. The very first Marranos came with Columbus, and in less than a century they had spread throughout the Caribbean and found their way into Mexico (New Spain) and South America, but the Inquisition made it impossible for them to establish viable communities. It was not until the mid-1600s that the first overt Jewish settlements sprang up in the New World—in Dutch Brazil and Surinam, on Curaçao, and on English Barbados and Jamaica. These were soon to become large and cultured metropolitan communities, for the Caribbean basin was at the time far more attractive and more populous than the mainland provinces to the north. The most important American Jewries of the eighteenth century were to develop in Surinam and in the Islands.

When the Portuguese recaptured Brazil, a handful of Dutch Jews, fleeing north, found refuge in the Dutch trading colony of New Amsterdam, soon to become English New York. Their arrival on the Hudson River in 1654 represents the beginning of North American Jewish life. These twenty-three Jewish "Pilgrim Fathers" were followed during the next hundred years by immigrants from the Islands and from Spain, Portugal, France, Holland, Germany, and England. By 1730, Jews of Central European origin outnumbered their Iberian coreligionists in North America. The first settlers in the 1600s were characteristically traders who had little desire to remain, but a permanent community had been established by the turn of the century. The Jewish businessmen married, settled down, and began to raise families. Throughout the Colonial period, however, American Jewry would remain an essentially immigrant group. Up to the Revolution, some 70 percent of the presidents of the New York synagogue were foreign-born, and the men who assumed leadership of Colonial American Jewish life were, with one notable exception, all immigrants. Many of the émigrés were competent merchandisers. Some of them had distinguished rabbinical ancestors; a few were unassorted misfits. The community's growth is reflected in the fact that there were about 250 Jews on the continent by the year 1700, whereas, by 1776, there were about 2,500. Jews never formed more than one-tenth of 1 percent of the Colonial population.

What prompted Jewish newcomers to set sail across the Atlantic? Was it a quest for religious freedom? The fact is that even the Dutch exiles from Brazil and the Spanish-Portuguese émigrés of converso ancestry who fled the Iberian Peninsula were not drawn to North American shores primarily for the sake of conscience; all of them could have found a haven in other lands, and if they came here, it was more often than not to better themselves economically. Nearly all of them sought, in addition, a measure of anonymity, an avoidance of public notice, for without exception they came from lands which still imposed disabilities on Jews and still enforced anti-Jewish laws of a medieval character. It is understood, of course, that these men would not have come to these shores if they had not been allowed to practice their faith. The immigrants took it for granted that they would be permitted to establish a community of their own.

Where did they settle? Some, to be sure, were found in the hinterland, but even they had trickled into the backcountry through the seacoast towns. Most Jews stayed well below the piedmont, in the tidewater areas. New Amsterdam–New York was the first and chief Jewish center, but only a short generation after the Brazilians arrived, a small settlement took shape at Newport, in the 1680s at the latest. That Rhode Island community did not last even a decade, however, and it was not until the 1740s that the New Yorkers, fanning out once again, reestablished Jewish life in Newport. Jewish newcomers, moving north, rarely bypassed the Rhode Island city; they tended to ignore Boston; apparently one center in New England sufficed them. That same decade of the 1740s saw the New Yorkers, in their southward trek, lay the foundations for a community at Philadelphia. Independently of New York, Charleston Jewry also established itself in the 1740s. Savannah, which had sheltered a substantial number of Jewish colonists in the 1730s, had already lost her first Jewish group by 1740, but, like Newport, would ultimately rebuild a durable Jewish settlement on the dead hopes of earlier émigrés. After the French and Indian War, New Yorkers moved up the Hudson and Lake Champlain to found a new congregation in Montreal.

It is obvious that nowhere in the fourteen provinces were Jews qua Jews ever openly denied the right to strike roots. By 1740, they were allowed the exercise of virtually every economic immunity and privilege. Not that such rights were obtained without a struggle! The Dutch in New Amsterdam, under the medieval-minded Stuyvesant, sought to deny them nearly all rights; yet it took no more than three years for them to wrest from the governor and his superiors in the Dutch West India Company the right to remain, to trade, to own land, and to hold worship services in private. These rights were extended under English rule, so that, even before the coming of the new century, England had, however reluctantly, accorded her American Jewish subjects full civil equality. In 1740, an imperial naturalization law confirmed the status of the Jew and offered him almost unlimited economic opportunity in the Empire as a whole as well as in the American provinces themselves.

Civil equality was not, of course, political equality. Jews in some colonies were certainly allowed the vote on a provincial and a local level, but they were nowhere permitted to hold honorific office. Such office was limited to Protestant Christians, especially those associated with the dominant or established church in each colony. On the whole, prior to the 1760s, the American Jew eschewed politics. Fourteen hundred years of Christian-imposed disabilities had taught him that political plums like lucrative offices were not within his reach, but this disability does not appear to have disturbed him before 1765. After all, the constant wars, the country's expanding economy, and the penetration of the West enabled the Jewish businessman to make a good living; he was simply too busy building an estate for himself and his family to concern himself with the fact that political appointments were denied him.

Still, when he was offered important communal committee assignments, he would seem to have gladly accepted them. Almost every town had some Jewish merchants of substance and wealth, and in the English world of mercantilism, the Jewish businessman, even if he could not sit in the Assembly, on the bench, or in the provincial council, was undeniably a part of the power structure. In Continental Europe, he could not have aspired to authority in the general community, for Jewry as an ethnic corporation was segregated by tradition and by the terms of separatist and divisive *privilegia*. The Colonial Jew, however, followed the developing pattern of English Jewry; he aspired to enter the general society within the ambit of a common unitary political system. He was not averse to office, to its opportunities and its responsibilities, nor was he indifferent to the improvement of his status. Ultimately the Jew here hoped to become one, politically at least, with the emerging American people and to be accepted as a full fellow citizen, but he was willing to bide his time. And his hopes achieved fulfillment, if as yet mainly on the federal level, in 1789.

The Jew of eighteenth-century America found his greatest opportunity in the world of commerce. Here, much more so than on the Continent, or even in England, he was almost exclusively a shopkeeper. To be sure, there were occasional dirt farmers in the northern provinces, and even an aristocratic planter on the South Carolina frontier, but farming was not the métier of these immigrants. Georgia Jewish merchants might hold good-sized ranches in the backcountry, and craftsmen, especially silversmiths, might be found in nearly every province, but the typical Jew was a businessman who owned a small shop. There he doled out credit to the customers who came to him for hardware, hard liquor, and dry goods. The successful shopkeeper became a merchant, and large-scale Jewish storekeepers were established even in the villages of Canada and as far west as Lancaster, Pennsylvania. The Montreal businessmen were primarily fur entrepreneurs, and Lancaster's outstanding merchant was well known as a supplier for the traders on the Ohio.

The important Jews in commerce were the tidewater merchant-shippers of Newport, New York, and Philadelphia. They exchanged American foods and forest products in Europe and the West Indies for consumer goods and for Caribbean staples like molasses, rum, sugar, and dyewoods. Sometimes, like the Jew who was Newport's commercial tycoon, they would participate in the African slave trade. Jewish merchant-shippers of that day were also industrialists, arranging through the put-out system for the manufacture of ships and barrels, the distillation of rum, the catching and processing of fish and whales, and the production of kosher and unkosher victuals for export. Above all, they were in the candle business. Indeed, it is no exaggeration to say that they constituted an important national factor in the manufacture of candles. Jews, however, were notably absent from the iron and tobacco industries, and though they included in their ranks substantial merchant-shippers, the total volume of their business, while it far exceeded their proportion to the population, was hardly determining in any field. The one exception, it might be said, was army supply: The most powerful Jewish commercial clan of the third quarter of the century was an Anglo-American family of army purveyors which reached its zenith during the French and Indian War. Like its Jewish counterparts in Europe, this clan carried on business operations reaching, at the very least, into the hundreds of thousands, if not millions, of pounds.

It may be fairly maintained that all but an infinitesimal number of North American Jews were to be included in a broadly conceived middle class. Some Jewish merchants were even wealthy by contemporary standards; practically none of the Jews were paupers, very few were proletarians, and a substantial number were lower-middle-class petit bourgeois shopkeepers and middle-class storekeepers and merchants. There were very few Jews who did not enjoy a degree of comfort; most of them made a "good living" and survived economically, though severe business reverses were by no means uncommon among them at some time or other.

The Colonial American Jewish community could be accurately described as a socioreligious group—or even a religiosocial group—whose members had grown up, for the most part, in the small towns of preindustrial Europe. Though they stopped to make no sharp distinctions between the religious and the secular, their orientation was definitely religious, and they were typically synagoguegoers. On their arrival here, they had immediately undertaken to set up de facto communities whose hub was, in every case, the house of worship. It was in a literal sense a meetinghouse. All newcomers were expected to join, to become paying members, or at least to attend the important services. Local Jewry was granted no state authority to compel membership, but social pressure generally saw to it that affiliation would be practically compulsory.

Even though religious devotions were undoubtedly held in every Jewish settlement as soon as the requisite quorum of ten adult males thirteen years of age or older could be mustered, the synagogue was not actually the first institution to be established. The first formal act was usually the acquisition of a plot of ground for a cemetery. Then came the synagogue. First the worshippers would rent a room, then a house; then they would purchase a building, and finally, they would erect a synagogue of their own. The synagogue-communal organization was of the simplest type, featuring a president, a small board, and at times a treasurer. Frequently the overburdened chief executive served also as secretary and treasurer; the major administrative duties were his. No rabbis—that is, no ordained, learned, professional officiants—were employed in North America prior to the second quarter of the nineteenth century. Colonial Jewry had no need for the services of experts to teach rabbinic lore to advanced students, or to sit as judges to adjudicate complex commercial disputes and matters touching on marriage, divorce, and estates. The chief salaried—or volunteer—officiant in every house of worship was the cantor, who chanted the liturgy. His ministrations were complemented by those of the shohet, who slaughtered food animals ritually, and the beadle, who served as the omnibus factotum for the board. These functionaries were certainly not overpaid, and all of them engaged in some form of gainful enterprise, on the side, to augment their incomes.

The liturgy employed by all the Colonial conventicles was the Sephardic or Spanish-Portuguese. Despite the fact that prerevolutionary American Jewry was overwhelmingly Ashkenazic (German-Polish) in ethnic origin, the Sephardic style had become the traditional American rite. Services were almost always held on the Sabbath and on all the holidays, though the difficulty of assembling ten busy adults often made it impossible to organize daily services. Ceremonial and ritual observance was expected of all Jews, even of those who lived in the backcountry, and the communal leaders attempted to exact conformity by threatening ecclesiastical punishments. The board was—or at least attempted to be—an authoritative body exercising discipline in religious matters over every confessing Jew in the region, but, unlike some of the Protestant sects, there was no effort to exercise surveillance in business concerns or even in the area of personal morals.

In the extant budgets of the country's chief synagogue, the largest items were salaries, pensions, and relief for the poor. It is true that congregants squabbled among themselves, often bitterly and vindictively, but generous provision was nearly always made for the needy and the impoverished. The

Jews took care of their own. Itinerants from the distant islands were "dispatched" back home at communal expense; Palestinian visitors were generously entertained and given gifts; and aspiring petitioners were granted modest loans to set them up in business. The sick received medical care, nursing, and hospitalization; the old were pensioned, and all the dead were buried at the expense of the community or for a purely nominal fee. Most Protestant groups also attempted to take care of their poor. Whether the Jews did more for their people than, for instance, Protestant sectarians like the Quakers, is difficult to determine, though a comparative study of budgets might answer this question.

Only to a limited degree was education associated with charity. Since the local community always included members who lacked the means to educate their children, the synagogal authorities never failed to provide a subsidized teacher for the children of the poor. Actually, however, the responsibility for providing instruction was the obligation of the head of the household; it was not a communal responsibility. Beyond question there had been private Hebrew instructors in New York City ever since the seventeenth century, and a communal Hebrew school was organized during the 1730s, at the latest, with all who had means paying tuition. Not all the children in the community had resort to the congregational school. Even in New York City—and this was certainly true of all the other Jewish communites as well—secular education was also acquired in private schools or through tutors.

The curriculum of the congregational school probably included the reading and translation of the prayer book and the Pentateuch, and at most some familiarity with the classical biblical commentaries. By the 1750s, this Hebrew school had become an all-day "publick school" teaching Spanish and the three "R's"—what we might call a "parochial" school. The language of instruction was English. The quality of the teaching in Hebrew was probably not too bad, for the first American-trained cantor is known to have had the capacity to consult the more elementary Hebrew codes. We have no way to gauge the quality of the instruction in "English reading, writing, and cyphering," but, since all Jewish children, even the humblest among them, were prepared for some form of business life, it may be assumed that the training the young natives acquired was adequate. Male immigrants with very few exceptions were literate. They could read English, write it phonetically at least, and keep a set of books. All were bilingual, for they knew English and Yiddish or German, or English and Spanish or Portuguese. A few had a third language at their command—Dutch, for instance—and some, if not many, were multilingual.

Exceedingly few young people were tempted to attend the country's colleges, although secondary schools were open to them in Rhode Island, New York, and Pennsylvania. Most Colonial Jews were not interested in the liberal arts as such, and professional training in law and medicine was not sought. The practice of medicine was not particularly lucrative, while lawyers were in bad repute throughout much of this period, and, if English precedent was determining, Jews would not have been permitted to practice in the courts. Prior to 1776, the American Jew wrote nothing in English worth preserving as a literary monument. The typical Colonial synagoguegoer, an immigrant, was too busy learning the language and making a living to achieve any facility or distinction in English letters; he could make no contribution even to the Jewish, let alone American, literary arts.

What did their neighbors think of the Jews? Every Christian who came to these shores brought with him "invisible baggage": his European and pagan traditions going back for millennia. The West India Company in New Amsterdam never hid its distaste for Jews; the New York rabble, headed by a "gentleman," attacked a Jewish funeral cortege on one occasion, and the desecration of cemeteries was not uncommon. "Jew" was still a dirty word, and it was hardly rare to see the Jews denigrated as such in the press. A distinguished lawyer speaking in the New York General Assembly did not find it too difficult to rouse his fellow-members against the Jews as a people guilty of the great crime of the Crucifixion.

Rejection does not tell the whole story, however, and one always does well to bear in mind that, if the Jewish businessman prospered in this land, it was because the Gentiles patronized him. Jews did not make a living by taking in each other's washing. There can be no question that the Jews here found more acceptance than in any other land in the world. Old-World traditions of Judeophobia were attenuated here. The Christian drama of salvation—a drama in which the Jew played the villain—was not dominant in molding public opinion in the colonies, for America offered everyone opportunity enough; there was no need to envy the Jew. In a society of Dunkers, Congregationalists, Moravian Brethren, Baptists, Christian Sabbatarians, Catholics, Methodists, Anglicans, Presbyterians (Old Side and New Side), Lutherans, Dutch Reformed, German Reformed, Mennonites, Schwenkfelders, a society of English, Scottish, Irish, German, Dutch, Welsh, Swiss, and Swedish settlers—not to mention Negroes and Indians—the Jew did not stand out too conspicuously. Christians in the villages and towns of the country discovered, sometimes to their dismay, that the Jews did not wear horns and that, if they had devil's tails and cloven feet, these were certainly not visible. The Christian who learned to know Mr. Judah, or Mr. Josephson, or Mr. Hays, or Mr. Gratz found that, after all, he was not so different, and the Jew was accepted. If he became a son-in-law, he was welcomed; he was a fine fellow.

The Jew was accepted, but did he accept America? What was this man like? What was happening to him on this side of the Atlantic? Was he different here? What had he gained for himself? What did he do for others, for this country that generously gave him a haven and a new home?

Apparently he was still the same "eternal" Jew, still the European traditionalist, equally untouched by deism and by Protestant religiosity, whether of the decorous Anglican kind or of the less conventional emotionalism of the Great Awakening. Yet he was different, if only because he found himself in a different milieu, and this was bound to influence and change him. It was not simply that, instead of speaking Yiddish or a bad German, he now spoke fractured English and dressed like any middle-class Englishman. This young American Jewish community of which he was a loyal and exuberant member shaped itself on a "frontier" far removed from the European *Judengasse* and its age-old classical traditions. The New World challenged his Old World. In order to survive here, the Jew found it expedient to extemporize, to compromise, and all this, in the final analysis, spelt a form of emancipation. Europe had never offered him more than a second-class citizenship; here in America, however, he encountered less paternalism and a more sympathetic government. Here, after 1700, he had full civil liberties and even a degree of civic recognition. By 1775, he had come very close to achieving first-class citizenship.

America connoted economic opportunity, and this was of paramount importance: "Bread to eat and a garment to wear." He was no longer a peddler, a petty trader, a cattle dealer; he was now a shopkeeper, even a merchant. If only because of the "wealth" he was often enough enabled to accumulate in America, he became something of a community figure. Here he could rise on the social ladder; he could improve his status and even enter into the world of Anglo-Saxon education and culture. Here the Jewish heritage reached out to absorb a new language and new ideals: "democracy," "natural freedom," "dictates of humanity," "constitutional trial by jury," "to live free or not at all," "rights, liberties and immunities." He had acquired a new vocabulary.

When the Jew left Europe, he left behind him there—physically at least—the all-pervasive authority of the Jewish community. Ultimately, his departure from the European home was to effect a measure of spiritual distance as well. If Jewish orthodoxy in its most classical form was to be found then in Poland, the Jews of these colonies were as remote from it physically as a sailing vessel could carry them. America signified the ultimate frontier of Jewish life. Religious controls were inevitably relaxed here. There was much less concern about observance and ritual. The individual was far freer to do as he pleased. He could if he wished—and most commonly he did wish—pay much less attention to the rabbinic learning which, for a thousand years, had been the leitmotif of European Jewish life. The new American Jew, who was beginning to emerge on the Colonial scene, much preferred to be a successful merchant than a talmudic scholar. Yet this very Jew was not estranged from his faith, and the communities that studded the North American coast from Montreal to Savannah are eloquent testimony to his determination not to abandon his heritage.

The typical Colonial Jew was true to his heritage because he was not pressed to be untrue to it. There was no overwhelming, monochromatic culture here to force itself upon him. There was no national ethos to exact conformity of him. If he acculturated, it was by his own choice. Free here to express his religious loyalties, since the outside world imposed no religious limitations upon him and extorted no price of emancipation, he assimilated almost unwittingly and without hesitation. Slowly but surely he sloughed off Europe. He felt completely at home here. The Jewish immigrant—and this was very probably not characteristic of him alone—manifested an aptitude for acculturation and even for total integration. Bear in mind that he had come originally from a Portuguese city, a German *Dorf*, or a Polish hamlet; yet, when he appeared as an urban businessman, he was already an urbane American. He had speedily become acquainted with English amenities and often had even acquired an Anglo-Saxon name. If he finally settled in a Colonial village, it was usually only a matter of time before he married a Christian and permitted his wife to rear his children as she thought fit. But conversion to Judaism, formal or informal on the part of the woman, might also occur, though with much less frequency. In a way, it is astounding how easy it was for many an observant European Jew to forswear in a few years nearly twenty-seven centuries of hallowed tradition—seemingly without a struggle.

The Jew *was* different here. He had left the "ghetto" to become a pioneer on the American "frontier," a frontier which according to Frederick Jackson Turner gave its people

> coarseness and strength combined with acuteness and inquisitiveness; that practical, inventive turn of mind, quick to find expedients; that masterful grasp of material things, lacking in the artistic but powerful to effect great ends; that restless, nervous energy; that dominant individualism, working for good and for evil, and withal that buoyancy and exuberance which comes with freedom.

For Turner, the frontier that effected these changes in the American psyche was the "Great West." Yet a moment's reflection will remind the student that these enumerated characteristics bespeak the successful American businessman, Jew or Christian. Think of Thomas Hancock! Certainly for the professing Jew—who was never to become a backwoods hunter or an Indian fighter—all of America was a frontier. If to be a frontiersman is to be a man who dares to hazard, then the Jews as a whole are America's urban frontiersmen par excellence. As a group, they are, more than others, a "nation of shopkeepers," gambling with their future. (Actually, of course, the Diaspora Jew had always lived as a marginal man on the "cutting edge," where he had to struggle for survival juridically, commercially, and spiritually.) The Western frontier is in no sense important for the development of the American Jew; the Atlantic frontier is all important. It was determinative in changing him. It gave him his greatest opportunity in centuries to give free play to those traits that he had already brought with him and which had long been characteristic of him.

For the Jew, the style of life was different here. He learned to dispense with Slavic obsequiousness and Germanic servility. There was no need for him here to be submissive. Here he could be assertive—if that was his nature. If he possessed physical courage, America offered him ample opportunity to manifest it. He learned not to be easily cowed. Is there any doubt that it required moral courage to cross the broad ocean and to traverse the lofty mountains and the dark forests to distant Michilimackinac or the Forks of the Ohio? For the first time in centuries, the Jew felt free. He was no longer faced with the problem of treading softly in the presence of a virulent Judeophobia. It may have been hard for him, but he began to trust his Christian neighbors; he became less suspicious of them. They were his customers; often enough they were his partners in business ventures, and he learned to believe in them, for there is no intimacy greater than that of two men who are prepared to share profits and losses.

The Jew of the European village who could only dream of a great future had the chance here to prove his mettle. He could be venturesome, daring, and enterprising. Here there was an open road for the man of ambition. It was not ludicrous here to project gargantuan schemes. No one looked askance at the Christian-Jewish consortium which proposed to establish a western colony of millions upon millions of acres. America was one land where, more than any other, the Jew could fulfill his inmost self by attempting whatever career he wished. Here he could be an individual. With opportunity and achievement and the regard of others came self-respect and dignity. The Jewish merchant was conscious of his own works; he knew what he was doing for the land and the people—and it was good in his eyes. He was giving and getting. He had the pride of a merchant, and he expected recognition, not only socially, but in rights and privileges.

It is undeniable: The American Jewish businessman *was* more than a European who dressed and spoke like an Anglo-Saxon. His children, too, were different. The father may have been a Spaniard or a Pole or a native Briton, but the children through intramarriage with Jews of other backgrounds were something new. This was a Jewish melting pot that fused together the Jews of half of Europe's lands to produce a new ethnic type—an "American" Jew. This American Jew "in becoming" struck a balance between his European religiocultural loyalties and his emotional identification with the spirit of this land. In Europe, he had been an outsider; in this land, he blended with the others. Here there were a dozen different breeds and stocks pouring into one another to become one in a common environment with common interests. This man was among that dozen, and though he would never have admitted it, he was becoming less of a Jew and more of an American.

In 1711, a number of New York's Jewish businessmen generously contributed to the building of an Anglican church; some fifty years later, the Jews of Savannah were active in a nondenominational charitable society. Such participation by Jews in American philanthropy can take on meaning only if we remember that in most European lands at that time the Jew was still held in disdain and that in some countries he was even outlawed and in danger of massacre. But here in the colonies, he believed, he knew, that he was part of the body politic. It is true that he had his own way of life, but, unlike others, particularly some of the Germans, he never locked himself behind the walls of a cultural enclave. Of course, he was fully conscious of the fact that he was not yet a first-class citizen. He realized it only too well, but his resentment never impelled him to withdraw into himself. He was very much moved by the political unrest of his neighbors and shared their hopes. Like all dissenters and all who labored under legal disabilities, he was not satisfied with the status quo; he sought more rights and more opportunities. A large measure of freedom had already been accorded him, but the Revolutionary spirit of the 1760s unleashed in him the desire for an even larger measure. It was this hope that prompted Jews to throw in their lot with the Whigs. By 1775, even many of the most recent newcomers thought of themselves as Americans, and "as a man thinketh in his heart, so is he."

By 1776, the typical Jew in this land was an urban shopkeeper of German provenance in the process of blotting out his German ethnic past. Yet he was firmly, proudly, and nostalgically rooted in his European religious traditions. He spoke English by preference, had regard for Anglo-Saxon culture, and enjoyed the same civil rights as did his Christian neighbors. Socially, he was a cut above the masses, the farmers and the mechanics, for he was a shopkeeper or merchant. As such, he expected—and he received—a measure of deference.

What did this man achieve for himself? He moved Europe across the Atlantic, no mean achievement. Synagogues, schools, charities, a "community" were transferred here, nailed down and fastened, firm and viable and visible enough to attract hundreds and thousands of others who never would have come to a "waste howling wilderness" where there were no Jewish institutions. A dozen families in seventeenth-century New York laid the foundations for a twentieth-century community of nearly six million Jews. Colonial Jewry wrote the pattern of acculturation that made it possible for the Jew to remain a Jew and to become an American. The pioneers of the eighteenth century succeeded in making an exemplary transition from a still medieval European Jewish life to the new American world of modernism and personal freedom.

What did this man achieve for the land? Not that this Jew was conscious of it, but together with all dissenters—and every American denomination suffered disabilities in one or another of the provinces—he helped teach his neighbor religious tolerance. The fruit of this tolerance was respect for the personality of the individual. The prerevolutionary Jew made no contribution to the literature of the colonies; he cleared no forests and ploughed no furrow—yet he, too, built the land. He, as much as any other, made American life more comfortable through the necessities and luxuries which he provided. It is true that the trader needed his customers, but it is equally true that neither city craftsmen nor toiling rustics could exist without him. It is true, too, that in a literal numerical sense the Jew was one man in a thousand, but, in an economy where an overwhelming majority of all who labored made their living on the soil, it is difficult to overstress the importance of the shopkeeper and the merchant.

CHAPTER 2

An earlier generation of American Jewish historians studied the Revolutionary era in order to find Jewish heroes. They worked assiduously to locate the name of every Jew who fought for the patriotic cause, and stressed the contributions to American freedom made by such men as Haym Salomon, whose activities as a broker brought much-needed funds into the new nation's treasury. Today, American Jewish historians have other concerns. What is most important to them, as the title of the essay here demonstrates, is the impact *of the American Revolution, how it affected the whole future shape of American Jewish life.*

As we now know, the American Revolution marked a turning point not only in American Jewish history, but in modern Jewish history generally. Never before had a major nation committed itself so definitively to the principles of democracy and freedom in general and to religious freedom in particular. The Constitution's twin assurances—that "no religious test shall ever be required as a qualification to any office or public trust under the United States (Article VI)," and that "Congress shall make no law respecting an establishment of religion, or prohibiting the free exercise thereof (Amendment 1)"—meant for Jews that they could claim true equality in America, not mere toleration as was accorded them in even the most liberal of European countries. Religious pluralism had become a reality in America. Jews and members of other minority religions could dissent from the religious views of the majority without fear of persecution.

Momentous as this guarantee of legal equality was, it did not immediately translate for Jews into full social equality. As the following article demonstrates, Jews still had to fight for their rights on the state level, and they continued to face various forms of prejudice nationwide. Yet at the same time, as the article also shows, many Jews benefited materially from the Revolution and interacted freely with their non-Jewish neighbors. Having shed blood for their country side by side with their Christian fellows, Jews as a group felt far more secure than they had in Colonial days. They asserted their rights openly, and if challenged, defended themselves both vigorously and self-confidently.

The changes wrought by the Constitution, the effort to weave Jews into the fabric of the nation's social and religious life, and the early struggles to maintain a Jewish life-style in the midst of a non-Jewish environment all serve as background to themes that appear over and over in the annals of American Jewish history. The number of Jews residing in America during this period may have been small, but the problems they faced were similar to those that Jews would always face in America's free environment. For this reason, the impact that the American Revolution had on American Jews is critical. It set in motion many of the forces that helped to shape the American Jewish community forever after.

The Impact of the American Revolution on American Jews

Jonathan D. Sarna

The American Jewish population in the late eighteenth century numbered about 2500, scarcely one-tenth of 1 percent of the national population. Jews' influence loomed far larger. Concentrated as they were in developing areas, Jews naturally became intimate with leading politicians and businessmen. Jewish merchants and non-Jewish merchants traded freely. Discriminatory legislation, though it existed in the colonies, rarely limited Jews' right to work and worship in peace. Indeed, Jews enjoyed far better conditions in the American colonies than in most other corners of the Diaspora.

Treatment of Jews did not, therefore, become the major factor determining Jewish loyalties in the struggle against Britain. Individuals based their decisions largely on business, national, and personal considerations. Many Jews vacillated, and pledged allegiance to both sides in the dispute for as long as they could. But when finally forced to choose, only a small minority sided wholeheartedly with the Crown. Most Jews came down on the side of the Whigs, and cast their lot for independence. They contributed what they could to the national struggle, shed blood on the field of battle, and, after the victory, joined their countrymen in jubilant celebration.

The Revolution had an enormous impact on Jewish life in America. Most immediately, wartime conditions caused massive human dislocations. Several families—among them the Gomezes, Frankses, Hayses, and Harts—divided into two hostile camps: Whig and Tory. A few British sympathizers, notably Isaac Touro, chazan of the synagogue in Newport, left the country altogether. Isaac Hart, a Jewish loyalist shipper who fled only as far as Long Island, was killed by patriotic Whigs. Some loyalists came in the other direction, from Europe to America. These were the Jewish Hessians, German soldiers employed by England's King George III (himself a German) to fight the rebellious colonists. Alexander Zuntz, the most famous Jewish Hessian, is credited with preserving Congregation Shearith Israel of New York's synagogue sanctuary during the period when the city was under British military control. Other Jewish Hessians settled farther south: in Charleston, South Carolina, and Richmond, Virginia. They seem to have met with mixed receptions from the Jews who preceded them there.

Supporters of the Revolution were no less mobile than their Tory opponents. A large contingent from Shearith Israel fled to Stratford, Connecticut, when the British moved on New York. Later, Philadelphia became the chief haven for patriotic refugees. Shearith Israel's minister, Gershom Seixas, moved there from Stratford in 1780. For Jews, as for non-Jews, war meant "fly[ing] with such things as were of the first necessity" when the British approached. Possessions that were left behind were usually lost forever.

These wartime migrations had lasting effects. People who never had met Jews discovered them for the first time, and learned how similar they were to everyone else. Jews from different parts of the country encountered one another, and cemented lasting unions. A succession of Jewish marriages took place, as Jewish children made new friends. Finally, the distribution of Jews in the colonies changed. Newport, Rhode Island, formerly one of the four largest Jewish communities in America, had its port destroyed in the war. Its Jews scattered. The Savannah Jewish community also suffered greatly from the war's decimating effects. On the other hand, two cities that were spared destruction, Philadelphia and Charleston, emerged from the war with larger and better organized Jewish communities than they had ever known before.

In addition to geographical mobility, the Revolution fostered economic mobility among American Jews. Trade disruptions and wartime hazards took their toll, especially on traditional, old-stock Jewish merchants like the Gomezes and Frankses. Their fortunes declined enormously. On the other hand, adventurous entrepreneurs—young, fearless and innovative upstarts—emerged from the war wealthy men. Haym Salomon bounded up the economic ladder by making the best both of his formidable linguistic talents and of his newly learned advertising and marketing techniques. He and his heirs seem not to have adapted so well to the inflationary postwar economy, for when he died his family became impoverished. Uriah Hendricks, and Hessian immigrants like Alexander Zuntz, Jacob and Philip Marc, and Joseph Darmstadt rose to the top more slowly. But by the early nineteenth century all were established and prospering. Generally speaking, the postwar decades were years of progress in the United States. Opportunities were available, and Jews, like their non-Jewish neighbors, made the most of them.

In order to take advantage of postwar economic opportunities, Jews sometimes compromised their ritual observances. They violated the Sabbath; they ate forbidden foods; and they ignored laws regarding family purity. War conditions had encouraged such laxities: The few Jews who struggled to observe the commandments while under arms are remembered precisely because they were so unique. Postwar America also encouraged such laxities.

While religious denominations scrambled to adapt to independence, many parishioners abandoned their churches for other activities. "Pious men complained that the war had been a great demoralizer. Instead of awakening the community to a lively sense of the goodness of God, the license of war made men weary of religious restraint," John B. McMaster observed. He likely exaggerated. Historians no longer believe that the postwar religious depression was quite so severe. Still, McMaster's comment demonstrates that Jews did not simply leave Shearith Israel empty on Saturday morning for business reasons. They also were caught up in the lackadaisical religious spirit of the age.

No matter how lax Jews may have become in their observances, they did not abandon them altogether. To the contrary, they remained proud Jews; more than ever, they expected recognition as such from their non-Jewish neighbors. Jews viewed the War for Independence (and later the War of 1812) as an initiation rite, an ordeal through battle. Having passed the test—having shed blood for God and country—they considered themselves due full equality. They felt that America owed them a debt, and they demanded payment. Jonas Phillips made this clear in his 1787 appeal for rights directed to the Federal Constitutional Convention meeting in Philadelphia:

> . . . the Jews have been true and faithful whigs, and during the late contest with England they have been foremost in aiding and assisting the states with their lifes and fortunes, they have supported the cause, have bravely fought and bled for liberty which they can not Enjoy.

Gershom Seixas, Haym Salomon, Mordecai Noah, and a host of other Jews employed precisely the same arguments in their battles for equal rights. In Maryland, where the debate over Jewish rights was particularly prolonged, even non-Jews appealed to the "Jews bled for liberty" plea. Thomas Kennedy reminded his fellow citizens that

> during the late war [1812], when Maryland was invaded, they were found in the ranks by the side of their Christian brethren fighting for those who have hitherto denied them the rights and privileges enjoyed by the veriest wretches.

Jews and sympathetic non-Jews thus appealed to their countrymen's patriotic piety. They demanded that the Jewish contribution to America's "sacred drama" be both recognized and rewarded.

It took time before these demands met with full compliance. Many Americans apparently felt that Jews' pre-Revolutionary gains sufficed. They wanted the old Colonial status quo in religion to remain in effect. Under the British, Jews had eventually won the rights—sometimes in law, sometimes in fact—to be naturalized, to participate in business and commerce, and to worship. They suffered from disabling Sunday closing laws, church taxes, and special oaths, and they were denied political liberties. But devout Protestants considered this only appropriate. In their eyes, God's chosen people still labored under a Divine curse.

Protestant Dissenters—Baptists, Methodists, Presbyterians, and smaller sects—were not content with the old status quo. Their interest in Jews was minimal; the reason that they opposed the Colonial system of religion was because it permitted church establishments. Since most established churches relegated Dissenters to an inferior status, or refused to recognize them at all, Dissenting Protestants insisted that church and state should be completely separate, and church contributions purely voluntary. They defended these positions by appealing to the arguments of British dissenters and Enlightenment philosophers.

Dissenters couched their rhetoric in the language of freedom. They endeavored to convince traditional forces that liberty of conscience and diversity of belief would not open the door to licentiousness and immorality. The question, as they saw it, was merely one of liberty—the very question that had been decided in the Revolution. "Every argument for civil liberty," Virginia Dissenters insisted, "gains additional strength when applied to liberty in the concerns of religion."

"Liberty in the concerns of religion," to these men, undoubtedly meant liberty in the concerns of the Protestant religion. With the exception of Roger Williams, whom succeeding Colonial generations viewed as a dangerous extremist, prominent Dissenters generally failed to fight for the rights of Catholics, non-Christians, or nonbelievers. They feared that admitting them to equality would threaten the safety and moral fiber of society. Logically, however, Dissentist arguments on behalf of liberty of conscience and church-state separation should have applied equally to non-Protestants. There was simply a disjunction between the radical ideas that Dissenters espoused, and the social realities which they were prepared to accept. The Baptist leader, Isaac Backus, for example, argued nobly that "every person has an unalienable right to act in all religious affairs according to the full persuasion of his own mind, where others are not injured thereby." Yet, he lauded Massachusetts lawmakers for decreeing that "no man can take a seat in our legislature till he solemnly declares, 'I believe the Christian religion and have a firm persuasion of its truth.' "

The development of complete church-state separation in America—the post-Revolutionary development that was of greatest significance to Jews—can thus not be credited to Protestant Dissenters. Though they spread the idea of religious liberty, and so helped all minority religions, their battle on behalf of this principle ended with the victory of Protestant pluralism over church establishment. Jewish rights rather came about through the work of a second group of Revolutionary-era thinkers: those inspired by the ideas of Enlightenment rationalism. Classic Enlightenment texts—among them the works of Locke, Rousseau, Grotius, Montesquieu, Harrington, and Voltaire—found many readers in America. Leading patriots like Franklin, Jefferson, Adams, and Paine openly avowed deistic or Unitarian principles. For these men, a utilitarian belief in the value of "all sound religion" was enough. Some argued that government should go so far as to encourage religion—though not any one particular religion—as a force for social good. Others, more radical advocates of church-state separation, felt sure that reason alone would guarantee society's moral order. Both agreed that Protestantism, for all its benefits, was *not* a prerequisite for good citizenship.

The Enlightenment view of religious liberty, in one of its two forms, eventually gained the upper hand in America, though Protestant pluralists continued to struggle—with various degrees of success—for many years. In 1777, New York became the first state to extend liberty of conscience to all native born, regardless of religion. An anti-Catholic test oath was required only of those born abroad. Virginia's justly famous "Act for Religious Freedom (1785)," written by Thomas Jefferson, was both more comprehensive and more influential. It carefully distinguished civil rights from religious opinions, and decreed that "all men shall be free to profess and by argument to maintain their opinions in matters of religion, and that the same shall in no wise diminish, enlarge or affect their civil capacities." Once the national Constitution, in Article Six and Amendment One, wrote Virginia's version of religious liberty into federal law, the claims of Revolutionary-era American Jews to equal rights were finally conceded. At least at the national level, an epochal change in Jews' legal status had come about.

Constitutional guarantees were not binding on the states; they could legislate as they pleased. As a result, some legislatures—notably those in New England, New Jersey, Maryland, and North Carolina—enacted into law only the principles of Protestant pluralism. Jews who refused to avow their faith in the Protestant religion were denied equality in state government. The implications of this were absurd: Theoretically, a Jew could be President of the United States, but ineligible to hold even the lowliest political office in Maryland. Realizing this, a majority of states granted Jews full rights by 1830 (though New Hampshire held out until 1877). Full rights, however, had only limited effects on social equality. Many Americans still viewed Jews with the greatest of suspicion.

Jews realized that they could win equality in popular eyes only by demonstrating that being Jewish in no way conflicted with being American. They had to prove that non-Christians could still be loyal and devoted citizens. As we have seen, they had taken major steps in this direction simply by fighting in America's great war. This justified their being granted legal equality in the first place. The fact that America's great orators associated the mission of the United States with that of the ancient Hebrews (King George was Pharaoh; America was the Holy Land; Americans were God's chosen people) may also have redounded to Jews' benefit. But no single action and no single speech could break down centuries of popular prejudice. Jews had *continually* to prove their patriotism. The battle against anti-Jewish stereotypes was a never-ending one.

Even before the Revolution, Jews had taken scrupulous care to display their loyalty through energetic participation in government-ordained religious ceremonies, both fast days and days of thanksgiving. New York's Congregation Shearith Israel, for example, held lengthy special services in 1760 on "the Day Appointed by Proclamation for a General Thanksgiving to Almighty God for the reducing of Canada in His Majesty's Dominions." In subsequent years, it, along with other congregations, celebrated or mourned at times of battle, times of victory, times of pestilence, and times of achievement. After the Revolution, the identical pattern prevailed. In 1784, 1789, and then almost annually, Jews gathered in their synagogues whenever governments ordained special days of prayer. They only demurred when insensitive politicians issued proclamations directed only at American Christians.

The two most famous early American Jewish displays of patriotism occurred outside the synagogue. They were the 1788 celebrations connected with the Grand Federal Procession in honor of the newly ratified Constitution, and the 1790 congregational letters to President George Washington. The former, held in Philadelphia, symbolized in remarkable fashion the tension between the Jewish desire to belong and the Jewish need to be separate. Jews participated fully in the celebrations, and their "rabbi"—probably Jacob R. Cohen—walked "arm in arm" with "the clergy of the different christian denominations." Yet, at the conclusion of the ceremony, Jews ate apart—at a special kosher table set aside for them at the end of the parade route. This was appropriate: In the eyes of the Constitution all religions were equal, yet each enjoyed the right to remain distinctive and unique.

Jews made the same point in their letters to the President. These letters, by their very nature, were sectarian expressions of support; they dealt largely with matters of Jewish concern. Yet, Jews did not wish to be considered a people apart. The Newport Congregation therefore assured Washington that its members intended to "join with our fellow-citizens" in welcoming him to the city. But they still wrote their own separate letter. The President understood. He hoped that Jews would "continue to merit and enjoy the good will of the other inhabitants," even as each Jew individually sat "in safety under his own vine and fig tree."

Besides these displays of loyalty, Jews sought to "merit and enjoy the good will of the other inhabitants" by organizing their synagogues on democratic principles. They may have done so unconsciously, following the example of those around them. They certainly knew, however, that Catholics and others resisted the temper of the times and in many cases continued to organize their churches on an autocratic model. By choosing to imitate patriotic Protestants, rather than the more traditionally oriented religious groups, Jews sided with the native-born majority; in so doing, of course, they subtly courted its favor.

Formerly, American Jews had imitated the example of the Anglican Church, the church that was officially established in many of the colonies. Synagogues modeled themselves on the Bevis Marks Synagogue in England, and looked to the Mother Country for guidance and assistance. After the Revolution, congregations prudently changed their constitutions (actually, they wrote "constitutions" for the first time; before 1776 they called the laws they were governed by "Hascamoth"). They became more independent and discarded as unfashionable leadership forms that looked undemocratic. At Shearith Israel, in 1790, the franchise was widened (though not as far as it would be in other synagogues), a new constitution was promulgated, and a "bill of rights" was drawn up. The new set of laws began with a ringing affirmation of popular sovereignty reminiscent of the American Constitution: "We the members of K. K. Shearith Israel." Another paragraph explicitly linked Shearith Israel with the "state happily constituted upon the principles of equal liberty, civil and religious." Still a third paragraph, the introduction to the new "bill of rights" (which may have been written at a different time) justified synagogue laws in terms that Americans would immediately have understood:

> Whereas in free states all power originates and is derived from the people, who always retain every right necessary for their well being individually, and, for the better ascertaining those rights with more precision and explicitly, from [form?] a declaration or bill of those rights. In a like manner the individuals of every society in such state are entitled to and retain their several rights, which ought to be preserved inviolate.
>
> Therefore we, the profession [professors] of the Divine Laws, members of this holy congregation of Shearith Israel, in the city of New York, conceive it our duty to make this declaration of our rights and privileges.

Congregation Beth Shalome of Richmond followed this same rhetorical practice. It began its 1789 constitution with the words "We the subscribers of the Israelite religion resident in this place desirous of promoting divine worship," and contined in awkward, seemingly immigrant English to justify synagogue laws in American terms:

> It is necessary that in all societies that certain rules and regulations be made for the government for the same as tend well to the proper decorum in a place dedicated to the worship of the Almighty God, peace and friendship among the same.

It then offered membership and voting privileges to "every free man residing in this city for the term of three months of the age of 21 years . . . who congregates with us."

By inviting, rather than obligating, all Jews to become members, Beth Shalome signaled its acceptance of the "voluntary principle" in religion. Like Protestant churches it began to depend on persuasion rather than coercion. This change did not come about without resistance. In 1805, Shearith Israel actually attempted to collect a tax of ten dollars from all New York Jews "that do not commune with us." But the trend was clear. The next few decades would see the slow transition from a coercive "synagogue-community" to a more voluntaristic "community of synagogues." As early as 1795, Philadelphia became the first city in America with two different synagogues. By 1850, the number of synagogues in New York alone numbered fifteen.

The voluntary principle and synagogue democracy naturally resulted in synagogues that paid greater heed to members' needs and desires. Congregational officers knew that dissatisfied Jews could abandon a synagogue or weaken it through competition. In response to congregant demands, some synagogues thus began to perform conversions, something they had previously hesitated to do for historical and halachic reasons. Other synagogues showed new leniency toward Jews who intermarried or violated the Sabbath. Leaders took their cue from congregants: they worried less about Jewish law, and more about "being ashamed for the Goyim . . . hav[ing] a stigma cast upon us and be[ing] derided."

The twin desires of post-Revolutionary American Jews—to conform and to gain acceptance—made decorum and Americanization central synagogue concerns. In the ensuing decades, mainstream Protestant customs, defined by Jews as respectable, exercised an ever greater influence on American Jewish congregational life. Not all changes, of course, reflect conscious imitation. When Christian dates replaced Jewish dates in some congregational minutes, for example, the shift probably reveals nothing more than the appointment of a new secretary—a more Americanized one. When Jewish leaders consulted "with different members of Religious Incorporated Societies in this city," and followed their standards, they also in all likelihood acted innocently, without giving a thought to how far social intercourse had evolved from the days when Jews only observed non-Jews in order to learn what *not* to do. Some, however, were fully conscious that Jews' accepted point of reference had become respectable Protestantism, and they turned this knowledge to their own advantage. When Gershom Seixas haggled with congregational officers about a raise, for example, he offered to submit his dispute to "three or five citizens of any religious society" for arbitration. He knew that an appeal to Christian practice was the easiest way to obtain redress from his fellow Jews.

In the heady atmosphere of post-Revolutionary America, it was easy for Jews to believe that they were witnessing the birth of a new age, one in which they would be accepted as perfect equals if only they proved themselves worthy and eager to conform. Jews had shed blood on the field of battle. The Constitution had promised them more than they had ever before been promised by any Diaspora nation. President Washington himself had assured them of "liberty of conscience and immunities of citizenship." All that America seemed to demand in return was loyalty, devotion, and obedience to law.

Jews kept their side of the bargain. They displayed their patriotism conspicuously, and diligently copied prevailing Protestant standards of behavior. In return, they won many new rights and opportunities. Yet, they failed to receive hoped-for equality. Instead, popular anti-Jewish suspicions lived on, and reaction set in. Missionaries arose to convert Jews, and succeeded in rekindling old hatreds. Many Americans, especially those affected by religious revivals ("the Second Great Awakening") and anti-Enlightenment romantic currents, insisted anew that America was a "Christian country."

Social, cultural, and political changes had taken place, of course, and Jews benefited from them. The Revolution did have a permanent impact—one that distinguished post-Revolutionary American Jewish life from its pre-Revolutionary counterpart. But, viewed retrospectively, the Revolution was no more than a single important step in a much longer evolutionary process. Many more steps would be needed in order to transform American Judaism from a barely tolerated Colonial religion into one of the twentieth century's three great American faiths.

CHAPTER 3

According to Malcolm Stern, American Jewry's leading genealogist, the 1820s were a time in American Jewish history somewhat akin to our own. In the 1820s, as in recent years, American Jews were native speakers of English, in most cases second-generation Americans or more. Sharing as they did in the culture and prosperity of the new nation, they sought to conform to its mores and trappings. The dilemma they faced—one that runs through all American Jewish history—was how properly to conform while still maintaining intact some measure of Jewish identity.

For many the dilemma was easily solved. They married non-Jews, raised their children to be Christians, and disappeared from the pages of Jewish history. Given the enormous difficulties many Jews had both in finding Jewish mates and in living Jewish lives—according to one researcher Jews formed less than 0.03 percent of the population—the greater wonder may be that more did not follow this route. This may be a tribute to tradition, identity, and Jews' stubborn insistence that they must somehow survive as a people. Whatever the case, it is clear that the survival strategies of these early Jews—their search for a viable American Jewish identity—anticipated much that would come later.

The leading American Jew of this period was Mordecai Noah, a man who at one time or another was a diplomat, journalist, politician, sheriff, playwright, and judge. While holding these lofty positions, he not only identified himself openly as a Jew, he also became a spokesman for the Jewish community. He worked to educate Christians about Jews, he sought to encourage increased Jewish immigration, and he defended Jews against those who sought to convert them. He once even tried to set up a Jewish colony—Ararat—on Grand Island, New York. But although Noah defended Jews, he also talked about the need for them to change some of their ways. He served as a living symbol of the fact that Jews could rise in American society without having to forfeit their faith, even as he implied that compromises with tradition could not be avoided.

This tension between tradition and change, between the lure of American life and the requirements of Jewish law, appeared simultaneously on many fronts in the 1820s. Stern cites demands for religious reform, particularly in

Charleston, remembered today as the place where American Reform Judaism was born. He also offers examples of traditional Jews whose religion had fallen into disuse. Yet at the same time, he presents striking expressions of Jewish pride of heritage, especially in response to those who attempted to deny Jews equal rights, or sought to convert them. The picture, in short, is a mixed one. Many native-born Jews found themselves torn by conflicting emotions, pulled simultaneously in different directions, and uncertain as to what the future would hold.

The 1820s: American Jewry Comes of Age

Malcolm H. Stern

The decade of the 1820s saw the development of a truly American Jewry. For the first and last time until our own generation, the majority of American Jews were English-speaking, many of them second- and even third-generation (or more) Americans. Some of them had the time and the means to advance themselves culturally and educationally. Their interests extended beyond making a livelihood. They were busy exploring ways of adjusting to their environment, concerned with their identity as Jews, and anxious to help their less fortunate Jewish brethren overseas.

Between 1790 and 1820 the general population of the United States grew from 3.9 million to 9.6 million, while the Jewish population—according to a conservative survey—grew only from 1,500 to 2,700. That period coincided in Europe with the French Revolution and Napoleon, with their promises of liberty, equality, and fraternity. The upheaval of war and the promise of civil betterment made emigration from Europe less appealing to the Jews of France and Germany. The flow of Jewish immigrants to America slowed to a bare trickle. The defeat of Napoleon and the subsequent Congress of Vienna brought the return of anti-Jewish legislation in many German states, but the postwar economy on both sides of the Atlantic was not conducive to emigration from Europe. Despite the revival of "Hep! Hep!" riots in South German towns in 1819 and increasingly burdensome restrictions against them, it was not until the 1830s that German Jews emigrated in any appreciable numbers. The Jewish immigrants who began coming in ever larger numbers in the 1820s were chiefly of Dutch and British origin. These had lived long enough in lands of emancipation to have thrown off ghetto traditions and, therefore, blended easily into the American scene.

Meanwhile, in the American communities, the children and grandchildren of the Colonial Jews were growing up as American Jews. The majority of those who resided in the cities where congregations existed were identified with the congregation, even when a mixed marriage occurred. Those in the more isolated communities found it more difficult to retain Jewish identification, but a number succeeded. Girls as well as boys were given classical education in academies or through private tutors. The arts were avidly pursued. One example of these trends is the Moses Myers family of Norfolk. Until he was impoverished by the impossibility of commercial shipping during the War of 1812, Moses Myers had been a prosperous merchant. In the first decade of the nineteenth century, he sent his oldest son, John, on a grand tour of Europe; his second son, Samuel, was the first Jewish matriculate at the College of William and Mary and became a lawyer; all his sons attended the Norfolk Academy; his daughters, tutored at home, could play the spinet and sing. Gilbert Stuart painted portraits of Moses and his wife; Thomas Sully painted one of John. Their Federal period home in Norfolk, Virginia, preserved with many of its furnishings, is a model of tastefulness. Their library, with volumes in French as well as English, and the nearly eight thousand letters that have survived, attest to the family's literate interests and abilities.

Perhaps the prototype of the evolving American Jew was Mordecai Manuel Noah, whose father and grandfather served in the Revolution. On his mother's side, he was a fifth-generation American. He grew up in his grandfather's Philadelphia home, taking advantage of Benjamin Franklin's Library Company of Philadelphia, the local theater, and "Poor Richard's" advice on manners and morals for a young man of character, while acquiring a passion for politics, journalism, and playwriting which became his joint career. With mixed success, Noah had already been by 1820 U.S. Consul at Tunis, editor of his uncle's pro-Tammany newspaper, and favorite orator of the New York Jewish community. The same environment that allowed Jews like Noah to feel truly American and to try any endeavor produced a growth of Protestant evangelism and conversionist activity among Jews in Europe and America. Jews invariably overreact to attempts at conversion of Jews, and Noah's reaction was to propose the creation of his proto-Zionist colony on an island in the Niagara River, Ararat. Although, in his lifetime, Noah was to achieve far greater prominence for his journalistic and political activities, it is for Ararat that he is best remembered. The experiment, and his dedication of it, as well as its failure, have been frequently noted and analyzed as idealistic, utopian, ridiculous, impractical, and the like. Suffice it to say here that it represents one of the flowerings of American Jewry's "coming of age." The dedicatory ceremony, so flamboyant and dramatic, is an early American public-relations scheme, the product of a fertile mind accustomed to journalism and drama.

Noah's Ararat is only the best known of a number of activities that evolved in the 1820s on the American Jewish scene. Another attempt at colonization and resettlement was carried on by Moses Elias Levy, a native of Morocco, who developed a successful lumber business in St. Thomas before becoming a purchasing agent for the Cuban government in 1816. Attracted by the potentialities of northern Florida, then under Cuban administration, Levy purchased a tract of land which he later traded for a more accessible plot. The latter carried with it the stipulation that at least two hundred colonists had to be settled on it within three years. This sent Levy traveling to Europe and the United States. He arrived in Philadelphia on June 28, 1818, and began to seek out leading Jews in the eastern seaboard communities, proposing the establishment of Jewish agricultural communities and a school for the education of Jewish children. He found enthusiasm for his project among the abovementioned Moses Myers family of Norfolk, especially with Samuel Myers, the father of two infant sons. Levy carried on a lively correspondence with Samuel Myers, suggesting that the religion in their proposed community be reformed in consonance with the efforts of Israel Jacobson in Prussia. Through the Myers family, Levy obtained an introduction to Rebecca Gratz of Philadelphia, but made an unfortunate impression on that lady by arriving a day late and failing to remember that it was Sukkot! The opening of government lands in Illinois led Israel Kursheedt of Richmond and Moses Myers of Norfolk to purchase thirty-four patents, consisting of 5,440 acres, with Levy holding a quarter interest in Kursheedt's twenty-one patents and a one-third share in Myers's thirteen patents. Unfortunately, Moses Myers and Son went into bankruptcy and the land was lost. Undaunted by this and by his own financial reverses, Levy succeeded in interesting the Reverend Moses Levy Maduro Peixotto, Mordecai Manuel Noah, and Judah Zuntz, of New York's Congregation Shearith Israel, in joining him in the call to establish at least the boarding school for Jewish children, and a circular to this effect, dated May 9, 1821, was sent to Moses and John Myers, and their son- and brother-in-law, Philip I. Cohen, in Norfolk. Nothing came of the project, due probably to the inability of those involved to raise funds and to the fact that Levy, the guiding spirit, had left for Florida, whose entrance into the United States had just been ratified. Levy's energies were subsequently devoted to the development of his Florida properties. Like Noah, he was unsuccessful in persuading European Jews to settle on his lands. He did, however, go to Europe for three years, 1825–1828, and engaged in active polemics in England against conversionist activities.

These conversionist activities instigated the creation of America's first Jewish periodical, *The Jew; being a Defense of Judaism against all Adversaries and Particularly against the Insidious Attacks of "Israel's Advocate."* In twelve issues, published between March 1823 and February 1825, editor Solomon Henry Jackson denounced and derided the leadership of the American Society for Ameliorating the Conditions of the Jews, founded 1820, and its publication,

Israel's Advocate. When that society's project of a Christian-Jewish community fell through because of lack of converts, Jackson felt that he had achieved his major purpose and stopped publishing.

To be as openly denunciatory of Christians in print as Jackson was testifies further to the security of the American Jew. So does the freedom with which Jews wrote directly to the President of the United States. On April 17, 1818, Mordecai Noah participated in the dedication of the second Mill Street Synagogue in New York. His discourse, a paean of praise for America and the Jewish religion, urged the Jew to take advantage of the opportunity America afforded for the development of the best in his faith and as a temporary Zion. When the address was printed, Noah sent copies to former Presidents Adams, Jefferson, and Madison, and received replies from all three. Noah's example was followed by Dr. Jacob De La Motta when he dedicated Savannah's first synagogue building on July 21, 1820. When his address, extolling the liberty enjoyed by the Jews in America, was printed, De La Motta sent copies to Jefferson and Madison and received complimentary replies. Joseph Marx of Richmond sent Jefferson a copy of the proceedings of the French Sanhedrin, convened by Napoleon to draft civil law for the Jews of his empire; this too was acknowledged with an expression of compassion for the Jews.

Jews were not hesitant about soliciting federal appointments. When bankruptcy hit in 1818, John Myers of Norfolk sought from President Monroe an appointment as commissioner of claims, citing his service in the War of 1812 as aide-de-camp to General Winfield Scott. This appointment was not forthcoming, but nine years later, John's father was recommended by John Quincy Adams to the Senate for appointment as collector of customs of the Port of Norfolk. The appointment was ratified on January 15, 1828, naming him also superintendent of lights and agent for the Marine Hospital, which Moses held until his resignation on March 28, 1830.

A reflection of the growing liberal spirit in American public life is the battle for ratification of the "Jew Bill" in Maryland. As early as 1797, Solomon Etting and his father-in-law, Barnard Gratz, prevailed upon Assemblyman William Pinkney to introduce a bill to abolish Maryland's requirement that anyone dealing with the law was required to declare his belief in the Christian religion. The bill, reintroduced annually, was defeated. In 1818, a Jeffersonian Democrat, Thomas Kennedy, took up the cause, but it was 1826 when a compromise version of the bill finally franchised the Jews of Maryland. Solomon Etting and Jacob I. Cohen were promptly elected members of the Baltimore City Council.

As indicated above in Moses Elias Levy's correspondence with Samuel Myers, the Jews were feeling a need to Americanize their religious practices. At a time when Christians were experimenting with new approaches to religion, Canadian-born Moses Hart, in 1815, published *General Universal*

Religion (republished in New York in 1818 as *Modern Religion*), in which he proposed a universal religion with special prayers, rites, theology, commandments, and nature festivals, all derived from the rationalism of the eighteenth-century Deists and the French Revolution. The book ran to a third printing and aroused interest, if not followers, at least as far south as Norfolk, for a copy of the 1818 edition was in the Myers family library.

A more serious attempt to remain within a Jewish traditional framework was the effort of forty-seven Jews of Charleston, South Carolina, to reform the worship in Congregation Beth Elohim. When the Adjunta (Board) rejected their request, the Reformed Society of Israelites was born on January 16, 1825, under the leadership of Isaac Harby. Their reforms were those which were to dominate Reform Judaism for more than a century and a quarter: sermons and prayers in the vernacular, abbreviating the service, the abolition of freewill offerings at worship to be replaced by dues, the abolition of auctioning *mitzvot*, dignity and decorum in the conduct of worship. As might be expected, the majority of this group were English-speaking, with at least thirteen native Charlestonians among them. The group grew to the point of raising funds for a synagogue, but economic problems in Charleston led to the migration of Harby and other leaders to New York, and the panic of 1837 brought the coup de grâce to the society.

Meanwhile, in 1825, rebellion against synagogue traditions began to appear in New York. So many members were abandoning the wearing of the *tallit* (prayer shawl) in Congregation Shearith Israel that the board voted to deny calling to the Torah anyone who failed to wear a tallit. It is significant that the punishment for infringement was so mild, an evidence of the breaking down of the authority of the synagogue. In another instance, Barrow E. Cohen, a comparative newcomer to the congregation from England, either willfully or from ignorance failed to make a charity pledge when called to the Torah. He was called on the carpet by the board. Partially as a result of the somewhat high-handed treatment of Cohen, a group calling itself *Chevra Chinuch Nearim* petitioned the Board for the right to hold services apart from the regular worship of Shearith Israel. Since the majority of the group were younger, recent arrivals from Europe, lacking the leisure to attend worship during working hours, they wanted pre-breakfast services. They also sought greater democracy in rotation of officers. This was a strictly Orthodox group; their one reform demand was for a person to preach weekly in English. Once again vested authority denied the right to change, so a new congregation was born, Ashkenazic B'nai Jeshurun, New York's second congregation. Such was the influence of America that the twenty-two-year-old Isaac Leeser, only four years out of Germany, could publish a series of six articles in defense of the Jew in the *Richmond* (Va.) *Whig*. These won for him a call, the following year, to serve as minister of Philadelphia's Congregation Mikveh Israel. A year later—in 1830—he began regular preaching in English, an innovation that was to earn him the epithet of "reformer" from his congregants, although to the later evolving Reform Judaism he was the champion of Orthodoxy.

The 1820s saw the movement of Jews away from the East Coast into the hinterland. A tiny group of English Jews met for High Holy Day worship in Cincinnati in 1819, but it was not until January 4, 1824, that they formed Bene Israel Congregation, now Rockdale Temple. Jews, chiefly from Charleston, moved into the South Carolina state capital at Columbia during the 1820s. In 1822 a burial society was organized, subsequently constituted as the Hebrew Benevolent Society. Presumably the Jews met also for worship, and Congregation Tree of Life dates itself from 1822. A pious Jew, Jacob S. Solis, came to New Orleans late in 1827 and was shocked to discover that although the community had at least twenty-five adult Jewish males, no congregation had been formed. Late that year or early in 1828, Solis succeeded in organizing "The Israelite Congregation of Shangarai-Chasset." As in New Orleans, Jews had been living in Baltimore since the last decades of the eighteenth century. The 1820s saw major growth of the Jewish community, but it was not until 1829, with the arrival of Zalma Rehiné from Richmond, that a minyan was formed—it convened in his home. The following year the Baltimore Hebrew Congregation was chartered.

The emergence of the Jew in the Christian communities in Europe and America, combined with the desire to convert him, led to a romanticization of the Jew. The thesis that the American Indian was a descendant of Israel's Ten Lost Tribes had long fascinated Protestants, producing such works as Elias Boudinot's *Star in the West* (Trenton, 1816). William Brown's two-volume *Antiquities of the Jews* (Philadelphia, 1823) paved the way for numerous editions of William Whiston's *The Genuine Works of Flavius Josephus*, which had been printed in America as far back as 1794. But no Jewish figure captured the popular imagination more than Rebecca of Walter Scott's *Ivanhoe*, published in American editions simultaneously in New York and Philadelphia in 1823.

Thus the 1820s can be seen as a productive, creative period for the tiny American Jewish community. Certainly word of Jewish freedom and self-assuredness must have reached abroad, for the following decade saw a new outpouring of immigrants from Europe.

What lasting results did the events of the 1820s have? Noah's dream of Ararat and Levy's colony for Jews in Florida, as well as the latter's Jewish boarding school, were too visionary. However, Levy did bring non-Jewish colonists to Florida at his own expense and developed some areas of that state. His son, from whom he became estranged, changed his name to Yulee and was elected Florida's first U.S. Senator. Levy Lake is named for the father, Levy County and the town of Yulee for the son. As the general and Jewish population of the United States grew, the relationships to the President became more formal, and fewer Jews sought and secured presidential appointments. The Maryland "Jew Bill," although not the last civil-rights stumbling block for Jews (it was 1877 before Jews and Catholics could hold office in New Hampshire), was undoubtedly the last in a state that had a sizable Jewish community. Jackson's periodical, *The Jew,* served its purpose and died; it was 1843 before its successor, Leeser's *Occident*, was born. Hart's *Modern Religion* was too radical and visionary to have an effect. The Reformed Society of Israelites was ahead of its time, but its goals penetrated into Beth Elohim, the Charleston congregation which had rejected them, and found fruition in Baltimore's Har Sinai (1843), New York's Emanu-El (1845), and Philadelphia's Keneseth Israel (1847)—although these groups were more influenced by ideas imported from Germany than by those planted in Charleston. New York's first Ashkenazic congregation, B'nai Jeshurun, was to spawn a whole series of landsmannschaften. Isaac Leeser, a product of 1820s thinking, became the most influential Jewish religious leader of his generation. The new congregations in Columbia, Cincinnati, New Orleans, and Baltimore were to provide manpower and inspiration for the creation of other congregations in the hinterland. The romantic image of the Jew was dissipated in the nativist Protestant-Catholic struggles of the 1840s and 1850s and in a growing anti-Semitic sentiment from which America has never been totally free. As for the American Jews of the 1820s in the succeeding decades, they found themselves inundated by German-born, German-speaking immigrant Jews with whom they had little in common. Consequently, the native-born Jews became more rapidly assimilated, often intermarried, and in many cases disappeared from the Jewish scene.

FOR FURTHER READING

The most comprehensive study of Jews in Colonial America is Jacob R. Marcus's three-volume opus, *The Colonial American Jew* (1970), summing up his lifetime of research in the field. Marcus's earlier two-volume work, *Early American Jewry* (1951, 1953), and his *American Jewry, Documents, Eighteenth Century* (1959) contain some of the source material upon which his later synthesis is based. Other documents are reprinted in Morris U. Schappes's invaluable *A Documentary History of the Jews in the United States, 1654–1875* (3rd ed. 1971), which contains primary sources relating to all the subjects dealt with here in parts one and two. The most recent scholarly synthesis of Colonial and Early American Jewish history is Eli Faber's *A Time for Planting* (1992).

Arnold Wiznitzer, "The Exodus from Brazil and Arrival in New Amsterdam of the Jewish Pilgrim Fathers," *Publications of the American Jewish Historical Society* 44 (1954), pp. 80–97, recounts the story of the 23 Jews who arrived in New Amsterdam in 1654. Leo Hershkowitz reexamines this evidence and questions prior assumptions in his "New Amsterdam's Twenty-three Jews—Myth or Reality?" in S. Goldman (ed.), *Hebrew and the Bible in America* (1993), pp. 171–183. Asser Levy, the most famous of the 1654 arrivals, is the subject of Malcolm Stern's "Asser Levy—A New Look at Our Jewish Founding Father," *American Jewish Archives* 26 (April 1974), pp. 66–77. Doris G. Daniels, "Colonial Jewry: Religion, Domestic and Social Relations," *American Jewish Historical Quarterly* 66 (March 1977), pp. 375–400, and Leo Hershkowitz, "Some Aspects of the New York Jewish Merchant and Community, 1654–1820," *American Jewish Historical Quarterly* 66 (September 1976), pp. 10–34, survey other social, economic, and religious aspects of Colonial American Jewry based on wide-ranging source materials. For a fascinating biographical study of the leading Colonial Jewish merchant in Newport, Rhode Island, see Stanley F. Chyet, *Lopez of Newport: Colonial American Merchant Prince* (1970).

The basic survey of Jews in the Revolutionary era is Samuel Rezneck's *Unrecognized Patriots: The Jews in the American Revolution* (1975). Richard B. Morris, "The Role of the Jew in the American Revolution," in Gladys Rosen (ed.), *Jewish Life in America* (1978), is a thoughtful, well-researched assessment by a leading American historian. For key documents, see Jacob R. Marcus (ed.), *The Jew and the*

American Revolution: A Bicentennial Documentary (1975), and Jonathan D. Sarna, Benny Kraut, and Samuel K. Joseph (eds.), *Jews and the Founding of the Republic* (1985).

The complex question of Jewish rights in early America has been studied colony by colony and state by state in Abraham V. Goodman, *American Overture: Jewish Rights in Colonial Times* (1947), and in Stanley Chyet's "The Political Rights of the Jews in the United States: 1776–1840," *American Jewish Archives* 10 (April 1958), pp. 14–75. Oscar and Mary Handlin surveyed the subject from a broader perspective in their "The Acquisition of Political and Social Rights by the Jews in the United States," *American Jewish Year Book* 56 (1955), pp. 43–98. For more recent assessments, see Morton Borden, *Jews, Turks and Infidels* (1984), and the early chapters of Naomi W. Cohen, *Jews in Christian America* (1992), a narrative history, and Jonathan D. Sarna and David G. Dalin, *Religion and State in the American Jewish Experience* (1997), a documentary history. The battle for Jewish rights in Maryland, a unique case, is carefully detailed in Edward Eitches, "Maryland's 'Jew Bill'," *American Jewish Historical Quarterly* 60 (March 1971), pp. 258–280.

The most comprehensive surveys of Jewish life in America in the decades immediately following the American Revolution are found in the first volume of Jacob R. Marcus's massive *United States Jewry, 1776–1985* (1989) and in the three-volume documentary edited by Joseph Blau and Salo W. Baron, *The Jews of the United States 1790–1840: A Documentary History* (1963). Three local histories are also very informative: Hyman P. Grinstein, *The Rise of the Jewish Community of New York* (1945), Edwin Wolf 2nd and Maxwell Whiteman, *The History of the Jews of Philadelphia from Colonial Times to the Age of Jackson* (1975), and James W. Hagy, *This Happy Land: The Jews of Colonial Antebellum Charleston* (1993). For demographic information, see Ira Rosenwaike, *On the Edge of Greatness: A Portrait of American Jewry in the Early National Period* (1985). *Jacksonian Jew: The Two Worlds of Mordecai Noah* (1981) by Jonathan D. Sarna details the life of the period's foremost Jewish leader in the context of his times. Sarna's "The American Jewish Response to Nineteenth Century Christian Missions," *Journal of American History* 68 (June 1981), pp. 35–51, and George L. Berlin, *Defending the Faith: Nineteenth-Century American Jewish Writings on Christianity and Jesus (1989)*, shed light on the subject of Jewish-Christian relations during this period, while Lou H. Silberman, "American Impact: Judaism in the United States in the Early Nineteenth Century," in A. Leland Jamison (ed.), *Tradition and Change in Jewish Experience* (1978), and Gary P. Zola, *Isaac Harby of Charleston* (1994), place Jewish religious reforms of the day into proper perspective.

PART TWO

THE "GERMAN PERIOD" IN AMERICAN JEWISH HISTORY

German Jews began to immigrate to American shores in substantial numbers in the 1840s. Their origins were humble, and many began life in America trudging wearily over back roads, heavily laden with peddlers' packs. But with the American economy growing at a rapid pace, opportunities soon knocked, and German Jews took advantage of them. Over the next eighty years they prospered, established Jewish settlements throughout the country, created new social, religious, and cultural institutions, assumed positions of communal leadership, and effectively reshaped the American Jewish community along new lines. So pronounced was German Jewry's influence on American Jewish life that the entire period of their hegemony is commonly referred to as American Jewish history's "German period." This is somewhat of a misnomer since Jews from German-speaking lands formed only a fraction of those immigrating. Other Jews came from Poland, elsewhere in Europe, and outside Europe too, and for the same reasons: economic distress, outrageous persecutions, restrictive laws, and the failure of movements aimed at revolution and reform. It was, however, largely German Jews writing in the German language who gave this period its distinctive character. In not a few cases, Jews born elsewhere passed themselves off as Germans—that was one way of achieving status.

The articles in this section trace the influence of German Jews in such widely diverse areas as religion, culture, politics, and business. They portray a community flushed with economic success, actively involved in the world around it, intensely proud of its German-Jewish heritage, and fiercely determined to gain acceptance into the American mainstream—but not at the cost of abandoning Judaism itself. In time, America's German Jews stopped being German; some also stopped being Jewish. But German Jewry's overall impact on American Jewish life continues to be felt. Reform Judaism, B'nai B'rith, the American Jewish Committee, the National Council of Jewish Women, Hebrew Union College, and a host of other movements, institutions, and organizations—religious, social, cultural, and philanthropic—testify to the rich inheritance that German Jews bequeathed to those who came later.

CHAPTER 4

The Jews who emigrated from Germany in the nineteenth century and sailed to the New World left generations of Jewish history behind them. Germany, home to a few Jews as early as the fourth century, became a center of Jewish culture during the Middle Ages. Few Diaspora countries created so profound an impact on Jewish life. With modernization, however, economic conditions in many of the German lands deteriorated. Germans, Jews and non-Jews alike, faced poverty as traditional village occupations disappeared and young people looked in vain for jobs.

Conditions for Jews proved particularly trying. Throughout Germany they faced discriminatory economic legislation that restricted them from trades and professions. Fifty percent of the Jewish community in 1848 lived in dire poverty. The province of Bavaria, seeking "not to enlarge the number of Jewish families in places where they exist," even limited Jews' right to settle and marry. "The combined effect of legal, social, and economic situations at home, and the promise of a better life across the ocean," historian Avraham Barkai concludes, set the stage for emigration.

Seeking to improve their lot, thousands of young Jews—an estimated 250,000 German-speaking Jews by World War I—embarked for America. There they found economic opportunity in abundance and more freedom than they had ever known before. The result, as Stefan Rohrbacher demonstrates in the article that follows, transformed Jewish life on both sides of the Atlantic. Using as a case study the small German village of Jebenhausen in Württemberg, he traces the motivations, scope, character, and implications of the migration. Information concerning America spread quickly, he shows, and Jewish emigrants followed in one another's footsteps, a phenomenon known as "chain migration." They assisted one another, sometimes married one another, and maintained Old World ties long after settling into their New World homes.

Some Jebenhausen Jews, to be sure, resisted pressures to emigrate and moved instead to urban areas within Germany itself—a reminder that emigration and urbanization are often closely linked. Over time, the condition of these and other German Jews improved markedly. Though Jebenhausen's synagogue closed in 1899, Germany remained an important center of Jewish life and culture until the Nazi era.

From Württemberg to America: A Nineteenth-Century German-Jewish Village on Its Way to the New World

Stefan Rohrbacher

Before the mass immigration of Jews from Eastern Europe toward the end of the nineteenth century, the vast majority of America's Jewry was of German descent. The bulk of the German-Jewish immigrants in the period prior to 1880 apparently came from small towns and villages in southern Germany. Apart from reports on individual careers, however, we have comparatively little source material concerning the influx of German Jews into America. There is also relatively little material regarding the background of these immigrants. We have a general idea of their living conditions and of the economic, social, and political factors which may be seen as having led them to emigrate. But only in rare instances do we have sufficient information to give us a more coherent and detailed picture of the development of German-Jewish mass emigration to America. The well-documented case of Jebenhausen, a village in Württemberg, therefore certainly deserves some attention.

Between 1830 and 1870 no less than 317 Jews from Jebenhausen went to America. Their emigration not only was recorded by the state authorities, but was also, and more regularly, noted in the family register of the Jewish community, and sometimes it was even publicized in the local and regional newspapers. Thus almost all of Jebenhausen's Jewish emigrants are known by name, and in most cases we are able to give their professions and their assets as well. We learn of entire families sailing to the New World, and of young children and elderly widows leaving on their own, of young women going overseas to contract prearranged marriages, of artisans fleeing competition and poverty. Thus in the exceptional case of Jebenhausen we are able to take a close look at the process of German-Jewish emigration; indeed, comparable data are not available for any other place in Germany.

The Jewish Community of Jebenhausen

The village of Jebenhausen, situated in the picturesque landscape of the Swabian Jura, about two miles south of the Württemberg town of Göppingen, had belonged to the family of the *Freiherren* (barons) of Liebenstein ever since 1467. But the revenues which could be extracted from the poor villagers were hardly worth mentioning, and in 1770 a mineral spring, which until then had been the barons' main source of income, was destroyed by a landslide. In order to make up for this loss it was decided to let Jews settle in the village. In July 1777 a contract was negotiated and signed by the barons and nine Jews, and the Jewish community was thus founded. The new inhabitants were allotted plots outside the village along the uphill road to Göppingen, and within a few years a separate Jewish settlement, the *Oberdorf* (upper village), had come into being.

The Jews of Jebenhausen were granted far-reaching liberties and had to pay comparatively moderate dues. It is not surprising, therefore, that in the first decades of its existence the Jewish settlement grew rapidly. As early as 1798, 178 Jews lived in Jebenhausen, and by 1830 the number had increased to 485, or 44.9 percent of the population. Most of the newcomers originated in villages in Bavaria and in the northern border regions of Baden and Württemberg. Since they came in such numbers, Jebenhausen must have seemed to them a most agreeable place. Yet life in Jebenhausen was far from easy. In 1793 the *Oberamtmann* (district bailiff) of Göppingen reported to the duke of Württemberg that only one Jewish family in Jebenhausen was well off and in a position to visit the Frankfurt and Leipzig fairs, whilst all the others were living in wretched poverty and had to wander as far as Switzerland, Saxony, and the Palatinate to eke out a meager existence from peddling or dealing in cattle. Even after the incorporation of Jebenhausen into the Kingdom of Württemberg in 1806 their lot improved only gradually.

Reasons for Emigration

At a time when pauperism, religious dissent, and political oppression caused a mass exodus of mostly poor people from Württemberg, Jews, and above all young Jews, had some additional reasons to consider emigration. They were still legally subordinate to their Christian countrymen, and in the course of the heated debates about the emancipation bill of 1828 they learned that the non-Jewish public generally opposed their legal and social advancement. The authorities demanded that they learn "productive" professions, and fined them if they engaged in any kind of *Schacherhandel* (petty trade); but their chances of being apprenticed to a Christian master craftsman or of receiving solid mercantile training were limited, and once they finished their apprenticeship they had to return to their home village, where there were already too many young Jews engaged in the same trades and hardly able to make a living.

The bitter experiences of young David Kohn, the son of a poor peddler, certainly were shared by many in this period. "He was sent to the village school for a short time and his remaining education was gained by self training. Apprenticed in a dry goods store some distance from home, he worked on a pittance several years for his board, being half starved most of the time." He left Jebenhausen in 1854, at the age of twenty-one, and followed his two elder brothers to Chicago.

Less drastic, yet equally significant, were the reasons given by young Louis Einstein for his emigration in a last letter to his parents in 1835. Einstein, a soap-boiler, had received thorough vocational training; yet he could never hope to make a decent living in his home village, to say nothing of raising a family. Since Jebenhausen was a rather isolated place some distance from the usual trade routes, he would have had to distribute his products by peddling or sell them in the village itself. But Jebenhausen's major grocer, Moses Ascher Frank, set the prices for soap and candles so low that they fell short of the actual production costs. Young Einstein assured his parents that if his father had obtained permission to establish a grocery, he would never have considered leaving. He claimed that the avaricious Frank, who was also a schoolteacher, had reproached parents who did not buy at his shop, and in some cases had even punished their children.

The Scope of Emigration

By Einstein's time, emigration to America already had a tradition in Jebenhausen. Several sources indicate that it started in 1803 or 1804. However, the first emigrant whose name has been handed down to us, Mayer Arnold, the eldest son of a cattle dealer, left for America as early as 1798. Since he was then only a lad of thirteen, we may assume either that he was a runaway or that he had set out from Jebenhausen in the company of others, or perhaps that he was to be taken care of by compatriots who already had arrived in the New World. Another early emigrant was Jekef Gutmann, son of a very poor cattle dealer, who around the turn of the century went to America as a redemptioner.

In 1839 Rabbi Abraham Waelder gave the following description of the local emigration movement:

> In 1804 several young people, sons of impecunious parents, emigrated to the United States of America. Every subsequent year they induced others, through recommendations, to follow there, establishing themselves there and regularly

> running businesses in public stores. By June of this year about 46 unmarried young men and women had in this manner emigrated to America, individually and one by one. Just *one* family went there last year and is included in this number. But in June of this year, 48 persons, among them six families with wives and children, have emigrated there *at one time.*

Liebman Levi, then schoolteacher in Jebenhausen, wrote this touching report on the exodus which took place on June 16, 1839:

> Today was a day of the most heartfelt sadness, of the bitterest pain for the local Israelite congregation. Six fathers of families with wives and children, altogether 44 individuals of the Mosaic faith, left home to find a new fatherland in far-off America. Not an eye remained without tears, not a soul unmoved, as the bitter hour of parting struck.

Up to this point emigration had only affected poor families. Of the group which left in June 1839, however,

> some were rather well-to-do, others belonged to the middle class, and no one could be called notoriously poor in the proper sense. They said that they were emigrating mainly because of their children. Since all trades are so very overcrowded everywhere and, moreover, they would have had to sacrifice their own property to let their children learn a trade, they feared that sooner or later they would be ruined, and that their children, who are studious of handicrafts, would not be able to feed themselves and their families from any trade in the countryside, owing to the numerous and heavy burdens and payments. Besides, they were given every aid and support by those who had already emigrated to America, since almost every family here has close or distant relatives among the emigrants. By now 94 individuals, or about one fifth of the 500 members of the local Israelite congregation, are in America. Already six fathers of families are determined to emigrate with their wives and children next spring.

The Decline of the Jebenhausen Community

In the following decades the exodus of Jews of all ages, occupations, and social strata, single people as well as whole families, led to a drastic decline in the Jewish population of Jebenhausen (see Table 1). To make matters worse for this community, after 1849 many of its members moved to nearby Göppingen, where they formed the bulk of the Jewish congregation founded in 1867 (see Table 2).

The temporary rise in the number of Jewish residents of Jebenhausen before its sudden decline after 1854 can be attributed to the high number of Jewish children born there during the first half of the nineteenth century,

TABLE 1. FAMILY STATUS AND OCCUPATION OF JEWISH EMIGRANTS FROM JEBENHAUSEN

		FAMILY STATUS			OCCUPATION			
Years	*No. of Emigrants*	*Single*	*Married, Widowed*	*Children*	*Artisan*	*Peddler, Trades-man, etc.*	*Cattle Dealer*	*Other*
1825–29	9	9	—	—	1	4	3	—
1830–34	8	8	—	—	1	3	—	1
1835–39	53	13	15	25	6	9	3	—
1840–44	19	11	4	4	2	2	2	2
1845–49	91	37	15	39	20	6	7	—
1850–54	73	47	14	12	13	11	5	3
1855–59	19	12	2	5	4	3	—	—
1860–64	16	14	2	—	1	5	—	1
1865–70	26	18	4	4	—	6	5	—
1825–70	314	169	56	89	48	49	25	7

Sources: Hauptstaatsarchiv Stuttgart E 143, files 486–491; E 146, files 1787–1790; Staatsarchiv Ludwigsburg F 170, files 281–288; *Familienbuch.*

TABLE 2. DECLINE OF THE JEWISH COMMUNITY OF JEBENHAUSEN

Year	*No. of Jews in Jebenhausen*	*Percentage of total population*	*No. of Jews from Jebenhausen in America*	*No. of Jews in Göppingen*
1830	485	44.9	32	—
1838	537	45.5	47	—
1846	496	42.7	126	—
1854	534	44.4	238	40
1862	392	35.9	291	90
1871	127	12.5	329	194
1880	74	6.2	—	242
1890	42	3.5	—	271
1900	9	0.7	—	324

Sources: Staatsarchiv Ludwigsburg E 212, file 362; Aron Tänzer, *Geschichte der Juden in Jebenhausen und Göppingen* (Berlin, 1927), pp. 97, 399; Alexander Dreher, *Göppingens Gewerbe im 19. Jahrhundert* (Göppingen, 1971), p. 119.

and to the number of Jews from other parts of the country who settled there for some time to find employment in one of Jebenhausen's Jewish-owned textile factories, which had come into being since the 1830s. At the same time many young people, and in most age-classes even a majority, had left

TABLE 3. PERCENTAGE OF EMIGRANTS TO AMERICA

Birth Years	*by age 25*	*by age 35**
1810–14	24.4	34.1
1815–19	19.1	36.2
1820–24	40.4	55.3
1825–29	55.6	61.9
1830–34	59.7	65.3
1835–39	57.4	59.0

*Includes figures in preceding column.

Sources: Haupstaatsarchiv Stuttgart E 143, files 486–491, E 146, files 1787–1790; Staatsarchiv Ludwigsburg F 170, files 279–283; *Familienbuch.*

for America (see Table 3). The whole demographic structure of the community had therefore become unbalanced, but the effects of this development appeared only during the second half of the century, when the number of families raising children dropped sharply.

Many families saw a more or less complete exodus of the younger generation. Of the fourteen children of the cattle dealer Aron Arnold, all but two sailed to America. Solomon Ottenheimer left for the New World in 1827; by 1835 all but one of his five brothers and sisters had followed him. In 1834 Moses Einstein set out for the United States, paving the way for seven of his ten brothers and sisters. The six daughters of the peddler Samuel Solomon Massenbacher, the five children of the innkeeper Abraham Moses Rosenheim, and the six children of the cattle dealer Benedict Rosenheim all went overseas, and so did seven of the nine children of the cattle dealer Juda Lindauer.

Sometimes young emigrants induced their parents to follow them. Isaac Bernheimer, a cotton manufacturer of rather modest background, had gone to Cincinnati in 1835 just to establish a business connection but "liked the country so much that he resolved to stay." America proved a most profitable ground for this enterprising mind, and when he sent for his aged parents in 1848, he was able to offer them a life of considerable luxury.

Like many others, young Moses Jacob Lindauer made several attempts at emigration, but after much hesitation he finally resolved to stay. His memoirs reflect the strain and sorrow the exodus meant for his family. Their relatives in Philadelphia and Baltimore repeatedly urged them to risk the voyage and start a new life.

> In 1854 my sister once again was to go, together with her husband, her brother-in-law, and our brother, but she could not do it. She stood in the kitchen and cried, while her brother-in-law reproached her because of the plans they had made. . . . Another brother-in-law, a butcher in New York, urged her husband to join him there. After some time he gave in, and in spite of all objections left my sister with her children. After two or three years he returned home with a nice little sum, but my sister never overcame her grief. . . . My brother David, who already had made some money in America, wanted to pay for my passage, but I did not want to part. Later on, however, I decided [to emigrate], as Erlanger & Blumgart, a firm from Jebenhausen, had promised to accept me into partnership in America. . . . Yet in the end I concluded that I had to stay, especially since at that time my brother-in-law had left for New York.

The Voyage to America

Jebenhausen's Jewish emigrants usually shunned the ill-famed seaports of Holland, from where the open sea could only be reached after a dangerous voyage through the English Channel. Like most other emigrants from southwestern Germany, they turned to Le Havre instead. In 1835 Louis Einstein gave the following description of the journey he had just made to the French seaport with David Arnold and Isaac Bernheimer; he included a passage concerning the emigrants' strict observance of the Sabbath, presumably aimed to comfort his parents.

> I inform you that the same day as we left my dear brother Baruch and Arnold, we went to Karlsruhe, from there the other day to Strasbourg, where we had to stop for one day because of the diligence. From there the trip to Paris cost us 52 francs a person, but had we come a fortnight earlier, we would have been able to ride for half this price. The reason for this is that a new diligence has been established, namely, the one we took. Those who had attended to transport before, Laffitte, Caillard & Co., wanted to ruin this one, but have not succeeded so far. Over Saturday we stayed in Chalons, where we had arrived on Friday evening at four o'clock. From there we traveled to Paris on Sunday, where we stayed until Tuesday. I already have seen several big cities, but Paris is indescribable. We have seen the greatest curiosities there, but in order to see everything one would need more time. Then we went to Rouen, and from Rouen we traveled here by steamboat, which was the most beautiful trip of the whole journey. We arrived in Havre on Wednesday evening, and yesterday we arranged for our

voyage on a mailboat named *Franc.* The captain of it is called Funk, he is an American. For 87 francs a person we get a partition by the side of the cabin.

Economic Status of the Emigrants

Einstein's report seems to indicate that the journey to Le Havre had turned out to be somewhat more expensive than the young travelers had expected. Of the 225 florins which he had taken along in addition to the money for travel expenses, Einstein probably saved only part for America. Many of his contemporaries, however, had even less to take along, and some virtually nothing (see Table 4).

TABLE 4. ASSETS OF JEWISH EMIGRANTS FROM JEBENHAUSEN: MONEY FOR TRAVEL EXPENSES, PER CAPITA

Year	*less than 100 florins*	*101–500 florins*	*501–1,000 florins*	*over 1,000 florins*
1825–34	7	6	—	—
1835–44	19	43	1	—
1845–54	53	63	19	3
1855–70	4	33	7	4
1825–70	83	145	27	7

Sources: Hauptstaatsarchiv Stuttgart E 143, files 486–491; E 146, files 1787–1790; Staatsarchiv Ludwigsburg F 170, files 281–288.

Sometimes emigration was a direct response to failure. Such was the case with Hirsch Ottenheimer, who left for the United States in 1848 with his wife and five children after he went bankrupt. In 1849 the authorities inquired about Benedict Lindauer, a thirty-five-year-old clothmaker who had run off, leaving his debts behind. Another emigrant who left with nothing but a ticket was seventy-three-year-old Solomon Seligman Lindauer, a peddler who in 1856 went overseas together with his daughter to join a son in the New World; and in spite of his alleged greed Moses Ascher Frank, the previously mentioned schoolteacher and grocer, had only 275 florins to take along when he left with his wife in 1841. On the average, families took along almost four times that amount.

It proves rather difficult to compare the economic situation of Jebenhausen's Jewish emigrants with that of their Christian fellow travelers. Unfortunately, data showing the average assets of emigrants from Württemberg are available only from 1854 onwards. After 1854, however, emigration from

Jebenhausen was quite low. Any attempt, therefore, to deduce much information from the limited number of cases we have in which the amount of assets was recorded may appear problematic. But if we take into account only those years in which a minimum of five individuals with recorded assets emigrated

TABLE 5. PER CAPITA ASSETS OF EMIGRANTS, IN FLORINS

Year	*All emigrants from Württemberg*	*Jewish emigrants from Jebenhausen*
1854	181	248
1859	434	422
1866	383	475
1870	516	875

Sources: Hauptstaatsarchiv Stuttgart E 143, files 489–491; Staatsarchiv Ludwigsburg F 170, files 284, 286–287; Wolfgang von Hippel, *Auswanderung aus Südwestdeutschland* (Stuttgart, 1984), p. 235.

from Jebenhausen, we arrive at the picture shown in Table 5. However cautiously we must approach its statistical foundation, the table appears to indicate that on the average Jebenhausen's Jewish emigrants were better off than their Christian companions. This is all the more likely as the figures in the first column refer to all emigrants from Württemberg regardless of their destination; and specified data for the year 1856 suggest that the figures for emigrants to the United States lay well below that average. While the per capita assets of all emigrants from Württemberg in 1856 amounted to 320 florins, the figure for emigrants to Bavaria was 1,030 florins, and for emigrants to Baden was 916 florins, whereas emigrants to America had only 215 florins per capita.

Who left, and who stayed behind? As Rabbi Waelder reported in 1839, until that year only the children of poor families had gone overseas, but now even the well-to-do took to emigration. It is apparent, however, that even after 1839 emigrants usually did not belong to the more affluent class amongst Jebenhausen's Jews. Their assets hardly ever exceeded 2,000 florins, whereas Jewish taxpayers in the village had an average property of 1,492 florins as early as 1826, and the figure must have been much higher in later years.

Economic prospects looked dim to most young people in the village, but some trades were particularly unpromising. Peddling was frowned upon by the authorities, and young people who took up this occupation were subject to severe restrictions on their civil liberties. Thus most of Jebenhausen's nineteen Jewish peddlers in 1845 were elderly men, and this may explain why, in spite of all the hardships they faced, comparatively few of them emigrated. By "encouraging" young people to turn to "productive" professions instead, the *Judengesetz* (Jews' Law) of 1828 had brought forth a multitude of Jewish bakers, dyers, plumbers, soap-boilers, shoemakers, tailors, weavers, and clothmakers, but as they were still restricted to the village they could hardly attain an equal footing with their Christian competitors. To those who had failed to obtain solid vocational training, the butcher's trade often seems to have been a last resort. As there were several Jewish master butchers in the village, a butcher's apprentice did not have to leave Jebenhausen or stay with a Christian master in order to learn his trade, and he probably did not have to pay a premium either. However, his skills were not worth much in a village where so many butchers tried so hard to make a living.

In 1845 and again in 1852, all Jewish male inhabitants above the age of fourteen were registered according to their occupations. It is most revealing

TABLE 6. EMIGRATION RATES, BY OCCUPATION

	In Jebenhausen, 1845	*In America by 1852*		*In Jebenhausen, 1852*	*In America by 1859*	
Occupation	*no.*	*no.*	*%*	*no.*	*no.*	*%*
Peddler	19	3	15.8	14	2	14.3
Butcher	16	7	43.7	11	5	45.5
Other artisan	41	16	39.0	14	2	14.3
Merchant	13	3	23.1	18	4	22.2
Manufacturer	5	—	—	11	—	—
Cattle dealer	40	6	15.0	29	1	3.4
Total	134	35	26.1	97	14	14.4

Sources: Staatsarchiv Ludwigsburg F 170 I, files 279–283; E 212, file 362.

to follow their traces over a couple of years. Table 6 shows the extent to which emigration was an answer to the lack of professional prospects. In 1845–1852 butchers, weavers, and other artisans showed much greater inclination to leave than those who earned their living as merchants or cattle dealers. By 1852 the situation of the weavers had improved considerably, as some of them had established themselves as textile manufacturers in Jebenhausen or Göppingen, and others were employed in the factories. Of the five weavers who remained in the village, only one emigrated subsequently. At the same time the number of Jewish bakers, tailors, dyers, furriers, and shoemakers in the village also dropped sharply, for many had left for America, and young people now were very reluctant to turn to these unprofitable crafts. Competition therefore pressed less heavily upon the few who remained, and only one of them left for America after 1852.

While the emigration rate receded markedly among weavers and other artisans, it remained high among butchers. Professional prospects for them were as unpromising as ever, and they could hardly hope to fare much better in nearby Göppingen, where old-established Christian butchers were determined to ward off unwelcome competition from newcomers.

During the third quarter of the nineteenth century most Jewish manufacturers moved from Jebenhausen to Göppingen, where they could employ steam power and make use of the railway, and so did the more affluent among the merchants. However, a considerable proportion of young merchants and apprentices sailed to America to seek their fortune there, some of them well-prepared and well-furnished with the pecuniary means for their future undertakings.

It was the cattle dealers who were least prepared to leave the village. Two reasons may be given: they were mostly elderly men, since few young people took up this strenuous trade; and their business was well-established and firmly rooted in the countryside. It was not until the 1870s that a substantial number of cattle dealers moved to Göppingen, Esslingen, Ulm, or Stuttgart. Characteristically enough, the last Jewish family to remain in the village after the turn of the century was that of a cattle dealer, Max Lauchheimer.

How They Fared in America

Once the Jews from Jebenhausen had safely arrived in the New World, where did they go, and how did they fare? We can give nothing but tentative answers to these questions. It is apparent that the newly arrived immigrant often sought the company of fellow countrymen who could help him accommodate to his new surroundings and perhaps aid him in making a fresh start. Indeed, the biographies of the few immigrants whose tracks we are able to follow often imply that a loose network of former inhabitants of Jebenhausen existed in America. By 1860 Jews from Jebenhausen were living in comparatively large numbers in Chicago and New York, but for many years they also maintained contacts with their brethren in such faraway places as St. Louis and even Donaldsonville, Louisiana. Marriages are known to have occurred between members of the Arnold and Bernheimer, Kohn and Levi, Rosenheim and Ottenheimer, Einstein and Rosenheim, Einstein and Rosenfeld, Rohrbacher and Strauss, and Erlanger and Dettelbacher families, and business connections were maintained between several others.

Mayer Arnold, who had come to the United States in 1798 at the tender age of thirteen, spent his early years in America in Kutztown, Pennsylvania, where he was apprenticed in a dry goods store. He soon established a store of his own, but it must have taken a while for him to feel economically secure, since he did not marry until 1822. Around 1835 he moved to Philadelphia, where he later joined his brother-in-law, Abraham S. Wolf, once his clerk, in the dry goods and clothing business. "He amassed wealth, and freely gave of his means to Congregational, charitable, and educational works." He soon became one of the most distinguished members of Philadelphia's Congregation Mikveh Israel, of which he was an officer, but he was also prominent in the German-Jewish congregation Rodeph Shalom. Arnold took an active interest in the work of the Hebrew Education Society and the first Jewish Publication Society. He died in 1868, a highly revered patriarch and millionaire.

Of Mayer Arnold's fifteen children, Simon W. Arnold, "well known for his intellectual capacities, executive ability, and earnest labors," was a successful businessman and a committed Democrat. He served as the first president of Philadelphia's United Hebrew Charities, and like his brothers Hezekiah, Edwin, and Ezra, was an active member of Congregation Mikveh Israel. The Reverend Isaac Leeser was closely attached to the family and, after his death in 1868, Hezekiah Arnold was one of the executors of his estate; the other was a distant relative of his, young Mayer Sulzberger, whose mother likewise came from Jebenhausen.

In 1832, Mayer Arnold's nephew, Abraham B. Arnold, then a boy of twelve, was sent across the ocean to live with his uncle. He later became a physician of some renown and for many years worked at the Jewish Hospital in Baltimore. In 1872 he was appointed to a professorship at Washington University. Abraham B. Arnold was a nonconformist who advocated abolition of the rite of circumcision, certainly much to the discomfort of some of his relatives who clung to strictly traditional ways. Isaac Mayer Wise later recalled that in 1854, when the publication of his *History of the Israelitish Nation* caused a general outcry among America's Jewry, Arnold was his sole defender. In 1860 "he arrayed himself with the Republican Party on the election of Lincoln and was made a member of the State Executive Committee of Maryland." He was a close friend of Rabbi David Einhorn with whom he stood united in the struggle for the abolition of slavery.

For a time the Arnold family was economically associated with the Kohn, Rothschild, and Rosenheim families in Chicago, New York, and Philadelphia, who had also come from Jebenhausen, and who had engaged in the wholesale clothing business as well. Abraham H. and David Rosenheim owned the very respectable firm of Rosenheim, Brooks & Co., millinery and straw goods, with stores in Philadelphia and New York. Abraham H. Rosenheim, who had come to America in 1838, was a delegate to the first Republican convention in 1856, which nominated Frémont for President. He died at Lake Placid in 1918, almost a centenarian.

In 1846 one of Mayer Arnold's daughters, Isabella, was married to Isaac Bernheimer, the previously mentioned cotton manufacturer from Jebenhausen. Together with his *Landsmann* and fellow émigré, Louis Einstein, Bernheimer had embarked on the career of a Cincinnati peddler during the late 1830s. By the time of his marriage he was a prosperous clothing and dry goods merchant. He moved to Philadelphia and eventually joined his brothers Simon, Herman, and Emanuel, who in the meantime had established a clothing business in New York. In the 1840s and 1850s Herman Bernheimer was a prominent member of New York's Congregation Anshe Chesed and of the German Hebrew Benevolent Society. None of the brothers suffered from want. In 1861 their clothing firm ranked high among New York's wealthiest companies, with a capital of $250,000. A few years later it was taken over by Isaac Bernheimer's brothers-in-law, Edwin and Eli Arnold, under the firm of Leon, Arnold & Co. Emanuel Bernheimer was also a brewer, and when he died his son, Simon E. Bernheimer, succeeded him in this capacity, making the brewery of Bernheimer & Schmid one of the largest in New York City.

Young Louis Einstein had not intended to leave his fatherland permanently, but planned to return home as soon as he had learned how to manufacture a specific kind of soap required by a firm in Göppingen and so far not manufactured anywhere in Württemberg—at least this is what he told his parents. He stayed, however, and for almost forty years engaged most successfully in the banking business and the manufacture of woolen goods. In 1847 Louis Einstein moved from Cincinnati to New York, where business prospects seemed even brighter. "Few men display more enterprise and sound judgment than did he, and The Raritan Woolen Mills became an important property under his management." For a long time Einstein was associated with Isaac Bernheimer, his companion from the days when they had set out for America. Their business partnership lasted from the late 1830s, when they peddled the countryside in the West, temporarily accompanied by Bernheimer's brother Simon, until late in the 1850s, when they ran a large wholesale clothing business, Bernheimer, Einstein & Co. They remained lifelong friends and close neighbors.

Of his eleven children, David L. Einstein, a shrewd and capable man, followed his father's vocation all his life and made more than a fortune. His son was Lewis D. Einstein, the well-known U.S. diplomat and author. Another son of Louis Einstein, Edwin, had an interest in several woolen and iron mills, and was also largely connected with banking interests. In 1878 Edwin Einstein was elected to Congress, and in 1892 he stood for the mayoralty of New York, receiving the greatest number of votes ever polled for a Republican candidate until that time. Theodore Roosevelt was a close friend of the family.

Louis Einstein's brother-in-law, Liebman Levi, the schoolteacher who had given so moving a report on the exodus from Jebenhausen in 1839, eventually settled in the United States, too. After some years in New Haven, Connecticut, Levi moved to Chicago in 1856 to serve as a reader and teacher in Congregation Anshe Maarabh. In 1861 his daughter, Theresa, was married to David Kohn, the poor peddler's son of whose sufferings we have already learned. Kohn had come to Chicago in 1854 to start on a remarkable career. "Obtaining a position as a clerk, he learned the customs and language of America and then started a small retail store. By industry and attention to business, he so increased his little savings, that, with his brothers, he was able to start in the clothing manufacturing business at his own risk, under the name of Kohn Bro's." He soon became very wealthy, and by 1890 he was "a large real estate holder, an owner of shares and bonds of the important street railroads, electric companies, etc."

In 1865 Louis Einstein's nephew and namesake, eighteen-year-old Louis W. Einstein, arrived in Memphis, Tennessee, where he engaged in the dry goods business. One year later he went to California at the request of a relative in San Francisco, and then established a wholesale liquor house in Portland, Oregon. In 1871 he moved to Visalia, California, and a few years later to Fresno, where he developed his pioneer store into "a business of enormous proportions." In 1887 Einstein founded the Bank of Central California.

Moses (Morris) Einstein, a butcher by profession, had come to the United States in 1846 together with a younger brother. After two years of peddling, during which he learned the English language and saved some money, he opened a store in Wellsburg, Virginia. One year later he moved to Tiffin, Ohio, and opened a store there. In 1851 he married his cousin, Jettle Rosenheim, who had just arrived from Jebenhausen. Shortly after their marriage, the store was destroyed by a fire, and Morris Einstein decided to follow the gold-miners' trail to California. There he played an active part in Sacramento's Jewish community, serving both the congregation and the Hebrew Benevolent Society as a secretary. After four years, he returned to Illinois and in 1856 opened a store in Joliet. In 1863 he moved to Chicago and began a wholesale and piece goods trade, which developed into a very successful business. His partners were Martin Clayburgh, a non-Jew, and Julius Kohn, a *Landsmann* from Jebenhausen. When Kohn left the firm in 1865, David Lindauer, also from Jebenhausen, was admitted as a partner. "Mr Einstein was frequently urged to run for office, but steadfastly declined, preferring to give his entire time to business. . . . He conducted his business with prudence and honor and was identified with many philanthropic movements in Chicago. He was one of the founders of the Michael Reese Hospital, the Sinai Congregation and Standard Club." One of his daughters was married to Morris S. Rosenfield, a grandson of Feissel Rosenfeld, who had emigrated from Jebenhausen in 1849. A daughter of the latter, Auguste Rosenfeld, was the wife of Einstein's later partner in business, B. Kuppenheimer.

Back in 1859 in Joliet, Baruch (Benjamin) Lindauer had crossed Einstein's path. Lindauer, a weaver by profession, had just arrived from Jebenhausen, and at that time was engaged in peddling goods between Chicago and Joliet, where Einstein may have employed his services. He later entered the employ of Martin Clayburgh, subsequently Einstein's partner in business. In 1861 Lindauer established himself as a dealer in general merchandise in Mount Carmel, Illinois. In 1866 he returned to Chicago, and in 1867 the wholesale clothing firm of Rohrbach, Lindauer & Co. was founded by Ulrich Rohrbacher, Lindauer, and Liebman Levi, all from Jebenhausen. In the old country Lindauer had attended the Academy of Weaving in Reutlingen and then had been the manager of the textile factory owned by his uncles, J. & S. Einstein, in Jebenhausen. His professional skill and experience now greatly benefited the company, which also embarked on the manufacture of woolen goods. In 1869 Rohrbacher left the firm, and Mayer E. Lindauer took his place. After the great fire of 1871, which caused the firm a total loss of $152,000, business was resumed at the residence of Mayer E. Lindauer, "where a cutting table was improvised from the door of a coal shed, supported on trestles, in order that employment might be at once furnished to their workpeople." In 1874 Seligman Lindauer, another brother, became a partner. By 1886 Lindauer Bros. & Co. ranked "as one of the largest establishments in the West"; in their manufacturing department alone, they employed about 400 people.

There is little reason to believe that such success stories were more typical for Jebenhausen's Jewish emigrants than for any other group of newcomers to the United States. This was simply the kind of biography that was likely to be recorded, whereas we know little or nothing about the fates of all the other immigrants. However, we may assume that many trod similar paths, although they may never have climbed the ultimate heights of success. The career of the peddler who established himself as a modest small-town storekeeper and eventually made it to the big city certainly reflects a more general pattern in the history of German-Jewish immigration. Moreover, these biographies reveal the importance of the ties which were upheld between *Landsleute* from the small village in Germany.

By 1870, emigration to America was no longer a major factor in the Jewish communities of southern Germany. Many rural communities had by then shrunk or even dissolved, and when young Jews left their home villages they now mostly turned to the bigger cities instead of going overseas. Between 1862 and 1866 alone, almost 200 members of the once-thriving Jewish community of Jebenhausen moved to Stuttgart, Ulm, and, above all, to nearby Göppingen. In 1899 a service was held for the last time in the beautiful village synagogue, and a few years later it was torn down.

CHAPTER 5

The American Jewish community was both religiously and culturally underdeveloped in the mid-nineteenth century. Few resources existed for those who sought to learn about their faith, and most of what did exist was imported. Germany, by contrast, stood at the center of Jewish life during this time. Its rabbis, scholars, and lay leaders won renown for their tireless efforts to bring Jewish life and culture into line with the demands of the modern age.

In the chapter that follows, Michael A. Meyer, a leading student of German Jewry and author of the definitive history of the Reform movement in Judaism, examines how nineteenth-century German-speaking Jewish religious leaders transformed American Jewish life through the ideas they disseminated, the innovations they introduced, and the institutions they created and shaped. Moving beyond the historical debate over whether the contributions of these men were primarily German or American in character, he demonstrates that "both Germanizing and Americanizing trends" were operative. Subsequently, he shows, American Jews did press for cultural independence. They insisted that they needed an American *Judaism—one that was uniquely their own.*

Meyer focuses particular attention on three American Jewish religious leaders from this period: the Orthodox activist Isaac Leeser, the Reform institution builder Isaac Mayer Wise, and the Radical Reform theologian David Einhorn. Differences among these men reflected broader ideological and religious conflicts raging through American Jewish life during this period, conflicts that divided both the rabbinate and the laity. Each man's followers confidently assumed that their strategy was best suited to preserve Judaism from the challenges it faced in its new American setting.

Ultimately, these conflicts paved the way for an American Judaism that exhibited a full spectrum of beliefs and practices: everything from thoroughgoing traditionalism to the most far-reaching of innovations. This spectrum, allowing for almost limitless diversity in Jewish life, still adheres. It is one of the German period's most lasting and important legacies to later generations.

America: The Reform Movement's Land of Promise

Michael A. Meyer

In the 1840s, the most prominent Jewish religious leader in America was Isaac Leeser (1806–1868). Leeser had come to the United States from Germany at the age of eighteen with only a limited knowledge of Jewish and secular subjects. But he read widely on his own, proved himself articulate, and within five years was chosen the chazan of the influential Sephardi Mikveh Israel congregation in Philadelphia. His *Occident,* begun in 1843, became the first American Jewish periodical of significance and it spread his name widely among the various communities. Later he translated the Bible and prayerbook into English, published a shelf of textbooks, and established a short-lived rabbinical school. He perpetually sought to achieve unity among American Jews. Leeser was an Orthodox Jew, but not of the old type. He pioneered the regular English sermon in his congregation, railed against mystical currents in East European Judaism, and favored eliminating those elements in the synagogue that detracted from its sanctity. He enthusiastically joined Rebecca Gratz in establishing the first Sunday school for Jewish children, though it admittedly followed the Christian model. But Leeser was also a halakhic Jew who insisted that change could be justified only in accordance with Jewish legal tradition. Historical development, either in modes of thinking or in the Jews' circumstances, was not to his mind sufficient grounds for religious reform. He vigorously defended those beliefs that Reform rejected: the personal messiah, the divinity of the Oral Law, bodily resurrection, the divinely initiated return to Palestine, and the reinstitution of animal sacrifices. Leeser advocated a purely formal accommodation to America, an enlightened orthodoxy of belief and practice which would adopt American dress without inner transformations. Like Samson Raphael Hirsch in Germany, the European religious leader whom he resembles most closely, Leeser favored a linguistic, cultural, and patriotic adaptation. But Judaism itself, because divine, was necessarily eternal. For some Reformers Leeser became at times a compatriot in the common effort to unify and strengthen Jewish life in America. But more often, and for all of them, he was the antagonist, rooted in America yet strident in his anti-Reform polemics, the symbol of an integration which they regarded as shallow or incomplete.

During the first years of Leeser's career there was little or no Reform with which to do battle, only the widespread lack of observance to be deplored and the need to defend against the persistent importunities of Christian missionaries. But by the decade of the 1840s the impulse for religious reform began to spread in America. It arose within existing congregations and it brought together new circles devoted to its principles from the start. By 1855 there were congregations with varying degrees of reformed ritual in Charleston, Baltimore, New York, Albany, and Cincinnati. In succeeding years the number and size of Reform congregations would increase at a rapid pace and reforms would become more radical.

The rise of the Reform movement in America after the initial Charleston episode must be attributed to both Germanizing and Americanizing trends. Neither trend alone will explain it. Of the immigrants who swelled the Jewish population from about 5,000 in 1825 to about 250,000 in 1875 the vast majority came from German-speaking lands. At first they were almost exclusively rural Jews, many of them from the small towns and villages of southern Germany. They possessed little secular education. They came to America in flight from restrictive legislation and in quest of economic betterment. Whether or not they were observant in their new homes often depended on the opportunities available where they settled, in American towns or along the advancing frontier. Only in the 1840s and 1850s did a significant number of relatively more educated and affluent Jews make their way to the United States. Some of them had gained acquaintance in Germany with at least a moderate reform—a more decorous synagogue, vernacular sermons, and a slightly abbreviated ritual. This second generation of German immigrants sought in America the same kind of ritual with which they were familiar in Germany, even as the earlier generation had sought to replicate their particular *minhagim,* whether of southern or northern Germany, in the United States. The desire of the later immigrants for modifications in the traditional service now encountered similar wishes on the part of those earlier settlers who had taken root in America and looked to reforms as a channel of religious Americanization. When religious leaders, familiar with the theory as well as the practice of the Reform movement in Germany, came to America they found a lay impetus for religious reform already present. The task the laymen assigned them—and they to themselves—was to give it an intellectual foundation and to direct its course.

In April 1842 a group of laymen in Baltimore formed the Har Sinai Verein, a society of German Jews dedicated from the start to creating a Reform congregation. One of the founders was an immigrant from Hamburg who was commissioned by his associates to familiarize them with the Hamburg Temple prayerbook, which was then adopted for the religious service. The Hamburg Temple just at that time had attracted fresh attention on account of its new building and revised prayerbook which provoked a lively and bitter controversy. No doubt the victory of the Hamburg Reformers was a topic of conversation among Baltimore Jews and brought the Hamburg Temple into active consideration as a possible model for their own worship. Another factor seems to have been the arrival in Baltimore in 1840 of Abraham Rice, the first ordained rabbi to settle in America and a staunch champion of Orthodoxy. Rice became rabbi of the *Stadt Schule* (Baltimore Hebrew Congregation) and apparently drove away some of the men who could not accept his views and authority.

The Har Sinai Verein held its first lay-led service at the High Holidays in the fall of 1842. We know that the congregation sang hymns from the Hamburg Temple hymnbook accompanied by a parlor organ. As in Hamburg, the men wore hats and sat apart from the women; the liturgy was mainly in Hebrew. After twelve years a more radical group broke off briefly in 1854 and for the first time in America held its weekly service on Sunday. But soon it rejoined Har Sinai, which then invited David Einhorn to become its rabbi.

Three years after the formation of Har Sinai, in 1845, Congregation Emanu-El was officially organized in New York. It emerged from a *Cultus-Verein* (worship association), similar to the Verein in Baltimore, whose purpose was to create a new congregation with a reformed ritual. The founders of Emanu-El were principally men who had arrived in America with some general intellectual background and liberal views. As in Baltimore, they were relatively young and were dissatisfied with the traditional German rite services in their city. They too did not initially tamper with head coverings or separate seating but immediately introduced German hymns, and once they had a proper building, installed an organ. Although for the first decade Emanu-El used the traditional prayerbook, it soon had a triennial reading of the Torah, confirmations, and a briefer service. It eliminated honors and blessings for individual congregants and by the fall of 1855 had instituted family pews and a mixed choir, and abolished the *talit* as well as observance of the second days of festivals. The congregation sponsored an elementary day school until 1854, then a religious school on Sabbaths and Sundays. Its synagogue in 1855 seated more than 1,000, and its attendance of about 300 on a Saturday morning was thought better than the average among other congregations in the city. Within the largest Jewish community in America, Emanu-El, after a decade, was already drawing the most successful and financially well-established Jews in the city.

Emanu-El differed from Har Sinai in that it was able from the beginning to employ a spiritual leader of some knowledge and ability. Leo Merzbacher

(1809 or 1810–1856), a Bavarian Jew, came to America in the early 1840s with the *morenu* degree of talmudic competence from the great traditionalist scholar and champion of antimodernist Orthodoxy, Moses Sofer. He had also studied at the universities of Erlangen and Munich. In New York, Merzbacher served two existing congregations, but they soon broke with him, at least partly because he openly advocated some mild reforms. His availability was a major factor in the organization of Congregation Emanu-El, where he was employed as rabbi and lecturer until his untimely death in 1856.

In 1849 the Emanu-El board directed Merzbacher to prepare a ritual especially for the congregation. When it finally appeared in 1855 as *Seder Tefilah: The Order of Prayer for Divine Service,* handsomely printed and bound in two volumes, it was the first American Reform liturgy compiled by a rabbi. It is striking that although Merzbacher preached exclusively in German, the literal prayerbook translation and its preface were in English. One can only speculate that the use of English may have been a concession to Americanization and perhaps also for non-Jewish visitors. In any case the service was conducted almost exclusively in Hebrew supplemented by German hymns from the Hamburg *Gesangbuch.*

In some respects Merzbacher's prayerbook was traditional. It opened from right to left and retained references to resurrection and the restoration of the Temple. But it radically abbreviated the services, omitting not only repetitions but a large portion of the less central elements in the liturgy. The Additional Service *(musaf)* was retained only on Yom Kippur. Angelology was excised as were references to the sacrifices, vengeance, and the exaltation of Israel above other peoples. There was no *kol nidre* for the eve of Atonement. While prayers for the messianic return to Zion were generally eliminated, Merzbacher somewhat inconsistently retained the formula translated as: "But because of our sins we have been carried captive from our land, and removed from our country." From the Hamburg prayerbook he took over the Aramaic addition to the *kaddish* which makes specific reference to the dead, and when Merzbacher's successor, Samuel Adler, revised the prayerbook in 1860, he introduced a novel Hebrew prayer for the comfort of mourners into the weekday petition when recited in a house of mourning. Merzbacher's liturgical work caused a bit of a stir. Bernard Illowy, an Orthodox rabbi then serving in St. Louis, when approached by several laymen who favored its adoption, replied it was not a Jewish prayerbook and that anyone using it was "entirely excluded from all religious communion." *Seder Tefilah* also had some influence on later American Reform Jewish liturgy. But perhaps because its author died a few months after publication and so could not tout its virtues, his prayerbook was soon eclipsed by those of David Einhorn and Isaac Mayer Wise. Only at Temple Emanu-El and a very few other synagogues, such as Anshe Mayriv in Chicago, did "Merzbacher-Adler" remain the standard liturgy until near the end of the century.

Of frail health, lacking dynamism, and very much dependent upon the will of Emanu-El's lay leadership, Merzbacher was not able to spread his reformist ideas widely. In Charleston, Gustavus Poznanski was seeking to withdraw from professional religious leadership. Nor during his New York period was Max Lilienthal (1815–1882), later a leading reformer, ready to play an active role. Lilienthal had arrived in America in 1845 at the age of thirty, having already achieved some notoriety. Armed with rabbinical ordination and a doctorate from the University of Munich, he had traveled to Russia in 1839 to become teacher and preacher of the Jewish community in Riga, which possessed a strongly German orientation. There he had introduced both regular sermons and the confirmation ceremony for girls. Later, at the behest of the Russian Minister of Education, he had undertaken a well-publicized venture to persuade Jews in the Tsarist Empire of the benefits they would derive from educational reform. Disillusioned by what he came to recognize as the government's bad faith, he left for the freer climate of America. But once in the United States Lilienthal did not immediately act the reformer. The terms of his position as rabbi of three German congregations in New York made him entirely subject to the will of traditionalist lay leaders. He could only introduce confirmation and rules of decorum. When the union of congregations dissolved in 1847, Lilienthal opened a private Jewish school and in 1854 began urging moderate reform guided by Jewish law. In the press he defended the Talmud as "not a system of immovable stability, but of progress and development." However, only after he came to Cincinnati in 1855 did Lilienthal become a Reform activist.

Thus the American Reform movement in the 1840s still lacked a leader who possessed the same influence as Isaac Leeser. Moderate reforms had begun in a few congregations; a growing number of laymen were seeking a religious expression of Judaism more in keeping with their heightened sense of being Americans. But there was no one as yet to transform individual local initiatives into a common cause.

It was Isaac Mayer Wise (1819–1900) who, more than anyone else, succeeded in stimulating, unifying, and giving direction to American Reform. Though not an outstanding intellectual or an original thinker, Wise was an uncommon man. Initially plagued by recurrent severe depressions, hypochondria, and the wish for death, he was able to overcome his debilitating self-doubts and assume a supreme, manic self-confidence that enabled him to face enemies and personal defeats with near equanimity, always certain that eventually he would succeed. In time, two thoughts fixed themselves firmly in his mind: "that I had a talent for all things, and that I was a child of destiny."

Wise's talents were indeed extraordinary. He could express himself easily, dramatically, and effectively in writing, lectures, and sermons. Though not a scholar by temperament, with a few weeks of reading he could present competent popular discussions on an astounding variety of topics, always supplying his own critical opinions. His memory was prodigious; he was acquainted with all the details of Jewish life in America and abroad. His knowledge of Jewish sources was sufficient to confront scholars greater than he when the need arose. He had read the basic works of German *Wissenschaft des Judentums* and kept up with the progress of Jewish scholarship. Wise also knew well how to deal with people, to win friends and supporters for his projects. He conducted polemics effectively, often simply overwhelming opponents with his outpourings of rhetoric or confusing the issue until they gave up in despair. Controversy did not discourage him; he thrived on it. A good fight stimulated interest, and it made Jews think. Above all, Wise reaped the advantage of a psyche that endowed him with boundless energy: he edited and did much of the writing for two weekly newspapers, led a large congregation, and traveled around the country dedicating synagogues, giving guest sermons, and gaining supporters for old and new projects. He wrote historical novels and histories of ancient Israel. And in addition to his other tasks, he eventually founded and became president and professor of theology at the first successful American rabbinical school. Wise was known everywhere in American Jewry, a powerful force that moved sometimes in this direction, sometimes in that, but was always driving toward some goal.

Wise was born in the Bohemian village of Steingrub, the son of a poor Jewish schoolmaster. He studied in a yeshivah near Prague and may have attended some university courses in Prague and Vienna. But Wise's formal education was meager. He did not learn Greek or Latin, did not earn a doctorate, and may not even have received a regular rabbinical degree. Yet his training was sufficient to qualify him as a schoolmaster, like his father, in the Bohemian village of Radnitz. There he remained for three years from 1843 to 1846. But apparently Wise soon became restless. Larger horizons had opened before him during his studies. In Vienna he had spent time in the homes of the preacher Isaac Noah Mannheimer and the cantor Solomon Sulzer. In 1845 he was a spectator at the Frankfurt Rabbinical Conference; he read the political writings of the German-Jewish liberal Gabriel Riesser and the religious philosophy of Samuel Hirsch. Teaching children and giving German sermons in the Radnitz Synagogue proved not very rewarding tasks and the prospects for a better position in Europe seemed bleak. Very likely Wise had also developed, as he later claimed, an intense desire for the freer atmosphere which America could offer him. In any case, with wife and child, he left Europe behind in 1846 and never looked back with any regret. Later he would insist that he was an American in spirit even while still in Bohemia.

In the United States Wise found an environment perfectly attuned to his own values and instincts. America, he quickly realized, was a land unburdened by hampering, hobbling traditions. It was a place where individuals could freely elaborate their own ideas and seek to convince others of their validity. Very little was fixed; almost everything was still being shaped. Religion was untrammeled by state control and no one faith was favored above others. Here American Judaism could compete equally with other denominations and prove its worth. It was only necessary to show that the ancestral faith was well suited to American values.

Wise became a persistent enthusiast of America, seldom its critic. For Jews caught up in the process of Americanization, his reformist ideas answered their question as to if and how Judaism could be related to the American milieu. Ancient Israel, he suggested to them, was the prototype of American democracy; loyalty to Judaism was therefore very good Americanism. In introducing his first book, *History of the Israelitish Nation,* Wise noted that Moses had already "promulgated the unsophisticated principles of democratic liberty and of stern justice in an age of general despotism and arbitrary rule. . . . Moses formed one pole and the American revolution the other, of an axis around which revolved the history of thirty-three centuries." Later Wise determined that "theocracy is identical with democracy," for in Ancient Israel, as in America, no earthly monarch stood between the individual and the word of God. Only if America should depart from its ideals and enact laws contrary to his personal religious conviction, then "I am an Israelite first and would treat my country as being in a state of rebellion against me. . . . First my God and then my country is as good a motto as any." Though sometimes forced to compromise, Wise opposed the desire of Jewish immigrants from Germany to perpetuate the German language in sermons, prayer, and Jewish education. While he recognized that Reform owed much to its European progenitors, he was convinced that only in America could it succeed fully. Here its ideas would necessarily gain ever greater acclaim, for here alone Judaism could participate fully in a national destiny.

Wise has generally been regarded as a moderate Reformer, though he has also been deemed a closet radical. There is some truth to each conception. Wise was not beyond dissembling traditionalism on some issues even as he remained genuinely conservative on others. But it must be emphasized that the precise ultimate course of Reform, whether moderate or radical, was not really Wise's basic concern. He was determined above all else to establish a strong and united Judaism in America, and he was quite ready to be flexible in utilizing whatever organizational means or unifying philosophy could most effectively achieve that end at any particular time. Of course there were limits. Wise never accepted the divinity of the Oral Law or even of the Torah in its totality. Nor could he, on the other hand, espouse a Judaism devoid of divine revelation, providence, and the traditional Sabbath. But within those boundaries he was ready to maneuver and to accept ambiguous formulations. Consistency, moreover, was simply not his highest value.

Some of Wise's vacillation was certainly self-serving. He possessed a strain of opportunism along with a penchant for self-aggrandizement. Unity would have to be achieved under his aegis. But some of Wise's inconsistency was also due to honest reconsideration, to varying polemical contexts, or simply to the use of a phrase for the sake of effect. Wise, for example, would at times stress that he was above all a Reformer, writing on one occasion with typical hyperbole: "The reforming spirit was innate in me; it was my foremost characteristic." Yet at other times he would call himself and his associates Orthodox Jews, by which he really meant that Reform Judaism was not an aberration or even merely a branch on Judaism's tree; it was the trunk itself. If Wise's expressed views, with regard to talmudic authority, for example, grew more radical in the course of time, it is less likely that he harbored such views secretly and consistently from the start than that his personal ideas on the subject became less conservative or that, in the absence of a firm conviction to the contrary, he was ready to shift his views forward toward the center of a progressively more radical movement.

Yet in one most important point of belief Wise remained consistent. He always maintained that God had directly revealed His will to Moses and that Moses himself, not later writers, had composed virtually all of the Pentateuch. To be sure, Wise was a rationalist. He did not believe in miracles that violated the laws of nature. The Red Sea, he argued, parted on account of natural causes; incredible myths made their way into the biblical text. But Sinai was a real event, "a direct revelation from on high" during which God literally transmitted the Ten Commandments, the "laws of the covenant," to Moses and to Israel. The truth of that event was sufficiently attested by the Bible itself, the entire people of Israel which witnessed it, and the faithful, uninterrupted tradition that preserved the memory. True, Wise did not call the event supernatural, but he rejected the notion of mere inspiration of a revelation that came only from within. Unlike more radical Reformers, he did not believe in a "progressive revelation." Sinai was unique and unrepeatable. Its revelation was not the product of evolution; it had burst into existence suddenly. Development and practical application, but not a new or higher religious truth, followed after it: "The truth established on Mount Sinai remains truth forever." The laws of Moses, apart from the Decalogue, represent the first expansion and application of the Sinaitic principles. The Talmud and later rabbinic literature continued that process. All laws and interpretations that came after Sinai were subject to change. In their time they had made unavoidable, though limited concessions to their age, in the case of the Bible to slavery, bigamy, blood vengeance, primitive modes of worship involving sacrifices, and a hereditary priesthood. But the Sinaitic revelation itself remained immutable, rooted in the divine. For all of his reformist stance, there was an undeniable strain of fundamentalism in Wise. Without the rockbed of Sinai as the firm ground of faith Judaism would fall victim to relativism and to dismemberment by biblical critics. For the individual too revelation provided the certainty that protected against "pessimism, misanthropism, despair and suicide." If the Pentateuch were, as some biblical critics claimed, a patchwork, stitched together by deceitful priests, then "whence do I know that there is an only, unique, and eternal God, who is merciful, just, loving and true?" The prophetic books were relatively less important to Wise. While other Reformers began speaking frequently of Prophetic Judaism, Wise continued to anchor his faith in Sinai.

Postbiblical Jewish history, for Wise, was a heroic tale: a glorious struggle for independence waged by the Maccabees, a desperate defiance of Rome, an unparalleled perseverance and a remarkable creativity in the Diaspora. The rabbinic literature, Wise recognized, was the bulk of Israel's productivity in the Diaspora and he paid it full tribute, but he linked modern Judaism especially to the medieval philosophical tradition. Beginning with Saadia in the tenth century, according to Wise, rabbinic hermeneutics ceased to be the sole authority for the exposition of Scripture. Philology and philosophy became "the final arbiters of scriptural teachings." According to Wise, "it may be truly maintained that the school now called Reform had its origin then and there." The trend continued via Maimonides—but not via the uncritical commentaries of Rashi—on to Mendelssohn and *Wissenschaft des Judentums,* wherever reason was the guiding light of exegesis. Wise gave relatively less credit to the German Reformers of the nineteenth century, for the future of the movement by then, he believed, lay in America. A new stage in Jewish history had begun on this side of the ocean. Late in life he wrote: "American Judaism, i.e., Judaism reformed and reconstructed by the beneficent influence of political liberty and progressive enlightenment, is the youngest offspring of the ancient and venerable faith of Israel. . . . It is the American phase of Judaism."

Wise had arrived in New York in the summer of 1846 at the age of twenty-seven. Thanks to the recommendation of Max Lilienthal, he was very soon elected rabbi of Beth El in Albany, founded in 1838. There he remained for four turbulent years. Supported by a faction of the congregation, Wise was able to introduce a mixed choir, confirmation, German and English hymns, and to eliminate *piyutim* and the sale of honors. But another faction opposed him. He aroused ire when he warned an officer of the congregation that unless he closed his business on the Sabbath, he must, according to a rule of the congregation, resign his position of leadership. Further antagonism resulted from a personal dispute with a kosher butcher, who also served as cantor of the congregation. Wise had dared to declare his meat unfit because he was an alleged gambler and frequenter of saloons. By 1850 Wise's opponents could also declare him an avowed heretic, since on a trip to Charleston he had denied belief in resurrection and a personal messiah.

Amid charges and countercharges Wise was dismissed from his position, but nonetheless appeared in clerical garb for the New Year service and insisted on performing his ceremonial tasks. Later he recalled what happened:

> Everything was quiet as the grave. Finally the choir sings Sulzer's great *En Komokho.* At the conclusion of the song I step before the ark in order to take out

> the scrolls of the law as usual, and to offer prayer. Spanier [the president] steps in my way, and, without saying a word, smites me with his fist so that my cap falls from my head. This was the terrible signal for an uproar the like of which I have never experienced.

The melee that followed was quelled only by a sheriff's posse that hurried to the scene. The faction favoring Wise now split off and formed a new congregation, Anshe Emeth, while the traditionalists remaining at Beth El speedily undid Wise's reforms.

Anshe Emeth, which soon numbered about eighty families, was thus a Reform congregation from the start. Here Wise's innovations found ready support. Here too he introduced an organ and, in 1851, for the first time anywhere in a synagogue, the family pew. Mixed seating, which took root in European Reform only much later, was to spread very broadly in the United States. Its adoption by the American Reform movement, and later by Conservative Judaism as well, reflected the practice of most American churches where it symbolized not only a higher degree of women's equality but also a link between religion and the values of family life.

During the Albany years, from 1846 to 1854, Wise frequently expressed views that were his heritage from German Reform. "Judaism acknowledges and permits rational progress," he wrote in 1849, "a development and interpretation of the given up to its highest potential." He forthrightly stated his belief that much of the ceremonial law had breathed its last, leaving behind lifeless rote observance. Only those rituals that could instill love of God and moral truth belonged to "the essence of Judaism." Ceremonials were means, not ends, and hence could be judged by their adequacy. Moreover, not all Jews required them to the same degree. Yet Wise was also defining himself quite conservatively: "I am a reformer, as much so as our age requires; because I am convinced that none can stop the stream of time, none can check the swift wheels of the age; but I have always the *Halacha* for my basis; I never sanction a reform against the *Din* [Jewish law]." Wise was clearly determined from the start to create a transformed Judaism, but he recognized that it could be successful only if built on the still widely accepted foundation of rabbinic authority.

In 1854 Wise left Albany to become the rabbi of Bene Yeshurun in Cincinnati, a traditional congregation in which a reformist party was on the ascendant. Cincinnati was then the largest metropolis west of the Alleghenies, a bustling commercial entrepôt on the Ohio River. Its Jewish community had reached 2,500 by 1854 and would more than double in the next decade. Its Jews were well established, though they would not be affluent until after the Civil War. Bene Yeshurun, organized in 1840, was composed mainly of Bavarian Jews; it differed in composition and rite from the older "English congregation," Bene Israel. In Cincinnati, where he remained the rest of his life, Wise could flourish in an atmosphere still redolent with the pioneering spirit that so well matched his own view of life. Here he could unleash his full energies and hope to find a sympathetic, even enthusiastic response. He insisted upon and received a life contract. But perhaps chastened by his experience in Albany, he was careful not to cause antagonism. Under his influence the congregation adopted reforms gradually and grew to 220 members by 1859, making it, after Emanu-El in New York, the second largest congregation in the United States. When Max Lilienthal came to Cincinnati as rabbi of Bene Israel in 1855, Wise gained a colleague and supporter. Bene Israel then began the introduction of its own synagogue reforms, so that the two largest of the four Cincinnati congregations were embarked on a similar course.

Wise was now ready to assume the role of national Jewish leadership to which he aspired. Only three months after taking over his new position in Cincinnati he founded the *Israelite,* a weekly Jewish newspaper that soon challenged Leeser's *Occident* in Philadelphia and Robert Lyon's *Asmonean* in New York as the chief sounding board for American Jewish opinion. To his readers Wise announced with typical bombast that he had put depression behind him: "The powerful impulse of the heart triumphed victoriously over fear and melancholy thought; and we re-appear before our friends as cheerful as ever, with an unchanged and immutable confidence in our cause, and with the firm determination to defend it at any and every risk." He was now intent on using all his energies for the sake of "our aged and venerable mother, Judaism," preparing the ancestral faith for its destined role as *"the religion* emphatically of the civilized world." Pretentiously but confidently, he applied Isaiah's words to himself: "And I heard the voice of the Lord saying: whom shall I send and who shall go for us? And I said: behold here I am, send me."

Early in 1855 Wise began agitating in the *Israelite* for a conference to unite American Jewry. His knowledge that earlier attempts to convene such a meeting, by Leeser in 1841 and by Wise himself in 1848, had failed to win support could not quell his ardor. He recognized, however, that only if Orthodox as well as Reform congregations could be induced to participate would such a gathering succeed. By August he had prepared the official call for a conference in Cleveland that October and he had gathered endorsements, not only from like-minded rabbis, but from traditionalist colleagues as well. All in all, nine rabbis signed the proposal, which called for deliberation on union, a regular synod, a common liturgy referred to as *Minhag America,* and a plan for Jewish education.

Although three of the Orthodox signatories did not attend the Cleveland conference, Isaac Leeser did, and there were other Orthodox delegates among the rabbinical and lay representatives from eight cities. Consequently, however, the chances of agreement seemed slim. The parties sat apart and glowered at each other with a suspicion unrelieved when Wise was elected president. Once it became apparent that the alternatives were forced compromise or failure, Wise chose the former, disarming Leeser by proposing that the conference agree on the divinity of the Bible and the obligatory authority of the Talmud. Merzbacher, Wise, and Leeser then discussed Wise's proposal through much of the night. The following day the conference adopted a call for a congregational synod that would be guided by common belief in the Bible as "of immediate divine origin" and the Talmud as containing "the traditional, legal, and logical exposition of the biblical laws which must be expounded and practiced according to the comments of the Talmud." Though he later defended the platform vigorously, this was probably a more traditional position than Wise's own, even at that time. But he recognized the value of committing the Orthodox to a common program with the Reformers, and he believed that within the projected synod the Reform faction would succeed in achieving its goals. Overcome with "glowing enthusiasm," Wise composed triumphal hymns. An "American Judaism, free, progressive, enlightened, united and respected," seemed within grasp.

Radical Reform in America—David Einhorn

Wise's hopes were speedily dashed. Upon his return to Philadelphia, Isaac Leeser was pressed to defend making common cause with avowed Reformers. It was not long until Leeser realized that Wise and his associates were proceeding to introduce liturgical and other innovations heedless of the conservatism he thought implied by the Cleveland principles. The union of moderate Reform and modernist Orthodoxy, represented by the presence of Wise and Leeser together at Cleveland, was crumbling on the right.

However, the fiercest opposition to the Cleveland platform did not come from Orthodoxy. It arose within that faction of the American Reform movement that was unwilling to give even lip service to talmudic authority for the sake of religious unity. Har Sinai in Baltimore and Emanu-El in New York formally dissociated themselves from the platform. Almost immediately there was criticism, as well, from the European Reformers Leopold Stein and Ludwig Philippson. Wise's compromise was seen as a betrayal of Reform ideology, an inconsistent and unconscionable step backwards. Thus Wise not only failed permanently to win over Orthodox moderates; in the attempt he seriously alienated the small but growing party of thoroughgoing Reformers in America and their sympathizers abroad.

By chance it was only a few weeks before the Cleveland conference that the first ideologue of European radical Reform Judaism arrived in America. David Einhorn (1809–1879) was already forty-six years old when he accepted the invitation of Har Sinai in Baltimore to become its rabbi; his Reform philosophy had crystallized abroad and would not change substantially in America. Einhorn almost immediately became Wise's severest critic, not only on account of his colleague's views, but also because of Wise's style of popular leadership. Einhorn was a very different sort of personality from Wise. While the Cincinnati rabbi was affable, dynamic, often careless in expression, Einhorn was reserved, scholarly, intensely serious, and careful to formulate his views in well qualified, often intricate German sentences. He attracted respect, not enthusiasm; he possessed the gifts of an intellectual, not of a popular leader. Einhorn's circle of influence would always remain limited to the few who could understand and appreciate his message. Yet it was Einhorn's uncompromising radicalism, rather than Wise's accommodating moderation, which by the end of the century would characterize American Reform.

David Einhorn was born in the Bavarian village of Dispeck near Fürth. A talmudic prodigy at the Fürth yeshivah, he received a rabbinical diploma there at the age of seventeen. But his studies at the universities of Würzburg, Munich, and Erlangen soon robbed him of his Orthodoxy, so that as a dreaded "neologue" he could find no rabbinical employment in Bavaria. Finally, in 1842, he was able to gain the rabbinate of Birkenfeld in the Grand Duchy of Oldenburg. After five years there, he assumed Holdheim's old position in Mecklenburg-Schwerin, and for a few months in 1852 he served as rabbi of the radical Reform congregation in Pest before the government closed it down. While in Birkenfeld, Einhorn had been among the European rabbis who defended Abraham Geiger's right to combine free scholarly inquiry with the rabbinical office in Breslau. In an erudite responsum he had expressed the view that while the Talmud was "a channel of the divine," it was not divine in and of itself. On the other hand, he had also joined rabbinical colleagues in condemning the radical Frankfurt *Reformfreunde* for failing to recognize the divinity of Mosaism and the progressive role played by the Talmud in its time. In 1845 and 1846 Einhorn participated actively in the rabbinical conferences at Frankfurt and Breslau. Here he was among the radicals. He wanted services conducted mostly in German, the "mother tongue" of German Jews, which alone could express their ideas and feelings. While recognizing that the Frankfurt conference quite properly stood on talmudic grounds, he insisted that the gathered rabbis were by no means bound to follow every talmudic dictate. At Breslau he agreed with Samuel Holdheim that Sabbath *rest* was merely symbolic and hence flexible to a point, though Sabbath *sanctification* was absolute. In his later years he would favor a supplementary Sunday service, but he would always insist on preserving the historical Saturday Sabbath.

Shortly before he left Europe, Einhorn published the first installment of what was intended to be a multivolume theoretical elaboration of Mosaism. Here he embarked on the task of explaining Mosaic laws in order to determine their essence, to trace them back to a single principle which he defined as a delicate balance of unity and individuality. Like his philosophical colleagues Steinheim, Formstecher, and Samuel Hirsch, Einhorn went on to set

Judaism sharply apart from pagan Greek philosophy. Against Mendelssohn and in keeping with Reform ideology, Einhorn here maintained that Judaism did indeed have dogmas and implied that these, rather than the laws, were Judaism's basic characteristics. What especially set Einhorn's work apart from other Reform writings was its focus on symbolism, its attempt to disclose the religious reality beneath ritual acts, especially the sacrificial service of the Temple. Einhorn noted that the synagogue quite rightly "always *felt* the importance of sacrifices, but without *comprehending* that importance, without grasping the eternally true idea on which the sacrifices were based and distinguishing the idea from the symbolic and hence transitory shell." Later he would name his prayerbook *Olat Tamid,* recalling the ancient perpetual offering.

Perhaps as early as his university years, and under the influence of the German philosopher Friedrich Schelling, Einhorn adopted the notion of a prebiblical, primordial monotheism that was the common possession of all humans. It was an idea that would persistently play a central role in Einhorn's religious thought. In 1857 he wrote that the "real shibboleth" of Reform Judaism was this:

> Judaism in its essence is older than the Israelites; as pure humanity, as the emanation of the inborn divine spirit, it is as old as the human race. The origin and development of the human spirit are also its own origin and its own development. It is rooted in Adam and culminates in a messianically perfected humanity. It was not a religion, but a religious people, that was *newly* created at Sinai, a priest people called upon, first of all, to impress the ancient divine teaching more deeply upon itself and then to bring it to universal dominion.

Here indeed was the essence of Einhorn's Reform Judaism, the nucleus of ideas which he chose especially to stress. Judaism, as Einhorn conceived it, begins and ends in universalism. Revelation is inherent in the human spirit from the beginning of universal, not Jewish history. It is never external, although the Bible pictures it that way at Sinai. God does not speak to human beings from outside themselves, but only from within to those who possess special gifts. Even Moses perceived God only in his spirit. The divine spirit brings light to its human counterpart; it mediates between God and man. While for Christianity the word becomes flesh, for Judaism it becomes spirit, a gift to all ages and all peoples. Thus Sinai revealed nothing new; it "simply disclosed to human nature its dearest and sweetest secrets." Revelation, understood in this way, is more process than event, more rediscovery and increased awareness than transmission. Within the Bible, Einhorn traced the advance of revelation from Noah to Abraham and Moses. But spiritual apprehension of the divine does not stop there. The basic religious and moral truths of the Torah do indeed remain immutable but the divine influence in the human spirit continues. There are "further revelations" which make the biblical doctrines more definite or clearer and the moral laws stricter. Revelation, then, is progressive, or put differently, the human spirit in its historical progress opens itself to God ever anew. Einhorn expressed this idea enthusiastically in relation to scientific achievement at the time the transatlantic cable was completed in 1866:

> Ceaselessly the word of God reveals itself in the advancing knowledge of His works, in the shaping of history! Never, never does the divine spring of revelation run dry among the children of man. And a time like the present, in which human research has given birth to a giant straddling the ocean, is not merely as filled, but in an incomparably greater degree more filled with God than was gray antiquity.

The most significant and novel element of the Sinaitic revelation was therefore neither theological nor moral. With regard to a conception of God, Sinai only elevated earlier notions of the unique Creator who is exalted above all creatures, purely spiritual, yet personal and always present. But at Sinai for the first time Israel accepted its moral responsibility as the chosen people of that God. Despite his universalism, Einhorn did not reject the controversial idea of the election of Israel. Already at the Frankfurt conference he had noted its practical value in the European context where it created "a beneficial self-esteem over against the reigning church." And at least as early as 1844, Einhorn had associated chosenness with the priesthood of the entire Jewish people in accordance with the biblical verse "You shall be to Me a kingdom of priests and a holy nation" (Exod. 19:6). The features of Jewish particularism—its ceremonials and its separation from the other religions of the world—were to Einhorn the Jews' priestly garb, which they were not free to remove until messianic times.

No one stressed more than Einhorn the mission of this priest people to the nations of the world. The destruction of its ancient temple and political institutions became the starting point of a universal and still unfinished task. Hence the events which had evoked mourning for nearly 2,000 years were in fact providential, not a punishment for sin but a necessary condition for universal priestly activity. The Ninth of Av, commemorating the destruction of both temples, became in Einhorn's prayerbook a day of joy as well as sadness. Einhorn's liturgy did not pass over the tragedy, but pointed beyond it to new light: "Not like an outcast son did Your firstborn go forth into the strange world, but as Your messenger for all the families of the earth." As once the Aaronide priests offered sacrifices in the ancient Temple, so the priesthood of all Israel was thenceforth required to present different sacrifices, more acceptable to God: love of God and humans, pure and holy conduct. Thus "the day of sorrow and fasting has become a day of gladness" and a time of rededication to building the "new Jerusalem" that will embrace all humanity. Einhorn did not believe in a personal messiah. All of Israel collectively was the messianic people. The phrase in the *ya'aleh ve-yavo* prayer for the festivals which speaks of "the remembrance of the messiah the son of David Your servant" in Einhorn's version became "the remembrance of all Your people the house of Israel, Your messiah."

On account of its mission, Israel was required to maintain its separate identity, however universal its religious faith. Einhorn usually spoke of the Jews as a *Stamm,* something more than a religious community, a group of common ancestry, to which he ascribed a common historical purpose. It was on account of his fervent belief in the Jewish mission that Einhorn was a lifelong opponent of mixed marriages and refused to officiate at such ceremonies even when pressed to do so. On one occasion he called mixed marriages "the nail in the coffin of the small Jewish race."

That Einhorn personally took the moral mission of Israel seriously is clear from his stand on slavery. Already in Germany he had castigated what he regarded as the enslavement of the Jews by a government that treated them like stepchildren. He had called, as well, for the religious emancipation of women. In America, within months of his arrival, he branded black slavery "the cancer of the Union." Applying his Reformer's distinction between principles and laws, he argued that while the Bible's laws tolerate slavery, its principle that all humanity is created in the image of the divine boldly militates against it. When Morris Raphall, the Orthodox rabbi of B'nai Jeshurun in New York, defended Negro slavery on the basis of the Bible in 1861, Einhorn was aroused to write a lengthy critique. Urged to keep politics from the pulpit, he asked rhetorically: "Is not the question of slavery above all a purely religious issue?" It was his outspoken stand on slavery that forced Einhorn to flee Baltimore for his life in April 1861. Later he claimed that it was also on account of his unwillingness to remain silent that *Sinai,* the German-language monthly he had founded shortly after his arrival in America, lost half its subscribers and died after seven volumes in January 1863.

Einhorn's feelings about the United States were ambivalent. On the one hand it represented to him the environment of freedom Judaism required in order to flourish. Therefore it was the land of Judaism's future. He developed the highest regard for its statesmen: Washington, Jefferson, Lincoln. But he would not subordinate religion to patriotism, and he was as often America's critic as its admirer. Despite the Constitution, there was a significant trend to foist Christianity on everyone, both in the schools and in public life. Americans neglected the education of their youth and worshiped the almighty dollar. They severely punished a poor man for stealing a crust of bread but allowed wealthy capitalists to steal millions. Einhorn detested American ostentatiousness, violence, and admiration for deeds rather than ideas. In nineteenth-century America success meant being a good showman, and a showman Einhorn was neither able nor willing to be. His favorite word for American popular culture was "humbug." To be called "reverend" in the United States, he once noted, often all you needed was a lot of impudence, a white neckerchief, a robe, and anyone's printed collection of sermons.

Unlike Wise, Einhorn looked to Germany and to German Reform Judaism for inspiration. He felt more comfortable with the greater value Germans placed on serious intellectual endeavor in religion as opposed to practical activity. The German language always remained for Einhorn the "language of our spirit and our heart . . . the language that brought the Reform idea to life and continued to bear it." For the foreseeable future German would have to remain the vehicle for liturgy and sermons. Einhorn personally used it without exception in his writings and from the pulpit. And in his final sermon he said of himself:

> Germany is my home. I am an *ivri,* a wanderer, and I journeyed with thousands of my brethren from there to this God blessed republic! As proud as I am of my adopted citizenship . . . I will never forget that the old home is the land of thinkers, presently the foremost land of culture, and above all the land of Mendelssohn, the birthplace of Reform Judaism. . . . If you sever from Reform the German spirit or—what amounts to the same thing—the German language, you will have torn it from its native soil and the lovely flower must wilt.

Einhorn was never fully at home in America. Despite his veneration for American ideals and his defense of its highest principles, he remained a stranger to the rough-and-tumble of its daily life. He really was, as he defined himself, a wandering Hebrew, justifying his own alienation by the Jewish mission still unfulfilled.

Not surprisingly, Einhorn had little regard for Isaac Mayer Wise. While in print he tried to ignore the popular Cincinnati rabbi, his letters abound in expressions like *shafel* (toady), "chief humbugger," and "Jewish pope." When Wise published his prayerbook, *Minhag America,* in 1857 and sent a copy off to Baltimore, Einhorn could not bear to even open it. Rather than ignore the prayerbook entirely, *Sinai* carried a critical review by Wise's more radical successor in Albany, Elkan Cohen. From the time of his arrival in America Einhorn sought to differentiate his brand of Reform from Wise's. He urged his congregants not to fear the specific designation "radical Reform." "Radical Reform," he told them, "wants a Judaism that bears the royal messianic mantle; moderate Reform—a Judaism swathed in Orthodox and reformist rags." Radical Reform was by nature uncompromising. Its motto was "first truth, then peace." For the radical Reformer "truth, which means peace with God, must stand higher than peace with humans and a stormy turbulent sea must be more precious than the calm of a stagnant swamp that exudes only polluting vapors." By nature radical Reform was decisive, unyielding, revolutionary. But, at the beginning in America, it was also rather lonely.

Einhorn's direct influence was very limited. Har Sinai, with seventy families, was not large, nor was Keneseth Israel in Philadelphia during the years Einhorn served it from 1861 to 1866. While at Har Sinai, Einhorn complained that although educated German Jews were coming to America in ever larger numbers, very few of them were settling in Baltimore. From time to time Einhorn was asked to speak in like-minded congregations: at Temple Emanu-El in New York and at Keneseth Israel in Philadelphia before he became its rabbi. But his carefully prepared German presentations were far less in demand than Wise's flamboyant addresses in English. *Sinai,* Einhorn's ponderous monthly, maintained itself precariously and was received by far fewer readers than those who every week read Wise's lively *Israelite.* During the fifties Einhorn had only two intellectually significant sympathizers. When Samuel Adler arrived in New York to assume the rabbinate of Temple Emanu-El in 1857, Einhorn welcomed the presence of a veteran, similarly inclined colleague. Likewise in Bernhard Felsenthal, who became preacher and teacher of Temple Sinai in Chicago, Einhorn discovered a talented and deep-thinking supporter and confidant. But there were few others. For at least a decade after his arrival, Einhorn's radical Reform remained a fringe phenomenon.

Einhorn had arrived in Baltimore virtually on the eve of the Cleveland conference. Though invited to attend, he stayed away, claiming the need to get settled. Yet the gathering had barely dispersed when Einhorn launched his *Sinai* with blasts at the conference's position on the Talmud. True, Einhorn held, the Talmud was one of the most significant phases in Judaism's development, had enriched it manifoldly, "reformed" Mosaic law, and introduced the welcome novel concept of the immortality of the soul. But it was also obsolete, morally narrow, and focused on the letter rather than the spirit of biblical Judaism. It misinterpreted biblical texts and had encumbered Judaism with a stifling array of petty religious regulations. Where the Talmud had made religious advances it had happened without conscious intent. Only when life wrested change did the Rabbis force new interpretations into the letter of the law.

But it was not only the Cleveland conference's acceptance of talmudic authority that irritated Einhorn. It was the very notion of religious authority, as much the proposed permanent synod as the imposition of rabbinic Judaism. Freedom, religious not less than political, was among Einhorn's most cherished values. He called Judaism "the religion of freedom" and remained ever suspicious of any attempt to infringe congregational autonomy or individual conscience. Any matter of hierarchy was anathema. Though later he favored the radicals formulating their own collective statement, Einhorn never himself put forward a plan for a general rabbinical synod or even for congregational union. One of the things he appreciated most about America was that, unlike in Germany, radical rabbis did not need to be hypocrites; they did not have to play at being Orthodox to avoid offending conservatives within a religious community seeking to serve all.

The men of Cleveland, he thought, had negotiated a "foul peace." Not only would the dead hand of the past choke the living spirit, but a collective will would impose itself on individual religious reflection. "Let the free American Israel be on its guard against such hierarchical strivings," Einhorn warned. At Cleveland, he asserted, the participants had constructed a "Tower of Babel" intended to serve as a pedestal for Wise's various initiatives, his Zion College in Cincinnati and his projected prayerbook. Einhorn was certain that their tower would never reach the heavens, that God had confounded their speech. As it turned out, on that point Einhorn proved correct: the tower was indeed a failure. But Wise was not dismayed. Undaunted, he simply picked up the bricks and kept on building elsewhere.

Rivalry and Rift

Not long after the furor over the Cleveland conference died down, the attention of American Jews was drawn to a larger rift that was tearing into the fabric of America. Slavery was a divisive issue for Jews no less than for Gentiles. The Orthodox rabbis Morris Raphall and Bernard Illowy defended it from Scripture; Einhorn, as we have seen, vigorously denounced it. So did the Reformers Bernhard Felsenthal and Liebmann Adler in Chicago. But Isaac Mayer Wise was among those who argued for states' rights. Cincinnati lay just north of the Mason-Dixon line. It was a station on the Underground Railroad, but its trade was largely with the South, where Wise's congregants had business associates and friends. Half of the subscribers to Wise's *Israelite* were Southerners at the time, and he had traveled extensively in the region. Wise did oppose slavery, but on this moral issue, as earlier and later on specific Jewish matters of belief and practice, he preferred unity—in this case of the American Union—over the provocation of separation for the sake of principle. Thus he remained silent or neutral as the Civil War raged about him. Not until well into the conflict did Wise come to venerate Abraham Lincoln, a man he had earlier despised along with abolitionists in general. Like his more conservative colleague Benjamin Szold in Baltimore, Wise deplored radical solutions.

The years immediately following the Civil War brought unparalleled prosperity to the United States and to American Jewry. Some Jews, indeed, had already managed to increase their wealth substantially during the war years. In one community after another they were soon ready to express their newfound status by constructing opulent, monumental synagogues. Wise's congregation in Cincinnati, with 220 families the second largest in America in 1859, undertook to build a grand structure as early as 1863, still in the midst of the war. Completed in 1866 at a cost of more than a quarter million dollars, it was modeled to a degree on the Moorish synagogues then fashionable in Germany. Two slender, minaret-like towers ascended from its multi-domed roof, while, somewhat later, the interior was lavishly decorated with Hebrew verses and geometrical designs. Similar grand structures were built at the same time or shortly thereafter in San Francisco, New York, Philadelphia, and other communities. While in 1860 there were, by one estimate, only 77 synagogues in the United States with a capacity of 34,412, by 1870 their number and capacity had more than doubled to 152 edifices capable of seating 73,265. The value of synagogue property had increased even more dramatically, by 354 percent. To help pay for the new structures pews were sold at public auction, the most desirable one at Temple Emanu-El in New York bringing $9,300.

With the construction of new synagogues or the renovation of old ones came a quickening of religious reform. The lavish buildings were thought incomplete without a magnificent organ. In 1860 Wise could claim only a dozen "organ congregations"; eight years later there were more than thirty. Temple Emanu-El in New York could now boast an instrument said to be the largest in the country except for Music Hall in Boston, while that of Bene Yeshurun in Cincinnati was acclaimed as the "best in the West." Even synagogues that were relatively traditional at the time, like Rodeph Shalom in Philadelphia and Baltimore Hebrew Congregation, adopted the organ in the early seventies. Less frequent as yet was the employment of non-Jewish choristers to assist, and sometimes to replace, the cantor and volunteer Jewish choir.

Mixed seating too became commonplace, as did the abolition of the second days of holidays. Many synagogues abbreviated the Torah reading by introduction of the triennial cycle and by the 1870s began to reduce it further, for example by reading only selected verses from the weekly portion and forgoing a complete reading entirely. Orthodox prayerbooks were increasingly put aside in favor of unorthodox. Relatively traditional synagogues chose the conservative prayerbook edited by Benjamin Szold and revised by Marcus Jastrow, middle-of-the-road ones Wise's *Minhag America,* and those drawn to radical Reform picked Einhorn's *Olat Tamid.* Use of vernacular in the liturgy became accepted practice, the relative proportion of Hebrew varying among the congregations. Gradually the explicitly Reform congregations also discarded the prayer shawl and then the headcovering for men. In some instances congregational boards allowed a period of choice before making bareheadedness mandatory. While the confirmation ceremony was very common by the late seventies, only a few congregations—Emanu-El in New York and Har Sinai in Baltimore, for example—had as yet gone so far as to prohibit the traditional Bar Mitzvah. In some instances it was a lay faction, eager for a style of worship appropriate to the congregants' rising status, that pressed for change; in other places rabbis sought the reforms for reasons of principle.

American Jewry was rapidly becoming both affluent and increasingly Reform. Wise could wax exultant: "Everywhere the temples of Israel, the monuments of progressive Judaism, as though touched by a magic wand, rise in proud magnificence, and proclaim with a thundering voice [against the opponents of Reform], we are right and you are wrong." Only "a small minority of our coreligionists still preserve some of the antiquated forms and overcome notions, but they are harmless remnants of bygone days." To Wise's mind, therefore, the struggle with Orthodoxy was over. It was dying a natural death. Against the radical Reformers he insisted that "Reform is no question any longer, and it is useless to harp away continually the outworn theme. With a very few and unimportant exceptions in the Atlantic cities, the American Hebrew community is decidedly progressive and in full sympathy with the best ideas of the age." Others shared Wise's conclusion. A New York correspondent for the German *Israelitische Wochenschrift* wrote in a similar vein: "Here in America attacks [upon talmudic Judaism, thought necessary in Germany] have become wholly superfluous. The meager residues of Orthodoxy which one still finds in this land are insignificant." For Wise and his supporters the really important objectives—now more clearly than ever—were Americanization and union.

Neither of these two goals could be easily attained. Americanization, so obvious an ideal for Wise, had its severest critics not in the traditionalist camp, but among the radicals. While Isaac Leeser and Wise fervently propagated it, opposition came from David Einhorn, from those rabbis associated with him, and from a portion of the Reform laity.

In the first half of the nineteenth century most German Jews who migrated to America had been only superficially Germanized. They had not gone to a German university; they spoke Judeo-German. Americanization was their first experience with integration into the modern world. It was otherwise with many of those who came later, from the forties until the Civil War. To a greater or lesser degree they carried German cultural baggage with them on the migration to America. In the United States they found a large non-Jewish community of German speakers, organized into a variety of social and fraternal societies. Jews could join such groups easily—indeed more easily than their prototypes in the old country. Often German Jews looked back with nostalgia to the physical and cultural landscape of their youth and they sought to preserve something of those memories in their new homeland. During the fifties, sixties, and even into the seventies German was frequently the language of Jewish schools, synagogue minutes, liturgy, and sermons.

Even as late as 1874 it was estimated that the German language predominated in the majority of the Jewish congregations in the United States.

To the minds of many of the later immigrants Reform Judaism was an integral part of their German heritage. They had been confirmed by German liberal rabbis; they were accustomed to a reformed liturgy, to the newer German synagogue melodies, and to the Reform ideas expounded from liberal German pulpits. While by necessity they learned to use English in business and on the street, they chose to preserve German in the home and, no less than Hebrew, as the sacred language of the synagogue. As we have seen, Einhorn's position on the religious necessity of maintaining German was clearcut. But he was not alone. Other radical Reformers, like Samuel Adler in New York and Bernhard Felsenthal and Isaac Löb Chronik in Chicago, shared his view that American Jewry was still not ready to strike out on its own, that its future, religiously and culturally, depended on the ability to transmit the heritage of German Jewry's religious values and the achievements of its Jewish scholarship. Every aspect of the way it was done in Germany remained important. At Har Sinai in Baltimore, a pioneer congregation of radical Reform, men and women continued to sit separately until 1873, simply because that was the custom in Germany. Only at the end of the sixties and thereafter did the most loyal Germanizers begin to waver. Their American-born children preferred to speak English and some of the children could not understand the German sermons. Moreover, the rabbis noted that German Reform, bound by the constraints of the local united community, had stagnated into conservatism. By the eighties they could also see more clearly how endemic anti-Semitism still was in German society while appreciating more fully how a freer American climate had enabled its Jews to rise socially and economically, to build their magnificent religious and philanthropic institutions. Although German consciousness would linger among Reform Jews for another generation and more, it was later increasingly defined as the special German identity of *American* Jews who had wrested religious hegemony from their brethren abroad. As Rabbi Adolf Moses of Mobile, Alabama put it—in German—in 1882: "From America salvation will go forth; in this land [and not in Germany] will the religion of Israel celebrate its greatest triumphs."

CHAPTER 6

The Civil War divided Jews much as it did the nation as a whole. There were Jews in the North and Jews in the South, Jews who supported slavery and Jews who condemned it, Jews who fought for the Union and Jews who fought for the Confederacy. While few Jews joined the ranks of the radical abolitionists—their Evangelical Christian rhetoric was distasteful to Jews and sometimes downright anti-Jewish—some did echo their views. At the same time, others, notably Judah P. Benjamin and David Yulee, assumed prominent positions in the Confederacy and defended slavery as a "positive good."

If in many respects the Civil War affected Jews much as it did other Americans, there were nevertheless three features of the struggle that affected Jews uniquely. First, wartime tensions led to an upsurge of racial and religious prejudice in America, and Jews, both in the North and in the South, proved to be convenient scapegoats. Even famous Americans slipped into anti-Semitic stereotypes when they meant to condemn one Jew alone. Second, Jews in the North (not in this case in the South) had to fight for their right to have a Jewish army chaplain—no easy task, since by law a military chaplain had to be a "regularly ordained minister of some Christian denomination." Although President Lincoln himself urged that this law be amended, it took heavy Jewish lobbying and over a year of hard work until the amendment was passed. Third, and most shocking of all to Jews, they had to face what was without doubt the most sweeping anti-Jewish official order in all of American history: General Order No. 11, published on December 17, 1862, that expelled all Jews from General Grant's military department. An irate and highly prejudiced response to wartime smuggling and speculating, crimes engaged in by Jews and non-Jews alike, it met with forceful Jewish protests. Within eighteen days, thanks to President Lincoln, the order was revoked.

Following the war, as the distinguished American Jewish historian Naomi W. Cohen shows in the essay that follows, communal self-defense became an ever-more-important priority for American Jews. Evangelical Protestants calling for a "Christian America" crusaded for an amendment to acknowledge "Almighty God" and "the Lord Jesus Christ" in the Constitution, advocated stronger Sunday closing laws, and promoted Bible readings and prayers in the public schools. Jewish leaders, spurred by the Board of Delegates of American Israelites, founded in 1859 to, among other things, "watch over occurrences at home and abroad relating to the Israelites," challenged each of these moves. They demanded equality for the nation's growing Jewish population and projected a vision of America where members of all faiths, Christians and non-Christians alike, enjoyed equal rights. Some also made common cause with those who advocated a secular state divorced from religion altogether. Church–state questions continued to spawn lively debates not only to the end of the nineteenth century, but throughout the twentieth as well. Through these debates, Jews helped to define both the nature of American society and their own unique place within it.

The Christian Agenda

Naomi W. Cohen

At the outbreak of the Civil War geography dictated loyalty: Jews, like their countrymen, fought for the Union or the Confederacy in the field and on the home front. During the war years, however, a wave of Judaeophobia swept both the North and the South. An upsurge in religious passion accompanying the national crisis reinforced the age-old negative stereotypes of the Jews—Christ killers, accursed and stiff-necked people, unscrupulous money changers, aliens, and traitors. Harassment and vilification culminated in General Grant's notorious Order No. 11, which in December 1862 expelled Jews "as a class" from the military department of Tennessee. A rare example of official discrimination aimed openly and exclusively against Jews, the order was readily accepted by Americans. The explanation, as a bitter Isaac Leeser found, lay in naked Christian prejudice: "The parties threatened with such ill-usage were not Christians, not even negroes, nothing but Jews! . . . and those, every one knows, are enemies of Christ and his apostles."

Although Lincoln quickly revoked the order, his administration was guilty of other slights against the Jews. One stemmed from an executive order which, studded with references to Christian servicemen and "a Christian people," called for Sunday observance in the armed forces. To concerned Jews it represented a breach of separation and, since no provision was made for the Jewish soldiers and their Sabbath, a violation of religious equality. Another threat to equality was Congress's failure to provide for Jewish chaplains. A conscious omission, it was challenged by Representative Clement Vallandigham on the floor of the House as a breach of the establishment clause of the First Amendment. "This is not a 'Christian *Government*,'" he said, "nor a Government which has any connection with any one form of religion in preference to any other form." A spirited public exchange ensued. While some Protestant groups shuddered at the thought of blasphemers as chaplains, the Board of Delegates of American Israelites (BDAI) contended that the act established a religious test for a federal office and thereby violated both Article VI of the Constitution and the First Amendment. Only after the board intervened with Congress and the president was the chaplaincy law revised.

Religious passions kindled during the war years fired visions of apocalypse and millennium. Both Northerners and Southerners put God center stage and read the wartime struggles in religious terms. Some devout northern Protestants explained that God was wreaking his vengeance upon a nation whose Constitution ignored his succor and indeed his very existence. Their solution: to engraft Christianity upon the Constitution. To be sure, regrets at the omission of references to the Almighty had been voiced at the first ratifying conventions and were revived periodically by individual crusaders. But only when the nation faced its most serious ordeal did the sentiment assume significant proportions.

Shortly after Lincoln's election, Senator Charles Sumner introduced a memorial from a Reformed Presbyterian synod in Pennsylvania that called for a constitutional amendment acknowledging the authority of Christ and the recognition of the paramount obligations of a divine law. Two years later representatives of eleven Protestant sects met in Xenia, Ohio, and launched what ultimately became a national movement to secure a religious amendment. Precisely because the Constitution ignored God, one position paper explained, a calamity had befallen the nation. In January 1864 the movement, under the name of National Association to Secure the Religious Amendment to the Constitution, formulated a petition to Congress. The sponsors asked that the preamble to the Constitution begin with the words: "We, the people of the United States, humbly acknowledging Almighty God as the source of all authority and power in civil government, the Lord Jesus Christ as the Ruler among the nations, his revealed will as the supreme law of the land, in order to constitute a Christian government. . . ." Endorsing appropriate changes in the body of the Constitution to conform to the revised preamble, they made short shrift of equality for non-Christians. At the same time, however, since they upheld liberty of conscience, they denied that they sought a union between church and state.

Lincoln adroitly withheld his support, and so did Congress. A second and almost identical memorial from the Presbytery of Cincinnati railed further against an "atheistical" Constitution and for a Christian nation. But despite the seeming groundswell of enthusiasm, Congress buried the petitions. Senator Lyman Trumbull reported in March 1865 that the Senate Judiciary Committee had not technically voted against the recognition of God in the Constitution but merely asked to be discharged from consideration of memorials both for and against the proposal. The committee thought a religious amendment was unnecessary and injudicious, "at this time, at any rate." Besides, they said, the Constitution already recognized the existence of God; it was assumed in the clause that required oaths of officials and in the religion clauses of the First Amendment.

The initial rebuff failed to deter the petitioners. From 1863 to 1869—the first phase of the movement—the crusades for a religious amendment held regional meetings and annual conventions. From the outset the cause attracted a good number of respected laymen and clergymen, decent men who could not be read off as extremists. Concomitantly, the crusaders launched an effective public relations drive through pulpits, periodicals, public meetings, and their own long-lived journal, the *Christian Statesman.* For a few years the theme of divine punishment for a godless Constitution persisted, but the war's end led the organization to amend its rhetoric and expand its horizons. By 1866 it had broadened its purpose to include religious amendments in state constitutions.

A call for a national convention in 1869 revealed a further expansion of aims. It cited those reprehensible views "which are now struggling for a baneful ascendancy in State and national politics: such as, That civil government is only a social compact; That it exists only for secular and material, not for moral ends; That Sabbath laws are unconstitutional; and that the Bible must be excluded from our Public Schools." Only a constitutional amendment affirming that the United States was a Christian nation whose fundamental law was Christian law could remedy the deplorable state of affairs. By carving out multiple and open-ended objectives, the crusaders for a religious amendment stood to augment their popular following at the same time that they ensured the movement's survival.

Although the actual chances for a religious amendment were very slim, the attempt reflected in extremist form the defensive posture of Protestantism in the last third of the nineteenth century. Sober Americans of many stripes wondered if and how a homogeneous Protestant America could withstand the challenges of rapid secularization, a by-product of urbanization and industrialization, and of the massive influx of non-Protestant immigrants. Those challenges, or "perils" in popular parlance, drove many to the side of organizations that worked actively at maintaining the Protestant character and institutions of the country. The amendment movement was the most radical, but the premises of two simultaneous campaigns, for Sunday observance and for religion in the public schools, were identical. In one fashion or another all three strove for the preservation of a Christian nation.

The years that later historians called the critical period in American religion constituted a critical period for postbellum American Jewry. Frightened by the major threats to church-state separation, Jews also felt the grip of a pervasive social anti-Semitism. In their view both developments rested on a common base: a militant and aggressive Christianity. Responses, however, varied.

Whereas timidity in the face of prejudice caused many to keep a low profile, others were led to a stricter separationist line on behalf of religious equality.

Concerned Jewish leaders carefully monitored the efforts to Christianize the Constitution. Still the principal defenders of Jewish rights, the Anglo-Jewish periodicals sensed the urgency of the Christian crusade, which was both all-encompassing and avowedly political. Isaac Leeser, who was among the most outspoken from the beginning, offered his readers an incisive analysis of how the war had generated religious passion as well as "*rishuth*" (the Hebrew word for wickedness, used by German Jews for anti-Semitism). A people understandably depressed by the war sought comfort and readily turned to legislators for solutions. The advocates of an amendment capitalized on that sentiment, and building on the political successes of the antebellum reform crusades—temperance, Sunday laws, abolition—they fed their "lust for dominion" by preparing to Christianize the law of the land. The rabbi warned of the movement's seriousness, for now a union of several Protestant groups, always a danger signal to a non-Christian minority, had been effected. It was not inconceivable, therefore, that the amendment crusade—an "intended inquisition"—would rally a popular majority. Even if rights were not rescinded, a Protestant alliance could well twist the law against Jews. Yet, despite the horrible consequences, the *Occident* had little to suggest by way of Jewish response other than "silent, yet energetic action through the ballot, and by pen and speech to rebuke the sacriligious [*sic*] attack [on] the Constitution."

Leeser's alarmist opinions frightened some Jews who doubtless believed that attacks on the amendment scheme might arouse further anti-Jewish animosity or afford free publicity to an undeserving movement. Since Jews were the "chief parties," as Leeser called them, in the opposition, the more timid souls preferred to keep silent unless non-Jewish supporters stepped forward and dispelled the notion of a "Jewish issue." The young BDAI took a wait-and-see attitude. The *Jewish Messenger,* a new periodical in New York, disputed the premises of the amendment group and soberly noted how it was linked to various components of the Christian-state idea. Simultaneously, however, the paper assured its readers that they had no real cause for alarm, and it apologized for any seemingly bellicose tone!

Isaac Wise of the *Israelite* ridiculed the first manifestations of the Christian movement. (In later years he pinpointed it as the immediate cause of the wave of social anti-Semitism which erupted full-blown in the fourth quarter of the century.) Nevertheless, recalling the agitation of the Know-Nothings and the temperance and abolition crusades, he warned the Jewish community to be on alert. Within a year Wise abandoned ridicule, calling the movement a "revolution" to destroy the basic tenet of religious liberty. In a series of lengthy editorials on church and state, he advanced many arguments, from the theological to the practical, on the unacceptability of the amendment. As the Jews were wont to do, he equated the Jewish with the national interest. The issue was an American one rather than one of Judaism against Christianity, and Jews, the defenders of American principles, took a position not as Jews but as lovers of liberty and justice. Since enlightened Americans also opposed the movement, Wise optimistically believed that the Christianizers would be "killed" at the ballot box.

The second memorial to Congress from the amendment group (1864), followed by a widely publicized convention, heightened Jewish apprehensiveness. A flurry of activity ensued. Isaac Leeser hastened to New York and as presiding officer of the BDAI called a meeting of the executive committee. All agreed that the board's inaction could no longer be justified; agitation might lend importance to the Protestant plan, but silence on the part of the Jews would endow it with greater determination. The board resolved, therefore, to present a counterstatement to Congress. Leeser also conferred with a self-constituted committee of prominent New York Jews on the amendment; they appointed a delegation to proceed to Washington, "to take such measures as may be necessary to defeat the object of the Petition." (The fact that the New York group preferred to function independently reflected the fragile unity represented by the BDAI.)

The BDAI's memorial, drafted by Leeser, charged that the amendment sponsors would deprive the Jews of their inalienable rights and the equal status intended for them by the Founding Fathers. In apologetic tones the memorialists invoked once again the military services of the Jews to the land as well as their incomparable virtue. Sumner presented the board's petition to the Senate, and both he and Trumbull assured the Jews that the proposed amendment had little chance of success in committee. They promised that if the question came before the Senate, the BDAI would be afforded an opportunity to testify. Still apprehensive, the board gloomily concluded that the "zealots and fanatics" would persist in their efforts for the evangelization of the country and for a union of church and state.

The cause of the Christianizers made rapid strides in the scandal-ridden decade of the 1870s. Adopting the name of National Reform Association (NRA), the crusaders drew up a constitution which, in addition to calling for a Christian amendment, pledged itself to promote needed reforms regarding "the Sabbath, the institution of the family, the religious element in Education, the Oath, and Public Morality as affected by the liquor traffic and other kindred evils." In this, its second phase, the society embraced multiple goals which enabled it to attract the various reform elements who constituted the "Moral Majority" of the post–Civil War era. Under the presidency of William Strong, who was appointed to the Supreme Court in 1870, the society's prestige soared, and other prominent figures added their names to the roster of officers. Nevertheless, the NRA failed to secure a hearing of a Christian amendment on the floor of Congress. The House Judiciary Committee reported in 1874 that an amendment ran counter to the intent of the Founding Fathers—who, the committee pointed out, were Christian—and thus did not merit consideration.

Jewish concern continued unabated. Leaders believed that the NRA's success in any area, even without an amendment, would both undermine Jewish equality and prove an entering wedge for furthering the overall Christian design. The Jewish press and the BDAI criticized the appointment of Strong to the Supreme Court and urged the Senate to withhold its consent. In 1872, when the agitation of the NRA crested, the irrepressible Wise asked for Strong's impeachment. Rabbis, despite their self-imposed code of political neutrality, publicly denounced the amendment movement. Wise, who charged that the "fanatics" intended not the union of church and state but—even worse—the subjugation of the state to the church, actively campaigned against an NRA sympathizer in 1876.

Wise's colleague Dr. Max Lilienthal sounded a different note. He invoked the "contract" between America and its Jews, whereby the country was required to maintain church-state separation, the prerequisite for liberty, equality, and intergroup harmony. Jews for their part had lived up to the bargain by totally effacing their Jewishness with an American identity: "Hence, we have given up all ideas of ever returning to Palestine. . . . Hence, we have given up our sectarian schools, and send our children to the free schools." The negative implication was clear: if America disavowed separationism and became like other nations, the transference of Jewish religious allegiance would have been in vain.

Jewish concern failed to trigger concerted communal action. Rabbis in Pittsburgh, joined by a few Christian ministers, attempted to cement a union of opponents to the amendment, but their efforts were barely recognized outside their city. In 1874, unlike its behavior nine years earlier, the BDAI presented no countermemorial to Congress to offset that of the NRA. It still relied on the sympathy of Senators Sumner and Trumbull and the promise that Jews would obtain a hearing should the amendment proposal reach that stage.

Anti-Semitic signals from the NRA accounted at least in part for Jewish wariness. At the NRA's national convention of 1873, for example, speaker after speaker lashed out against the enemies of the movement. One minister attacked those who impeded America's progress as a Christian civilization by opposing Sunday laws, Bible reading in the classroom, and legislation to enforce Christian morality. A second speaker was more explicit: "The enemies of our movement naturally draw into their ranks all infidels, Jews, Jesuits, and all opposers of Him who is Lord over all, our Lord Jesus Christ." A third participant observed that there was a "confederacy of the Jesuit and Jew, infidel and atheist, in their attacks upon the Bible in our schools." Disparate elements without a common cause, they nevertheless had "stricken hands like Herod and Pontius Pilate in the common work of crucifying Christ." A year later, the NRA was horrified at the appointment of Felix Adler to a visiting professorship of Hebrew and Oriental literature at Cornell University. The naming of a Jew clearly imperiled Christian interests. Within a short time representatives of the society also admitted openly that a Christian Constitution "would disenfranchise every logically consistent infidel."

Jewish inaction was somewhat offset by the appearance of a welcome ally, Francis E. Abbott. Abbott, a Unitarian turned self-proclaimed anti-Christian, actively worked with other freethinkers on behalf of the Free Religious Association. A firm believer in separationism, he reported in his newspaper, the *Index,* on disabilities suffered by Jews that were grounded in religion. One of his numerous liberal projects was a petition campaign in 1872 against the Christian amendment. The petition amassed some thirty thousand names, and, forwarded to a sympathetic Senator Sumner, it helped to undercut the NRA. Ever disinclined to agitate without assurance of non-Jewish sympathy, appreciative Jews hailed Abbott's efforts. Some influential rabbis and laymen supported his local Liberty Leagues as well as the establishment of the National Liberty League (1876). The direct opposite of the NRA, the League pressed for a "religious freedom amendment" that would put an end to Sunday laws and religious instruction in the schools.

Jewish identification with Abbott, albeit short-lived, departed from earlier Jewish criticisms of agnostics and atheists. It revealed, first, that Jews themselves were succumbing to new intellectual currents, and, second, they could not afford to spurn any support in the crucial struggle against a Christian amendment. The friendships that were forged in that common effort inevitably led some Jews to the camp of the secularists.

How much influence the NRA exerted on moderate Protestants is impossible to gauge. At the very least, it doubtless confirmed the popular belief that the United States was a Christian nation whose freedoms rested on Christian precepts. In 1888 the *New York Tribune* candidly articulated that view. It fully appreciated the value and virtues of "our Hebrew fellow-citizens," the paper said, but

> they should recognize . . . that the Republic which offers a refuge and the broadest religious freedom to all men, expresses, in so doing, the highest teaching of Christ—the brotherhood of humanity. If it had not done so they (the Hebrews) would have had no foothold here. The United States . . . is Christian in its foundation, its structure and its development, and none . . . who have taken refuge here have more reason to thank God for its Christian spirit than the Hebrews.

The drive for a Christian amendment subsided until the 1890s, but under the encouragement of the NRA pressures escalated for stricter Sunday observance and for religious instruction in the public schools.

Sunday Laws

As a recent study noted, the theocratic ideas of the NRA permeated the post–Civil War Sunday movement. Its supporters looked upon Sunday legislation not only as a means of inculcating public religion but as a symbolic recognition of Jesus Christ as the nation's ruler. To be sure, moderate Protestants who rejected the notions of a theocracy and a religious amendment also upheld the imperative of Sunday laws. The oft-cited Philip Schaff, eminent church historian and theologian whose views on liberty of conscience were unimpeachable, believed that Christianity played a pivotal role in shaping the religious freedoms of the Constitution. He agreed that the church and the state moved in separate orbits, but they met on moral issues, and therefore absolute separation was impossible. Schaff preferred a "friendly separation," a system under which both church and state preserved Sunday laws and religion in the schools. The only alternative that he and other prominent Protestants saw was an "infidel" separation, which rested on hatred of religion and wrought havoc with morality. The polarity thus constructed better suited an earlier homogeneous community when religious meant Christian and when all agreed that church and government served identical ends. The reality was fast changing, but on the simplistic dualities of Christian-infidel, religious-atheist, majority-minority, the defenders of American Protestantism still rested their case. Religious minorities had to yield to the Protestant majority, for a minority that challenged the Protestant design risked the stigma of heathen or godless.

From the minority's point of view it made little difference if support of Sunday laws or religion in the schools came from a Schaff or an NRA member. The success of those causes, irrespective of their supporters, presaged a larger danger, the entrenchment of other public Christian usages. As Rabbi Max Samfield of Memphis argued, if Sunday laws, grounded as they were in religion, were validated by law, religious instruction in the public schools and a religious amendment to the Constitution would be equally legitimate.

With the cooperation of both national and local societies, in 1879 the NRA began the drive for a national Sunday law to reverse the currents of religious laxity. Its larger purpose was to retain an America uncorrupted by secularism and unyielding to the influences of non-Protestant immigrants. Agitating now on both state and federal levels, Sunday law advocates encountered serious obstacles, for the same social currents that had increased nonobservance in the first place escalated opposition to the Sunday crusade. A highly politicized issue, the Sunday question heightened the visibility of the Jews, principally as violators or potential violators of the laws.

Unlike the amendment issue, the subject of Sunday laws failed to muster Jewish unity. Aside from a mild recommendation for exempting Sabbath observers, the Board of Delegates kept silent. Among the Anglo-Jewish journals, which carefully monitored the subject, opinions differed. The *Jewish Messenger* upheld Sunday laws as police regulations which ensured the necessary day of rest for all. It favored moderate Sunday laws, permitting opportunities to those who desired to rest and those who preferred to use Sundays for recreation. That Sunday was a Christian institution was irrelevant; Sunday laws did not make the United States a Christian nation. The statutes, with proper exemptions for Sabbatarians, were hardly too onerous for the minority, who, out of respect for the religious sensibilities of their neighbors, were obliged not to add to the secularization of Sunday. Far worse than the laws were two kinds of Jews: those who violated their own Sabbath yet claimed exemption from the laws, and those whose attacks on the laws cast doubts on Jews as law-abiding citizens.

The *Messenger*'s views were of little comfort to concerned separationists or to observant Jews forced to eke out a subsistence living in five days. In keeping with its approach to all public issues of a controversial nature, the accommodationist journal refused to challenge the majority's acceptance of Sunday laws. Its Jewish traditionalist posture doubtless fed the *Messenger*'s forceful denunciation of Jews who violated their own Sabbath as well as its aversion to a secular nation wherein a vibrant Judaism could hardly flourish.

Isaac Wise's *American Israelite* (the paper's name was changed in 1874) entertained no defense of legalized Sunday observance. "All Sunday laws, together with the penalties attached to them," one editorial stated flatly, "are unjust, despotic, and damnable." In an unending stream of arguments, Wise appealed primarily to principle: Sunday laws were religious in nature and intent, they were a salient component of the Christian-state idea, they nurtured the movement for a Christian amendment, and, alien to the American republican spirit, they aimed at a union of church and state. Not only did the actual laws defy logic and consistency, but, since neither morality nor true Christianity could be advanced by legislation, they were utterly pointless. Jews in particular had cause to distrust the Sunday law movement, for some agitators readily resorted to anti-Semitic slurs. His readers would do well, Wise advised, to respond actively, petitioning legislators and cooperating with other Sabbatarians.

Just as the *American Israelite* differed from the *Jewish Messenger*, so did differences exist within the Reform camp itself. At a public meeting on Sunday laws, Rabbi Samuel Sale of Baltimore advocated not the abolition of the laws but modifications to permit recreation and amusements. Lawyer Simon

Wolf of Washington agreed that Puritanical laws were unsuitable to the spirit of the age, but, stressing principle, he interpreted all Sunday legislation to be an encroachment on individual liberties. By the turn of the century, when the new immigrant presence intensified the focus on Sunday observance, Reform opinion ran the gamut from those who desired total repudiation of religious legislation to those who preferred to soft-pedal the issue in light of the new urban problems.

Despite his ideological rhetoric, Rabbi Wise realistically acknowledged that Jews could attain no more than exemptions. In 1876, at the annual meeting of Reform's Union of American Hebrew Congregations, he introduced a resolution which called for petitions to state legislatures asking for exemptions of Sabbath-observing Jews. When specific attempts for exemptions were made in Pennsylvania, he counseled Jews to repudiate the opponents at the polls. The Reform leader's forceful and defiant tone, and his consideration of Sunday laws as part of a larger Christian design, may have distanced him from the timid, accommodationist *Jewish Messenger*, but at bottom both worked for the same objective—exemptions.

The two papers were joined by a third influential journal in 1879, when a group of Conservative Jews founded the *American Hebrew* of New York. The new weekly was centrist with respect to Sunday laws as it was in religion. On one occasion it sounded like the *Israelite:* "But even if we did not keep the Sabbath . . . we claim that the law has no right 'to select the day that shall be the day of rest.'" For the most part, however, it limited its rhetoric to demands for fair exemptions and even-handed enforcement. Legislation without exemptions, the journal elaborated, especially for the poorer classes, surpassed even the cruelties of the missionaries. How honest were July Fourth orations on religious liberty, and how meaningful was the First Amendment, if Sabbath observers were arrested for Sunday labor? Where the *Israelite* fought the theory of all Sunday laws, the *Hebrew* implied that proper exemptions fulfilled the requirements of religious liberty and equality. Neither was yet prepared to agitate for the growing number of Jews who violated their own Sabbath but on grounds of principle objected to the observance of the Christian Sunday.

Although it is tempting to correlate Jewish reactions with religious orientation, it would be inaccurate to conclude from the sampling of the journals that Reform Jews were consistently "hard" separationists, the Orthodox "soft" separationists, and the Conservatives somewhere between. The timidity of the *Messenger* did not necessarily follow from the traditionalist posture of its founder, S. M. Isaacs; Isaac Leeser had been a traditionalist too. Indeed, Wise the Reformer rather than Isaacs had inherited Leeser's mantle and his belief that justification of Sunday laws as police regulations was an outright subterfuge. Two other factors doubtless accounted for the different approaches: personality—Wise the noisy and ubiquitous crusader—and politics—the *Messenger* was Republican, the *Israelite* was Democratic, the editorial board of the *Hebrew* was mixed. It is probably most accurate to conclude that the nexus forged by Reform between Judaism and Americanism made its spokesmen especially sensitive to matters of church and state. Generally more affluent and acculturated than the traditionalists, and better unified, Reformers shaped the response of the community on all significant church-state issues for fifty years after the Civil War.

In anticipation of the centennial in 1876 commemorating American independence, the BDAI advised Jews to contribute to the occasion "by concurrent and distinctive action." B'nai B'rith suggested a work of art underwritten by the Jewish community, and it commissioned sculptor Moses Ezekiel to execute the project. Some Jews were opposed. Why they and not any other religious group? To suggest, even unintentionally, that Jews owed a special debt of gratitude to the government for the freedoms they enjoyed, when equality was theirs by right, showed an undignified lack of self-respect. Despite the opposition, Ezekiel's statue, named *Religious Liberty,* was contributed by B'nai B'rith to the centennial exposition in Philadelphia.

Agitation over Christianity as the public religion marred Jewish enjoyment of the celebration. In the spring of 1876 the legislature of Pennsylvania, the host state of the exposition, overwhelmingly rejected a proposal to exempt Sabbatarians from Sunday laws. In the shadow of the NRA's crusade, many Jews also resented Bishop Matthew Simpson's opening prayer at the centennial exposition, in which the United States was called a Christian nation. The *Messenger* attempted to defuse opposition; fearful lest Jews be distanced from the rest of the citizenry, especially in the centennial year, the journal admitted that except in the crucial area of law it was not incorrect to refer to America as a Christian country. At the other extreme, the *American Israelite* termed Simpson's statement a "falsehood" and bitterly criticized the use of the exposition for "sectarian advertisement."

More upsetting was the decision of civil authorities to keep the exposition closed on Sundays. Again the leading Jewish journals reacted in characteristic fashion. The *Jewish Messenger* suggested a compromise: forbid the operation of machinery and sale of liquor but permit a limited number of exhibits for the benefit of workers, not exclusively Sabbatarians, who had no other day of leisure. The *American Israelite* fumed over the disregard of constitutional liberties and noted bitingly how comfortable the regulation would be for visitors from despotic lands. Wise suggested that in accordance with the principle of religious equality the fair should also be closed on Fridays and Saturdays. Reform Rabbi David Einhorn, prominent civil libertarian and ally of Isaac Wise on that subject, addressed the fair's closing in a centennial sermon. How free was America, he asked, if bigotry forbade "to citizens who earn their livings honestly by the sweat of their countenances, every recreation on Sunday, even the sight of the world exposition."

Einhorn's sermon went on to discuss the social problems of the nation, and he also pointed to a grave inequity that troubled Jews in particular: "While the Declaration of Independence knows of no religion and does not even mention the word 'Christian' a single time . . . there has for years resounded in your midst with ever greater intensity the ominous cry: 'The United States is a Christian country.'" Hence, America, "Where is your equality?"

In the last two decades of the century, no uniform trend with respect to Sunday laws developed. The statutes were liberalized in some states and toughened in others. The pattern of enforcement also varied, not only from state to state but within a single state. State and federal courts generally upheld Sunday laws, but they too emitted contradictory signals. Although some judges invoked religious reasons, most found the laws to be a proper exercise of state police powers. Judicial refusal to countenance religious legislation may have gratified the Jewish minority, but, as discussed earlier, the police power rationale weakened their case. Accommodationist Jews could not very well challenge the authority of elected lawmakers to provide for the well-being of society, particularly when a guaranteed day of rest for the American worker was at stake. Their repeated argument that the laws under any guise were religious in intent rang hollow, and pragmatically the best chances for relief lay in securing immunity for Sabbatarians.

Over twenty states provided for exemptions, but some were narrowly limited to servile labor, as opposed to business or shopkeeping, or to occupations that caused no public disturbance. Efforts to broaden exemptions usually encountered vigorous opposition from Sunday law defenders. Among other reasons, they argued that the majority's choice of Sunday had to be honored uniformly. One Sunday law supporter stated: "We want but *one* Sabbath in this country. We don't want any Judaizing here." Nonconformists not only violated the mood of the day, but they enticed Christians to desecrate the Christian Sabbath. Besides, exemptions for Sabbatarians provided them with a distinct economic advantage over their competitors. Clearly, those who most blatantly resisted a Christian Sunday were the Jews.

Admittedly, exemptions alone did not erase all hardships. Enforcement generally threw the burden of proof upon the Jew, who had to prove to the satisfaction of the charging officer or court that he was in fact a conscientious Sabbath observer. Furthermore, under the requirement that exempted activities cause no public disturbance, exemptions were dependent on who was disturbed. In New York, for example, a Sabbath-observing Jew who operated a sewing machine in his own house on Sundays was charged with willful disturbance by a Methodist church next door. According to one city newspaper, the case revealed a glaring inequity: "Suppose, for instance, a Christian coppersmith or boiler maker has his shop near a Jewish synagogue, can he be compelled to stop work during the hours of service in the synagogue on Saturdays?" Had the Jew lived elsewhere, his activity might have gone unchallenged. Such seemingly trivial episodes revealed countless variations in the Sunday law structure as well as different levels of intergroup tension.

Shortly after the Civil War, two cases in the South considered the Jewish position under Sunday laws. A court in Alabama, a state without exemptions, ruled that an owner of a dry-goods store, a Sabbath-observing Jew, could not be excused from Sunday closing regulations. Basing its decision on the state police powers, the court explained that "acts must . . . be . . . *in fact* religious, in order that an immunity from legislative prohibition may be claimed." In Louisiana the court weighed the constitutionality of a Shreveport ordinance that exempted those who closed their stores on Saturdays. The judges noted the large number of Jewish merchants in Shreveport, but they found the exemption invalid. A law that gave a special privilege to Jews alone violated the constitutional guarantees of equality for Jews and gentiles.

In northern cities, where the Jewish population far exceeded that of Mobile and Shreveport, broad exemptions were hard sought. *Commonwealth v. Has,* a test case in Massachusetts that excited Jews in various parts of the country, failed to secure a broad interpretation of exemptions. The court upheld the right of Sabbath observers to labor or do business on Sunday, but it said that doing business did not permit them to keep open their stores and thus encourage others to violate the Sunday law. Nor did the court pay serious attention to Has's argument that the Sunday laws operated to subordinate one religion to another. Although the judge consistently referred to Sunday as the "Lord's day," he insisted that Sunday laws were civil rather than religious enactments. A Jew had to conform, not because his religion was subordinate but because he was required to submit to the rules of the community.

The usually timid *Jewish Messenger* denounced the decision, calling it an affirmation of a "State religion." The furious *American Israelite* lashed out against the hypocrisy of Massachusetts, which on the one hand avowed Christian love for "Negroes, Chinese, Fiji Islanders, or Hottentots" but on the other denied Jews the rights of man. It suggested that Jews along with liberals petition the state legislature repeatedly until public opinion compelled an amendment. The journal's Washington correspondent advised a different remedy: a concerted campaign by Boston's Jews to make all conform to the letter of the law—not even concerts, traveling, or unnecessary walking on Sunday. "Make the odious law odious to all." All protests, however, were futile. Ten years later the same court, citing the *Has* decision, ruled that immunity did not even extend to a Jewish ritual slaughterer who opened his butcher shop on Sundays to supply meat only to other Sabbath-observing Jews.

Tighter enforcement and narrower interpretation of exemptions also troubled Sunday law opponents in New York. In the largest center of American Jews, acceptable exemptions for Sabbatarians had existed until 1882. That year, however, a new penal code provided: "It is a sufficient defense to a prosecution for servile labor on the first day of the week, that the defendant uniformly keeps another day of the week as holy time. . . ." Narrower than the earlier law, it specified "servile labor" and not work, and it restricted immunity to defense only *after* an offender had been charged.

Upon the promulgation of the code, New York City police promised a crackdown on Jewish merchants who did business on Sundays. The police commissioner of Brooklyn said that "you cannot allow a Jew to sell goods which a Gentile may not sell." Shopkeepers pondered the warnings, but many decided to risk a violation rather than lose one day's income. Sunday, they said, was the only free day for workers and hence the busiest day for the stores. True to their word, the police, whose anti-Jewish prejudice contributed to their zeal, swooped down on the violators. "There are a great many of this shrewd people . . . who are expected to play double," they announced. To prevent "deception" on the part of Jews, the police quietly made a count of those businesses that were shut on Saturday. Within a week, a group of thirteen East Side merchants obtained temporary injunctions to halt police harassment that forced them to close on Sundays. Twelve were Jews, and eleven of these, joined shortly by five others, kept closed on Saturdays.

At the trial in the Superior Court, one of the attorneys for the Jews agreed that there should be a legal day of rest, but that Jews had the right to choose their day. For those who chose to observe Saturday, doing business on Sunday was "a work of necessity" (the typical exception made by Sunday laws to what was proscribed). Justice William Arnoux ruled otherwise. The exempting clause in the code referred only to servile labor and correctly so, for a Jew who opened his store on Sunday was presenting non-Jews with the temptation to violate the law. Moreover, the clause did not protect even the Jewish laborer from arrest but only provided him with a defense to his prosecution. Citing the Shreveport case, Arnoux added that broad exemptions gave Jews an unfair advantage.

New York Jews as well as the Board of Delegates charged that the law was unconstitutional. Submitting its own proposal to the legislature, the board called repeatedly but unsuccessfully for broad exemptions. Christian journals disagreed, and the influential *Independent* candidly suggested that if the Jews did not like it, they were free to leave. The offensive law lasted well into the twentieth century, compelling the Jews, as one observer said, "to labor surreptitiously on Sunday."

As if to compound the injury with insult, the New York Court of Appeals in 1893 defined the "Christian Sabbath" as a civil institution whose desecration the state was empowered to prevent. The police power rationale notwithstanding, the Christian aura around Sunday legislation still lingered.

CHAPTER 7

"Our Crowd"—a term that Stephen Birmingham made famous—was, in fact, only a small crowd composed of the leading German-Jewish families in New York. By the end of the nineteenth century, it had coalesced into a homogeneous elite, at once part of and distinct from general upper-class life in the city. Members were wealthy and heavily involved in finance and commerce, belonged to the same temples and the same clubs, took part in the same philanthropic and communal activities, and with some notable exceptions chose their friends and spouses from within the same limited sphere. They all lived in the golden age of German Jewry in America, an age when Jewish notables used their minds, money, and power to make their influence felt.

In the path-breaking article that follows, business historian Barry E. Supple explores the social and economic forces that shaped the members of this unified elite. He explains their rise in America in terms of their origins, early activities, ideologies, and habits, and shows how their similarities became more and more evident once they settled down in New York. For those outside New York, many of Supple's conclusions apply equally well. Sharing as they did common interests, common backgrounds, and a common faith, leading Jewish businessmen in numerous cities banded together into fraternal networks, depending upon one another for information, credit, and mutual aid. In some cases, acting according to the tradition of noblesse oblige, *leading Jews assumed the burdens of "stewardship," involving themselves in Jewish charitable, educational, and community relations work. Members of the Jewish elite also played active roles in general community affairs, especially in cities such as San Francisco, where they faced relatively little prejudice. Some even rose to prominent positions in local and national politics, the prime example being Oscar Straus, who served as Secretary of Commerce and Labor under President Theodore Roosevelt.*

Yet, the contributions of the German-Jewish elite were soon overshadowed. Assimilationist tendencies, the passing of the immigrant generation, World War I, and the new situation engendered by the mass migration from Eastern Europe weakened "our crowd." While individual German-Jewish families continued to wield influence, the community that once existed in New York fragmented. Power passed to a new elite, a less colorful and more heterogeneous one.

A Business Elite: German-Jewish Financiers in Nineteenth-Century New York

Barry E. Supple

Although the German-Jewish immigrant of the mid-nineteenth century was rarely very wealthy, he usually had some small capital. The journey alone, in the years before steam revolutionized the cost of transport, demanded some money. To live during the passage was in itself a drain on resources: Joseph Seligman (the first of eight brothers to come) set out from Baiersdorf, Bavaria, in July 1837, at the age of seventeen, with about one-hundred dollars. Traveling with a small group and camping at the roadside, he took eighteen days to reach Bremen. From there he sailed steerage at a cost of forty dollars (which included only one meal a day), and took sixty-six days to cross the Atlantic—landing on September 24, 1837, and proceeding immediately to Pennsylvania.

Once in the United States, with his capital steadily dwindling, the immigrant who typically made a success of his economic activities usually had sufficient means or friends to find his way to one of many scattered regions throughout the land—unlike later generations of East European Jews, whose destitute immobility kept them concentrated in New York. In fact, the mid-century Jewish immigration as a whole produced a rapid growth of small communities from the East to the West Coast and from Chicago to New Orleans—although, naturally enough, there was a higher concentration in the East. By 1820 there was already a small community in Cincinnati, and the 1820s and 1830s saw a further penetration of the Midwest, while a few immigrants reached Louisville, Kentucky. In 1826 a congregation had been founded in New Orleans, and in the 1840s Texas and in the 1850s California were reached by Jewish settlers. The thirty-seven reported synagogues of 1850 increased to sixty-seven in 1860—and they were found for the first time in California, Alabama, Georgia, Illinois, Indiana, Maryland, New Jersey, Wisconsin, and the District of Columbia.

One reason for this distribution was that the contemporary Jewish immigrant often followed the frontier of peddling and petty retailing. The original occupation structure of the German Jew had led him, unlike the peasant, to appreciate the significance of income as capital—as the potential source of further income; he, "even in the old country, had learned to reckon, to direct earnings toward a purpose." This grasp of a central proposition of entrepreneurship meant that he was less likely than the erstwhile peasant to feel economically rootless in the new environment. Once in America, then, he cast around energetically for a means of livelihood and capital accumulation. Peddling (if the immigrant had little capital) and settled retailing or wholesaling (which would, in any case, follow upon peddling as quickly as possible) naturally attracted a great number—and it seems possible that by 1860 a majority of the peddlers in the United States were Jewish.

An itinerant life was something which, historically, was not too strange a mode of existence for the Jews. Initial difficulties with the language might militate against many other occupations. Historical social pressures and attitudes made Jews reluctant to enter unskilled manual occupations or go onto the land. Where the desire to keep their Sabbath free for worship was so strong, independence was a goal well worth striving for. And where family life and solidarity played such an important social role, any occupation in which the family as a whole might participate was the more welcome. In addition, since Jews were accustomed to being a persecuted minority group they had no compulsion to look outside their own community for social approval. The criteria against which actions were significantly measured lay within the circle of coreligionists; social snobbery from outside was the norm—and was therefore not a meaningful variant that conditioned their lives. If peddling was a menial task in the eyes of the majority, it was not so to the poor Jewish immigrant—in fact it might be a convenient means of escaping from the *real* degradation of working for others.

As everywhere in the West "the rapid march of settlement outdistanced the ability of the towns to supply the rural districts with needed goods," as the development of markets outpaced the rise of sophisticated and institutionalized retail distribution, so Jews were attracted into the field, selling notions, trinkets, dry goods, and old clothes, opening stores if they could, buying a pack (or even a wagon) if they could not. Most of the group under discussion here participated in this development, and as a consequence became well distributed geographically—although each peddler needed a base for his operations and each storekeeper wished to tap the richest market. Hence the rise of Jewish communities in strategic regional urban centers, usually near water routes. Especially remarkable in this sense were the Ohio Valley region (centering on Cincinnati), the Chicago area, the Pennsylvania mining towns and Philadelphia, the West Coast, and some southern areas.

The father of the founders of J. S. Bache & Co., Semon Bache, worked in a Mississippi store (owned by his uncle) after his landing in New Orleans. Marcus Goldman, who ultimately started Goldman, Sachs & Co., proceeded to Philadelphia in 1848 and there peddled for two years before opening a men's clothing store which prospered greatly until his temporary retirement in 1867. Meyer Guggenheim, after his landing in New York in 1848, also peddled in Pennsylvania (in the mining areas), selling shoestrings, lace, stove and furniture polish, safety pins, needles, spices, and so forth; he then turned to the sale of home-manufactured stove polish, traveling with samples by train and horsecar; and about 1852 opened, in Philadelphia, a wholesale store for household products, ultimately importing goods from Europe. Philip Heidelbach peddled in Ohio and then went into the clothing trade (probably as a manufacturer) in Cincinnati; from a venture in local banking he ultimately graduated, in 1876, to a banking house in New York. Abraham Kuhn and Solomon Loeb, the founders of Kuhn, Loeb & Co., commenced with a commercial partnership in Lafayette, Indiana, about 1850, before moving to Cincinnati with a general merchandising store, which lasted until their temporary retirement in 1865. Henry Lehman immigrated in 1844, peddled in Alabama for a year and then opened a general store in Montgomery; he was joined by his brothers Emanuel and Mayer Lehman within five or six years and the firm expanded through the years into cotton brokerage with a New York branch; after the war the firm extended its commodity dealings to include coffee and petroleum, being joined by the second generation in the 1880s. Samuel Rosenwald, father of the future president of Sears, Roebuck, peddled in the South, on foot and then with the help of a horse and wagon, until the outbreak of the Civil War, when he moved North to Springfield, Illinois, and established what was to be one of the town's leading stores. Lazarus Straus landed in Philadelphia in 1852 and went to Oglethorpe, Georgia; after peddling for some months he settled in a general store in Talbotton. His family joined him in 1854 and in 1863 he moved to Columbus—returning North after the war to establish a wholesale crockery business. William Scholle, who arrived with little means in 1841, eventually came to deal on a large scale in clothing and woolens, opened a branch in San Francisco, and in 1850 moved there himself; at which point the firm developed a banking business—presumably under the influence of the gold discoveries. California after the gold discoveries also attracted the Seligman brothers and they, in fact, provide us with an archetype of geographical dispersion.

Joseph Seligman, the eldest of the eight, immigrated in 1837 and worked for a year as an assistant in Asa Packer's store in Mauch Chunk, Pennsylvania. Then he resigned and occupied himself with peddling in the locality. By spring 1839 he had amassed five hundred dollars and was joined by his brothers William and James, who also became peddlers. Next, Joseph and William opened a small store in Lancaster and James went South as an itinerant merchant, centering his peddling in Alabama. His success stimulated the others (together with Jesse who had, meanwhile, left Bavaria for

America) to accompany him back, and in 1841 the four brothers opened a store in Selma, Alabama—which, with one brother left in charge, they used as a base for peddling. By 1843 they had extended their activities to include four stores—in Selma, Greensboro, Eutaw, and Clinton—each managed by one brother who left his store in charge of an employee in order to peddle. After 1846, feeling restricted in Alabama, they opened a drygoods importing house in New York. Soon William went to St. Louis to establish a clothing business with his brother-in-law Max Stettheimer, and Jesse and Henry (who had come over in 1843) opened a branch of the New York house in Watertown, New York. In 1850 Jesse and Leopold were bitten by the gold bug—or at least by the prospect of commercial profit in California—and in the fall they moved to San Francisco with twenty thousand dollars' worth of merchandise. The fifties were to see some movement of Seligman personnel between branches, but up to the Civil War the framework remained essentially unchanged: The Seligmans had succeeded in establishing a network which placed them—even if fortuitously—in a preeminent position so far as the realities of distribution were concerned.

Thus, by the late 1850s, the initial phase of economic integration was largely completed. Twenty years had witnessed the arrival of a generation of German Jews with little capital. Among them were men who, seeing their opportunity in the field of distribution, launched forth inland yet more hundreds of miles. Some stayed out in the West and the South and their children established permanent communities, but another cluster also emerged: men who, back in New York with capital and commercial experience, would ultimately participate to no small extent in the critical development of the American capital market in the decades after the Civil War.

Within a relatively few years of their arrival in the United States, most of our men were firmly established in one aspect or another of the distribution system—retail or wholesale or overseas trade.

For most of them the Civil War brought prosperity—at least to some degree. Even where, as in the case of Straus and the Lehman brothers, operating within the southern economy, they had to bear the brunt of commercial dislocation and general insecurity, there might be some counterbalancing benefits. Thus, Lazarus Straus's son Isidor was in Europe for the last two years of the war with a commission to buy supplies for the Confederacy and, it appears, made a profit of several thousand dollars on the sale of Confederate bonds. But for most, the period was one of relatively uncomplicated prosperity. A boom in textiles helped those whose business was in clothing, and the general war inflation naturally aided those whose principal economic activity lay in buying and selling. The Seligmans, as always, could not go wrong. In the early years of the war, partly owing to their influence in government circles and their prominence in the Republican party, they obtained lucrative clothing contracts; and from 1 August 1861 to 30 July 1862, the government paid them, on this account, almost $1½ million. Later on in the war they were large-scale participants in the flotation of federal loans—principally in Europe. As early as April 1862, the brothers had a capital of just under $1 million; by March 1864, this had been augmented by over $250,000.

In general, then, the postwar position of these men was buoyant—and in two instances (Kuhn and Loeb in 1865 and Marcus Goldman in 1867) there was even a retirement from economic activity. But when Kuhn and Loeb, in 1867, and Goldman, in 1869, reentered business, it was in a way that typified the general movement: to New York and into finance. For most of the group who immigrated before the war with little money and no financial experience, the postwar decade was seminal. Private banking, commercial paper discounting, exchange transactions, stock dealings, all exerted a strong pull on men with agile minds and the requisite capital. Kuhn and Loeb, it has been estimated, had a capital of half a million dollars and some experience in extending credits, and we have seen how wealthy the Seligmans were—while their financial experience was extensive. It seems that Marcus Goldman's wife played a not unimportant role in persuading him to make the move. But his entry into the commercial paper field was made possible only by the attraction of New York as a financial center and by the capital which he had accumulated in Philadelphia. The Seligmans, of course, had long had their base in the metropolis, but as conditions changed it is possible to witness the long and purposeful thought which went into their decision to leave the importing of dry goods and to enter wholeheartedly into international investment banking.

It was at this stage of their development that the path of the originally unqualified men crossed that of the group who immigrated qualified, either with capital or experience, for the banking field. They, too, were consciously gravitating to a young and flourishing field, and they provide even more obvious examples of the mobility of factors of production. The two Speyer brothers (Philip and Gustav) had come in 1837 and 1845 respectively and established Philip Speyer & Co. They, like the Seligmans, sold federal bonds in Europe during the Civil War. In 1878 the firm name was changed to Speyer & Co., and it was by no means an insignificant factor in the American underwriting world. Ladenburg, Thalmann was established in 1880—as the successor of Limburger & Thalmann (1873)—Ernst Thalmann having been in banking since his immigration in 1868. Jacob Schiff had entered in 1865, already had a brokerage partnership in 1866, went back to Frankfort in 1872, and in 1875 returned, for good, to join Kuhn, Loeb & Co.

Once established in New York, both types of firm—all houses stemming from German-Jewish families—experienced a development parallel to that of the New York money and capital markets. Leopold Cahn & Co. (1879), which Semon Bache's son Jules S. joined in 1880, became J. S. Bache & Co. in 1892 and developed into a prosperous stockbroking business which is still on Wall

Street, operated by Jules's nephew Harold L. Bache. Goldman, Sachs and Co. (originally, in 1869, M. Goldman, Banker & Broker) dealt for many years in note-discounting, branched out into the handling of letters of credit and bills of exchange, started to buy railroad bonds, and under the leadership of Marcus's son Henry Goldman, and with the help of Samuel Sachs and his three sons, went into investment banking in the first decade of this century. In the latter venture Lehman Brothers joined Goldman, Sachs. The Lehmans had started with commodity transactions, and in the 1880s had commenced stock and bond dealings, railroad investment, and industrial banking—by which time the second generation was in control. Kuhn, Loeb's private banking house (established 1867), especially under the invigorating leadership of Jacob Schiff, gradually gave more attention to securities and helped establish a market for American government obligations and railroad bonds—until at the end of the century it was numbered among the six leading investment banking houses in the land. Hallgarten, Speyer, and Ladenburg, Thalmann were also outstanding in the financing of railroads, utilities, and industry.

Why this particular group should have been as successful as it was in this particular field is not a question that permits of a satisfying answer. Clearly they were not concerned in a conspiracy to monopolize the money market. To some extent, as will be seen, the common background facilitated their dealings with each other and with some clients; but this was not a continuous process, and it could not explain their success in financial transactions involving non-Jews. Neither can it be proved that personal experience in European finance counted for something in every case: the backgrounds of most of these men, before they went into finance, were not such as to provide them with a mastery of European techniques. However, it is more interesting that, besides the few who came to America with abilities based on years of family banking, many of the group were fully alive to the lessons to be learned from European experience. Schiff was undoubtedly aided by his early work in Frankfort banking and by his stay in Europe in 1872–1875, while Kuhn, Loeb in later years *continued* to call on European talent in the shape of Otto Kahn and the Warburgs. More than this, there were frequent visits to Europe for further education in finance even when the American firm was well established: Ernst Thalmann, Goldman, Sachs personnel, the Seligmans, all learned valuable lessons there. Of course, as J. P. Morgan's early history demonstrates, this interplay of ideas was by no means confined to German-Jewish houses. But, with their strong orientation to German culture and their continuous attachment to Europe, there can be no doubt that this particular group was in an especially favorable position to benefit from the advanced practices across the Atlantic. As will be seen in the final section, this cosmopolitan frame of mind enabled them to profit from the contemporary need to import capital from Europe, by establishing trans-Atlantic connections. In general, this particular result of their cultural background is not something to be underestimated, and therefore the fact of their having been *German* Jews was clearly significant.

To some extent, of course, the "open mind" had been important from the early days of their settlement in America. An ability to grasp the concept of productive capital which exceeded that of their fellow immigrants, a willingness to risk even more of the unknown in order to achieve economic and social independence, an historical aversion to unskilled manual labor or agricultural pursuits: all these factors go toward explaining their ultimate position in the interstices of trade organization. As America after 1865 came to provide for men of capital in the field of finance the opportunity and promise for which a host of other immigrants had looked, and were to look, in vain, these families easily made the transition into the new world, confident that it would fulfill its promises. The road that had led from the dusty lane to Main Street now pointed toward Wall Street and even more security. Scattered over much of America, these families could not but have felt socially isolated. Back in New York they set about building their own in-group. To the bases of this structure the next section is devoted.

Once in New York, the families who had originally arrived poor coalesced with those who had arrived with capital to form an elite differentiated in background, in culture, in religious observance, in social outlook and activities, from other groups around it. That Henry R. Ickelheimer, Jules S. Bache, three Seligman brothers, and James Speyer were all present at the marriage of Jacob Schiff's son, Mortimer, was more than evidence of business good manners: it demonstrated a strong social solidarity. That Mortimer, in fact, married the daughter of a Hallgarten partner, or that Henry R. Ickelheimer, four years later, married Pauline Lehman, were more than coincidences, for these young people went to the same clubs, worshipped at the same temple, and continually gathered at each other's houses. The elements which, at bottom, drew them all together were principally three: their business interests, their German background, their Judaism.

In some respects, the group adopted habits common to families of equivalent income. But much of its social life was basically insular, oriented around each other's homes or such clubs as the Harmonie. Founded in 1852, the *Harmonie Gesellschaft* was patronized almost exclusively by German Jews: Not until 1893 did German cease to be its official language. Interesting in this respect, and as reflecting the economic interests of club members, is the following quotation from one of Henry Seligman's letters, after Pacific Mail stock had tumbled 15 points in March 1885: "The Jews in particular have been badly nipped. . . . They are down on Ed Lauterbach who is on the board and at the Harmonie the members are going about singing *On Lauterbach hab ich mein gelt verloren*."

The social solidarity of the German-Jewish banking community was in no way better exemplified, and furthered, than by the tendency—common to all unified elites—to intermarriage. Chart I represents the genealogies and marital ties of the families under consideration. As can be seen, one result was that the business *was* the family—in its economic aspect. To some extent the added strength which partnerships derived from marriage vows antedated the final rise to social and business success. Thus, Solomon Loeb's first wife was Abraham Kuhn's sister Fannie, and the marriage took place well before the move to New York and the establishment, by the brothers-in-law, of the famous investment banking house. On other occasions a new partner's entry into the established firm would follow on or be coincident with his marriage to an older partner's daughter, as in the case of Jacob Schiff's partnership in Kuhn, Loeb. Indeed, this firm was so interwoven by marriage relationships that from 1869 through 1911 it had no partners who were not related to Solomon Loeb or Abraham Wolff, and as late as 1931 this rule held good of three new partners: John M. Schiff (grandson of Jacob and therefore great-grandson of Solomon Loeb), Frederick M. Warburg (son of Felix and therefore, again, grandson of Solomon Loeb), and Gilbert W. Kahn (grandson of Abraham Wolff). In Goldman, Sachs & Co. it was not until 1915 that a person outside the two families was brought into the firm and the family histories show an early intertwining—two Sachs boys (who had been orphans under the care of their future father-in-law) marrying two of Goldman's daughters. Similar intrafirm unifications occurred in the Seligman enterprises and Heidelbach, Ickelheimer & Co., which was founded in 1876 after the marriage of Isaac Ickelheimer to Philip Heidelbach's daughter. Four of Hallgarten's partners, Bernard Mainzer (1864), Charles Hallgarten (1872), Sigmund Neustadt (1872), and Casimer Stralem, were also tightly knit—Mainzer's sister married Charles Hallgarten, and Neustadt's daughter married Stralem. Sometimes a business did not even need marriages to secure family continuity in partnership: Until 1924 all the eleven partners in Lehman Brothers bore the family surname!

The broken lines on Chart I also demonstrate that the marriage ties connecting both families *and* banking houses were of no less importance. In the resulting interlocking structure, the fecund Seligmans occupied an "anchoring" position, having connections with the Lewisohns, the Lehmans, Kuhn, Loeb, and the Guggenheims—the marriage of Benjamin Guggenheim and Florette Seligman in 1894 uniting the two most important families in American Jewry. Jacob Schiff, so closely tied by marriage to his own firm and the brother-in-law of a Hallgarten partner, who was the son-in-law of another partner, who, in his turn, was the father-in-law of an Ickelheimer!

Clearly, the marriages were not entirely consciously arranged with an eye to business solidarity. The formation of the group was the initial step. With the consequent participation in an insular social world—with a constant meeting in the same homes, the same clubs, and the same restaurants—it was inevitable that the younger generations should choose their spouses as they did. These ties, in any case, were only the framework upon which was built a towering structure of mutual friendships. Descendants of the families today, who were then conscious of such things, can remember from their childhood a period when most of these people were intimate acquaintances—when Jacob Wertheim, for instance, was a close friend of Daniel Guggenheim, the Hallgartens, Julius Rosenwald, the Seligmans, the Ickelheimers, the Loebs, Jacob Schiff, the Strauses, the Lehmans, Felix Warburg, and Henry Goldman. The firmness of the group's social position cannot be doubted. Springing from religion, nationality, occupation, and wealth, it was strengthened by education, culture, club membership, and religious observance. It was, perhaps, almost as much a matter of defense as of spontaneity. This cluster of families had a background and cultural acquisitions pushing them toward the conventional social graces; but they carried an ethnic stigma which, at least in the first generations, prevented their moving into the graceful echelons of New York society for which they no doubt considered themselves fitted. For only a small minority was assimilation an acceptable solution to the problem. In rare instances an individual might participate in two communities. But for the great majority the answer was a society within a society, an elite perhaps equal but certainly separate, forced into being by prejudice and buttressed by participation in a specialized culture.

Nevertheless, it would be wrong to claim that the German-Jewish group had been completely divorced from some aspects of American society. Most of their friendships and much of their social activity *was* insular. But the Seligmans knew Lincoln and loved him well, they helped arrange a pension for his widow, and they were extremely close to President Grant; Oscar S. Straus is best known as someone who made his mark in government circles—as Ambassador to Turkey and the first Jewish member of the Cabinet; Jacob Schiff was ultimately considered the equal of the Yankee financial aristocracy, and was very close to Edward H. Harriman, and Nathan Straus was on the best of terms with President Cleveland. Equally, too, and as a corollary of their devotion to Reform Judaism, these men fought hard against any tendency to "separatism" in American Jewry. Schiff's opinion was that "we are all Americans," and Oscar Straus, although he felt his ethnic background very keenly, was no less devoted to America: Jews, he said, "are not less patriotic Americans because they are Jews, nor any less loyal Jews because they are primarily patriotic Americans." For this reason too, because they saw the clash with Americanism, most of these men were opposed to the Zionist movement, which they viewed as dangerous in so far as it established a prior lien on citizenship.

In spite of these early trends to Americanization and in spite of the ultimate crumblings of social demarcations, it is possible to see at the end of the nineteenth century a social elite based primarily on ethnic factors: strong

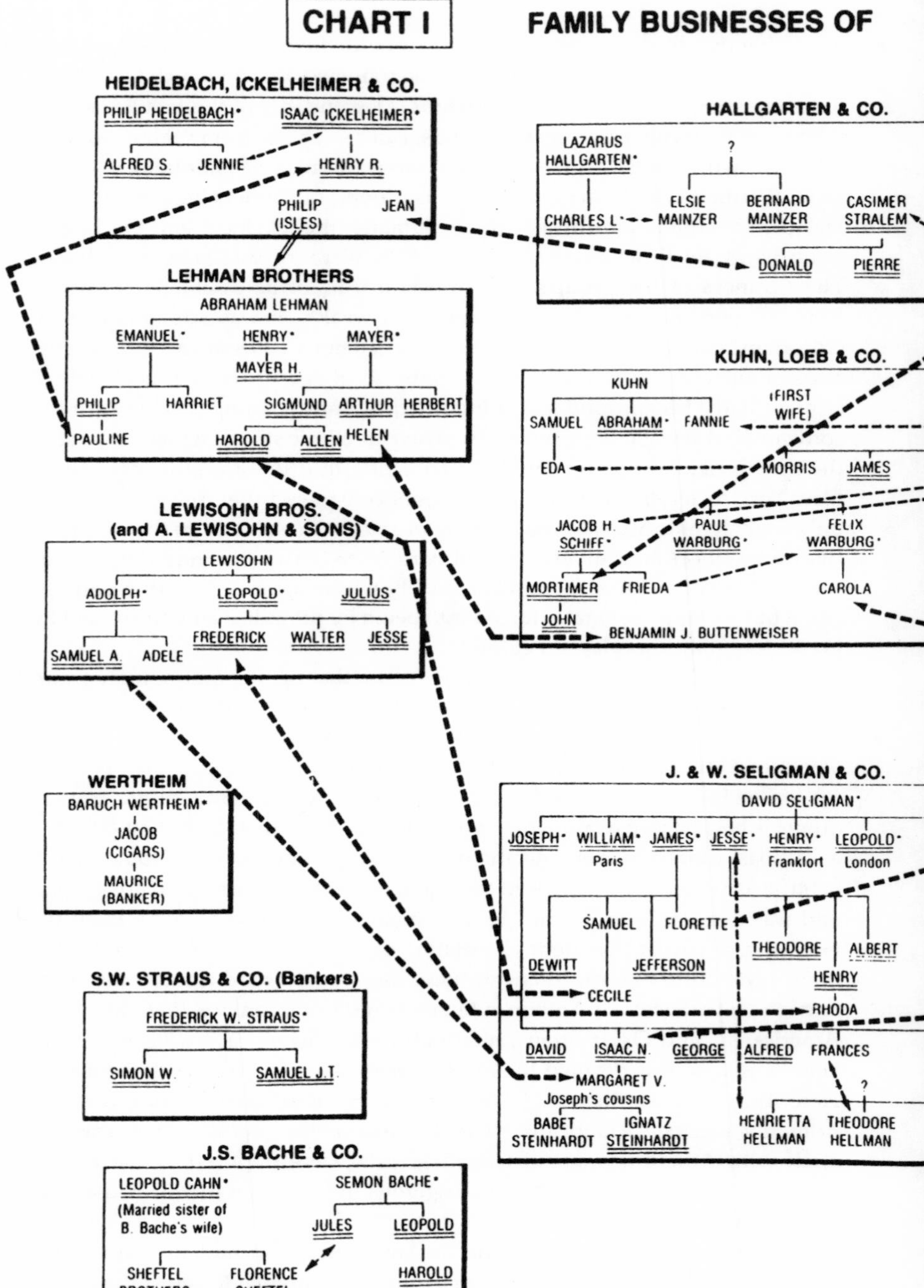
CHART I
FAMILY BUSINESSES OF
HEIDELBACH, ICKELHEIMER & CO.
PHILIP HEIDELBACH*
ISAAC ICKELHEIMER*
ALFRED S.
JENNIE
HENRY R.
PHILIP (ISLES)
JEAN
HALLGARTEN & CO.
LAZARUS HALLGARTEN*
?
CHARLES L.
ELSIE MAINZER
BERNARD MAINZER
CASIMER STRALEM
DONALD
PIERRE
LEHMAN BROTHERS
ABRAHAM LEHMAN
EMANUEL*
HENRY*
MAYER*
MAYER H.
PHILIP
HARRIET
SIGMUND
ARTHUR
HERBERT
PAULINE
HAROLD
ALLEN
HELEN
KUHN, LOEB & CO.
KUHN
SAMUEL
ABRAHAM*
FANNIE
(FIRST WIFE)
EDA
MORRIS
JAMES
JACOB H. SCHIFF*
PAUL WARBURG*
FELIX WARBURG*
MORTIMER
FRIEDA
CAROLA
JOHN
BENJAMIN J. BUTTENWEISER
LEWISOHN BROS. (and A. LEWISOHN & SONS)
LEWISOHN
ADOLPH*
LEOPOLD*
JULIUS*
SAMUEL A.
ADELE
FREDERICK
WALTER
JESSE
WERTHEIM
BARUCH WERTHEIM*
JACOB (CIGARS)
MAURICE (BANKER)
J. & W. SELIGMAN & CO.
DAVID SELIGMAN*
JOSEPH*
WILLIAM* Paris
JAMES*
JESSE*
HENRY* Frankfort
LEOPOLD* London
SAMUEL
FLORETTE
THEODORE
ALBERT
DEWITT
JEFFERSON
HENRY
CECILE
RHODA
DAVID
ISAAC N.
GEORGE
ALFRED
FRANCES
MARGARET V.
Joseph's cousins
BABET STEINHARDT
IGNATZ STEINHARDT
?
HENRIETTA HELLMAN
THEODORE HELLMAN
S.W. STRAUS & CO. (Bankers)
FREDERICK W. STRAUS*
SIMON W.
SAMUEL J.T.
J.S. BACHE & CO.
LEOPOLD CAHN*
(Married sister of B. Bache's wife)
SEMON BACHE*
JULES
LEOPOLD
SHEFTEL BROTHERS
FLORENCE SHEFTEL
HAROLD

GERMAN–JEWISH ORIGIN

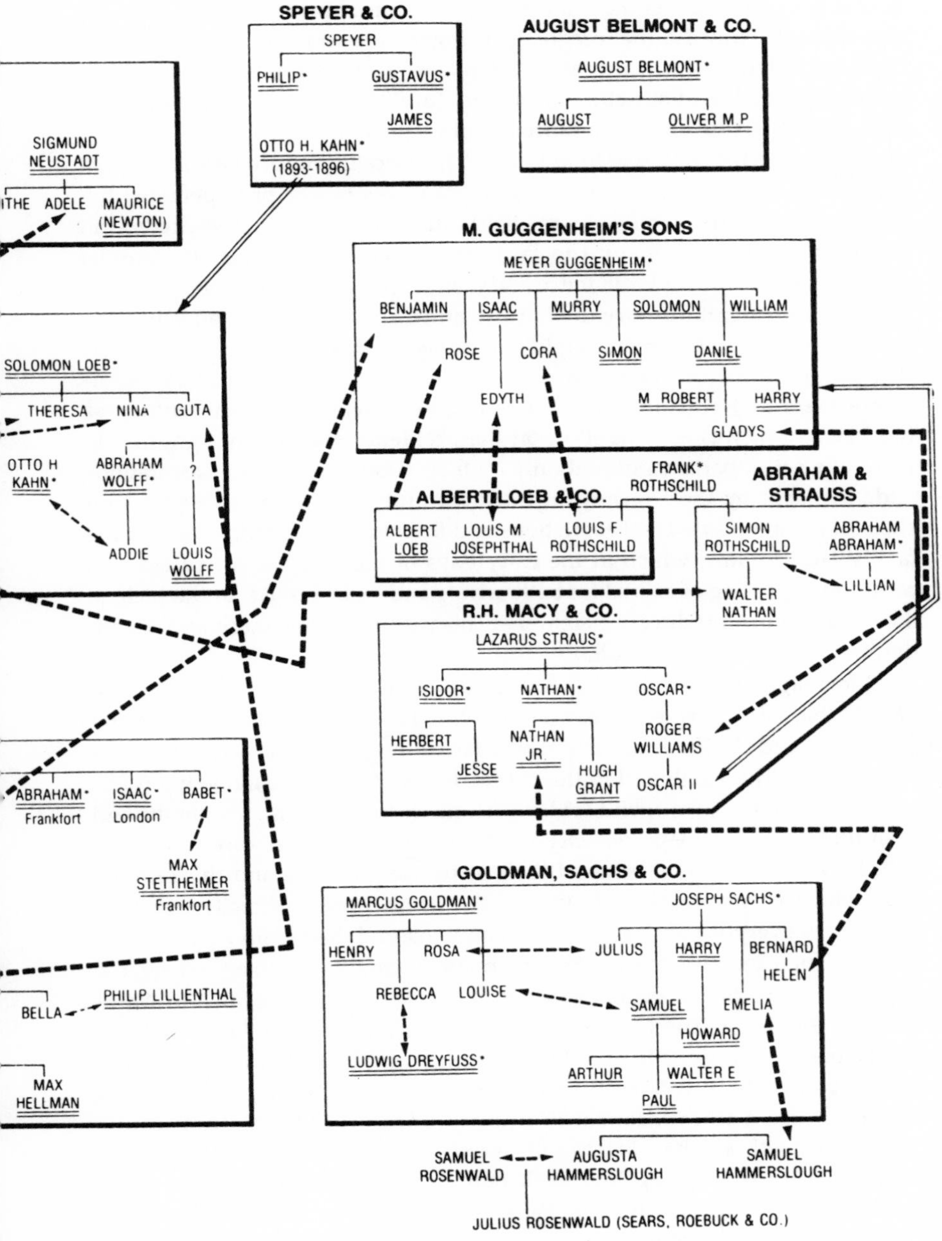

SAMUEL ROSENWALD — AUGUSTA HAMMERSLOUGH — SAMUEL HAMMERSLOUGH

JULIUS ROSENWALD (SEARS, ROEBUCK & CO.)

NOTES: BROKEN LINES INDICATE MARRIAGES. DOUBLE UNBROKEN LINES INDICATE MEMBERS OF A FIRM. ASTERISKS INDICATE ACTUAL IMMIGRANTS, IF KNOWN. NOT ALL MEMBERS OF FAMILIES ARE SHOWN.

and united, a series of interlocking kinship groups revolving around the New York financial scene. Yet the important question for business history remains unanswered. How did the foregoing arrangements and attitudes impinge on business activity? This can best be considered from two points of view: the internal strength and structure of the firm, and the relationship between the individual business and the financial world outside it.

It is, perhaps, possible to argue that historically the primary social unit for business organization before the recent development of impersonal bureaucracies was the family. In medieval Italy the Bardi or the Medici, in sixteenth-century Germany the Fuggers or the Hochstetters, in colonial America the Browns of Providence and many other mercantile enterprises, in the early nineteenth century the Lowells and Cabots in textiles, all substantiate the proposition that men sought in marriage or blood relationships the ties that strengthened and gave security to the structure of their business enterprises. German-Jewish investment banking in the late nineteenth century, as has been seen, was also based upon the proliferation of kinship groups. In place of a set of partners united only by their common economic aspirations and, perhaps, by their regard for business unity, there was created a firm skein of common universal aspirations and interests—an identification of the family and the firm which in the early days of the Seligmans had led to a continuous pooling of capital for both private and business use, and which, at the least, would produce a heightened regard for the business and a continuity of entrepreneurial skill.

Most significant in this respect was an attitude imported from the Old World: that of family solidarity and unity. For the Seligmans, the Guggenheims, and Schiff, Friday night was family night—a time when children and grandchildren gathered in the patriarch's house. "I have made it a rule," wrote Schiff in 1890, "to spend Friday evening exclusively with my family, and I can under no circumstances vary from this." All members were concerned with the affairs and well-being of their respective families, and this orientation, which is noticeable in nearly all the firms, sprang directly from the structure of everyday life—nothing was more natural than to find a place for a relative. For example, Joseph Seligman for a period was plagued by the necessity of creating a position in the Seligman enterprises for Max Stettheimer, who had married Joseph's sister Babet. Thus in 1863 he reported that Stettheimer was anxious to go into importing, "and if we do not enter into it as largely as of old he will try to get other partners. . . . Nothing would please me more, were it not for dear Babet; who says as soon as Max ceases business connections with us, she will face a life more insupportable than hitherto, and begs of me, to try to keep him in. If only for her sake I deem it my duty, provided I cannot place him in Paris or Frankfort as I would prefer, to commence importing again."

The repercussions of this attitude were complicated. On the one hand there can be little doubt that it served to provide a powerful, although intangible, motivation to accept entrepreneurial training; and for business activity the identity of kinship group and firm meant an added strength and unity of purpose. This coincidence, in fact, as was clearly demonstrated in the case of the Seligmans, produced a dedication, almost a compulsion, to commercial activity, which might otherwise not have been present. "I think it is our duty toward our children," wrote Joseph Seligman, "to have a decent business for them." Although not every descendant came into the business, for many years it was considered normal for son to follow father, nephew to cooperate with uncle, son-in-law to participate in this particular field of economic endeavor. And this was applicable, to some extent, to the whole of American business, as well as to other types of investment banking houses, an outstanding example being the Boston firm of Lee, Higginson & Co., which, from 1848 to 1918 drew twelve of its twenty-two partners from the two Yankee families who gave the house its name. In an activity so dependent upon confidence and trust as finance, it was to be expected that family participation should have been considered an economic advantage.

On the other hand, there were distinct disadvantages. Primary among these was the fact that the facilitation of the entry of relatives into a business might mean assuming the burden of a poor businessman. This most often must have happened unknowingly, but (as in the case of the Seligman brother-in-law) there might be little to be done even if the fact were realized. However, this drawback need not have been disastrous. Businesses and families were organized along patriarchal lines: As long as decision-making could be concentrated, as long as the number of sellers and purchasers of securities was small, the personality of the head of the firm—his ability, contacts, and reputation—was all-important. Underneath him there might be (within reason) any number of poor businessmen who could do little lasting harm to the business because they were not near the center of decision-making. In the long run, too, there was no hesitation about bringing in outside talent when it was needed—which was often tantamount to going outside the circle of blood relatives and choosing or creating relatives by marriage in order to bolster the business. Finally, it is most probable that it was only the existence of unified German-Jewish houses which enabled men to enter the realm of high finance who might otherwise have been prevented from so doing on the basis of their race and background, for it is a remarkable feature of the rest of the financial world that other prominent firms never had Jewish partners.

On the whole in the late nineteenth century there were two basic groups of investment bankers: the New Englanders and the German Jews. It is to be hoped that one day the former will be analyzed and compared with the latter. But initially it seems possible to say that the German-Jewish groups had a strategic role to play in the provision of capital from Germany for America's industrial development. While the Yankee bankers were able to tap the capital resources of old England, it was the Germans who were able, through cultural, social, and linguistic affinities, to draw German capital across the Atlantic. As early as the Civil War the Speyers and the Seligmans had played a major role—overcoming Rhineland reluctance to subscribe to federal loans. Indeed, a remarkable feature of the bankers' operations was their cosmopolitan outlook. Goldman, Sachs created intimate relationships with houses in London, Amsterdam, Berlin, and Zurich. The Speyers, of course, were from the beginning closely tied to Speyer-Ellison in Frankfort and, later on, to Speyer Brothers in London. Kuhn, Loeb & Co. had close connections with Europe—one with *Disconto Gesellschaft*, and another very strong one with Sir Ernest Cassel, which was well buttressed by a personal friendship between him and Schiff, and which also led to Cologne and Frankfort. Hallgarten & Co. was allied with the Darmstaedter Bank. The Seligmans constructed the strongest network of all—not even relying on existing firms abroad. Once the decision to enter international banking had been made in the 1860s, the eight brothers, under Joseph's patriarchal guidance, set up houses in London, Paris, and Frankfort, each house controlled by one or more brothers. With J. & W. Seligman & Co. in New York (1864), J. Seligman & Co. in San Francisco (which became a fully fledged banking house in 1867), Seligman, Hellman & Co. in New Orleans (1865), Seligman Brothers in London (1864), Seligman & Stettheimer in Frankfort (1864), and *Seligman Frères et Cie* in Paris (1868), the family was unrivaled in its international framework. Throughout the last decades of the century houses such as Kuhn, Loeb or Hallgarten demonstrated a supreme ability to establish contact with sources of supply of German capital.

From this point of view, the rise of an investment market, with all that that meant in terms of economic growth, might have been very different without the influence of these men, and without the solidarity and progress of this particular financial and social grouping.

FOR FURTHER READING

Four book-length studies of the "German period" in American Jewish history have appeared in recent years: Naomi W. Cohen's *Encounter with Emancipation: The German Jews in the United States, 1830–1914* (1984); Hasia Diner's *A Time for Gathering: The Second Migration* (1992); Avraham Barkai's *Branching Out* (1994); and the middle volumes of Jacob R. Marcus's *United States Jewry 1776–1985* (1989–93).

Earlier, Rudolf Glanz authored some of the most important studies dealing with the German period in American Jewish history. He collected the bulk of them in his *Studies in Judaica Americana* (1970), but two more recent ones also merit close attention: "The German Jewish Mass Emigration: 1820–1880," *Americn Jewish Archives* 20 (April 1970), pp. 49–66; and "Vanguard to the Russians: The Poseners in America," *Yivo Annual of Jewish Social Science* 18 (1983), pp. 1–38. Glanz's 2,500-item bibliography, *The German Jew in America* (1969), lists a wealth of primary materials in this area, most of them, of course, in German.

Eric E. Hirshler (ed.), *Jews from Germany in the United States* (1955), is one of the best collections of its kind, and contains several fine articles. Briefer surveys include H. G. Riessner's comprehensive study "The German-American Jews (1800–1850)," in the *Leo Baeck Institute Year Book* 19 (1965), pp. 57–116, which includes a valuable bibliography; and Bertram W. Korn's more loosely focused "German-Jewish Intellectual Influences on American Jewish Life, 1824–1972," in A. Leland Jamison (ed.), *Tradition and Change in Jewish Experience* (1977). Some of Korn's other articles dealing with this period are collected in his *Eventful Years and Experiences* (1954). Robert Ernst's book *Immigrant Life in New York City 1825–1863* (1949) puts Jewish life into broader perspective, but does not duplicate Hyman B. Grinstein's *The Rise of the Jewish Community of New York 1654–1860* (1945). For differing perspectives on the identity of German Jews in the United States, see Stanley Nadel, "Jewish Race and German Soul in Nineteenth-Century America," *American Jewish History* 77 (1987), pp. 6–26, and Michael A. Meyer, "German-Jewish Identity in Nineteenth-Century America," in Jacob Katz (ed.), *Toward Modernity: The European Jewish Model* (1987).

American Judaism in the German period has formed the subject of three important books: Moshe Davis, *The Emergence of Conservative*

Judaism (1965), which is much broader than its title implies; Michael A. Meyer, *Response to Modernity: A History of the Reform Movement in Judaism* (1988), which is excerpted here in Chapter Five; and Leon A. Jick, *The Americanization of the Synagogue* (1976). Lance Sussman's *Isaac Leeser and the Making of American Judaism* (1995) and Sefton Temkin's *Isaac Mayer Wise: Shaping American Judaism* (1992) portray the era's foremost Jewish leaders within the context of their time. The religious lives of American Jewish women, a neglected subject, is considered in different ways in Ann Braude, "The Jewish Woman's Encounter with American Culture," in R. Reuther and R. S. Keller (eds.), *Women and Religion in America* I (1981), pp. 150–192; Ellen M. Umansky and Diane Ashton, *Four Centuries of Jewish Women's Spirituality* (1992); Riv-Ellen Prell, "The Vision of Woman in Classical Reform Judaism," *The Journal of the American Academy of Religion* 50:4 (1982), pp. 575–592; and Karla A. Goldman, "The Ambivalence of Reform Judaism: Kaufmann Kohler and the Ideal Jewish Woman," *American Jewish History* 79 (Summer 1990), pp. 477–499.

The Civil War forms the subject of two of the best books ever written in American Jewish history, Bertram W. Korn's *American Jewry and the Civil War* (1951; rev. ed. 1971) and Eli Evan's *Judah P. Benjamin: The Jewish Confederate* (1988). The new edition of Korn's book includes a valuable chapter on "Jews and Negro Slavery in the Old South," which should be read in conjunction with Maxwell Whiteman's "Jews in the Antislavery Movement," published as an introduction to the reprint edition of Peter Still, *The Kidnapped and the Ransomed* (1970), and Louis Ruchames's "The Abolitionists and the Jews: Some Further Thoughts," in Bertram W. Korn (ed.), *A Bicentennial Festschrift for Jacob Rader Marcus* (1976). The whole subject of Jews and slavery has received heightened attention in recent years. Two articles by leading historians of slavery stand out in importance: David Brion Davis, "The Slave Trade and the Jews," *New York Review of Books* 41:21 (1995), pp. 14–16; and Seymour Drescher, "The Role of Jews in the Transatlantic Slave Trade," *Immigrants and Minorities* 12:2 (1993), pp. 113–125. Sefton D. Temkin, "Isaac Mayer Wise and the Civil War," *American Jewish Archives* 15 (November 1963), pp. 120–142, puts into perspective one leading rabbi's obvious ambivalence toward the war effort; and F. S. Frank, "Nashville Jewry During the Civil War," *Tennessee Historical Quarterly* 39 (Fall 1980), pp. 310–322, examines the war's impact on one Jewish community. Stephen V. Ash, "Civil War Exodus: The Jews and Grant's General Order No. 11," *The Historian* 44 (August 1982), pp. 505–523, is the finest single study of Grant's anti-Jewish order, and brings to light much new information. For the order's impact on Grant's subsequent career, see Joakim Isaacs,

"Candidate Grant and the Jews," *American Jewish Archives* 17 (April 1965), pp. 3–15. Louis Schmier, "Notes and Documents on the 1862 Expulsion of Jews from Thomasville, Georgia," *American Jewish Archives* 32 (April 1980), pp. 9–22, makes clear that such incidents were by no means limited to the North alone.

The broader question of Jewish-Christian relations during this period is treated in Egal Feldman, *Dual Destinies: The Jewish Encounter with Protestant America* (1990), and Naomi W. Cohen, *Jews in Christian America* (1992); see also Benny Kraut, "Judaism Triumphant: Isaac Mayer Wise on Unitarianism and Liberal Christianity," *AJS Review* 7–8 (1982–1983), pp. 179–230, and his "Reform Judaism and the Unitarian Challenge," *Journal of Ecumenical Studies* 23 (Winter 1986). On anti-Semitism during these years, the best sources are David Gerber, *Anti-Semitism in American History* (1986), and Leonard Dinnerstein, *Antisemitism in America* (1994).

A serious economic history of American Jewish life during this period has still to be written. Stephen Birmingham's *Our Crowd* (1967), David Black's *The King of Fifth Avenue* (1982), and Leon Harris's *Merchant Princes* (1979) offer popular accounts of financiers and department store magnates; and Allan Tarshish has surveyed "The Economic Life of the American Jew in the Middle Nineteenth Century," in *Essays in American Jewish History* (1958). Lucy Dawidowicz's "The Business of American Jews," in Neal Kozodoy (ed.), *What Is the Use of Jewish History?* (1992), pp. 237–253, is highly suggestive, and Elliot Ashkenazi, *The Business of Jews in Louisiana, 1840–1875* (1988), serves as a valuable case study. Other more narrowly focused monographs appear in two special issues of *American Jewish History* 66 (September 1976) devoted to "American Jewish business enterprise," and vol. 72 (March 1983) devoted to quantification (with a bibliography).

PART THREE

THE ERA OF EAST EUROPEAN IMMIGRATION

East European Jewish immigration to America dates all the way back to Colonial times. Thereafter, every decade saw some *Ostjuden* (Eastern Jews) trickle into the country, but their numbers down to the Civil War remained far too small to be noticeable. In the 1860s and 1870s East European Jews arrived in greater numbers, particularly in the wake of persecutions, and they soon set up their own synagogues and fraternal organizations. They remained, however, no threat at all to German-Jewish hegemony. Then, in 1881, came the assassination of Russia's Tsar Alexander II, and the resulting government-inspired anti-Jewish pogroms. Suddenly, the trickle of East European Jewish immigrants turned into a flood.

If anti-Jewish violence sparked many a decision to risk life and fortune in the New World, the root causes of the mass immigration lay deeper—in overpopulation, oppressive legislation, economic dislocation, wretched poverty, and crushing despair, coupled with tales of wondrous opportunity in America and offers of cut-rate tickets from steamship companies plying the Atlantic. By the time restrictive immigration quotas took effect, in 1924, well over two million Jews from Russia, Austria-Hungary, and Rumania had journied to America's shores. The nation's German-Jewish community was effectively overwhelmed.

The articles in this section focus on the inner world of East European Jewish immigrants: how they lived, how they worked, how they interacted with other American Jews, how they struggled to overcome the many hurdles that stood between them and the American dream of success. The East European Jews seen here were doing far more than just passively Americanizing. To a considerable degree they were also actively transforming the American Jewish community: changing its composition and geographical distribution, realigning its politics and priorities, injecting new elements of tradition, nationalism, and socialism into its religious life, and seasoning its culture with liberal dashes of Yiddish civilization and East European

Jewish folkways. One generation later, when the new American Jewish community emerged, it retained elements of the German and Sephardic pasts and was as heterogeneous as ever, but it looked altogether different. It was this refashioned community—large, wealthy, and influential—that became the foremost Jewish community in the world.

CHAPTER 8

The saga of the East European Jewish immigrant has been recounted many times, most recently in Irving Howe's best-seller, The World of Our Fathers. *Here, historian Deborah Dwork surveys immigrant Jewish life from a unique perspective, that of a medical historian. After noting three features that distinguished Jewish immigrants from their non-Jewish counterparts—a larger percentage of Jews immigrated with the intention of staying, brought their families with them, and came equipped with marketable skills—she concentrates on conditions that affected the immigrants' life and health. "Living conditions," she rightly warns, "must not be romanticized. . . . Poverty, as it existed on the Lower East Side of New York, was noisy, foul smelling, diseased, hungry." Dwork's later research—not reproduced in these pages—demonstrates that living conditions formed only part of the story. The psychic toll exacted by immigration was even heavier:*

> *Despite the foul housing and work conditions, Jews on the whole were physically healthier than their neighbors, both immigrant and Yankee. . . . However, they were not spared the emotional illnesses and conditions which stemmed from the rupture with tradition and the pain of dislocation. Depression, suicide, gonorrhea, and nervous disorders were more common among European Jews in America than in the old country. Neurasthenia, hysteria, and mental alienation were more common among Jews than among their non-Jewish neighbors.*

Swept into a new and alien culture, cut off from loved ones left behind, and, in many cases, forced to violate religious tenets once held dear, immigrants frequently spent lifetimes trying to reconcile what they had left behind with what they had gained. Many cursed Columbus and wondered aloud if the travail they had put themselves to was justified. A few returned to Europe. But in the wake of the infamous Kishinev pogrom of 1903 and subsequent persecutions in Russia and elsewhere, the promise of American life shined ever brighter. Most Jewish immigrants struggled on, hoping for a better life for their children.

Immigrant Jews On the Lower East Side of New York: 1880–1914

Deborah Dwork

The mass immigration of Eastern European Jews to the United States occurred between 1880 and 1914. From 1881 to 1900, 675,000 Jews entered the United States; from 1901 to 1914 the number doubled to approximately 1,346,000. The dates 1881–1914 are related to specific historical events: the assassination of Tsar Alexander II with its subsequent pogroms, and the beginning of World War I. In the thirty-three years between these two events, over two million Jews, or one-third of the Jewish population of Eastern Europe, came to the United States. Prior to 1881, Jews emigrated in search of a less oppressive society. Then, as a result of three events, the character of Jewish emigration changed. First, the assassination of Tsar Alexander II unleashed a fury of pogroms, which continued intermittently at least until World War I. A mass exodus of Russian Jews occurred following the 1881 pogroms, the 1903 Kishinev massacre, and pogroms following the unsuccessful revolution of 1905. Second, the increased legal restrictions on Jews, such as the so-called May Laws of the 1880s, forced Jews to abandon their previous employments and way of life and to migrate to urban centres. Prohibited from owning or renting land outside towns and cities, industrialization encroaching rapidly on their occupations as artisans and craftsmen, Jews turned to the industrial labour force. The population of Jews in Lodz soared from eleven in 1793 to 98,677 in 1897 and 166,628 in 1910. Similarly, Warsaw had 3,532 Jewish inhabitants in 1781 and 219,141 in 1891. These migrations within Russia and Poland were often only temporary solutions to the problem of survival, especially for young skilled Jews who saw no future in the cities. Finally, the decline of Central European emigration to America encouraged the German transatlantic passage companies to seek out Eastern Europeans as new passengers.

There were also more private reasons for leaving: to escape military service; lack of a dowry; hunger. They left because the others were dead, or had left already. They left because "the struggle for living was too great and hard. . . . The persecution of the Jews became unbearable." "People who got it good in the old country don't hunger for the new."

The Jewish immigration was a movement of families. Between 1886 and 1896, an average of 41.6 percent of Jewish immigrants entering the port of New York were women, and 33.8 percent were children under sixteen years of age. This continued after the turn of the century. From 1899 to 1910, women accounted for 43.4 percent of the Jewish immigrant population, and children under fourteen years of age for 24.9 percent. Nearly 70 percent of Jewish immigrants were between the ages of fourteen and forty-four.

For most, it was a permanent move. A smaller percentage of Jews returned to the Old World than of any other immigrant group. Between 1908 and 1924, 94.8 percent of the Jewish immigrants, as contrasted with two-thirds of the total immigrant population, remained in the United States.

The occupational training of Jewish immigrants changed considerably before and after 1900. Prior to 1900, there were fewer industrial workers and more artisans and people engaged in middleman occupations. The years between 1880 and 1900, however, saw great industrial and urban development in both Eastern Europe and the United States. Thus, later immigrants had the opportunity to learn industrial skills in Europe. Immigrants wrote to their family and friends still in Europe, extolling the virtues and necessity of industrial skills. For example, due to the geometric growth of the U.S. garment industry, young people began to take sewing lessons in preparation for emigration. "By 1900 even the daughters of respectable householders had turned their energies and talents to it." The hero of Abraham Cahan's novel, *The Rise of David Levinsky,* recounts his arrival in New York:

> "You're a tailor, aren't you?" [the contractor] questioned him.
>
> My steerage companion nodded. "I'm a ladies' tailor, but I have worked on men's clothing, too," he said.
>
> "A ladies' tailor?" the well-dressed stranger echoed, with ill-concealed delight. "Very well; come along. I have work for you."
>
> . . . "And what was your occupation? You have no trade, have you?"
>
> "I read Talmud," I said confusedly.
>
> "I see, but that's no business in America." . . .

The immigration statistics verify this emphasis on skilled labour. Although Jews constituted only 10.3 percent of the total immigrant population between 1900 and 1925, they accounted for one-quarter of the skilled industrial workers entering the United States—nearly one-half of the clothing workers, jewellers, and watchmakers; one-third of the printers; 41.4 percent of the leather workers; and one-fifth of the shopkeepers and merchants. From 1899 to 1914, "Jews ranked first in 26 out of 47 trades tabulated by the Immigration Commission, comprising an absolute majority in eight."

Immigrants often encountered great difficulties arranging passage to America. Often the male members of the family would leave first, sometimes one at a time, and live depriving themselves of all but bare necessities until they had enough money to "bring over" their wives, mothers, sisters, and children. In Anzia Yezierska's short story, *Brothers*, the hero Moisheh tries to save money for ship tickets for his mother and two brothers:

> . . . Moisheh the Schnorrer they call him. He washes himself his own shirts and sews together the holes from his socks to save a penny. Think only! He cooks himself his own meat once a week for Sabbath and the rest of the time it's cabbage and potatoes or bread and herring. And the herring what he buys are the squashed and smashed ones from the bottom of the barrel. And the bread he gets is so old and hard he's got to break it with a hammer.

Even if a ticket were sent, money was needed for travel from the village or town to a port of embarkation. People simply sold all their possessions and left for America by cart, train, or on foot, with packs on their backs held in feather bedding—if that hadn't already been sold as well. If the immigrant was male and of conscription age, he had to be smuggled out of the country, and often left with no passport or identifying papers. Steerage from Hamburg, Bremen, or Antwerp cost $34; from Liverpool, $25. Bribing various officials was another major expense.

At the port the immigrants were examined by a physician. This was not done for their health, but rather with an eye to the ship company's profit: upon arrival at Castle Garden, and after 1892 Ellis Island, immigrants with incurable or contagious diseases or conditions had to return to Europe at the ship company's expense. The medical examination is the subject of the short story *Off for the Golden Land* by the great Yiddish author Sholem Aleichem:

> The time comes to go on board the ship. People tell them that they should take a walk to the doctor. So they go to the doctor. The doctor examines them and finds they are all hale and hearty and can go to America, but she, that is Goldele, cannot go, because she has trachomas on her eyes. At first her family did not understand. Only later did they realize it. That meant that they could all go to America but she, Goldele, would have to remain here in Antwerp. So there began a wailing, a weeping, a moaning. Three times her mamma fainted. Her papa wanted to stay here, but he couldn't. All the ship tickets would be lost. So they had to go off to America and leave her, Goldele, here until the trachomas would go away from her eyes. . . .

The vast majority of immigrants travelled steerage class. They were crammed into the bowels of the ship; some companies even locked them in to prevent them from going on the upper decks and mingling with the second-class passengers. For many the food was inedible since it was not kosher. The nonobservant found it equally inedible because it was so disgusting and decayed. Many people subsisted on a diet of black bread, herring, and tea. Some were fortunate enough to have cheese and butter. Sanitation was terrible, with a few saltwater basins used as dishpans, laundry tubs, and for personal hygiene. The condition of the toilets was worse—open troughs that were rarely flushed and even more rarely cleaned. Throughout their memoirs and oral histories, people recounted tales of terrible seasickness, explaining that the filth and foul smell of their surroundings alone caused nausea.

The voyage lasted anywhere from ten days to three weeks; usually it was a two-week trip. They arrived dazed, confused, weak from hunger and seasickness, at "The Island of Tears," Ellis Island. From all reports—those of the immigrants, officials, and the Hebrew Immigrant Aid Society—Ellis Island was a bewildering experience, full of the pain of displacement. During the late nineteenth century, a few thousand immigrants had arrived at Castle Garden each week; throughout the early years of the twentieth century, tens of thousands arrived at Ellis Island each week.

Each immigrant was given a medical and cursory mental examination. People with suspected problems were marked with symbols drawn in chalk on their outer garments. One immigrant recalled that day with horror:

> It was so crowded and noisy. I was a small child then and held fast to my mother's hand. A man in uniform leaned down and drew a letter on my coat. I was frightened. My mother made as if it was hot and opened her cloak wide, doubling it back over her shoulders. Then, after we passed that man, she did the same to me. There were so many people, no one noticed. That's how I got into America.

Trachoma was the cause of more than half the medical detentions, and according to a contemporary article in Scribner's magazine, "most of those detained by the physicians for trachoma are Jews."

Some immigrants were met by relatives, others, sometimes unexpectedly, by landsmen, or fellow-villagers. One immigrant writes that his rabbi in Russia had written to the *landsmanshaften* (a fraternal organization or lodge composed of fellow townspeople) in New York on his behalf. Thus, to his surprise, he was met at the pier by an old neighbour. Still others were met by contractors on the watch for "greenhorns" (newcomers) experienced at their trade but not in American ways. And finally there were those, like David Levinsky, Abraham Cahan's fictional protagonist, who were simply pointed in the direction of the Lower East Side, and walked until they were greeted with recognizable signs and understandable speech.

Between 70 percent and 90 percent of the Jewish immigrants remained in

New York, for a number of reasons. Social ties were very important. Family, friends, or neighbours might have already established themselves there. The desire to settle in a Jewish community was also of great importance. Despite a decrease in strict religious observance, certain essentials were necessary: kosher meat, a rabbi, a minyan (the mandatory minimum of ten men necessary to hold religious services). Many immigrants recalled the great uprooting and intense loneliness mitigated by homely companionship and customs. And, finally, New York was attractive because industrial work was more readily available there than in other parts of the country.

The Jewish immigrant population concentrated in the seventh, tenth, eleventh, and thirteenth wards of lower Manhattan. By 1900, Jews comprised an average of 79 percent of the population of these wards, or an estimated 252,821 individuals. Thus, these can be considered "Jewish" wards.

The living conditions in these wards must not be romanticized. There is a common notion that poor today is not like poor then; old-time poverty was clean, honest, and upright. This is utter nonsense. Poverty, as it existed on the Lower East Side of New York, was noisy, foul-smelling, diseased, hungry:

> The squalid humans that swarmed about . . . the raucous orchestra of voices, the metallic bedlam of elevated trains, the pounding of horses . . . the teeming ghetto . . . haggling pushcart peddlars . . . the dirt and din of screaming hucksters. . . . The slattern yentehs lounging on the stoops, their dirty babies at their breasts. . . . Wedged in, jumbled shops and dwellings, pawn shops and herring-stalls, strained together. . . . Broken stoves, beds, three-legged chairs sprawled upon the sidewalk.

The congestion was overwhelming. The *New York Times* reported on 18 January 1895 that sections of the Lower East Side were more densely populated than the most crowded areas of Bombay or Prague, and immigration had not yet reached its peak. The tenth ward was more densely populated than any European city, with 626.25 persons per acre as compared with 485.4 in Prague and 125.2 in Paris.

In 1905, there were 115 blocks on the Lower East Side with an average density of 750 or more persons per acre, and 39 with a density of 1,000 or more per acre. In Manhattan in the early years of this century, 70 percent of all workers engaged in manufacturing, 67 percent of the factories, and 28 percent of the city's inhabitants were located below 14th Street on one one-hundredth of the city's land area. Furthermore, the Lower East Side had only 29.8 acres of park space, or 2 percent of the city's total park area.

There was an astounding variety of activity in the Lower East Side. The University Settlement Report of 1896 included a social census of the tenth ward. There were 989 tenement houses; eight public schools; three theatres, with a total seating capacity of 9,500; sixteen stables, with a capacity of 210;

thirteen pawnshops; seventy-two restaurants; forty-one churches, of which thirty-one were synagogues; sixty-five factories; 172 garment makers' shops; 236 saloons, of which 108 were Raines Law Hotels, a combination saloon and brothel of the seediest type; and eighteen "disorderly places." There were thirty-four bathtubs; four in private houses, twelve in barber shops, and eighteen in lodging houses. In 1904 David Blaustein, superintendent of the Educational Alliance, took a private census of approximately thirty-two streets south of Houston Street and east of the Bowery. He found 5,007 tenements housing 64,268 families engaged in eighty-four different occupations. There were 306 synagogues, and so few public schools in comparison to need that the children could only attend half-day sessions.

The Lower East Side also had a burgeoning red-light district centred on Allen Street. As the neighbourhood became increasingly Jewish in character, the saloons moved out; Jews were temperate, and business became slack. The red-light district, by contrast, became more prominent. Allen Street was not simply a spectacle in the ghetto. It was part of the way of life of the poor. Michael Gold, an active Communist, remembers the neighbourhood in which he grew up:

> The East Side of New York was then the city's red light district, a vast 606 playground under the business management of Tammany Hall. . . .There were hundreds of prostitutes on my street. They occupied vacant stores, they crowded into flats and apartments in all the tenements. . . .On sun-shiny days the whores sat on chairs along the sidewalks. They sprawled indolently, their legs taking up half the pavements. People stumbled over a gauntlet of whores' meaty legs. . . .Earth's trees, grass, flowers could not grow on my street; but the rose of syphilis bloomed by night and by day.

Living conditions for the families of the Lower East Side were dictated largely by the conditions of their homes. The tenements, in turn, were fundamental to the health conditions of Lower East Side inhabitants. Legally, "tenement house" was defined in 1867 as, "any house, building . . . occupied as the home or residence of more than three families living independently of one another, and doing their own cooking on the premises, or by more than two families upon a floor, so living and cooking and having a common right in the halls, stairways, yards, water-closets, or privies, or some of them. . . ."This definition could also suit flats and apartment houses, which were not then or now known as tenements. Jacob Riis, an ardent reformer and pioneer photographer-journalist, described the tenement:

> It is generally a brick building from four to six storeys high on the street, frequently with a store on the first floor which, when used for the sale of liquor, has a side opening for the benefit of the inmates and to evade the Sunday law;

four families occupy each floor, and a set of rooms consists of one or two dark closets, used as bedrooms, with a living room twelve feet by ten. The staircase is too often a dark well in the centre of the house, and no direct ventilation is possible. . . .

The immigrants' descriptions were more pithy, if less precise. "Our tenement was nothing but a junk-heap of rotten lumber and brick. . . .The plaster was always falling down, the stairs broken and dirty. . . .There was no drinking water in the tenement for days." "The bedbugs lived and bred in the rotten walls of the tenement, with the rats, fleas, roaches. . . ." "In America were rooms without sunlight."

The number of houses without light, ventilation, hot running water, baths, or water closets was overwhelming. In 1900, the Tenement House Committee of the Charity Organization Society illustrated this problem by exhibiting a cardboard model of an entire block. The chosen block, bounded by Chrystie, Forsyth, Canal, and Bayard streets, was in the tenth ward. The 80,000 square foot area boasted thirty-nine tenement houses (nearly all six storeys high) with 605 apartments. These buildings housed 2,781 people, 2,315 over five years of age and 466 under five. There were 264 water closets; only forty apartments had hot water. The one bathtub on the block, wedged in an air shaft, was obviously unusable. Of the total 1,588 rooms, 441 or 27.7 percent were completely dark, with no access to outer air; 635 rooms or 40 percent were ventilated only by dark, narrow air shafts. The rent roll was high, at $113,964 a year. The disease toll was also high. During the preceding year (1899), thirteen cases of diptheria had been reported to the health department; during the past five years (1895–1900), thirty-two cases of tuberculosis had been reported. It was estimated that "not over two-thirds of the cases are actually reported to the department." Startling as they may seem, these conditions were by no means unique. The block was typical.

The tenement house was not a new invention at the turn of the century, manufactured to accommodate the late mass immigrations. Tenement houses had been a social, political, and health problem in New York City since the early 1800s. Public action, however, was not taken until the middle of the century. In 1842, Dr. John H. Griscom, a city inspector of the State Board of Health, drew attention to tenement house conditions and urged that legislative action be taken to ameliorate the situation. Although this was not done, in 1846 the New York Association for Improving the Condition of the Poor (AICP) began investigating slum conditions. An 1854 report disclosed the startling extent of poverty and disease which the AICP had found, and prodded the public conscience by stressing the great need for reform. As a result of this report, the State Legislature appointed a commission to study the tenement situation and to propose ameliorative legislation. However, in 1857, the legislature turned down the commission's reform bill.

Public interest waned until the draft riots of 1863 and high death rates stimulated a group of prominent New Yorkers to form a Citizens' Association. A sub-committee on sanitary conditions, the Council of Hygiene and Public Health, included eminent physicians. Despite the council's reports on the loathsome sanitary conditions of New York City, the State Legislature still did not act. Finally, in 1865, after cholera appeared in Europe, fear of an epidemic in New York convinced the legislature to establish a Metropolitan Board of Health for New York City (1866), and a Tenement House Law (1867).

The fact that these measures were passed at all was highly significant. It demonstrated the development of a legal consciousness of the importance of the public health. With the Tenement House Law, society recognized the right to limit the entrepreneurial freedom of builders in the interest of public health. However, the law itself was vague, and standards were low. Most requirements could be altered at the discretion of the Board of Health; and the requirements themselves were not sufficient to protect the inhabitants. Among the major provisions: tenements had to have fire escapes or some other means of egress; a water tap had to be furnished either indoors or outside. Only one water closet or privy had to be provided for each twenty inhabitants, and it could be located outdoors (usually in the rear yard). Water closets and privies had to connect with sewers, but only if such existed. Cesspools were forbidden, except where necessary. There was no limit on the percentage of the lot which the building might cover.

In 1879, the history of the tenements took a sharp turn. During December of the previous year, editor Charles F. Wingate held a $500 competition in Henry C. Mayer's new trade journal, the *Plumber and Sanitary Engineer.* The competition, entitled "Improved Homes for Workingmen" or "The Model Home Competition," called for erection on a standard city lot (25 × 100 feet) of a brick building which provided "security against conflagration (including fireproof staircases open to the air), distribution of light, ventilation, drainage and other sanitary appointments . . . inexpensiveness."

James E. Ware won first prize; his construction, commonly known as the "dumbbell" or "double-decker" tenement, was published in March 1879. Despite the magazine's exhortations that "it is irrational to suppose that a commodious and healthful house for a large number of families can be built upon an ordinary lot 25 × 100" and that "the present competition has demonstrated that stringent restrictions should be made upon the erection of houses of this class," the dumbbell tenement was mass-produced for the working class in New York between 1879 and 1901.

The competition stimulated public interest in tenement house reform. On Tenement House Sunday (23 February 1879), concerned New York clergy preached on the subject. On 28 February, at Cooper's Union, Mayor Cooper presided over a large public meeting, again dealing with tenement house reform. Within days, the Mayor's Committee of Nine was formed with a mandate to devise reform measures. Approximately one month later, it introduced a successful bill amending the Tenement House Law of 1867. While the bill modified various regulations of the preceding law and provided for thirty sanitary police to enforce the housing code, it still subjected all requirements to the discretionary power of the Board of Health. It did, however, limit the percentage of space a new building could occupy to 65 percent of the lot, and required a window measuring a minimum of twelve square feet in rooms used for sleeping.

There was no new legislation or important public agitation until 1884, when Professor Felix Adler, founder of the Society for Ethical Culture, again roused public interest and energy with a series of lectures decrying the tenement blight. This renewed public concern forced the legislature to appoint a second legislative commission, whose recommendations stimulated the passage of further amendments to the Tenement House Law in 1887. The number of sanitary police was increased to forty-five. Running water on every floor and one water closet per fifteen inhabitants were now required. The board also took responsibility for inspecting every tenement semiannually.

The mayoral Tenement House Commissions of 1894 and 1900 produced further landmarks of tenement house reform. The 1894 commission was created due to public anger caused by a series of exposés published by a newspaper, the *Press*. The resulting Tenement House Law of 1895 provided for two small parks on the Lower East Side and five recreation piers to be built along the river.

The commission of 1900 grew out of interest stimulated by the Charity Organization Society's (COS) Tenement House Committee exhibit. Lawrence Veiller, who directed this committee, was appointed secretary of the commission. Its recommendations, adopted in their entirety in 1901, prohibited the future erection of dumbbell-type tenements. In new construction, the space between buildings was to be enlarged from an air shaft to a court. A separate water closet had to be installed in each apartment. Although baths were not required, an inspection of 311 new tenement houses revealed that 125 of them, or 40 percent, had a private bath for each apartment. Veiller also reported that many landlords voluntarily improved the plumbing on their property. Clearly, the tenement population desired toilets, sinks with running water, and baths, and were willing to repay the landlord for his investment through increased rent.

Unfortunately, at least initially, the majority of Jewish immigrants were not in a position to take advantage of the major innovations of the 1901 law. For example, the tenth ward had been built up during the last decades of the nineteenth century, and by 1901 little land was left for new construction. The few new apartments built after 1901 were in great demand, especially by those immigrants who had been in New York for a number of years and could afford the luxury. Often, the apartments were rented even before they were completed.

In existing tenements, landlords were required by the 1901 law to install a window in any room which had none. School sinks (sewer-connected privies) and privy vaults had to be replaced with individual water closets. The commission also detailed specifications for fireproofing, fire escapes, and the lighting of public hallways of existing and future tenements. These measures to safeguard the public health were influenced by contemporary medical knowledge. The bacteriological origins of disease set forth by Koch and Pasteur in the 1870s were by this time becoming popularly understood and accepted. The importance of sunlight and ventilation in destroying the tubercle bacillus was stressed in the commission's report.

Within the Jewish wards the dumbbell tenement was the predominant housing structure, and there were a significant number of rear buildings as well. The latter were built prior to 1879 and, without direct access to the street, were less well ventilated and sunlit, and more of a fire hazard than the dumbbell tenement. The dumbbell structure, built between 1879 and 1901, was characterized by an air shaft which was supposed to provide light and air to the rear rooms. In fact, the air shaft was as much a hazard as a convenience. It conveyed noise and odours, and acted like a huge flue in a fire. According to Jacob Riis, "more than half of all fires in New York occur in tenement houses," and the air shaft, functioning like a chimney, "added enormously to the fireman's work and risk." The air shaft also served as a garbage dump, and, consequently, was even more infested with rats and vermin than the other parts of the tenement structure. Statistics prove that landlords were slow to comply with the 1901 window requirements, designed to succeed where the air shaft had failed in providing light and air. There were 350,000 dark interior rooms in Manhattan in 1902. In 1908, there were still 300,000 south of Houston Street alone.

Tenement houses were not just inadequate, unsanitary homes, they were also inadequate, unsanitary work sites. It was not possible to separate "workshop" from "living quarters" among immigrant Jews.

> Let us follow one [immigrant man] to his home and see how Sunday passes in a Ludlow Street tenement.
>
> Up two flights of stairs, three, four, with new smells of cabbage, of onions, of frying fish, on every landing, whirring sewing machines behind closed doors betraying what goes on within, to the door that opens to admit the bundle [of unfinished garments] and the man. A sweater, this, in a small way. Five men and a woman, two young girls, not fifteen, and a boy who says unasked that he is fifteen and lies in saying it, are at the machines sewing knickerbockers, "knee-pants" in the Ludlow Street dialect. The floor is littered ankle-deep with half-sewn garments. In the alcove, on a couch of many dozens of "pants" ready for

> the finisher, a bare legged baby with pinched face is asleep. A fence of piled-up clothing keeps him from rolling off on the floor. The faces, hands, and arms to the elbows of everyone in the room are black with the colour of the cloth on which they are working. . . .
>
> They are "learners," all of them, say the woman . . . and have "come over" only a few weeks ago.

The immigrants arriving in New York found employment wherever they could. "Everyone grabbed the type of job he could get, and changed it very often. . . . Today, one can be a shoemaker; tomorrow, a tailor, and the day after tomorrow he is forced to become a farmer; later a bookkeeper and so on ad infinitum," wrote George Price. Price himself worked in six different types of factories, taught, did manual labour, worked in ditches and on trains, and finally became a prominent physician in the trade union movement.

The majority of immigrant Jews found work in the needle trades shortly after arrival. Tailoring was easy to learn and was not physically demanding—an excellent combination for the immigrants. Some were snatched up by a contractor at Castle Garden or Ellis Island. Many others entered the needle trades following the example of family or friends who had preceded them. By and large they sought employment among other Jews. This enabled them to observe religious law and eliminated a formidable language barrier. An 1890 survey by the Baron de Hirsch Fund found that 14,316 or 55 percent of the employed permanent residents of wards 7, 10, and 13 worked as tailors, cloakmakers, and labourers in white goods and other branches of the needle trades. There were also 452 furriers and 309 dealers in clothing. Peddling, the second most common occupation, employed another 9.3 percent or 2,440 people. The survey found 1,382 clerks, 976 cigarmakers, 633 shoemakers, and 500 who owned tailor stores. By 1897, according to the 12th Annual Report of the Factory Inspector of New York, 75 percent of the 66,500 workers in the clothing industry in Manhattan and 80 percent of the 15,000 cloakmakers were Jewish. Manhattan was rapidly becoming the hub of the industry; by 1905, half of the clothing manufactured in the United States was produced in New York. The predominance of Jews in the needle trades continued well into the closing years of our study. The fur trade in 1910 was 75 percent Jewish. In 1911, the Joint Board of Sanitary Control in the Cloak, Suit, and Skirt Industry reported that 85 to 90 percent of its workers were Jewish. The dress and waist industry reported in 1913 that 77.7 percent of its workers were female, and that 56.16 of these women were Jewish.

By the late nineteenth century, the needle industry in New York was also overwhelmingly owned and operated by Jews. Historically, Jews had always been involved in the clothing industry. Christians in the United States had allowed Jews to deal in secondhand clothing because this was considered a despicable occupation. This traditional foothold in the clothing industry enabled Jews to take advantage of its fantastic growth during the second half of the nineteenth century.

Three factors greatly stimulated this growth: the Civil War created an unprecedented demand for mass-produced uniforms, the invention of the sewing machine in 1846 provided a means of manufacture, and the large influx of Irish and, later, German immigrants during the mid-century provided the labour force. After the Civil War, the demand for uniforms decreased, but the industry created a consumer market by providing fashionable clothing at much lower cost than custom tailoring. Until the early 1880s skilled German tailors and Irish cutters controlled production. Then competition arrived in the form of Eastern European Jews who had spent time in London learning not only the tailor's craft but also English language and customs. These tailors broke into the production business and paved the way for future immigrants. The clothing industry thus became one of the few in which Jews were employers.

Within the American needle industry, there were three systems and three sites of production. Most antiquated was the so-called "family system," which had become the dominant system of production under German immigrant influence in the mid-nineteenth century. Irish tailors worked in shops, but the Germans worked at home, dividing the labour among family members. Usually the husband was the most skilled worker, the master tailor. He operated the sewing machine while his wife and children did the basting, buttonholes, and finishing touches. This "homework" was done in the family's tenement apartment.

The contracting or "sweatshop" system grew out of the family system. As competition and the volume of work increased, much time had to be spent obtaining work to do; picking up the cloth or, more commonly, pre-cut, unsewn garments; and then delivering the completed product to the warehouse. Enter the contractor. He knew English and had lived in America at least longer than the greenhorns. He contracted with the manufacturer to do X work for Y price by Z date, and was then free to conduct his business as he chose. This seemed ideal to newly arrived immigrants; they could communicate in their own language, observe the Sabbath on Saturday, and maintain other religious laws.

There were a few variants to the contracting system. The contractor could act as a middleman between the working family and the manufacturer, or hire labourers of his own (who would also work in the tenement, either in the contractor's own apartment, or one rented for work purposes), or he could sell the job to a sub-contractor who performed the same function as the contractor himself. Until the last decade of the nineteenth century, the cloak, suit, and skirt trade was primarily controlled by these petty manufacturers. One estimate ascribed 90 percent of all ladies' coats and suits produced in

New York City in 1890 to the contractor. Dr. George Price, by then chairman of the investigative committee of the Joint Board of Sanitary Control in the Cloak, Suit, and Skirt Industry, explained the proliferation of contractors. "Very little capital was needed for the establishment of a shop, as the workers were compelled to furnish their own machines, which were run with foot power. The workers were also often compelled to pay deposits for the privilege of work. All the enterprising manufacturer had to invest was his ability to get work, and perhaps capital enough to pay for the rent of his 'factory.' " These factories were located in lofts, tenement house apartments "converted" for industrial use, or in the tenement home itself. A "cockroach sweater" was the lowest man on the contractor totem pole; his was a small business with few employees, usually run in his own tenement apartment.

The third production site was the inside shop, in which the manufacturer dealt directly with the store buyer, hired his own workers, and ran his own factory. The manufacturer usually worked with a designer, who created fashions or imitated famous designs. The manufacturer displayed these models to the store buyer, who ordered them for the season.

As was generally the case in industry, the physical conditions in which garment workers laboured ranged from poor to foul. The lack of light, space, ventilation, plumbing, and sanitation in tenements has been described already. This situation was exacerbated by the use of the tenements for manufacture. Jacob Riis described the filth and penury over and over again in prose and with photographs. The third annual report (1888) of the New York factory inspectors also discussed the problem of Jewish homework. "They usually eat and sleep in the same room where the work is carried on, and the dinginess, squalor and filth surrounding them is abominable." Annie S. Daniel (1858–1944), an eloquent physician interested in the welfare of the poor and particularly concerned about public health, perceived the problem in 1904–5 from another standpoint:

> These "homes" of working men and women consist of from two to four rooms. In one room, that which opens on the street or yard, is carried on all the domestic life. This room serves for parlor, dining-room, and kitchen; and in this room in addition is carried on the manufacturing. It is quite obvious that the word home was never intended to apply to such an apartment. . . . Every garment worn by a woman is found being manufactured in tenement rooms. . . . [Some] I have seen being made in the presence of small-pox, on the lounge with the patient. . . . Among the 150 families [I attended who did] manufacturing in the living rooms, 66 continued to work during the entire course of the contagious disease.

Conditions in the sweatshops and most factories were equally abominable. In his memoirs, Gregory Weinstein describes a printshop of the 1880s: "Dark shops in rickety buildings; climbing up four, five and six flights of wooden stairs; cases full of dust and rat dirt; working under gas-light from seven o'clock in the morning till six in the evening." Nearly twenty years later, in 1903, conditions in the needle trades were just as bad. Yetta, the heroine of Arthur Bullard's *roman á clef, Comrade Yetta*, views her surroundings: "She saw the broken door to the shamefully filthy toilet, saw the closed, unwashed windows, which meant vitiated, tuberculosis-laden air, saw the backs of the women bent into unhealthy attitudes, saw the strained look in their eyes."

By 1910, homework was in Italian immigrant hands: Jewish labour had moved into inside shops. Unfortunately, most workshops were not a great improvement. In 1910, inspection of 228 waist shops employing 11,000 workers showed that 62 percent used inadequate artificial light, and 60 percent provided no protection against the glare. Thirty percent had filthy water closets with no light or ventilation, and in 28 percent of the shops the general conditions were labelled "extremely dirty". Loft buildings housed 91 percent of the inspected establishments, and over one-half of the employees worked above the sixth floor. This was basically the case in all branches of the needle trades. Loft buildings had improved sanitary conditions in the industry; they were new edifices with large windows providing natural illumination and ventilation, and had up-to-date plumbing facilities. But they posed a much greater fire hazard than previous work sites. Building materials were flammable, fire escapes were either not provided or inadequate, and the loft buildings were simply too high—the Fire Department could not handle fires above the seventh floor. This dilemma was horribly illustrated by the famous fire at the Triangle Waist Company on 25 March 1911, which killed 146 employees.

A 1913 inspection of 700 dress and waist shops revealed that 97.3 percent were located in loft buildings, 2.7 percent in converted buildings, and none in tenements or cellars. The sanitary conditions of the loft buildings were considered very good with only 5 percent using artificial light and 3 percent having no protection from glare. Only 4.5 percent had dirty water closets. However, if anything, the danger from fire had increased, as there were now more people working at greater heights. A little over 50 percent of those in the industry, or 18,417 persons, worked on or above the sixth floor, and nearly 10 percent, or 3,530 persons, worked on or above the twelfth floor. The Fire Department was still incapable of handling fires at these heights, and only 7 percent of the shops practised fire drills. Fifteen shops had no fire escapes; forty-seven had obstructed access to the fire escape; and forty-six had no safe means to escape from the fire escape, which meant that workers could be trapped in an enclosed courtyard or alley—a tunnel of fire. A full 30 percent of the shops had doors which opened inward, making escape difficult and dangerous. Finally, as in the Triangle fire, a few employers still illegally locked their employees in the work room, making escape impossible.

Similar conditions prevailed in the predominantly male cloak, suit, and skirt industry. After the great cloakmakers' strike in 1910, a Joint Board of Sanitary Control was established to study and ameliorate shop conditions. In 1911, the committee of investigation published its report on 1,738 shops. Two-thirds were found deficient in fire protection and/or sanitary conditions. At a time when chewing tobacco was common and spitting was not considered impolite, over 99 percent of the shops had no cuspidors (in direct opposition to the law), thus increasing the risk of tubercular infection. The legal limit of one water closet for every twenty-five persons was also largely ignored—some shops had only one water closet for eighty-five workers. Hot water, towels, and rubbish bins were nearly unheard of, and 6.8 percent of the shops were poorly ventilated. Lunch was eaten in the shop room itself. As in the dress and waist industry, however, fire was by far a greater danger to the workers than were the poor sanitary conditions. Loft buildings housed 90 percent of workers, 50 percent between the sixth and twelfth floors. The interiors of the buildings were hazardous, and rapid escape difficult. The halls were narrow; there were only 1,951 stairways in 1,738 buildings. Thus, most shops had only one means of egress, built either of stone, which heated quickly and then crumbled when wetted, or of wood, which burned easily. The vast majority of shops (84 percent) had only one fire escape, often narrow, leading into an enclosed courtyard or alley.

In 1911, the Joint Board of Sanitary Control adopted sanitary standards which included fire precaution and prevention regulations. Certificates were given to worthy shops. In February 1912, shops employing 40 percent of the workers were so certified, and in September 1912, shops employing 61 percent of the workers were found sanitary. By September 1913, 79 percent of the workers were employed in certified shops. In May of the same year the Joint Board published an alphabetical list of approved establishments.

Thus far, we have primarily examined the physical and sanitary conditions of two branches of the ladies' garment industry. While the great majority of Jewish immigrants were industrial workers, not all were employed in the clothing industry. Industrial conditions in general were on a par with those of the needle trades prior to the 1910 cloakmakers' strike and subsequent formation of the Joint Board of Sanitary Control. George Price, reporting in 1912 for the Factory Investigating Commission (which had been established in response to the public's outcry after the Triangle fire), noted that 54 percent of the shops had no, or insufficient, washing facilities, and an even larger percentage had no hot water. Few had lunch rooms; the great majority of workers ate in the work room. Poor toilet accommodations were the rule. Very few shops had emergency rooms or first aid facilities in case of illness or accident. The worst offender was the food industry, with baking, nutpicking, and ice cream manufacture commonly done in the tenement.

Not only were the physical conditions of the workplace disgusting, degrading, and unhealthful, but the long hours and low wages increased the strain on the worker's constitution. Lillian Wald, founder of the Henry Street Settlement, wrote:

> From the windows of our tenement home we could look upon figures bent over the whirring footpower machines. One room in particular almost unnerved us. Never did we go to bed so late or rise so early that we saw the machines at rest, and the unpleasant conditions where manufacturing was carried on in the overcrowded rooms of the families we nursed disquieted us more than the disease we were trying to combat.

It is impossible to discern exactly how many hours per day or week people worked. Hours differed from industry to industry, from "outside" shop to "inside" factory, and from rush to slack seasons. In 1891, New York factory inspectors reported a sixty-six-to-seventy-two-hour minimum work week during the slack season in the clothing industry (if the worker was lucky enough to maintain his position), and sixteen to nineteen hours a day, seven days a week during the busy season. Dr. Annie Daniel reported women working at home nineteen hours a day, seven days a week during the busy season in 1904–5. Workers were hard put to decide which was worse: the anxiety and poverty of the slack season with little or no employment, or the hours and tension of the rush season with greater and greater work demands. Hours in the factories were slightly better. In 1894 the cloakmakers' union went on strike for—and won—a ten-hour day, reduced from the standard twelve to fifteen hours. In 1901, nearly all clothing union workers sought a fifty-nine-hour week.

Wages depended upon position, piecework, sex, and whether the worker was employed by a contractor or in a factory. In all cases, wages were low, the difference being between poverty and penury. In 1888, male cloakmakers in inside shops earned an average weekly wage of $12. Annie Daniel reported that female homeworker wages averaged $1.04 a week in 1904–5, and the average weekly income from the man's work was $3.81. Jacob Riis gives various piecework prices: there were knee pants "for which the manufacturer pays seventy cents a dozen," or another grade of kneepants at 42¢ a dozen. The finisher of the garment "gets ten and the ironer eight cents a dozen: button-holes are extra, at eight to ten cents a hundred." According to the United States Industrial Reports, between 1880 and 1901 the weekly wage of New York coatmakers in task shops fell nearly 17 percent. The work day increased by 20 percent and productivity increased by 66 percent. There were no significant technical advances during this period, nor any improvement in the division of labour. The workers simply worked harder and longer.

CHAPTER 9

The tension between the native and the newcomer is a perennial theme in immigration history. What makes the case of late nineteenth century American Jews different is the fact that the natives and the newcomers were kinfolk: German Jews and East Europeans. Enmity between them went back to Europe, where German Jews habitually viewed Ostjuden *(Eastern Jews) as unenlightened medievals, and* Ostjuden *in turn viewed them as assimilated and godless. But such stereotypes did not prevent German Jews from being both sympathetic to the plight of the East Europeans and eager to help them.*

The rift between the two groups—referred to as the split between "uptown" and "downtown," or between the "Yahudi" and the "immigrant"—developed in America early in the 1880s. German Jews feared that immigration would provoke anti-Semitism, saw newcomers as social inferiors, recognized that their own community was fast becoming outnumbered, and, at least in the early years, discouraged East European Jews from immigrating, doubting that they could succeed. East European Jews were naturally resentful, notwithstanding the material support that German Jews extended to them, and many bristled at being the objects of charity, much as they may have needed it. Some projected onto German Jews their frustrations about America as a whole, and sought as a matter of right the kind of social equality that time alone could create for them.

Yet, bad as feelings sometimes became, German-Jewish leaders continued to work long and hard on behalf of the East Europeans. The great "uptown" leader and lawyer, Louis Marshall, actually learned Yiddish—and he was not alone. As time went on, individuals in both camps grew to respect one another. When critical issues arose, such as immigration legislation and bills aimed at abrogating America's commercial treaty with Russia, German Jews and Eastern European Jews stood shoulder to shoulder; they planned strategy together. In the end, bonds of kinship proved far stronger than petty in-group squabbles.

Moses Rischin, in the essay that follows, traces these developments as they took place in New York. Moving beyond an earlier generation of historians concerned only to affix blame, Rischin sees the interplay between native Jews and immigrants in its full complexity: negative images as well as positive actions, altruism as well as self-interest. He describes the manifold institutions created by Germans and *by East Europeans, and shows how they functioned together to promote Jewish unity.*

As Rischin realizes, a fascinating process was taking place in New York. Though scarcely recognized at the time, German Jews and East European Jews, by coming together, were paving the way for a new community. Leaving behind one riddled with inner divisions that fractured even immigrant enclaves, they were forging what would become known as an ethnic *community. It divided along ideological and religious lines, and left old-world geographical ones behind.*

Germans versus Russians

Moses Rischin

At a time when established Jews were becoming acutely sensitive to the opinions of their fellow New Yorkers, they were faced with the prospect of a mass migration of coreligionists from Eastern Europe, whose coming seemed to threaten their hard-won respectability. German Jews had shed the tradesman's mien and were acquiring the higher mercantile manner. As they became Americanized, their ties with the German community in New York became less pronounced and they, along with Jews of American origin, were discovering a common identity as Jews that they had not known earlier.

Yet in the years of the great Jewish migration, to be identified as a Jew became more and more irksome. The hosts of uncouth strangers, shunned by respectable New Yorkers, seemed to cast a pall upon all Jews. Disturbed native and German Jews, heirs to the age of reason and science, condemned everything that emanated from the downtown quarter.

It had not been so earlier, when disparities had been less marked and less consequential. East Europeans, few and far between, blended into the immigrant city and created no problems. Place of origin, family pride, clan solidarity, and intellectual tastes loosely defined business and social relations, but differences were in degree rather than in kind and fleeting contacts minimized friction. Gruff-mannered East Europeans tended to hover on the edge of more elegant "German" society despite mutual animosities. The Russian-Polish Jew, assuming German airs, became the "Kavalier Datch." Selig became Sigmund, eager to dwell in the shadow of German respectability, at last to claim, "Mayn waib is gevoren ah datchke un ich bin gevoren ah datch" (My wife has become a lady and I a gentleman). As the East European colony took shape, the German model persisted; but it lost its primacy, for Russian pioneers could now turn to their own circles to satisfy their social needs.

Established New York Jews made every effort to become one with progress. In 1870 the *New York Times* saluted Temple Emanu-El in its new Moorish edifice as one of the globe's leading congregations, "the first to stand forward before the world and proclaim the dominion of reason over blind and bigoted faith." Clearly an age was dawning when all men, regardless of race or ancestral faith, would come together in universal communion. "In the erection and dedication of the Fifth Avenue Temple, it was not only the congregation that was triumphant, it was Judaism that triumphed, the Judaism of the heart, the Judaism which proclaims the spirit of religion as being of more importance than the letter." In 1873 German Emanu-El turned to Manchester, England, and called Gustav Gottheil to its pulpit to preach Judaism's universal message in impeccably English accents, comprehensible to all New Yorkers.

European events sustained in German Jews the conviction of the supreme merit and eventual acceptance of all things German—all, regrettably, but language. With the rise of a new Germany, New York Germans, even as they became more American, compensated for earlier rebuffs with a rising flamboyance. Jews shared in the elation and further celebrated the removal of lingering disabilities upon their kin in the new empire. They took new pride in their roots and vicariously partook of German imperial prestige, assured that the German Empire meant "peace, liberty, progress, and civilization." German Jews, insisted Rabbi Kaufmann Kohler, free of the "shackles of medievalism," their minds "impregnated with German sentiment . . . no longer Oriental," stood convinced of their superiority to East Europeans and regarded all vestiges of a segregated past with discomfort.

The fears of uptowners, colored with racist phraseology, smoldered in the Anglo-Jewish press. There anti-Russian sentiment assumed a withering metaphysical rationale as "a piece of Oriental antiquity in the midst of an ever-Progressive Occidental civilization" called forth the ghost of a happily forgotten past. Uptown Jews, sensitive to the reverberations of the new German anti-Semitism, were far more distressed by the "un-American" ways of the "wild Asiatics" than were non-Jews. "Are we waiting for the natural process of assimilation between Orientalism and Americanism? This will perhaps never take place," exclaimed the *American Hebrew.* The *Hebrew Standard* echoed these misgivings: "The thoroughly acclimated American Jew . . . has no religious, social or intellectual sympathies with them. He is closer to the Christian sentiment around him than to the Judaism of these miserable darkened Hebrews." Even Emma Lazarus in her sonnet inscribed to the Statue of Liberty, "Mother of Exiles," called the immigrants of the 1880s "the wretched refuse of your teeming shore."

Nothing in the newcomers seemed worthy of approval. Yiddish, or Judeo-German, "a language only understood by Polish and Russian Jews," though intelligible to non-Jewish Germans, was denounced as "piggish jargon." Immigrant dress, ceremonials, and rabbinical divorces were anathema.

Yiddish theaters were barbarous, Yiddish newspapers, collectively stigmatized as "socialistic," even worse. Furthermore, "dangerous principles" were "innate in the Russian Jew." Mounting newspaper publicity proved especially distasteful. "The condition of the Jewish quarter . . . has too often been the subject of extravagant word-painting." Lincoln Steffens's reports of East Side life in the *Evening Post* and *Commercial Advertiser* were resented equally with Abraham Cahan's realist fictional essays.

> Our newspapers have daily records of misdemeanors, marital misery, and petty quarrels that may largely be attributed to the same source. The efforts of intelligent brethren to raise the standards of Judaism have been frustrated by the efforts of misguided people who regard all teaching and criticism, as an outrage on their suddenly acquired and misunderstood liberty.

Most intolerable of all was that "anomaly in America, 'Jewish' trades unions." Germans, embarrassed by Russian business competition, dismissed their rivals, whose names often ended with "ki," as "kikes." So Russians often were forced to Germanize their names in order to escape the stigma among German credit men. "Uptown" and "downtown" separated employers from employees, desirable from undesirable, "classes" from "masses," "Americans" from "foreigners," and icily confirmed the most categorical judgments.

Making New Americans

Yet, uptowners of means spared no effort to assist downtowners. "The uptown mansion never forgets the downtown tenement in its distress." Uptowners, taken unawares by the heavy immigration of terror-stricken refugees in 1881 and fearful of a pauper problem, attempted to restrain further immigration. But as the tide could not be stemmed, the Jewish charities of the city, aided considerably by West European Jewry, chafingly accepted their new responsibilities. The *American Hebrew* urged: "All of us should be sensible of what we owe not only to these . . . coreligionists, but to ourselves, who will be looked upon by our gentile neighbors as the natural sponsors for these, our brethren."

The established Jewish charities proved unequal to the new demands. The United Hebrew Charities, formed in 1874 during the economic crisis, had efficiently administered extra-institutional relief, but so moderate had been the claims made upon it, that in 1880 its treasury showed a balance of $14,000. Mass migration transformed the scope of Jewish charity. The Hebrew Emigrant Aid Society, improvised for the crisis, raised $300,000 to succor the first contingents of refugees. In a single year, the HEAS expended as much as had the United Hebrew Charities in its seven-year existence. "Assistance was no longer claimed as a fraternal right, nor extended as a kin-like obligation," recalled Professor Jacob H. Hollander two decades later at the Fifth Biennial Session of the National Conference of Jewish Charities.

> It was the imperious demand of stricken humanity. But, as the situation lost its bitter novelty and the burden settled in onerous pressure, benevolence waned and something akin to patronage grew. The charitable association became no longer a semi-social device whereby the more prosperous members of the community relieved the misfortunes of neighbors and associates, but a tax-like charge for the indefinite relief of misery and dependence of a distinct class, different in speech, tradition and origin, unsought in arrival and unwelcome in presence, whose only claim was a tenuous tie of emotional appeal and an identical negation in religious belief.

Help continued nevertheless. Local groups and individuals, aided by the Independent Order of B'nai B'rith, the Baron de Hirsch Fund, and the Union of American Hebrew Congregations, ministered to the needs of immigrants. The Forty-Eighter Michael Heilprin of the *Nation* came to a premature end as a result of his exertions to settle immigrants on the land. When refugees overflowed Castle Garden and the lodging houses nearby, the State Commissioners of Emigration opened the Ward's Island buildings to the newcomers and Jacob H. Schiff contributed $10,000 for the erection of auxiliary barracks. The United Hebrew Charities provided free lodgings, meals, medical and midwife care, and, for countless unfortunates, free burial. The UHC's employment bureau did its best, even when "the market was overladen with the kind of work offered" and "applicants were nearly all without special trade or calling and . . . physically unable to comply with the conditions demanded in this country." In 1885, despite depressed trade conditions, the UHC's employment bureau turned away only 744 of 3036 applicants as unemployable.

German Jews devised comprehensive schemes to divest downtown brethren of the marks of oppression and to remodel them in the uptown image. Mrs. Minnie D. Louis's sixteen-verse poem outlining uptown's Americanizing mission, "What it is to be a Jew," opened with the image of the ghetto Jew,

> To wear the yellow badge, the locks,
> The caftan-long, the low-bent head,
> To pocket unprovoked knocks
> And shamble on in servile dread—
> 'Tis not this to be a Jew

and closed with a portrait of the American Jew, fully realized,

> Among the ranks of men to stand
> Full noble with the noblest there;

> To aid the right in every land
> With mind, with might, with heart, with prayer—
> *This* is the eternal Jew!

First and foremost came vocational preparation, training not available to immigrants under other auspices, and tutelage in American customs. With these goals in mind, the United Hebrew Charities had organized special classes in the domestic and sewing arts for girls as early as 1875, and a few years later the Hebrew Free School Association had opened the Hebrew Technical School for girls. After 1890 the Baron de Hirsch Fund supervised and supported an array of educational facilities that included the Hebrew Technical Institute for boys, an evening technical school, and evening English classes, initiated by the YMHA to supplement the public evening schools. "Jargon journalists, Hebrew teachers, musicians" anxious to qualify for admission to professional schools, were given special instruction; in 1896, of a class of eighteen, eight were admitted to medical school, three to law school, and four to special technical schools. Earlier as later, insufficient classrooms postponed for many months admission to public education, and a preparatory school was organized to drill the fundamentals into children who waited to be admitted to the bulging city schools. Between 1905 and 1910 school buildings on the Lower East Side were so strained that the Camp Huddleston Hospital Ship at the foot of Corlears Hook was converted into a city school where ten thousand children received instruction.

The zeal to Americanize underlay all educational endeavor, from kindergartens first organized in 1882, on up through the grades. The Hebrew Free School Association, originally founded to discourage Christian missionizing among the children of the poor, recast the course of study of its afternoon schools. Training in the amenities, cleanliness, and the practical home and industrial arts crowded aside the curriculum of Jewish history, Jewish religion, and the Hebrew elements. The Reverend Clifton Harby Levy's advice to the trustees of the Baron de Hirsch classes that the addition of Hebrew to the curriculum would enlist parental support was ignored. The Federation of Temple Sisterhoods, originating in 1887 with the Emanu-El Sisterhood, sponsored classes of like pattern and maintained day nurseries as well. But in 1905 only one Jewish-sponsored crèche, the Brightside Nursery, served the entire Lower East Side.

Uptown reached the summit of its Americanization program in the Hebrew Institute. This Jewish-sponsored community house, hailed by its founders as a "center of sweetness and light, an oasis in the desert of degradation and despair," was organized jointly in 1889 by the Hebrew Free School Association, the Young Men's Hebrew Association, and the Aguilar Free Library Society. In 1891 it was housed in an impressive five-story structure at the northeast corner of Jefferson Street and East Broadway, and in 1893 it was renamed the Educational Alliance. From 9 A.M. to 10 P.M., class and meeting rooms, an auditorium seating seven hundred, library, gymnasium, shower baths, and a roof garden entertained a wide range of activities. While adults learned "the privileges and duties of American citizenship," youngsters received the benefits of its many advantages. Vocational courses, classes in English, civics, American history, and English literature, and Edward King's especially popular classes in Greek and Roman history were augmented by sermons, public lectures sponsored by the Board of Education, and flag-waving exercises on the national holidays.

Not until the first decade of the twentieth century was the Educational Alliance to bridge the gap between modern, urban New York and the psychological world of Torah and ghetto by conducting its courses in Yiddish. But its initial program remained an outstanding unifier. A host of clubs, each with patron author, poet, scientist, statesman, or philosopher—including the George Eliot Circle for girls—crowded the calendar and vied for the never-adequate meeting rooms. In a city growing more sensitive to the collective pleasures given by music, musical training especially was encouraged. Piano, violin, mandolin, and singing classes met regularly and the melodic din of rehearsing trios, quartets, orchestras, choral groups, and a children's symphony echoed through its halls. If drawing classes elicited a poor response, art exhibitions jointly sponsored with the University Settlement, assisted by the public schools, set unprecedented attendance records. A ten-cent admission charge to Saturday evening concerts and entertainments discouraged only the mischief makers from attending. The first English performances in the Jewish quarter, "As You Like It" and "The Tempest," added Shakespearean fare to Purim and Hanukkah plays. Physical exercise, slighted by serious youngsters, was promoted by a full and vigorous athletic program. Dr. Jane Robbins, a founder of the College Settlement, spoke to young women on personal health and feminine hygiene in 1898, and leading physicians lectured to young men on "The Marriage Question: Its Physical and Moral Sides." A few years later the Henry Street Settlement welcomed similar talks, presaging the introduction of such education into the public schools. In the first decade of the new century, a few hundred paid and voluntary workers descended upon the Alliance, its annex, and its two subbranches to direct and supervise a beehive of activity that weekly attracted some 37,000 adults and youngsters.

Deeply influencing the children, the Educational Alliance remained alien to the adult East Side, more so perhaps than the public schools and settlements, for these at least did not represent themselves as Jewish. At the Alliance, English was the official language and at the Alliance's People's Synagogue Dr. Adolph Radin conducted religious services in Hebrew and German. Yiddish, in immigrant eyes the touchstone of Jewishness, was taboo. Although the Alliance's successive Russian-born directors, Isaac Spectorsky and David Blaustein, could do little to affect the major lines of institutional policy, they were sensitive to the needs of their countrymen. The reading room, visited by a thousand persons daily, bulged with over one hundred Hebrew, Russian, and Yiddish journals. The Zionist Hebrew Literary Society, where youngsters sampled their first Hebrew idyl or renewed a romance with a reborn Hebrew literature, "is certainly in the line of moral culture," noted David Blaustein apologetically in the Alliance's annual report. The Russian-American Hebrew Association, founded in 1890 by Dr. Radin, its president and sole officer, "to exercise a civilizing and elevating influence upon the immigrants and to Americanize them," broke precedent to permit Zevi H. Masliansky, the East Side's magnetic Zionist preacher, to lecture in his native Yiddish. No less than Hebrew and Yiddish, Russian, the language of the intelligentsia, was unwelcome at the Alliance, although on occasion Russian-speaking societies met on the premises. Radin, a Posen Jew, felt moved to explain that "Russian" simply designated the place of origin of the immigrants, not the "half-barbarous civilization often signified by that name."

Philanthropy versus Self-Help

Despite their failings, German-Jewish charitable institutions aroused the admiration of all New Yorkers. Echoing Andrew Carnegie, Jacob H. Schiff, writing in the *Independent*, reaffirmed the stewardship of wealth with Jewish overtones. "Philanthropy as the aim and ideal of Judaism," succinctly described the path taken by the religious impulse.

Few human needs were overlooked. Old institutions were modernized and expanded and new ones were established to meet unanticipated requirements. Mount Sinai, formerly the Jews' Hospital, admitted more free clients than any other private institution in the city; nearly nine-tenths of its patients in the 1880s were treated without charge. The Hebrew Orphan Asylum Society and the Hebrew Sheltering and Guardian Society generously provided for orphans, while the Clara de Hirsch Home for Working Girls provided adolescents with recreational facilities. The Association for the Improved Instruction of Deaf Mutes—the oldest oral and only Jewish school for the deaf in the country—and societies for the blind and the crippled aided the handicapped. In 1893 a Jewish Prisoners' Aid Association was formed reluctantly to minister to the relatively small but growing number of Jewish prison inmates. Before the turn of the century offending Jewish lads had been sent to the state-maintained House of Refuge or to the Catholic Protectory, as Jews proved laggard in providing for their youthful transgressors. But a precipitous rise in juvenile delinquency led to the founding in 1907 of the Hawthorne School of the Jewish Protectory and Aid Society. The Lakeview Home for Jewish unmarried mothers followed; and a few years later, the

Jewish Big Brother and the Jewish Big Sister associations were formed to supervise youngsters on probation. Rounding out the major Jewish social agencies organized primarily to care for immigrant needs was the National Desertion Bureau, founded in 1911 to locate missing husbands.

Uptown institutions, however proficient and commendable, did not satisfy downtowners. East Europeans, treated as mendicants, were hardly grateful for the bounty bestowed. Efficient charity, with its documents and inquests, seemed incapable of performing the religious obligation of *Zedakah*—on its highest plane, pure loving-kindness. Prying strangers outraged the sense of decency of folk who in their home circles were often persons of consequence. As soon as it was possible, self-respecting immigrants made every effort to assist their own.

> In the philanthropic institutions of our aristocratic German Jews you see beautiful offices, desks, all decorated, but strict and angry faces. Every poor man is questioned like a criminal, is looked down upon; every unfortunate suffers self-degradation and shivers like a leaf, just as if he were standing before a Russian official. When the same Russian Jew is in an institution of Russian Jews, no matter how poor and small the building, it will seem to him big and comfortable. He feels at home among his own brethren who speak his tongue, understand his thoughts and feel his heart.

From their earliest coming, immigrants in need instinctively turned to their fellow townsmen. "The amount of small charity given directly from the poor to the poorer will never be known." The many-sided *landsmanshafts*, uniting the features of the Old World burial, study, and visitors-of-the-sick societies, bound the immigrant to his *shtetl* and birthplace. At first these societies had been coextensive with synagogues. But with the onset of the great migration each town and village asserted its individuality. As early as 1892 a contemporary directory listed 136 religious societies in the Lower East Side and doubtless there were more. Ninety-three were registered as Russian-Polish; the rest, classified as Austro-Hungarian, embraced Austrian, Hungarian, Rumanian, and some German congregations. The Beth Hamedrash Hagadol on Norfolk Street alone welcomed all Jews.

After 1880 *landsmanshafts* independent of synagogue ties began to supersede the religious societies. The better managed benevolent societies furnished insurance, sick benefits, and interest-free loans, as well as cherished cemetery rights. In time, women's auxiliary aid societies were founded, whose members were tutored in the parliamentary amenities by their male sponsors. In 1914, 534 benevolent societies, with from fifty to five-hundred members each, embraced virtually every immigrant household in New York City. When *landsmanshafts* affiliated with fraternal orders, they were transformed into familiar American lodges. Since the established German associations discouraged the entrance of newcomers, East Europeans formed their own. In 1887 Hungarians organized the Independent Order Brith Abraham, which conducted its business in German, but welcomed all comers; this organization soon became the largest of all Jewish fraternal orders. In 1900 the Workmen's Circle and in 1912 the Jewish National Workers' Alliance were founded by Jewish trade unionists dissatisfied with the quasi-religious ritual and tone of the existing orders.

By the late 1880s, East Europeans had already begun to organize their own communal charities. Russians and Austro-Hungarians founded their respective free burial societies. The cathedral Russian congregation established the Passover Relief Committee of the Beth Hamedrash Hagadol and prided itself on its catholicity: "In dispensing money and matzos to the poor, all are recognized as the children of one Father, and no lines are drawn between natives of different countries." The *Hevra Hachnosas Orchim* (the Hebrew Sheltering Society), formed in 1890, undertook to feed, lodge, and clothe friendless immigrants and to aid them in finding employment or in seeking out *landsleit*. In 1909 the Hebrew Sheltering Society was united with the Hebrew Immigrant Aid Society, founded in 1902 to ease the entrance of newcomers into the country. The expanded HIAS was to serve the needs of immigrants for over half a century.

The self-help principle took characteristic communal form in 1892 in the *Gemillat Hasodim* Association, the Hebrew Free Loan Society. The Society, relying solely on the endorsement of merchants of standing, made interest-free loans of from $10 to $200 to immigrants eager to set up independently in business. Within little more than a decade, the society's funds soared to over $100,000 as grateful borrowers, recalling the source of their success, contributed to its capital.

East Europeans also founded their own hospitals. Beth Israel, beginning in 1889 as a dispensary on Birmingham Alley, "the shortest and most dismal street in the whole city," grew to become the Lower East Side's leading hospital. Lebanon Hospital, Beth David, and the Hungarian People's Hospital followed, and in 1904 Galicians and Bukovinians undertook to found Har Moriah. Despite the opposition of the United Hebrew Charities, East Side physicians organized the Jewish Maternity Hospital in 1906 so that East Side mothers no longer had to depend on the New York Lying-In Hospital. These East Side institutions could be trusted to be kosher and to treat East European patients and physicians as equals. (Although 90 percent of Mount Sinai's patients were East Europeans, East European physicians were not admitted to that hospital's staff.) In 1897 institutional care for the aged poor also was inaugurated with the founding of the Home of the Daughters of Jacob.

Levantine Jews maintained an existence independent of Yiddish New York. As early as 1884 Gibraltans, culturally akin to the Levantines, founded Congregation Moses Montefiore in East Harlem. However, the number of true Levantines did not become significant until over two decades later when unrest within the Turkish empire brought a mixed multitude of ten thousand to the city. Dominantly Judeo-Spanish (Ladino) in speech, they included several hundred Greek-speaking Jews, and one thousand Arabic-speaking Jews from Aleppo in Syria. At first they were aided especially by the sisterhood of the city's oldest congregation, the Sephardic Shearith Israel, distant kin indeed to the newcomers. But in 1913 these latest immigrants organized a mutual benefit society and the Oriental Ozer Dalim Society to care for their own needy.

The religious urgency to provide a genuinely Jewish education for their sons drove downtowners to trust to their own resources. Half the Lower East Side children receiving a religious education in the 1890s attended the classes of the Hebrew Free School Association, but most of them were girls, for these classes did not answer the needs of East Europeans (many of whom even suspected that the cookie-laden Mrs. Minnie Louis of the Downtown Sabbath School was a Christian missionary). Parents gladly sacrificed to send their sons to the traditional Hebrew schools; the registration in 1903 at the Lower East Side's 307 *cheders* (religious elementary schools) was 8616 boys and only 361 girls. There the *rebbe* (religious teacher) linked the generations in intimacy of mood, ritual, and language, and slaked the consciences of parents who welcomed the opportunities thrown open to their children by the public schools, but who dreaded the impiety and the emptiness created between generations.

Late afternoon and early evening, pedagogues in basements or tenement flats, above saloons and dance halls, drove youngsters through the mechanics of prayer-book reading, rarely understood in the Old World, but in the New not even feared or respected. More ambitious and systematic were the Talmud Torahs which at first dispensed shoes and clothing along with a traditional religious education. In 1886 the Machzike Talmud Torah acquired its own building on East Broadway and soon shed its charitable aspect. In the same year the Yeshiva Etz Chaim was founded as an all-day school where a small number of youngsters pursued talmudical learning. In 1901 the Americanized Jacob Joseph Yeshiva was organized "to prepare Hebrew boys for life in this country." Finally, the Yeshiva Isaac Elchanan, organized in 1896 for the pursuit of advanced talmudical studies, completed the educational ladder for traditional Jewish learning. While most parents strained to pay the small fees, many were neglectful or unable to meet their obligations. The announcements in 1908 that three out of every four children received no religious education was doubtless exaggerated. Even so, it did reflect poverty, indifference, and weakened parental control. A dismal literal translation of the Talmud testified to the hopelessness of inspiring respect for traditional knowledge among the American-born.

A few enthusiasts, disgusted with formalistic Jewish studies, pioneered modern Jewish schools in an effort to link son to father, to breathe meaning into an ancient heritage in the modes of a new age. Zionists opened modern Hebrew schools in the 1890s while Jewish nationalists founded Yiddish folk schools around 1910, both groups searching for bridges over the chasm separating the generations that would unite the most advanced democratic ideals to a transvalued Jewish tradition. Random trials also were made with socialist Sunday schools, sponsored by the Socialist party, where lessons in "capitalist ethics" were replaced by lessons in "socialist ethics." At Emma Goldman and Alexander Berkman's Ferrer Center and School, two dozen youngsters were regaled with the lessons of anarcho-communism and listened to lectures by Clarence Darrow, Edwin Markham, and Lincoln Steffens that pointed to the free development of the individual. However humanitarian in intent, these experiments remained on the fringe of the immigrant community and acquired but a small and uncertain following.

The Larger Giving

Traditions of Jewish communal responsibility left little need for outside aid. Despite seasonal unemployment and acute poverty in the mid-nineties and during the 1907 and 1914 depressions, the resources of city, state, and non-Jewish private agencies were lightly taxed. In crisis years, aroused private citizens lent a hand, and examples of nonsectarian charity were many. In 1882 non-Jewish merchants and bankers contributed to the Hebrew Emigrant Aid Society, while in 1891, at a banquet honoring Jesse Seligman, non-Jews contributed to the Russian Transportation Fund for the Moscow refugees. In the depressed nineties Mrs. Josephine Shaw Lowell's East Side Relief Work "put our poor 'Hebrew Jews' at work to clothe the poor Negroes of the Sea Islands," and John B. Devins, pastor of Hope Chapel, transformed the East Side Relief Workers' Committee into the Federation of East Side Workers that included Protestants, Catholics, and Jews. In 1907 Mrs. Russell Sage and Warner Van Norden made substantial gifts to the United Hebrew Charities; Henry Phipps, too, proved a generous and steady supporter of the Legal Aid Bureau of the Educational Alliance.

Where municipal, state, and private institutions felt the pressure of the newcomers, they shared the burdens with the Jewish agencies. The City's Board of Estimate annually allotted a small sum to the United Hebrew Charities; and the state earmarked more subsantial amounts for the Hebrew Orphan Asylum Society, the Hebrew Sheltering and Guardian Society, the Aguilar Free Library Society, and the Jewish hospitals. The Charity Organization Society, the New York Association for Improving the Condition of the Poor, the Children's Aid Society, and the Society for the Prevention of Cruelty to Children cooperated with the United Hebrew Charities. The Sloane Maternity, the New York Lying-In, and the Mother and Babies' hospitals aided expectant mothers in out-patient departments. The *Tribune* Fresh Air Fund, the *Herald* Ice Fund, the spectacular fund-raising of the *World* and the *Journal*, and Nathan Straus's sterilized milk for the children of the tenements also contributed to the well-being of the immigrant East Side.

Two nonsectarian agencies proved especially useful. The Deutscher Rechts Schutz Verein, founded in 1876 by German immigrants, became the Legal Aid Society in 1894. By then most of its litigated cases were recorded on the East Side, and in 1899 an East Side branch was opened at the University Settlement. The society's panel of prominent attorneys, cooperating with the Legal Aid Council of the United Hebrew Charities and the Legal Aid Bureau of the Educational Alliance, arbitrated petty disputes without charge and kept thousands of cases from reaching the court dockets. The Provident Loan Society, authorized by a select committee of the Charity Organization Society, also performed a special service. Operating as a small loan association, it proposed to reduce the high interest rates of pawnbrokers, permitted to charge 3 percent per month, by charging 1 percent. By 1911 there were three Provident Loan Society branches on the Lower East Side and one each in the Bronx, Williamsburg, and Brownsville, the major foci of East European Jewish settlement.

Promise of Community

At the turn of the century all East Europeans, despite their diversity, were characterized as "Russians." Russian immigrants, with their numbers, variety, intellectual drive, and sense of historical exigency, defined and redefined the quarter's horizons of heart and mind. Despite their nostalgia for the scenes of their childhood and youth, having fled a despotic homeland to which there was no returning, they were quick to embrace America as their first true homeland. Galicians, however, harbored a genuine affection for the benevolent Austrian empire and could easily return. While idealistic Russians formed the Lermontoff Benevolent Society and a host of liberty-loving clubs, celebrating the Russia to be, wistful Galicians founded the Crown Prince Rudolph Verein, the Franz Joseph Kranken Unterstutzung Verein, and the Franz Ferdinand Benevolent Society, honoring the Hapsburg empire as it was. In 1884 Hungarians organized the Magyar Tarsulat (Society) and in the same year lonely Rumanians banded together in the Roumanisch-Amerikanischer Bruderbund. The huge Russian colony, agitated by the winds of the world to come rather than by monuments to attained liberties, overshadowed the lesser enclaves. In 1904 immigrants isolated from the main currents of the quarter formed the Federation of Galician and Bukovinian Jews to promote intercourse with culturally more energetic Russians.

The low intermarriage rate, even between individuals of the diverse East

European Jewries, reflected their group solidarity. After 1900 the equipoise between the sexes in each group and a clan-centered social life especially limited contacts. The barriers that separated East European Jews from non-Jewish New Yorkers militated against marriage outside the fold. After 1900, however, the association of Jewish women with Italians and non-Jewish Russians in the apparel trades led to some marriages. The highly publicized nuptials of Americanized "emancipated" Jewish women and social reformers were unusual. Yet, in these years, such alliances were only slightly less frequent than marriages between uptowners and downtowners.

In time bridges of communication formed between Germans and Russians. Yet only a complex transformation wrought on both groups by American and world experiences over more than half a century was to boil away the mutual incomprehension and intolerance that kept Jews apart. In these years, cooperation was rare and halfhearted in the lone area of social encounter between uptown and downtown—charitable endeavor. In 1901 the downtown Auxiliary Society of the United Hebrew Charities disbanded, no longer content with a subordinate, mere fund-collecting role. In the same year the Downtown Burial Society, *Chesed Shel Emes*, assumed full responsiblity for the Lower East Side, and the United Hebrew Charities dissolved its Free Burial branch. After 1904 requests for aid to the UHC declined; inadequate relief discouraged those in desperate need, while the galaxy of mutual aid societies provided for those less seriously distressed. Yet, even as Germans and Russians pulled apart, the rise of an American-trained generation of Russians spelled the onset of a new equilibrium. Indeed, as early as 1901 downtowners envisioned a United Hebrew Community, "to effect a union of Jewish societies and congregations in New York City."

In the early years of the twentieth century, the beginnings of accommodation between Germans and Russians were discernible, as the spirit of American reform penetrated both groups.

CHAPTER 10

The study of immigrant Jewish women has proceeded rapidly in recent years. No longer are they seen as mere passive extensions of their immigrant husbands. In fact, evidence now reveals that many women immigrated to America unmarried. What's more, immigrant Jewish women often assumed assertive roles: they educated themselves, obtained paying jobs, and in some cases played active roles in the labor movement and in community politics. Where other immigrant women found themselves barred from participation in what was considered to be the "male sphere," Jewish women faced far fewer restrictions. They could appear unescorted at evening lectures and classes and participate in public demonstrations without giving rise to scandal.

Once married, Jewish women did not so frequently leave home to enter the marketplace. But while a 1911 study from New York contends that only a paltry 1 percent of immigrant Jewish wives were employed "officially," many more were certainly working in fact, either at home or in so-called "Mom and Pop" businesses like groceries, delicatessens, or candy stores. Nor were married women necessarily inhibited from participating in community politics. To the contrary, Jewish housewives operating at the grass-roots level led various strikes and boycotts. As Paula E. Hyman, a modern Jewish historian who specializes in women's history, points out, they expressed their political concerns in their own neighborhoods, "where they pioneered in local community organizing."

Professor Hyman focuses here on a women-led kosher meat boycott. Kosher meat—meat slaughtered and prepared according to the dietary requirements set forth in Jewish law—gave rise to various scandals in the immigrant period (and later), as unscrupulous merchants sought to exploit an essentially captive market by price-fixing; some even passed non-kosher meat off as kosher and sold it at great profit. In the absence both of state consumer legislation and effective Jewish community controls, shoppers—women, in the main—had to fend for themselves. In May 1902, as the retail price of kosher meat soared, they did just that, and undertook to boycott kosher meat in an effort to force prices down.

As an incident, the meat boycott quickly faded; attention turned to other problems. As a case study, however, the boycott has lingering significance for it portrays immigrant Jewish women in a new light. It shows, for example, that even those who were married with growing families and years of experience on American soil could if provoked assert themselves and organize effectively, using traditional friendship groups as their base. It also shows that women had developed considerable political savvy—a valuable asset in America, and one that Jewish women activists both in the labor movement and in Jewish women's organizations would later exploit with success.

Immigrant Women and Consumer Protest: The New York City Kosher Meat Boycott of 1902

Paula E. Hyman

Women have always participated in politics. Despite their eclipse in the conventional seats of political power, women in preindustrial societies frequently engaged in popular protest, particularly when the price, or availability, of basic foodstuffs was at issue. As one English historian of the working class and of popular culture has pointed out regarding eighteenth-century food riots, women were "those most involved in face-to-face marketing [and hence] most sensitive to price significancies. . . ." In fact, he adds, "it is probable that the women most frequently precipitated the spontaneous actions." In the popular ferment of the early days of the French Revolution, women were also conspicuous by their presence. The image of grim-faced market women on the march to Versailles to bring the royal family back to Paris has been sharply etched in the mind of every student of history or enthusiast of historical dramas. Even before the emergence of modern political movements committed to the recruitment of women into the political process, the "crowd" was an important means of expression for women's economic and political interests.

Immigrant Jewish women, too, took to the streets in spontaneous food riots on several occasions. Like their British and French forerunners more than a century before, they were reacting to the sharp rise in the price of food. Most noted and flamboyant of these incidents were the 1902 kosher meat riots in New York City. Erupting in mid-May, they precipitated political activity which continued for almost a month, attracting considerable attention within both the Jewish community and the larger urban society. Indeed, in a fierce and vitriolic editorial of May 24, 1902, the *New York Times* called for a speedy and determined police repression of this "dangerous class . . . especially the women [who] are very ignorant [and] . . mostly speak a foreign language. . . . It will not do," the editorial continued, "to have a swarm of ignorant and infuriated women going about any part of this city with petroleum destroying goods and trying to set fire to the shops of those against whom they are angry."

What impelled immigrant Jewish housewives to take to the streets (of Williamsburg, in this case) with bottles of kerosene in their hands? Was this simply an act of spontaneous rage, a corroboration of the English writer Robert Southey's comment that "women are more disposed to be mutinous [than men]"? Are the kosher meat riots a late manifestation, as Herbert Gutman has suggested, of a preindustrial sensibility that focused upon the illegitimacy of violating a fair price for food? Finally, and most importantly, what can we learn of the self-perceptions, political consciousness, and sense of community of immigrant Jewish women by examining their role in this incident?

Despite their superficial similarity to earlier food riots, the kosher meat riots of 1902 give evidence of a modern and sophisticated political mentality emerging in a rapidly changing community. With this issue of the high price of food, immigrant housewives found a vehicle for political organization. They articulated a rudimentary grasp of their power as consumers and domestic managers. And, combining both traditional and modern tactics, they temporarily turned their status as housewives to good advantage, and used the neighborhood network to stage a successful three-week boycott of kosher meat shops throughout the Lower East Side, parts of upper Manhattan and the Bronx, and Brooklyn. The dynamics of the kosher meat boycott suggest that by focusing almost exclusively upon organized political activity in the labor movement and the socialist parties, historians have overlooked the role of women. Although for a great part of their life absent from the wage-earning market, immigrant Jewish women were not apolitical. They simply expressed their political concerns in a different, less historically accessible arena—the neighborhood—where they pioneered in local community organizing.

In early May, 1902, the retail price of kosher meat had soared from twelve cents to eighteen cents a pound. Small retail butchers, concerned that their customers would not be able to afford their produce, refused to sell meat for a week to pressure the wholesalers (commonly referred to as the Meat Trust) to lower their prices. When their May 14 settlement with the wholesalers brought no reduction in the retail price of meat, Lower East Side housewives, milling in the street, began to call for a strike against the butchers. As one activist, Mrs. Levy, the wife of a cloakmaker, shouted, "This is their strike? Look at the good it has brought! Now, if *we women* make a strike, then it will be a strike." Gathering support on the block—Monroe Street and Pike Street—Mrs. Levy and Sarah Edelson, owner of a small restaurant, called a mass meeting to spread the word of the planned boycott.

The next day, after a neighborhood canvas staged by the organizing committee, thousands of women streamed through the streets of the Lower East Side, breaking into butcher shops, flinging meat into the streets, and declaring a boycott. "Women were the ringleaders at all hours," noted the *New York Herald*. Customers who tried to carry their purchased meat from the butcher shops were forced to drop it. One woman emerging from a butcher store with meat for her sick husband was vociferously chided by an elderly woman wearing the traditional sheitel that "a sick man can eat tref meat." Within half an hour, the *Forward* reported, the strike had spread from one block through the entire area. Twenty thousand people were reported to have massed in front of the New Irving Hall. "Women were pushed and hustled about [by the police], thrown to the pavement . . . and trampled upon," wrote the *Herald*. One policeman, trying to rescue those buying meat, had "an unpleasant moist piece of liver slapped in his face." Patrol wagons filled the streets, hauling women, some bleeding from their encounters with the police, into court. About seventy women and fifteen men were arrested on charges of disorderly conduct.

After the first day of street rioting, a mass meeting to rally support and map strategy was held at the initiative of the women activists, who had formed a committee. Two of their number addressed the crowd, as did the popular figure Joseph Barondess and the Zionist leader Rabbi Zeft. The next day, May 16, Lower East Side women again went from house to house to strengthen the boycott. Individuals were urged not to enter butcher shops or purchase meat. Pickets were appointed to stand in front of each butcher shop. On each block funds were collected to pay the fines of those arrested and to reimburse those customers whose meat had been confiscated in the first day of rioting. The *Tribune* reported that "an excitable and aroused crowd roamed the streets. . . . As was the case on the previous day, the main disturbance was caused by the women. Armed with sticks, vocabularies and well sharpened nails, they made life miserable for the policemen." On the second day of rioting another hundred people were arrested. The boycott also spread, under local leadership, to the Bronx and to Harlem, where a mass meeting was held at Central Hall.

On Saturday, May 17, the women leaders of the boycott continued their efforts, going from synagogue to synagogue to agitate on behalf of the boycott. Using the traditional communal tactic of interrupting the Torah reading when a matter of justice was at stake, they called on the men in each congregation to encourage their wives not to buy meat and sought rabbinic endorsement of their efforts. For once, urged a boycott leader, citing a biblical passage, let the men use the power of "And he shall rule over her" to the good—by seeing to it that their wives refrain from purchasing meat.

By Sunday, May 18, most butcher shops on the Lower East Side bowed to reality and closed their doors. And the boycott had spread to Brooklyn, where the store windows of open butcher shops had been broken and meat burned. That night, the women held another meeting, attended by more than five hundred persons, to consolidate their organization, now named the Ladies' Anti-Beef Trust Association. Under the presidency of Mrs. Caroline Schatzburg, it proposed to continue house-to-house patrols, keep watch over butcher stores, and begin agitating for similar action among Christian women. Circulars bearing a skull and crossbones and the slogan "Eat no meat while the Trust is taking meat from the bones of your women and children" were distributed throughout the Jewish quarters of the city. The association established six similar committees to consolidate the boycott in Brownsville, East New York, and the Bronx. Other committees were set up to visit the labor and benevolent societies, labor union meetings, and lodges and to plan the establishment of cooperative stores. The association also sent a delegation to the mayor's office to seek permission for an open-air rally. Local groups of women continued to enforce the boycott in their neighborhoods. In Brooklyn four hundred women signed up to patrol neighborhood butcher stores. Buyers of meat continued to be assaulted and butcher shop windows smashed. In Harlem two women were arrested when they lay down on the elevated tracks to prevent a local butcher from heading downtown with meat for sale. Throughout the city's Jewish neighborhoods restaurants had ceased serving meat.

However, competition between Sarah Edelson, one of the founders of the boycott, and Caroline Schatzburg, the president of the Ladies' Anti-Beef Trust Association, erupted by May 18 into open quarrels between their followers at meetings. Taking advantage of this rivalry and winning the support of Edelson and her backers, on May 21 male communal leaders, with David Blaustein of the Educational Alliance presiding, held a conference of three hundred representatives of synagogues, *hevras*, landsmanshaften, and unions "to bring order to the great struggle for cheap meat." In his remarks at the conference meeting, Joseph Barondess made explicit that a new leadership was asserting itself. Urging the women to be quiet and leave the fighting to the men, he noted that otherwise the women would be held responsible in the event of the boycott's defeat. Calling themselves the Allied Conference for Cheap Kosher Meat, the male conference leaders appointed a ten-person steering committee, among whom were only three women. (Women continued, however, to engage in propaganda activities and sporadic rioting in their neighborhoods.) The Allied Conference published a circular in both Yiddish and English, noting that "brave and honest men [were] now aiding the women" and declaring that the conference had "decided to help those butchers who [would] sell cheap kosher meat under the supervision of the rabbis and the conference." "The people feel very justly," continued the statement, "that they are being ground down, not only by the Beef Trust of the country, but also by the Jewish Beef Trust of the City."

On May 22, the Retail Butchers Association succumbed and affiliated itself with the boycott against the Trust. On May 27, Orthodox leaders, who had hesitated to express formal endorsement of the boycott, joined the fray. By June 5 the strike was concluded. The wholesale price of kosher meat was rolled back to nine cents a pound so that the retail price would be pegged at fourteen cents a pound. Kosher meat cooperatives, which were established during the strike in both Brooklyn and Harlem, continued in existence. While meat prices began to rise inexorably again in the period following the conclusion of the boycott, the movement can still be considered a qualified success.

The leaders of the boycott were not typical of other women political activists of the period. Unlike the majority of women organized in the nascent garment unions, they were not young. Unlike the female union leaders, they were housewives with chidren. The mean age of those boycott leaders who could be traced in the 1905 New York state manuscript census was thirty-nine. They ranged from Mamie Ghilman, the thirty-two-year-old Russian-born wife of a tailor, to Mrs. L. Finkelstein, a fifty-four-year-old member of the Women's Committee. All but two were more than thirty-five years of age at the time of the boycott. These women were mothers of large families, averaging 4.3 children apiece living at home. Fannie Levy, who initiated the call for the strike, was the mother of six children, all below the age of thirteen. None had fewer than three children. While only two women were United States citizens, the strike leaders were not, for the most part, recent arrivals to America. They had been living in New York City from three to twenty-seven years, with a median residence of eleven years. Having had sufficient time to accommodate themselves to the American scene, they were not simply expressing traditional forms of cultural resistance to industrial society imported from the Old Country.

In socioeconomic terms, the women initiators of the boycott appear representative of the larger immigrant Jewish community of the Lower East Side. Their husbands were, by and large, employed as artisans in the garment industry, though three were self-employed small businessmen. The husband of Annie Block, a member of the Women's Committee, was a tailor, as were three other husbands. Fannie Levy's husband was a cloakmaker and Bessie Norkin's a carpenter, while J. Jaffe's husband, Meyer, and Annie Levine's husband, Morris, topped the occupational scale as a real estate agent and storekeeper respectively. With one exception, all of their children above the age of sixteen were working—two-thirds of them in artisan trades and the remainder as clerks or low-level business employees (e.g., salesladies). Only the eighteen-year-old son of the real estate agent was still in school (though his older brothers were employed as garment-industry operators). Thus, the women formed not an elite in their community, but a true grass-roots leadership.

It is clear from their statements and their activity that the women who led the boycott had a distinct economic objective in mind and a clear political strategy for achieving their goal. Unlike traditional food rioters, the Lower East Side housewives were not demanding the imposition of a just and popular price on retailers. Nor were they forcibly appropriating meat for purchase at a popularly determined fair price, though they did retain a traditional sense of a moral economy in which food should be available at prices which the working classes could afford. Rather, recognizing that prices were set by the operation of the laws of supply and demand, as modified, in this case, by the concentration of the wholesale meat industry, they hit upon a boycott of meat as the most effective way to dramatically curtail demand. They referred to themselves as strikers; those who did not comply with the boycott were called "scabs." When they were harassed in the street by police, they complained that denial by police of their right to assemble was an attack on their freedom of speech. Thus, Lower East Side women were familiar with the political rhetoric of their day, with the workings of the market economy, and with the potential of consumers to affect the market.

While the impulse for the boycott originated in spontaneous outrage of women consumers at the price of kosher meat and their sense that they had been manipulated (or swindled, as they put it) by the retail butchers, who had sold out their customers in their agreement with the wholesalers, this incident was not simply an explosion of rage. It was a sustained, though limited, movement whose success lay in its careful organization. As the *New York Herald* rightly commented, "These women were in earnest. For days they had been considering the situation, and when they decided on action, they perfected an organization, elected officers, . . . and even went so far as to take coins from their slender purses until there was an expense fund of eighty dollars with which to carry on the fight."

In fact, the neighborhood focus of the boycott organization proved to be its source of strength. The initial boycott committee, composed of nineteen women, numbered nine neighbors from Monroe Street, four from Cherry Street, and six from adjacent blocks. This was not the anonymous city so often portrayed by antiurban polemicists and historians but a neighborhood community whose residents maintained close ties. The first show of strength on May 15 was preceded by an early morning house-to-house canvas of housewives in the heart of the boycott area. A similar canvas occurred the next day in Harlem under the aegis of local women. Rooted in the neighborhood, where many activities were quasi-public rather than strictly private, housewives were able to exert moral (as well as physical) suasion upon the women whom they saw on a daily basis. They assumed the existence of collective goals and the right to demand shared sacrifices. Individual desires for the consumption of meat were to be subordinated to the larger public good. As one boycott enthusiast stated while grabbing meat from a girl leaving a butcher store, "If we can't eat meat, the customers can't eat meat."

Shouting similar sentiments in another incident, striking women attempted to remove the meat from cholent pots which their neighbors had brought to a local bakery on a Friday afternoon. Participants in the boycott picketed local butchers and also resolved not to speak to the "scabs" in their midst. The constant presence in the neighborhood of the housewife leaders of the boycott made it difficult for individuals to evade their surveillance. The neighborhood, a form of female network, thus provided the locus of community for the boycott: all were giving up meat together, celebrating dairy shabbosim together, and contributing together to the boycott fund.

The women who organized and led the boycott considered themselves the natural leaders of such an enterprise. As consumers and housewives, they saw their task as complementary to that of their wage-earning spouses: "Our husbands work hard," stated one of the leaders at the initial planning meeting. "They try their best to bring a few cents into the house. We must manage to spend as little as possible. We will not give away our last few cents to the butcher and let our children go barefoot." In response, the women shouted, "We will not be silent; we will overturn the world." Describing themselves as soldiers, they determined to circulate leaflets calling upon all women to "join the great women's war." An appeal to their "worthy sisters," published by the Ladies' Anti-Beef Trust in the *Forward*, expressed similar sentiments, calling for "help . . . in the name of humanity in this great struggle which we have undertaken out of need."

Sharper formulations of class resentment mingled with pride in their own talents in some of the women's shouts in the street demonstrations. One woman was heard lamenting to another, "Your children must go to work, and the millionaires snatch the last bit from our mouths." Another called out, "My husband brings me eight dollars a week. Should I give it away to the butcher? What would the landlord say?" Still another screamed, "They think women aren't people, that they can bluff us; we'll show them that we are more people than the fat millionaires who suck our blood." When the son of the Chief Rabbi, who supervised the kashrut of the meat, passed through the area, he was met with shouts of "Trust—Kosher *Korobke*," a reference to the kosher meat tax, much despised by the poor in Czarist Russia.

The ringleaders who were arrested and charged with disorderly conduct defined their behavior in political terms and considered it both just and appropriate to their status as housewives. "Did you throw meat on the street?" Rosa Peskin was asked. "Certainly," she replied. "I should have looked it in the teeth?" When the judge condescendingly commented, "What do you know of a trust? It's no business of yours," she responded, "Whose business is it, then, that our pockets are empty . . .?" "What do you have against a woman who has bought meat," the judge persisted. "I have nothing against her," retorted Peskin. "It doesn't matter to me what others want to do. But it's because of others that we must suffer." Rebecca Ablowitz also presented the boycotters' rationale to the judge: "We're not rioting. Only see how thin our children are, our husbands have no more strength to work harder. . . . If we stay home and cry, what good will that do us?"

Of similar conviction and eloquence was Mrs. Silver, one of the most articulate spokeswomen of the boycott, who headed the campaign to interrupt services in the synagogues. When one irate opponent roared that her speaking thus from the bima was an effrontery *(chutzpa)* and a desecration of God's name *(chillul ha-Shem),* Mrs. Silver coolly responded that the Torah would pardon her.

The climate of the immigrant Jewish community facilitated the resolute behavior of the women. While a few rabbis, particularly those with close ties to the meat industry, were hostile to the boycott enterprise, they were the exception. Support for the boycott was widespread within the community. Friendly crowds packed the courtroom to cheer the arrested women. In every one of the synagogues on the Lower East Side, it was reported, "the uprising of the Hebrew women was referred to by the rabbis." Most synagogue members warmly greeted the women who brought their cause to the congregation. When police were brought in to arrest Mrs. Silver after a disturbance erupted in one synagogue, a congregant rose to compare the woman to the prophet Zachariah, "who preached truly and whose blood demanded vengeance." So persuasive was he that Mrs. Silver was released. Feeling that they could count upon the support of the traditionally observant community, the Ladies' Anti-Beef Trust Association, in an appeal printed by the *Forward,* called for communal ostracism of the one prominent rabbi, Dr. Adolph N. Radin of the People's Synagogue, who had not only refused to approve the boycott but had treated representatives of the association rudely in his synagogue. He should be removed from his position as chaplain to Jewish prisoners, urged the women, for if this "half-German" could refer publicly to the boycotting women as "beasts" and receive them so coarsely in front of his congregation, how must he treat the unfortunate Jewish inmates he sees within the confines of the prison?

Both the socialist *Forward* and the Orthodox *Yiddishes Tageblat* portrayed the initial disturbances as well as the later movement in a sympathetic manner and were offended by the rough treatment meted out to the women and their families by the police as well as by the unsympathetic attitude of much of the English language press. Jewish socialists, in particular, stood squarely behind the protest. The *Forward* heralded the boycott with the banner headline, "Bravo, bravo, bravo, Jewish women!" To the *Forward,* the boycott provided an opportunity not only to support a grass-roots protest action but also to level an attack upon the collusion of the rabbis with the German-Jewish meat trust. There was little reason for the differential between kosher and non-kosher meat to stand at five to six cents a pound, proclaimed the newspaper's editorial. Those who raised the prices "are Yahudim with gilded beards, who never eat kosher. Why are they suddenly so *frum* (pious)? Since when is there a partnership between those who give rabbinic endorsements in the Chief Rabbi's name and those Yahudi meat handlers? . . . The Chief Rabbi's son is merely a salesman for the Trust," continued the editorial. "He goes about in carriages collecting money in the name of his unfortunate father's endorsement. . . . Whether the strike of the good Jewish women brings down the prices or not," concluded the *Forward*, "one thing remains certain, the bond between the Trust and the rabbis must end. If they are truly pious, let them serve their religion and not the Trust in whose pay they are in." In Russian Poland, noted the paper the next day, the meat tax was seven cents a pound, but at least there the *korobke* supported all kehilla (communal) activities. Here, on the other hand, it went only to the Trust.

While the *Forward* conducted its pro-boycott campaign, the labor movement as a whole extended monetary donations and aid to the boycott; two men active in the Ladies' Garment Workers' Union were appointed as vice president and secretary of the Ladies' Anti-Beef Trust Association, while the posts of president and treasurer remained in women's hands. In Harlem it was the Women's Branch No. Two of the Workmen's Circle, with the support of the parent organization, that coordinated local boycott activity.

Communal support was not, however, without its limits. Jewish communal leaders were clearly upset by the initiative assumed by the women activists. The sight of Jewish women engaged in picketing and in the physical coercion of butcher shop customers as well as their arrest at the hands of a none too gentle police force aroused concern. "Don't give the Trust and the police an opportunity to break heads," cautioned the *Forward*. "More can be accomplished lawfully than not. . . . Agitate quietly in your homes." Moreover, when the boycott was recognized as a force to be reckoned with, men tried to wrest control of the movement from its female leaders. However, the women were never entirely displaced, and the Yiddish language media continued, if somewhat ambivalently, to view the success of the boycott as a legitimate example of the "power of women." (On the other hand, the *American Hebrew*, the organ of the Uptown Jews, studiously ignored the kosher meat riots.)

In a larger sense, the immigrant Jewish community was quite supportive of women's political activity. East European Jewish immigrants were highly politicized; just how highly can be seen in the meat boycott, whose participants were sufficiently traditional to buy kosher meat and to use the synagogues and *hevras* as areas for potential recruitment. Indeed, the development of the boycott suggests that the compartmentalization of the immigrant community by historians into Orthodox, socialist and anarchist, and Zionist sectors does not do justice to the interplay among the groups. Boundary lines were fluid, and socialist rhetoric tripped easily from the tongues of women who still cared about kosher meat, could cite biblical passages in Hebrew, and felt at ease in the synagogue. Moreover, the boycotters consciously addressed themselves to several different constituencies—synagogues, landsmanshaften, the labor movement, and socialist groups.

Even within the traditional community, women had never been banned from the *secular* public sphere. In developing cadres of female activists, both the Jewish labor and Zionist movements in Russia built upon the relative freedom of public activity accorded women within the Jewish community. As Mary Van Kleeck of the Russell Sage Foundation commented in her study of one Lower East Side trade that employed Jewish women, "The Jewish girl . . . has a distinct sense of her social responsibility and often displays an eager zest for discussion of labor problems. . . . Her attitude is likely to be that of an agitator. Nevertheless, she has the foundation of that admirable trait, 'public spirit,' and a sense of relationship to a community larger than the family or the personal group of which she happens to be a member." Sufficient toleration existed within the family circle to enable Jewish women to express their "public spirit," to permit wives and mothers to attend evening meetings and to demonstrate in the streets. As the *Yiddishes Tageblat* put it, somewhat condescendingly, at the beginning of the boycott, "The women this time let the men play at home with the children while they went to attend the meeting." While this was clearly a situation worthy of comment, it was not a violation of communal values.

If the immigrant Jewish community helped to sustain the meat boycott, the English-language socialist press was far more ambivalent in its attitude to this form of political activity. Indeed, it saw the only appropriate weapon for workers in the struggle against capitalism in the organization of producers rather than consumers. As *The Worker* commented,

> The Meat Trust does not care two-cents for such opposition as this, no matter how sincere the boycotters may be. . . . [A boycott] is so orderly and law-abiding, so free from all taint of socialism or confiscation or class hatred, so truly individualistic, and above all, so perfectly harmless—to all except the poor workingmen. . . . We cannot oppose the aggression of twentieth century capitalism with weapons fitted to the petty conflicts of eighteenth century small producers.

Added the *Daily People*, organ of the Socialist Labor Party, "It does not make the capitalist hungry if the workingman goes without food. . . ." Such an attitude overlooked the potential of community organization outside the workplace. It precluded reaching out to the neighborhood as a possible secondary locus of political activism, and incidentally resulted in an inability on the part of the socialists to tap the ranks of the politically conscious housewife.

The difference in attitudes between the Yiddish-speaking and English-language socialists is also of broader interest. While the Jewish socialists were often seen as assimilationist, they remained closer to the shared value of their own immigrant community than to the perhaps ideologically purer stance of the American radicals.

The boycott movement enables us to look at the potential for political organization among Lower East Side women, the majority of whom were housewives unaffiliated in any formal sense with the trade-union movement. But it also raises questions for which there are no readily available answers.

Was there any precedent for this type of direct action among married women in Eastern Europe? One can find a tenuous connection to the Eastern European scene in reference to the *korobke*, the meat tax, which in the nineteenth century constituted as much as one-third of the budget of some Jewish communities and was passionately resented. Some Hasidic rebbes in the first half of the last century urged passive resistance against the tax, even including a boycott on the purchase of meat. Clearly, the ability to draw an analogy, as both the women activists and the *Forward* editorials did, between the *korobke* and the high price of kosher meat caused by collusion between the meat trust and rabbis selling their hechsher (certification of kashrut) was an appealing propaganda device. It linked the 1902 boycott to the long-standing disaffection of the poor with the authorities of the Eastern European kehilla. However, the boycott's leaders do not refer to earlier Eastern European examples of reaction against the *korobke*, nor is there any other evidence of direct influence from the Eastern European to the American scene.

As interesting as the boycott is as a vehicle for examining the political sensibilities and assessing the political potential of Jewish housewives on the Lower East Side, the fading away of the Ladies' Anti-Beef Trust Association is as significant as its sudden appearance. If the neighborhood network was so effective a means to reach women and mobilize them, why was it not sustained to deal with other social problems? True, the 1904 and 1907–8 rent strikes on the Lower East Side espoused similar tactics and hailed the meat boycott as their model. Beginning with a house-to-house canvas initiated by women, strike leaders promoted neighborhood solidarity by collecting written pledges of refusal to pay rent. In 1908 women also lent their support to retail butchers protesting the rising cost in wholesale meat prices. These further incidents of local activism confirm the growing consumer consciousness of Lower East Side women. However, there appears to be no overlap in leadership between these several expressions of female popular protest. Were women co-opted into already established fraternal and political organizations, or did the politics of crisis bring with it inertia once the crisis had passed?

Because its leaders faded into obscurity with the conclusion of the boycott, because of the very nature of a short-lived grass-roots movement, it is impossible to assess the impact of the movement upon its participants. However, it is likely that the political awareness expressed by the boycotters was no isolated phenomenon but was communicated effectively, if quietly and informally, to their younger sisters and daughters. The boycott alerted the immigrant community as a whole and the labor movement in particular to the political potential of women. Moreover, the communal support of the boycott could only have encouraged women themselves to further activity. As Alice Kessler-Harris notes of Jewish women in the garment trades, whose numbers in the unions exceeded their proportion in the industry as a whole, they "unionized at their own initiative" and were "responsible for at least one quarter of the increased number of unionized women [in America] in the second decade of the twentieth century." In that sense the kosher meat boycott should be seen not as an isolated incident but as a prelude to the explosion of women activists in the great garment industry strikes at the end of the decade.

CHAPTER 11

East European Jews characterized America as being both a goldene medinah, *a golden land, and a* treifene medinah, *a profane ("unkosher") one. Both portrayals, of course, were exaggerations, but as the historian Andrew Heinze argues in the selection that follows, both also contained vivid elements of truth. America did appear to Jewish immigrants to be something of a cornucopia, brimming with more consumer goods than they had ever known before. This abundance, he shows, dramatically transformed and Americanized many aspects of their lives, particularly holiday observances.*

Chanukah, traditionally a minor Jewish festival celebrated in early winter, provides the best example of this process. By introducing the American "rite of consumption" into this holiday through the practice of gift giving, immigrant Jews sought to accommodate the pervasive Christmas spirit of America's Yuletide season while still distinguishing Judaism from the nation's majority Christian faith. In related ways, as the article shows, immigrant Jews also Americanized other Jewish festivals, even as they managed to inject distinctively Jewish elements into such American holidays as Independence Day and Thanksgiving.

Heinze's analysis refines our understanding of East European Jewish immigrant life in the United States in at least two important ways. First, it highlights the impact of rising economic mobility on Jewish immigrants, a reminder that suffering and victimhood form only one side of their history. Second, it illuminates the kinds of religious issues that Jewish immigrants to the United States confronted, the ongoing conflicts between Jewish and American norms that affected and transformed numerous aspects of immigrant Jewish religious life, from the mundane to the exotic.

Adapting to Abundance: Luxuries, Holidays, and Jewish Identity

Andrew R. Heinze

Jews relied on the holidays of Sukkot, Chanukah, and Passover to express an American Jewish identity and, by the 1890s, they were altering each one in response to the condition of American abundance. As a celebration of the earth's bounty, Sukkot naturally expanded to include the new awareness of mass-marketed plenty in America. By proximity to the secularized American Christmas, Chanukah rose to importance in the United States, where it allowed Jewish newcomers to integrate themselves more fully into the larger society through the ritual of holiday shopping and gift giving. In the cause of spiritual purification, Passover raised the concept of festive luxury to a high point where it would blend with the American emphasis on a rising standard of living. This premier festival became an occasion not just to commemorate the liberation from Egypt but also to overhaul household and personal possessions. As Chanukah allowed Jews to share in American festivities while nominally respecting tradition, Passover watched the old command for purity give way to the new quest for a higher standard of living.

Respect for Jewish tradition and appreciation of American life were suitably mixed in the celebration of Sukkot (pronounced "Sukkos" in Yiddish), the Feast of Booths. This holiday combined a harvest festival with the commemoration of the forty years wandering in the wilderness, the period after the exodus from Egypt in which the Israelites dwelled in *sukkot*, or booths. Sukkot was venerated in scripture as the time appointed by Moses for the public reading of the Torah that he had committed to writing. The occasion of great pilgrimages to the ancient Temple, the festival gained additional esteem from the prophecy of Zechariah (14:16) that all nations would one day come to Jerusalem to celebrate Sukkot with the Jews. After the destruction of the Temple, Jews were supposed to construct their own loosely roofed sukkahs. These temporary dwellings were customarily well furnished and, if the weather permitted, primary domestic activities took place within the structure for the seven days of early autumn when the holiday occurred. Sukkot recalled and celebrated both the protection given by God in the aftermath of liberation from Egypt and the bounty that awaited Jews in the promised land. Reverence for a sacred past and hope for a secure and satisfying future found a home in the sukkah.

Against the inhospitable background of the modern city, the effort of Jewish immigrants to perpetuate Sukkot showed a deep respect for tradition. Describing the holiday as a bulwark of Jewish identity, the New York *Yiddishes Tageblatt* declared that Judaism did not use weapons of destruction in the struggle of the great religions—it fought instead with "weapons of the spirit," of which a vital one was the observance of Sukkot. Under the harsh conditions of American life, Sukkot may have been, as Abraham Cahan expressed it, a time of "tortured joy," but newcomers considered the festival well worth preserving. In the courtyards and on the rooftops of tenements, they erected booths in the urban wilderness, using planks of wood and imported boughs of fir trees, as well as boxes, sheets, shawls, quilts, wicker, green-painted cane, and any other materials fit for the task. "Each back yard of the East Side these last six days . . . with hardly an exception," the *New York Tribune* stated on September 24, 1899, "has possessed one of these houses of boughs, the tents of the Judeans in the wilderness modernized, yet of the spirit of centuries bygone."

The effect of the modern sukkah as a haven of traditional Judaism in strange surroundings was evoked by a reporter covering the Lower East Side for the *Tribune* in October 1895. "Down in the street, far below, the noise of traffic and the tumult of the city made a deafening roar," the journalist recorded, "but up by the tabernacles on the reddened roofs all was peace and quiet, except for the children who were enjoying the novelty of the occasion, and the voices of the householders as they spoke of the festival and its meaning." Welcomed into an unusually elaborate sukkah by a matron who spoke little English, the writer was struck by the interior, which was illuminated by three "walls" of orange, crimson, and purple stained glass, and covered by a tent like roof of plaited wicker. On a side table, there were prayer books and candles in burnished candlesticks, and over the substantial rear wall of the booth the customary inscription for Sukkot was emblazoned in Hebrew letters: "Seven Days Shalt Thou Sit in the Tabernacle." Set against the chilling depression of 1895, the impression of domestic warmth was completed by a host of delicious foods—"golden pears, ruddy-cheeked peaches, apples and clusters of grapes hung from the matter roof, and decanters of wine, plates of fruit and fancy cake stood ready to be served on the hospitable table."

Described so vividly in the *New York Tribune,* the elegant sukkah carried its own message about the changing nature of this holiday in urban America. The tabernacle stood as a visible reminder of the contrast between Jewish life in the United States and Jewish life in the "wilderness," which referred not only to the desert of ancient Palestine but also to contemporary regions of persecution, most notably Russia. Delicate and vulnerable to the elements, the sukkah served as a perfect symbol of Jewish life among the nations of the world, and it gave newcomers to America a vehicle through which to express their appreciation of the relative security they had found. In 1912, the *Tageblatt* considered "Our American Sukkah" symbolically, stating that the Jews "have never had in any place such a comfortable, such a solid Sukkah" as that which they had in America.

As a time of thanksgiving for both plenty and security, Sukkot gained a new dimension not only from the political character of the United States but also from the influence of material abundance. Formerly an acknowledgment of nature's bounty, the festival accommodated the keen awareness of manufactured plenty as an element of American society. After the depression of the 1890s, renewed optimism about the future generated a new lavishness in the holiday. As the commodities of city life entered into the sukkah, mingling with the fruits of nature, the two forms of abundance struck a balance that was mirrored in the title of a Yiddish feature story of 1904, "The Green Horn of Plenty: The Piano in the Sukkah." Mandated by the Torah to be an occasion of great feasting, Sukkot seemed a good occasion for the appreciation of luxuries acquired by newcomers in the American city. Posed to reinforce the contrast between the hardships of a nomadic existence and the comforts of a settled life, the holiday, in one sense, culminated in America.

Whereas Sukkot achieved a measure of harmony between the traditional Jewish and the modern American identity, Chanukah plunged into the complexity of Jewish adaptation to American society. In contrast to Sukkot, which was rooted in the Bible, this holiday derived not from scripture but from a historical conflict between Judaism and paganism.

In the period 175–164 B.C.E., when Antiochus IV assumed the leadership of the Seleucid dynasty that controlled Palestine, the Jews of Jerusalem and surrounding areas were confronted with a nemesis who would provoke the Maccabean rebellion commemorated on Chanukah. Abetted by the willingness of some Jews, particularly those in prominent positions, to accept Greek customs as a way of increasing their political power and social prestige, Antiochus IV encouraged the growth of paganism in Jerusalem and turned the venerable position of the High Priest into an object of barter. The assault on Jewish tradition climaxed in 167 B.C.E., when the king outlawed Jewish worship and instituted pagan rites in the Temple. While some Jews deferred to royal decree, many pietists rebelled, and the struggle against the Seleucid forces began, at first with little success.

The prospects of the religious rebels turned upon an uprising against royal officials and soldiers in the town of Modin to the northwest of Jerusalem. There, a Jewish priest named Mattathias appears to have incited a riot against the authorities who had demanded that the Jews make sacrifices to idols. After the slaughter of the king's agents and soldiers, groups of Jews fled to the nearby mountains, from which they waged guerrilla warfare against troops dispatched from Syria, the base of the Antiochene empire. After two years of war under the command of one of Mattathias's sons, Judah, who was given the honorary surname Maccabeus, which may have derived from the Hebrew word for "hammer," the Jews defeated the ostensibly more powerful Syrians. Jerusalem was reclaimed and, in the autumn of 164 B.C.E., the Temple was rededicated. Sustaining the legendary miracle of the cruse of oil that was sufficient only to light the Temple for one day yet lasted for eight, the Festival of Lights, as Chanukah quickly came to be known, focused on the ritual of lighting candles for eight days.

Illuminating the problem of cultural assimilation, Chanukah found new relevance and popularity among Jewish newcomers to America. With the rise of Zionism as a response to European persecution at the end of the nineteenth century, the heroism of the Maccabean struggle was emphasized by ideologically minded Jews who envisioned the creation of a Jewish nation based on a tough-minded attitude of self-determination. But, among the multitude of American Jews, the popularity of Chanukah had little to do with ideology. It stemmed instead from the powerful presence of Christmas as the American rite of consumption.

The approximation of Chanukah to Christmas was based on the desire of Jewish newcomers to adopt secular American holidays. Labor Day harmonized with the socialist leanings and organizational flair of Jewish workers, and it fit well into the rhythmic alteration of working and vacationing that would define Jewish life under the American calendar. The holiday called for the end of summer relaxation and the renewal of hard work during the colder seasons of autumn and winter. The Fourth of July was a jubilee for Jewish immigrants, who had a visceral respect for American pluralism. Unlike their native countries of Eastern Europe, where citizenship was often defined in opposition to Judaism, the United States seemed to welcome the participation of those newcomers whose politics were not disturbingly radical. Consequently, as the *Tageblatt* editorialized in 1904, the Jews felt they had "a place in America" and celebrated "the great holiday of July 4th."

The gradual acceptance of Thanksgiving showed a willingness to fuse Jewish and American rituals. Elizabeth Stern, a social worker whose family had immigrated from Russia to New York City in 1892 when she was two years old, remembered how Thanksgiving was adopted in her home. As the children grew up and began to speak English at home, their parents tried to adapt to some American ways. One Thanksgiving, Stern's father brought home a turkey, which her mother repeatedly compared to a duck and a chicken, the poultry that Jews had traditionally enjoyed on holidays and festive occasions. In a further blending of American and Jewish features, the table was set with a white cloth, "as if it were a holy day," and her father, who made a meager living teaching Hebrew, recited tales from the Talmud. Afterward, the young Stern explained the meaning of Thanksgiving. Her mother responded with approval but managed to give Judaism the last word by reminding the inquisitive daughter that "one must not give thanks only on one day and for one bird!"

With the rise of Christmas as the primary secular holiday of urban Americans, the preconditions for an American Chanukah were established. Originally, the predominantly Protestant populace of America did not consider Christmas to be an occasion worth honoring. In 1659, the Puritan colony of Massachusetts made the celebration of Christmas, through abstention from work or feasting, an offense punishable by a fine of five shillings. Although this law was ultimately repealed, people continued to work on Christmas Day at least until the end of the seventeenth century, and the holiday had minimal effect until the second half of the nineteenth century. By that time, the great immigration of Germans had begun to boost the nation's interest in Christmas. After the Civil War, department stores began to stay open late on the days before Christmas, ornaments for trees became popular, and the first American Christmas cards appeared, following the example set by German immigrant Louis Prang, a leading maker of color lithographs, who started the trade in Christmas cards in 1874. Within a few years, Prang was producing millions of cards each season. The stirrings of a great interest in the holiday were prompted by entrepreneurs rather than ministers.

By the late 1880s, Christmas appears to have asserted itself as the primary holiday of the United States. In 1888, *Good Housekeeping* lamented the fact that the simplicity of Thanksgiving, which commemorated a time of material hardship, had been overcome by the extravagance of the American urban Christmas. Although Thanksgiving was distinctive to America, Christmas bore seeds—in the ritual of gift giving—that would be nourished in the uniquely American climate of consumption. The increasing sophistication of retail displays, the growing mythology of Santa Claus as a grand dispenser of merchandise, the ornamentation of the home and the tree, the development of card sending as a social obligation, all of these qualities of the secular Christmas insured the superiority of the day in the hierarchy of festivals. One week after the Christmas of 1897, the *New York Tribune* indicted the intriguing commercial atmosphere of "the modern Christmas," which was fast becoming "a time for barter, for display, for acquisitiveness."

The drama of Christmas exerted a strong influence on Jewish newcomers, as the spectacle of the Christmas tree and the rite of gift giving altered the celebration of Chanukah. In December 1900, the *Tageblatt* contended that the ancient struggle of the Jews against the "turbulent forces of Antiochus" found no better parallel than "the struggle between the poor, quiet, little Chanukah lights and the brightly illuminated, dressed-up and decorated Christmas tree." On the awareness of Jewish children, the impact of the splendid tree was inestimable. The ritual of decorating Christmas trees established itself in the public schools and settlement houses. In 1906, Abraham Stern, a member of the New York City Board of Education, noted that most of the kindergartens in Jewish neighborhoods had trees. Jewish youngsters apparently enjoyed the festivity of decoration and, Stern added, "in many cases the Jewish mothers helped in trimming the trees."

The charm of the Christmas tree was best reflected in the introduction of trees into some Jewish homes. Reformed Jews in the United States, like the affluent and cosmopolitan Jews of Odessa, St. Petersburg, and Moscow, had already adopted certain features of Christmas. Yet, when Rabbi Judah Magnes of New York City's prestigious Temple Emanu-El denounced the "cringing" behavior of those who brought Christmas trees into their homes, an action that constituted, in his opinion, "one more step in their gradual disappearance as Jews," the respected leader may well have been referring to newcomers from Eastern Europe as well as to the affluent congregants of his Reformed synagogue. Addressing the influence of Christmas upon immigrants, a reporter for the *Tageblatt* claimed at the start of 1899 that it was not necessary to travel uptown to witness the holiday's effect, because "East Broadway and Henry Street showed quite a number of Christmas trees in Jewish houses." Four years later, the Yiddish press regretted to report that "the Christmas-tree parade in Jewish homes" was growing, and, if the tree itself were not present, it was likely that "the holly and the mistletoe" would be.

Yet, despite the appearance of the emblems of a Christian holiday in the tenements of the Lower East Side, Jews had no intention of adopting Christmas. As the festival had become secular in nature, its symbols posed a minimal threat to Judaism. The impact of Christmas could be measured most effectively in terms of changes in the celebration of Chanukah. Largely as a result of the popularity of the secular Christmas in America, the Jews developed a new enthusiasm for the Festival of Lights.

A view of the Lower East Side in the 1890s showed that Chanukah had survived the shocks of immigration. During that time, passengers on the Second Avenue "El" train heading down toward First Street in the darkness of a December evening were struck by the rows of burning candles that illuminated the windows of tenement house after tenement house. In the Chanukah season of 1897, the downtown press made reference to the upsurge of interest in the holiday among Eastern European Jews. "The tendency has been of late years to celebrate the festival quite generally, only it is given over for the most part to the little ones," a newspaper explained, suggesting the resemblance to the child-centered day of Christmas, and advocating the new emphasis on festivities with the declaration that "the Jews, too, even in our day, must have an occasion for merry-making, and here it is."

Traditionally, Jews had not suffered from a lack of "merry-making," but the focus of fun-filled celebration apparently shifted in America. Although the Eastern Europeans rejoiced on a variety of occasions, the leading time for unrestrained fun was Purim. Celebrated a month before Passover, Purim commemorated the legendary rescue of Persian Jews from annihilation at the whim of an evil prime minister, by virtue of the intervention of the Jewish Queen Esther. Marked by an enthusiastic reading of the Book of Esther in synagogue, by *spiels*, or plays, rendering the cataclysmic events of the story, by the generous exchange of delicious treats, and by parading in masks and costumes, this special day was the only time in which transvestism, a violation of biblical law, was permitted, and in which the normally sober Jews were enjoined to become drunk to the point that they were unable to tell the difference between the phrases "cursed be Haman," referring to the legendary hater of the Jews, and "blessed be Mordecai," referring to the heroic cousin of Esther. Recalling the celebration of Purim in the Russian shtetl of Lida in the 1870s, David Blaustein explained that the fun-filled occasion was the climactic point of the year for children. Although the holiday continued to be observed with the accustomed enthusiasm in Eastern Europe, in the United States it had become "a lost day."

Had Christmas been in March, Purim would undoubtedly have held a high position in the calendar of American Jews. Although it included activities that paralleled those of Christmas—the exchange of gifts, the entertainment of children, the production of plays—Purim failed to synchronize with the American calendar of festive consumption. If this day of merriment waned in the face of an insurgent Chanukah, it was not for lack of substance.

In contrast to Purim, Chanukah did not originally include the custom of gift giving that had become so prominent a part of the American Christmas. The giving of coins, or "Chanukah gelt," to children in honor of the holiday had gained popularity in Eastern Europe, having derived from the seventeenth-century Polish practice of sending a sum of money with children for the benefit of local teachers. And, although Chanukah was not a particularly important holiday, it was anticipated by children. The excitement of visiting relatives to receive small sums of money provided the motif for Sholom Aleichem's short story "Chanukah Gelt," in which two brothers endure the bothersome conversation, the gratuitous squeezes, the peculiar personalities, and the worthless pieces of old Russian money inevitably donated by their Uncle Moishe-Aaron, in their pursuit of coins for the holiday. Possessing some of the excitement that Christian children associated with Christmas, Chanukah nonetheless lacked the emphasis on presents that made the gentile festival a rite of consumption. The introduction of retail products into the Jewish holiday was spurred by the exotic commercial atmosphere of the secular Christmas.

The mystique and the drama of Christmas shopping exerted tremendous pressure on Jewish newcomers in the city. In 1898, a "large proportion" of the Jewish population of New York was observed shopping in the major retail stores during December. These shoppers apparently considered Christmas to be a holiday in which they were "to an appreciable degree interested."

Not restricted to retail stores, the commercial attractions of the holiday season pervaded the city's street markets as well. During the weeks before Christmas, peddlers competed intensely for spaces on the street. Many camped out overnight in their desired locations and made fires to keep themselves warm. Some alternated nights with fellow merchants, watching each other's wares in turn. Still others hired proxies who, for fifteen cents per night, agreed to guard merchandise while the vendors went home to sleep. Often garnished with wreaths of holly and evergreen boughs, the displays of pushcarts were carefully and colorfully designed to attract urban customers. Jewish wholesalers on the Lower East Side distributed large stocks of Christmas ornaments and treats for the outdoor markets. The infusion of bright color and wintergreen fragrance into the normally drab streets of the city affected all but the most reclusive of Jewish immigrants. As a daughter of Serbian Jews remembered of her youth in New York City, "for us a need was filled at Christmas time by the gaily decorated wares that were spread out by the street merchants."

Accentuated by the yearnings of children exposed to the ubiquitous ritual of gift giving, the impulse to buy Christmas presents welled up among the multitude of Jewish newcomers. On Christmas Day, 1904, feature stories in the *New York Tribune* and the New York *Forward* documented the extent to which the alien custom had been adopted by Jews. "Santa Claus visited the East Side last night, and hardly missed a tenement house," the *Tribune* declared, adding the patronizing remark that "in the greatness of his heart . . . he forgot that there was a religious significance to the day for which he has come to be the patron saint, and dispensed his favors regardless of creed or caste." In the same fatuous tone, the newspaper stated that "in the homes of the poor Hebrews, as well as of the well to do, Christmas is being celebrated with never a thought that it is the birthday of Him whom their forebears crucified more than nineteen centuries ago."

Despite the attitude of pretentious bigotry behind this report, its findings were substantiated by the Jewish press. Under the title "They Are Pious, But They Observe Christmas Too," the Yiddish daily *Forward* claimed that many Jewish families, including "freethinkers" as well as observers of the faith, bought Christmas presents to satisfy the demands of their children. Yet children were not the only recipients of Christmas presents. Spouses and neighbors in the tenement houses were also seen exchanging gifts, some of which, expensive beyond the purchasers' means, were bought on the installment plan.

The sudden popularity of gift giving among Jewish newcomers reflected not an inclination toward Christianity but an effort to embrace the American spirit. "Who says that we are not Americanizing?" the *Forward* asked rhetorically, in the knowledge that the buying of presents in the Christmas season, for which Jewish newcomers showed such passion, constituted "the first thing that demonstrates that one is not a greenhorn." Through the ritual of gift giving, newcomers demonstrated their devotion to the belief in monetary generosity that reflected the American perspective of material abundance. Acknowledging the importance of liberal spending to the urban American, an official of a large East Side synagogue reported that many local leaders encouraged the practice of holiday gift giving on the premise that "it will do one no harm to open up his purse once a year and give generously where friendship dictates."

Sometimes oblivious to the motive that led newcomers to accept the idea of the Christmas present, local critics made a ritual of hurling condemnations at the multitude each December. Parents were rebuked for giving gifts to settlement workers, for contributing toys for the decoration of public Christmas trees, and, of course, for exchanging gifts within their own circles. Appalled that devout Jews would indulge their children's desires for Christmas presents, one social commentator imagined "how the soul-commanding voice of Isaiah . . . would chide the people for this error—could he but speak today." The scriptural theme of religious backsliding was evinced poignantly in a 1907 editorial called "Our Greatest Enemy." Arguing that the subtle influence of American habits of consumption posed as great a problem as the tyrannical force of religious persecution, the commentary admonished that "we do not want death from pleasure, just as we have not wanted death from trouble."

These spirited prophecies reflected the confusion that had arisen from the proximity of the secular Christmas to Chanukah, but they would not be borne out by the course of events. The adoption of gift giving implied the alteration of a Jewish festival, not the acceptance of a Christian belief. It was this practice that identified the American Chanukah. Despite the fiery criticism that poured from its pages, the tradition-minded *Yiddishes Tageblatt* itself sanctioned the shift in popular custom. Striking an analogy between the ancient conflict of Greek and Jewish culture and the struggle taking place in urban America, the newspaper called not for the abolition of gift giving among Jews, but, instead, for the use of presents as a means of bolstering the enthusiasm surrounding Chanukah.

Ridley's department store on Grand Street, a major retailer of the Lower East Side and a faithful advertiser in the *Tageblatt,* articulated the alteration of Chanukah in an advertisement of December 1897. "The spirit with which all Americans wait for the joyous Christmas grows ever stronger and stronger with the passage of time," Ridley's exclaimed, "and Chanukah gifts with Christmas presents go hand in hand. There is only a difference in name." The spirit of Christmas to which the advertiser referred was clearly not that of a single religion. It seemed to be an ecumenical spirit of buying and giving, of festive consumption tempered by the flame of generosity.

In the ethic of consumption, Chanukah and Christmas had discovered a common denominator. Advertising in the Yiddish press mirrored that of the metropolitan newspapers, promoting the notion that new products were as pertinent to Chanukah as they were to Christmas. The fundamentally secular content of the festival was illustrated in an advertisement of the Schubert Piano Company, a firm with stores on West 33rd Street in Manhattan and on Fulton Street in Brooklyn. Appearing in 1911, the advertisement urged "A Piano or Player Piano for Chanukah" and showed a picture of Santa Claus moving a piano into the living room of a young couple. In the European setting, it would have been inconceivable that a Christian saint enter the psychic world of Jews. In urban America, where Saint Nicholas had been stripped of religious significance and converted into a herald of consumers, he could be accepted gracefully by the multitude of Jewish newcomers.

Through the winter rite of consumption, the majority of newcomers found the easiest way to incorporate an American attitude into Chanukah. The Jewish and American traditions could also be combined in the sphere of art, but this required an effort that many people were not prepared to make. In December 1900, the Educational Alliance of the Lower East Side staged a dramatic production that exemplified the artistic method of seeking such a harmony. Founded in 1889 as the Hebrew Institute, moved in 1891 to a stately five-story building on the corner of East Broadway and Jefferson Street, and renamed in 1893, the Educational Alliance was a civic center designed by affluent and well-established German Jews to expose the Eastern Europeans to American beliefs and values, and to the fine arts. The primary cultural event of the holiday season in 1900 was the pantomime performance of Henry Wadsworth Longfellow's poetic five-act play *Judas Maccabeus.*

Composed in December 1871, with the spirit of Chanukah inspiring the poet's imagination, Longfellow's work contained a number of poignant scenes evoking the desperation of Jews besieged by Greek culture. Highlighting the dilemma of the Jew who submitted to the ways of the politically dominant Syrians, the high priest Jason mourns his own downfall, near the end of the play, by crying, "I am neither Jew nor Greek, but stand between them both, a renegade to each in turn." Amplifying the play's message about the dangers of assimilation, the passion of the performers elicited a strong response from several audiences, which were composed mainly of young Russian Jews.

In the production of *Judas Maccabeus,* the spirit of Chanukah was expressed through American art. Satisfying to the few who enjoyed serious theater, the Alliance's presentation was missed by the multitude of Jewish immigrants who honored the holiday in the arena of the department store and the street market. In their activities, the spirit of the American consumer was expressed through the holiday of Chanukah.

Whereas art served to heighten the spiritual meaning of Chanukah, the popular approach to fusing Jewish and American culture required that the essence of the holiday be discounted. Although Chanukah could appropriately be called the Festival of Lights as long as the menorah endured, the holiday's other traditional name, Festival of Dedication, sounded hollow in America. As a commemoration of the heroic rededication of the Second Temple, the festival had lapsed. Even in the Jewish calendar of Eastern Europe, the message of Chanukah may have been subordinated to the festivities of dreidel-spinning and cardplaying that had been grafted onto the holiday during the Middle Ages. Yet, in America, the omnipresence of Jewish values had been shattered, and the spiritual basis of Chanukah had been obscured all the more by the focus of gift giving. The festival fell prey to the same charge of superficiality that plagued the secular Christmas. For many newcomers, it had apparently become a time of celebrations that were not specifically Jewish and that had no relevance to the character of the holiday.

The evolution of Chanukah during the first generation of immigration from Eastern Europe reflected the effort of Jews to balance the flexibility of American urban culture against the rigidity of ideological commitment. By infusing an essentially American practice and attitude into the traditional form of Chanukah, newcomers tried to bridge the yawning chasm between their old world and their new one. Preferring involvement in American society to seclusion from it, they inevitably blunted the Jewish point of view. Their approach stifled the meaning of Judah the Maccabee, but it generated an Irving Berlin, the immigrant from Siberia who composed the popular song of 1909 *Christmas Time Seems Years and Years Away* and whose 1942 classic *White Christmas* would show the potential of American city culture for fusing the traditions of residents and newcomers.

Whereas Chanukah was altered in order to facilitate the Jews' participation in the central American rite of consumption, and Sukkot was modified in order to express the Jews' appreciation of American abundance, Passover infused the Jewish belief in the dignifying power of luxury into the American concept of the standard of living. On account of Passover's prestige among the Jewish holidays, this festival played a singular role in the revision of Jewish identity in America.

No Jewish holiday contained more regulations, required more preparation, and enjoyed more popularity than Passover. Commemorating the miraculous deliverance of the Jews from bondage in Egypt, this seven-day occasion was the foremost acknowledgment of God's covenant with the Jews. After the destruction of the Second Temple in 70 C.E., the unleavened bread, or matzoh, came to take the place of the sacrificial lamb as the symbol of the redemption assured by belief in the God of Abraham and Moses. Neglect of the laws of Passover, which focused on the removal of all *khomets*, or leavened foods, from the home, was considered tantamount to rejection of the divine covenant. Unlike other holidays, Passover had its own code of purity, which excluded a variety of foods that could conceivably rise from exposure to moisture, prohibited all contact with such foods, and required the purification of all vessels and utensils that had come into contact with them. The uniqueness of the festival was exemplified by the practice of a Hasidic rabbi of late nineteenth-century Poland, who reserved special apartments of his two-story home for use only on Passover.

The holiday stirred a profound sense of religious devotion and historical identity among Eastern European Jews. The elaborate housecleaning and preparation of the feast for the Seder, the ceremonial meal that initiated the holiday, made the weeks before Passover a time of heady anticipation. An immigrant from Lithuania recalled that the people of his former shtetl "lived the whole winter for Pesach." After the furniture of the household had been taken to the river for a cleaning, the dirt floor covered with fresh yellow sand from nearby hills and caves, the utensils of ordinary days replaced by special wine goblets, dishes, and tableware taken out of storage, and regular clothes replaced by the best available garments and shoes, the humble dwellings of Jews radiated a spirit of purity and holiness. On Passover, the joyous serenity of the Sabbath was intensified.

Newcomers to America had special reasons for perpetuating this gem of the Jewish holidays. In Russia, the beauty of Passover had been accompanied by a peculiar anxiety, for, at this time of year, the underlying anti-Semitism of the populace was most likely to be aroused into an outburst of violence. Fear of the blood libel, the hideous accusation that Jews would kill a Christian child in order to get blood for the preparation of the Passover matzoh, filled the air of early spring with horrible visions of mass slaughter at the hands of a superstitious peasantry. As late as 1913, a Russian Jew, Mendel Beilis, was subjected to the absurd charge of committing the ritual murder of a young boy. In the United States, the specter of Christian fanaticism was weaker.

Coincidentally, in the same year of 1913, American Jews witnessed the trial of Leo Frank, the Jewish superintendent of an Atlanta pencil factory who was spuriously accused of murdering a young female employee and who, two years later, was dragged from the state penitentiary by twenty-five armed men and lynched. Yet, this famous instance of rabid anti-Semitism was, as Abraham Cahan noted several years afterward, an interruption of the general climate of religious tolerance prevailing in the decades before World War I, when "the Jewish immigrant almost did not know that there actually was such a thing as anti-Semitism here."

The American Passover became an important time of reflection on the new conditions of Jewish life. Emphasizing the continued plight of his people in Russia, a journalist stated in 1898 that the Jews of the United States "as in no other country in the world," ought to celebrate "this feast of the deliverance of our forefathers, as a free people, with deep felt gratitude." The comparative comfort of immigrants in urban America yielded a sense of thanksgiving, but it dulled the edge of a distinct Jewish identity that in Eastern Europe was continually sharpened by oppression.

In the atmosphere of the American city, Passover came to serve as a bulkhead of Jewish identity, checking the powerful tendency to identify with American ways. It reminded Jews that they possessed a culture different from that of their "host" society. The ongoing struggle of relatives left behind in Russia, Austria-Hungary, and Rumania became a focus for the collective memory of American Jews, whose relatively benign situation harbored the risk of forgetting about the social marginality that had long defined the Jewish people.

Designated by the Torah (Deut. 6:20–25) to be a time in which parents were obliged to inspire children with the history and principle of Judaism, Passover emerged also as the annual occasion for bridging the gap that separated American-reared children from their elders. Although restlessness impelled some young people to leave the table before the conclusion of the lengthy Seder, virtually all Jews attended a ceremony at the home of a relative or friend, if not a parent. Moreover, the fact that youngsters were observed singing traditional melodies "with greater earnestness" than they devoted to "Donkey-Monkey Business" showed that at least the rudimentary feelings of Jewish identity crossed the barrier of the generations.

Finally, the symbolic matzoh was maintained in the uncongenial setting of urban America. "Even Jews who do not uphold Passover strictly," the *Forward* claimed in 1902, "concern themselves with the matzohs, because of the fear of embarrassing themselves before the neighbors." By exerting pressure on each other at Passover, newcomers kept the anchors of cultural identity.

Although Passover continued to be a key to Jewish existence in the United States, its aura of sanctity disappeared. In a newspaper article that appeared before Passover of 1907, one newcomer pinpointed the corrosive effect of American material conditions upon the holiday. In Europe, he recalled, he used to look forward to Passover as soon as Sukkot ended in the autumn. His wife would then buy hens and chickens in preparation for the great holiday, and new dishes, spoons, glasses, pots, and pans would also be purchased well in advance. In America, however, the festival was prepared at the last minute. With two trips to the stores, his wife could prepare a complete Seder. There was no scouring and liming to do, because the walls were covered with wallpaper, as was the floor with oil cloth and carpets. "The whole year is by me Passover," he exclaimed, "clean and kosher!" By narrowing the gap between the holy and the mundane, the ease of shopping and the commonness of luxury in the American city had eroded the distinction of Passover, dethroning the queen of Jewish festivals.

The decline of purification as the dominant theme of Passover was also rooted in the neglect of the special Sabbaths preceding the holiday. With special readings from the Torah and the Prophets, Sabbath Parah and Sabbath Hahodesh anticipate this theme. In particular, Sabbath Parah, which was named after the account of the red heifer (*parah adumah*), dwelled on passages from Numbers (1:22) that detailed a mysterious rite for purifying the defiled, and on passages from Ezekiel (16:38) that prophesied the time when God will purify the Jews and infuse in them a new spirit. The prefatory emphasis on purification appears to have been lost on many Jews in America, where Sabbath Parah, along with other special Sabbaths in proximity to it, was not well observed.

As the theme of purification waned in the American Passover, the luxuries of the festival acquired a different meaning. Facilitated by the atmosphere of urban abundance, the acquisition of new things developed into an annual ritual that cohered with the American emphasis on the rising standard of living. Progress, rather than purity, came to be an important theme of the American Passover.

Although Chanukah had begun to gain importance as a time for shopping, Passover was the holiday that affirmed the dignifying power of luxuries, and, in America, this festival outpaced the others as an occasion for buying new things. The parade of people on the Lower East Side's main thoroughfare, Grand Street, around Passover in 1907, was likened to a "sea of new hats and new dresses . . . of beautiful color from the drugstore on the cheeks and beautiful color from nature on the faces." The bright appearance of Jews, enhanced "with jewelry both genuine and false," seemed to reflect "the holiday soul" that had come over them. By donning fashionable new hats, a prominent part of dress at the turn of the century and one in which style changed quickly, "greenhorns" fresh from Europe could fit into the Passover crowd of Jews already familiar with American ways. The American Passover gave newcomers an opportunity to measure their acquisition of the basic luxuries of city life.

In addition to the traditional idea of sanctifying oneself and one's household through the acquisition of luxuries, the practice of gift giving seems to have entered into Passover and escalated the importance of shopping for the occasion. Although Passover in Europe had not included the exchange of presents, the *Tageblatt* encouraged Jews, particularly young Jews, to augment the spirit of the holiday by giving gifts to their parents. For older immigrants who had difficulty adjusting to American life, Passover provided a welcome period of joy. The younger generation, it was argued, could increase the happiness of the holiday by honoring elders with a thing of beauty and value.

The pulse of retail commerce in Jewish neighborhoods rose in the early autumn, for the High Holidays and Sukkot, and in December for Chanukah, but the intensity of shopping for Passover was distinctive. By late March, the advertising sections of Yiddish newspapers swelled to twice their normal size, and the street markets bristled with activity. Peddlers who usually sold fish or produce often discontinued these lines during the weeks before Passover, in order to sell new chinaware, tinware, and crockery, the products for which the holiday created a special demand. The curbside inventory of all types of merchandise grew, as clothing, laces, ribbons, pictures, lamps, baskets, oilcloth, and fine foods all found a place in the "reconstruction" of the Jewish home and the material rehabilitation of its members. "The ambition of every Jewish housewife to have as many new furnishings in her home on this occasion as her purse can buy," a reporter observed in 1906, had turned the shopping weeks before Passover into a "harvest" for the street merchants.

A novel ritual, the dumping of household furnishings into the city streets, showed that Passover in America had become a time in which many Jews upgraded their standard of living. With the holiday, the people of the East Side became "new and clean," the New York *Tribune* stated in a report on the Passover of 1902. They displayed new clothes and furniture, and the area took on "an unusual air of brightness," after the New York City street cleaning department "cleaned the streets into which all the abandoned furniture and bedding" had been thrown. Gone were the days of hauling furniture to the river bank of the shtetl for a thorough cleaning. The rhythm of shopping in urban America demanded the replacement rather than the refurbishing of possessions.

Although not every item of every home was discarded at Passover, the dumping of merchandise on the streets assumed a remarkable scale, touching the poor as well as the affluent. In 1898, the "thorough renovating of Jewish homes once (at least) every year," was applauded as being of great psychological benefit, especially to poorer Jews whose existence in small and ill-ventilated tenement rooms was eased by the renewal of furnishings. Well-to-do families tended to keep a special set of Passover dishes and utensils, but the majority of people reportedly took advantage of mass-marketed luxuries by discarding their wares, buying new ones, and then, after the holiday, using the newly acquired items on a daily basis for the rest of the year.

The annual transformation of the household had become a well-established custom by the 1890s. In April 1896, while the great depression of the decade continued to burden urban workers, the dumping of possessions on the streets of New York was described as "A Jewish Custom that Gives Colonel Waring's Men Trouble," in reference to the industrious new head of the street cleaning department, Colonel George Waring. It apparently took municipal workers several weeks to clear the Lower East Side of the tremendous amount of bedding, furniture, and kitchenware left on the pavement before and during Passover, an amount that was already considered typical despite the economically depressed conditions of the preceding years.

By providing an annual occasion for the acquisition of new products, Passover underscored the American belief in the value of a rising standard of living. Given the decline of traditional Judaism in America, luxuries served no longer to substantiate the Jewish sense of holiness. Instead, they symbolized the faith in social progress that moved many Jews seeking to fit into American society. The ritualized demand for new products gave newcomers reason to believe that they were "greening themselves out," upgrading their level of material life in the manner of urban Americans. Passover thus enabled immigrants to retain an important element of communal identity while it sanctioned a basic American attitude.

As Jews secularized their view of festive consumption, they inspired a democratic appreciation of luxuries that suited the new society. The Sabbath had long been viewed as a respite from the monotonous and degrading aspects of daily life, a time in which individual Jews were dignified by the "additional soul" that entered them on Friday evenings. Yet it was on Passover that the notion of dignifying the ordinary person through celebration attained highest expression. The Passover Seder was thought to confer an aspect of royalty upon its participants. Jewish fathers, mothers, daughters, and sons were commonly referred to at this time as kings, queens, princesses, and princes. In the Old World, the elevated dignity of the individual derived from the veneration of the Lord to which the Jewish holidays were devoted. As a subscriber to the divine covenant, the humblest Jew was entitled to a status of grandeur.

In urban America, as the cloak of religious sensibility fell away, and as the dignity of the individual became purely a secular matter, the consumption of products in honor of Passover inevitably took on a different light. Simply by virtue of being an American consumer, the individual was endowed with luxuries that had once been intended for the keeper of the Jewish faith.

The subtle shift of attitudes was illustrated in the advertising of clothier Moe Levy, an immigrant from Russia who was one of the few clothing retailers to achieve a broad regional following prior to 1920. In the Passover season of 1906, by which time Moe Levy and Company owned three stores, two on the Lower East Side and one in Brooklyn, one of the retailer's full-page Yiddish advertisements declared: "On Passover the man is a king, the woman is a queen, and the children are princes and princesses. When the king sits on his Passover cushion and his royal children ask him the four questions, and the queen smiles and becomes full of delight, one feels then a rare pleasure and one wants to pour a sixth glass and toast 'To Life' to Moe Levy and Co. who clothes all well-dressed Jews and their children with the best and finest clothes . . . in honor of Passover." In the secular setting of the

United States, the acquisition of fine products ceased to uphold the dignity of the Jew as a Jew. Instead, it dignified the Jew as a consumer.

In altering the symbolism of luxury that sustained the holidays of Sukkot, Chanukah, and Passover, Jews demonstrated an eagerness to create a new cultural identity that would combine aspects of Judaism with an American sensibility. As clothiers like Moe Levy were well aware, the act of dressing stylishly was fundamental to the quest for identity in the American city. For most newcomers, it would be the foremost symbol of Jewish commitment to the principle of becoming an American.

CHAPTER 12

"Without question," writes Irving Howe, "the most important secular institutions created by the [Jewish] immigrants were the Jewish *trade unions." All agree that there was some special Jewish flavor to these unions, traits that distinguished them from other labor-movement unions developing at the same time. Howe argues that these traits stemmed from the way Jewish unions served immigrants not only as bargaining agencies defending their rights as workers, but also as "homes away from home"—as "social centers, political forums, and training schools." Historian Lucy Dawidowicz, in her essay here, points to Jewish values and traditions as being what made Jewish unions different: "that welfare, education and philanthropy became union concerns in Jewish unions demonstrated the ways through which the Jewish workers transferred the social responsibilities of the East European Jewish community to the labor movement."*

Dawidowicz stresses other characteristically Jewish features of the Jewish labor movement as well. In the first place, Jews formed a unique kind of working class. They concentrated in a few industries, particularly the garment trades, and were eager to advance or at least to see their children advance to a higher socioeconomic status—an aspiration that made class consciousness difficult to achieve. Second, Jews continually faced tensions between their class identities and their Jewish identities, especially on issues such as immigration restriction, where class interests and Jewish interests diverged. This problem became particularly acute whenever anti-Semitism reared up in labor's ranks. Finally, Jews came from a tradition that long emphasized arbitration and conciliation as means of resolving intragroup conflicts. While not alone in this, Jews, being an endangered minority group, did have a special interest in preserving communal solidarity and social stability. By accepting the principles of "industrial peace" as set forth in the so-called "Protocol of Peace" that ended the cloakmakers' strike of 1910, the Jewish labor movement set an example of how harmonious relations between employers and workers might be achieved in the future—without strikes.

The influence of the Protocol of Peace, as Dawidowicz points out, was lasting—especially in the garment industry, where Jews continued to play a central role. The social-welfare programs pioneered by Jewish labor unions may have had even more impact, since the New Deal made many of them standard employee benefits, available nationwide, and sponsored in some cases by the government. Of course, the Jewish labor movement itself declined with the widespread entry of Jews into the middle class. But while it lasted it embodied something of American Jewry's ideals: offering a way for immigrant Jews to help themselves, their countrymen, and humanity, even as they remained rooted in a thoroughly Jewish environment, open to the wide world beyond.

The Jewishness of the Jewish Labor Movement in the United States

Lucy S. Dawidowicz

According to the findings of the National Jewish Population Study, nearly 90 percent of American Jews in the labor force in 1971 were white-collar workers, whereas fewer than 10 percent were blue-collar craftsmen and operatives. But half a century ago the proportions were different. Not only did Jewish blue-collar workers preponderate over Jewish white-collar workers, but in centers of Jewish immigrant concentration, Jewish workers were actually a plurality in the total industrial labor force.

Over 1,500,000 Jews were part of the great stream of immigrants that expanded and transformed the industrial and commercial structure of the United States. For the most part they came from the towns and villages of the Russian Pale of Settlement, from the Galician backwaters of the Hapsburg empire, and from the Moldavian heartland of Rumania. In the old country they had been artisans or merchants, but in America most of them became shopworkers, primarily in the clothing industry. (In the 1880s German Jews owned 234 of 241 clothing factories in New York City. The statistic facilitated the influx of the Russian Jews in tailoring.)

From 1881 to 1910 nearly eighteen million immigrants arrived in America. These were the "new" immigrants who came from Southern and Eastern Europe—the Italians, Slovaks, Croats, Poles, Ruthenians, Greeks, Hungarians, and Jews. The "old" immigrants who had come before the Civil War from Northwestern Europe—the English, Scotch, Welsh, Irish, Germans, and Scandinavians—had become assimilated into the native population.

The new immigrants began to replace the old immigrants and the native Americans in the coal fields and in the steel mills. They crowded America's great manufacturing and mining centers—New York, Detroit, Chicago, Pittsburgh, Buffalo, Cleveland, bringing their own ethnic flavor, linguistic variety, religious practices, and political traditions, which still linger, giving each urban community its unique character. Each wave of new immigrants followed their compatriots into the same neighborhoods of the same cities and the same industries, clinging together for comfort and aid in alien urban America. Tensions multiplied between old immigrants and natives, on the one hand, and the new immigrants, on the other. Old-timers resented newcomers, aliens speaking foreign tongues, who displaced them on the job, underbid them in wages, worked longer hours, and were, to boot, full of dangerous ideologies.

The early labor movement incorporated the prejudices of its members, sharing their nativism, xenophobia, and even anti-Semitism. Narrowly construing its interests, the organized labor movement vociferously opposed free immigration. It was not unexpected, then, that the Jewish immigrants from Eastern Europe, long habituated to exclusion from social institutions and to the separatism of their own institutions, should set about forming their own "Jewish" unions. The United Hebrew Trades, organized in 1888, was a natural outgrowth of the inhospitality on the American labor scene to immigrant Jewish workers. Even a quarter of a century later, the formation of the Amalgamated Clothing Workers Union as a split-off from the United Garment Workers reflected the unabating tension between Jewish and non-Jewish workers in the men's clothing industry. Among the hat workers, too, the Jewish and non-Jewish unions had developed in mutual hostility for over thirty years, until 1934 when they finally combined, the conflicts between the "old" and "new" immigrants finally having subsided.

These Jewish unions in the garment trades, born in the struggles of the Jewish immigrant workers to find their place in America's industrial society, eventually helped to shape an enlightened trade unionism in America. In addition, they served as a way station on the road to acculturation. Fortuitously these unions became the vehicle through which the Jewish immigrant workers expressed their values and transmitted their traditions. Blending Russian radicalism with Jewish messianism, these unions sounded an alien note on the American labor scene at the turn of the century. They were too radical for the American Federation of Labor and its head, Samuel Gompers—an English Jew—who feared that the Russian Jewish socialists forever chanting about a better world were jeopardizing the here-and-now of pure-and-simple trade unionism. But the ideological vocabulary of the Russian Jewish radical movement, with its thick overlay of German philosophy, French political slogans, and English economic theories, obscured its emotional impulse and fundamental character.

The Jewish revolutionary passion—whether for socialism, anarchism, and even, finally, communism—originated in the Jewish situation. Anti-Semitism, pogroms, discrimination, had alienated the Jews from Russian society. In the revolutionary movement, the Russian Jews protested against Russia's tyranny, its denial of the common humanity of all men and particularly of Jews, and its refusal to grant the basic political rights already commonplace in most of Western Europe—freedom of speech, press, and assembly, the right to vote and to elect representatives to a legislative assembly, and freedom from arbitrary arrest. The economic goals of the radicals were in fact modest: the right to organize, to work only a twelve-hour day, for a living wage to be paid each week. The Jewish radicals in Russia were not engaged in a class war against a ruthless industrial capitalism, for it did not exist there. They hoped for a revolution that would create a constitutional state and guarantee political equality. These Jewish radicals embraced a liberal-humanitarian utopianism, rational and this-worldly, in contradistinction to the chiliastic utopianism of the *hasidim*, who computed the coming of the messiah by the extent of Jewish suffering.

In America, where they found most of their political utopia already in existence, the Jewish immigrants directed their revolutionary energy toward economic utopia. They talked in class-war terms about redistributing the wealth and taking over the means of production, but in practice they fought on the barricades only for union recognition. That was the American equivalent of the struggle for the dignity of man, the dignity of the worker, and his parity with the boss as a human being. These Russian Jewish immigrants were not really as class-conscious as they sounded and did not perceive their position in the class structure in Marxist terms. Not content to remain proletarians, many "sweated" workers quickly became entrepreneurs—from worker to subcontractor, to contractor, to manufacturer, to jobber, to wholesaler. No group had a more fluid class structure than the immigrant Russian Jews. They soon outranked all other immigrant groups in attaining, in their own generation, a socioeconomic status as high as or higher than third-generation Americans.

Not all Jewish immigrants succeeded in escaping from the sweatshop. Those who remained concentrated on educating their children for something better than the shop. They formed a one-generation working class, being "neither the sons nor the fathers of workers." For themselves they sought dignity and community in their unions and the institutions associated with Jewish labor. In Russia the Jewish community had been an organic whole, and most Jews, however alienated, found their place within it, whether as upholders of the tradition or as secularists. In America, however, Jewish communal life was atomized and the immigrant had to recreate a community of his own. The Jewish labor movement and its institutions became the secular substitute for the old community. In many ways, the Jewish immigrant workers looked upon the institutions of the Jewish labor movement—the unions; their fraternal order, the Workman's Circle; their Yiddish daily newspaper, the *Forverts*—as their contribution to Jewish continuity. They brought Yiddish into their unions and sustained a Yiddish labor press for many decades. They were the consumers of a "proletarian" literature in Yiddish (largely revolutionary didacticism tempered with self-pity). They established Yiddish schools with a labor orientation. The labor movement was their vehicle to preserve Jewish values and traditions as they understood them.

François Guizot once wrote that peoples with a long history are influenced by their past and their national traditions at the very moment when they are working to destroy them. In the midst of the most striking transformations, he said, they remain fundamentally what their history has made them, for no revolution, however powerful, can wipe out long-established national traditions. The Jewish revolutionaries who fled Tsarist prisons and Siberian exile were hostile to the Jewish religious tradition, which they rejected as clerical and superstitious. They sought desperately to break out of what to them was its constricting mold. Yet even they had been shaped by that Jewish mold. David Dubinsky, at the convention of the International Ladies Garment Workers' Union (ILGWU) in May, 1962, when he was reelected president, conjured up his youthful dreams, in which Jewish messianism and the perfect society had appeared in a Jewish Labor Bundist guise. "I was sent to Siberia," Dubinsky said, "because I dreamt at that time of a better world. I dreamt of being free, of not being under the domination of a czar and dictatorship." He then recalled that his father, a religious man, used to read to him from the Bible on Saturday afternoons. In reading, his father used to stress that "a good name is better than precious oil." He had heard it so often, Dubinsky confessed, that it became part of him and of the movement with which he was identified: "When we saw the labor movement imperilled because of lack of ethics, I realized a good name is better than all the riches and all the offices to which one could aspire." Like many other Jewish labor leaders, Dubinsky had lived only briefly within the Jewish tradition he wistfully recalled, and had rebelled against it. Yet this Jewish tradition, discarded and unacknowledged, significantly affected the way the Jewish labor movement developed.

In America, shortly after World War I, the Jewish unions pioneered with their social welfare programs: medical care, housing, unemployment insurance, health insurance, vacations (and vacation resorts), and retirement benefits. They were the first to develop educational programs and the first to make philanthropy a union practice. Such activities became accepted in the general labor movement only after the New Deal. That welfare, education, and philanthropy became union concerns in Jewish unions demonstrated the ways through which the Jewish workers transferred the social responsibilities of the East European Jewish community to the labor movement. In the Jewish world of Eastern Europe, the community took care of its sick and its poor, its old and needy, and created the institutions to administer this care. This tradition the unions took over. It was only natural, then, that the ILGWU started the first union health center in 1916 and the Amalgamated started the first *gemilut-hesed* in 1923. The Amalgamated Bank was not the first labor bank; a few labor banks had been established a little earlier, in the hope that banking might yield large profits and make the unions independent. But the Amalgamated Bank was the first to offer union members low-interest loans, without collateral, which they could not get elsewhere. This was the sort of *tsedakah* which Maimonides might have designated as the highest degree.

In 1927 the Amalgamated built the first cooperative houses in New York to provide some of its members with housing that was not only decent but also attractive. Thirty years later other unions followed that example. Probably the most paradoxical episode in union housing occurred in 1957 when the ILGWU lent a corporation headed by Nelson A. Rockefeller $2.6 millions to help finance a workers' housing development in Puerto Rico.

The Russian immigrant passion for learning had been stilled partly by the revolutionary movement, which had been teacher as well as agitator, publishing popular science and philosophy along with political tracts. In America Jews had more educational opportunities. Hutchins Hapgood wrote in 1902 in *The Spirit of the Ghetto* that "the public schools are filled with little Jews; the night schools of the east side are practically used by no other race. City College, New York University, and Columbia University are graduating Russian Jews in numbers rapidly increasing." Despite classes, lectures, and debates at the settlement houses, at the Americanizing agencies like the Educational Alliance, at Cooper Union and the Rand School, the immigrant workers continued to look to the labor movement for learning, so the Amalgamated and the ILGWU gave courses in English and economics, history and philosophy. They were indeed labor colleges. It took a quarter of a century, during Roosevelt's New Deal, for other unions to sponsor labor education.

Philanthropy, too, as the Jewish unions practiced it, demonstrated the pervasiveness of Jewish tradition. For many decades, a small portion of union dues has been set aside for donations—to labor organizations, health and welfare agencies, educational and cultural institutions, civic and political causes, and finally to the ethnic beneficiaries—Jewish organizations, Italian, and later, as a consequence of ethnic succession, Negro and Puerto Rican. During the Nazi period and in the immediate postwar era, the unions distributed colossal sums of money for relief and rescue, mostly for Jews, but also for non-Jewish labor leaders and unionists. Jewish causes—the Jewish Labor Committee and the United Jewish Appeal being the top beneficiaries—enjoyed the support of the ILGWU. The Histadrut and many Israeli labor projects have been the richer for gifts from the Jewish labor movement.

The Jewish influence has perhaps been deepest in the realization of industrial peace in the garment industry, though industrial peace was not particularly a

Jewish idea. The National Civic Federation, founded at the turn of the century, had brought together representatives of labor, capital, and the public to head off strikes by mediation and to use conciliation to settle disputes. But the federation had limited success, being accepted, at best, on a temporary basis by some segments of capital and labor, because labor for the most part suspected that cooperation meant sellout, and capital thought conciliation meant surrender. But the situation was different with regard to Jewish labor and capital in the clothing industry.

In 1910 the Protocol of Peace settled the "Great Revolt," an eight-week strike of some sixty thousand cloakmakers in New York. The strike involved mostly Jewish workers (with a substantial minority of Italians) and nearly all Jewish manufacturers. The mediators were Jewish community leaders, many associated with the Ethical Culture Society. The most active in the settlement were Louis D. Brandeis, distinguished Jewish lawyer and political liberal; leading Boston merchant and Ethical Culturist A. Lincoln Filene, who was also a member of the National Civic Federation; pioneer Jewish social workers like Meyer Bloomfield in Boston and Henry Moskowitz in New York; and the most prominent of Jewish community leaders, Jacob Schiff and Louis Marshall, of the American Jewish Committee. The manufacturers and the union alike were torn between the militants and the compromisers. Yet a precedent-setting settlement was reached, which, besides increasing wages and decreasing hours, established a preferential union shop, a union-management joint board of sanitary control in the factories, a grievance committee, and a board of arbitration. The arbitration board was to consist of one representative of the union, one of the manufacturers, and one of the public. To be sure, the protocol broke down, was repaired, and broke down again after some years. But most scholars agree that its influence was lasting.

Several months thereafter, a four-month strike of some eight thousand workers at Hart, Schaffner and Marx, the world's largest men's clothing manufacturer, in Chicago, was settled by establishing a three-man arbitration board. As in New York, most of the workers were Jews and nearly all the manufacturers were Jewish. That settlement started a tradition of such harmonious labor-management relations between Hart, Schaffner and Marx and the Amalgamated that, in 1960, the late Meyer Kestenbaum, then president of the company, spoke at the Amalgamated's convention commemorating fifty years of collective bargaining.

Exceptional in this history of cooperation between labor and capital have been its liberal, humanitarian qualities. The unions did not "sell out" their workers nor did they "compromise" their ideals. On the contrary, they succeeded in enlisting the employers' support for economic and social programs once considered eccentric and visionary, turning these into commonplace realities.

Was Jewishness the determinant? The existential Jewish situation, Jewish workers and Jewish bosses in a gentile world, must have had an effect, entangling them in one community. They could not extricate themselves, even if they chose, from each other's fate. Nor could they divest themselves of the habits and outlooks of centuries-old traditions. This is not to minimize the specific conditions in the garment industry. Professor Selig Perlman has pointed to its special character—the multitude of small shops in an industry that had not quite reached the factory stage, the cutthroat competition of highly individualistic employers, the industry's seasonal character, in which a strike meant unemployment for the worker and financial calamity for the employer.

But the Jewish differential remains. Jews in a gentile world, despite class differences, workers and bosses felt responsible for one another. The wealthy Jews may have been more sensitive to the Jewish situation, feeling their position and prestige imperiled by the flow of immigration from Eastern Europe. They were ashamed of the appearance, the language, and the manners of the Russian Jews, aghast at their political ideologies, and terrified lest the world crumble by the mad act of a Jewish radical. (The fear was not entirely unfounded: a crazy Polish anarchist had assassinated President McKinley.) Unhappily and involuntarily identified with the immigrant community, the American Jews sought to restrain and tranquilize the revolutionary temper of the immigrant workers with Americanization programs and traditional Jewish education. Afraid to be accused of burdening the public charities with immigrant Jewish paupers, they contributed to Jewish relief societies and to welfare and educational institutions. But they knew that employment and labor peace were better guarantees against economic hardship than charity. In the long run, it may have been cheaper to pay higher wages than to make bigger donations. Besides, labor unrest was bad for the Jewish name and for the reputation of the Jewish employers. The dignity of man and the dignity of labor were as high in the system of values of the Jewish capitalist as the Jewish worker, for it was Judaism itself that endowed labor with divine attributes ("Israel was charged to do work on the six days, just as they were ordered to rest on the seventh day"). Louis Marshall, who had not much sympathy for radical ideologies, nonetheless had a deep sense of the dignity of labor and the working man. Some months after the Protocol of Peace had been signed, he chided a manufacturer whose workers had struck: "So long as the manufacturer considers his employees as mere serfs and chattels, so long as they are considered as unworthy of being brought into conference or consultation, so long as their feelings and aspirations as human beings are lost sight of, so long will labor troubles be rampant and a feeling of dislike, if not of hatred, will be engendered against the employer in the hearts of the employees."

The practice of Judaism, as well as its principles, helped bridge the gulf between worker and boss. Sholem Asch's Uncle Moses, who brought his whole *shtetl* over to work in his factory, prayed with his workers at the evening services, if only to encourage them to work overtime. Lillian Wald reported an incident about a Jewish union leader who met Jacob Schiff. At first the union man was uncomfortable about his shabby clothing, but this was forgotten when, arguing an issue, both he and Schiff began to quote Bible and Talmud, trying to outdo each other. This kind of familiarity reduced the workers' awe for the boss and made discussion between them not only possible but even likely.

The Jewish situation had made many wealthy American Jews receptive to liberal and humanitarian ideas. They befriended the pioneering social workers of their day and were willing to learn from them about the conditions of the industrial poor. Lillian Wald in New York City taught Jacob Schiff; Judge Julian W. Mack and Jane Addams educated Julius Rosenwald in Chicago. Little wonder, then, that Schiff used to contribute anonymously, through Lillian Wald, for the relief of striking workers and sometimes even to a union treasury. Back in 1897 during a garment workers' strike, he asked Lillian Wald, "Is it not possible that representatives of workers, contractors, and manufacturers meet to discuss ways and means in which a better condition of affairs could permanently be brought about?"

The question may have seemed novel or naive in those days of labor's unrest and capital's indifference. Yet in a short period radical Jewish unions, conservative Jewish community leaders, and profit-seeking Jewish manufacturers answered Schiff's question affirmatively. Perhaps the most curious milestone on this path was erected in 1929, when three great Jewish financiers and philanthropists—Julius Rosenwald, Herbert H. Lehman, and Felix Warburg—lent the ILGWU $100,000 to help the union's reconstruction after its locals had been rewon from Communist capture.

The Jewish tradition of arbitration and conciliation had cut a broad swath. Originating in talmudic times, incorporated in the *Shulchan Aruch*, practiced for centuries in all Jewish communities, these principles of compromise, arbitration, and settlement were familiar and venerable to worker and boss alike. The rabbi and *dayanim* decided in the *beth din*, the religious court, but disputants frequently took their case to communal leaders who acted as arbitrators, *borerim*. The procedure must have seemed commonplace to most Jewish workers, not long from the old country and the old culture. As for the manufacturers, they, too, were responsive to the teachings that peaceful compromise was preferable to the humiliation of a court and that Jews should settle their disputes within the Jewish community.

Jewish solidarity and the Jewish tradition, albeit secularized, bred innovations in the institutions of modern American labor. The Jewish situation itself—the Jew poised on the margins of gentile society, in an existential

Galut—created the energy and the impetus for those innovations. Whereas lower-class anti-Semitism had separated Jewish workers from the non-Jews, anxiety among upper-class Jews about anti-Semitism had more securely fixed their solidarity with the Jewish workers. The tension of Jews living in a gentile world has accounted for much of Jewish creativity in modern society. The Jewish labor movement, too, shared in that creativity.

FOR FURTHER READING

World of Our Fathers (1976), Irving Howe's epic history of East European Jewish immigration to the United States, is *the* book that anyone seriously interested in this subject should turn to first. Susan A. Glenn, *Daughters of the Shtetl* (1990), and Sydney Stahl Weinberg, *The World of Our Mothers* (1988), fill in missing details concerning Jewish immigrant women. For briefer surveys, see Gerald Sorin, *A Time for Building: The Third Migration, 1880–1920* (1992); Salo Baron, "United States, 1880–1914," in Jeanette Baron (ed.), *Steeled by Adversity* (1971); Bernard D. Weinryb, "East European Immigration to the United States," *Jewish Quarterly Review* 45 (April 1955), pp. 497–528; and Oscar and Mary Handlin, "A Century of Jewish Immigration to the United States," *American Jewish Year Book* 50 (1948–1949). These may be supplemented by various documentary histories of the period, including Irving Howe and Kenneth Libo, *How We Lived* (1979); Abraham J. Karp, *Golden Door to America* (1976); and Uri D. Herscher's collection of immigrant memoirs, *The East European Jewish Experience in America* (1983).

Moses Rischin's *The Promised City* (1962) is an essential volume that offers a panoramic portrait of East European Jewish immigrants in the city that almost all of them either lived in or passed through: New York. Indeed, New York has been the focus of a great many studies of Jewish immigration. Thomas Kessner, *The Golden Door* (1977), demonstrates statistically the relatively rapid occupational mobility of New York Jews. Arthur Goren, *New York Jews and the Quest for Community* (1970), illuminates the early-twentieth-century effort to forge a united Jewish community or *kehillah* in New York by wedding traditional Jewish forms to contemporary American ideals. Ronald Sanders, *The Downtown Jews* (1969), Hutchins Hapgood's classic, *The Spirit of the Ghetto* (1902, reprinted 1965), and Allon Schoener, *Portal to America* (1967), a collection of photographs and newspaper articles, evoke the flavor of New York's old Lower East Side. Isaac Metzker (ed.), *A Bintel Brief* (1971), translates "help" letters to the *Jewish Daily Forward,* shedding light on the heartaches of Jewish newcomers. Jenna W. Joselit's *Our Gang* (1983) chronicles "Jewish crime in the New York Community, 1900–1940." And Jonathan D. Sarna (ed.), *People Walk on Their Heads* (1981), presents in translation an early critique of Jews and Judaism in New York by an Orthodox immigrant rabbi, while discussing in his introduction the transition from immigrant Judaism to American Judaism. For a sense of how different immigrant Jewish life was outside of New York, see Ewa Morawska, *Insecure Prosperity: Smalltown Jews in Industrial America 1890–1940* (1996).

Literary portrayals of Jewish immigration to America abound. Abraham Cahan's *The Rise of David Levinsky* (1917, 1960) is certainly the best, and may be supplemented by Cahan's earlier efforts, notably *Yekl* (1896, 1970)—the basis for the movie "Hester Street." Anzia Yezierska views immigration through a woman's eye, particularly in her early stories and her novel, *Bread Givers* (1925, 1975). Other literature from the period has been gathered by Milton Hindus in *The Old East Side: An Anthology* (1969), and listed by Carole S. Kessner, "Jewish-American Immigrant Fiction Written in English Between 1867 and 1920," *Bulletin of Research in the Humanities* 81 (1978), pp. 406–430.

Focused studies on selective aspects of immigration are too numerous to list. Eli M. Lederhendler reviews some of the most important ones in his "Jewish Immigration to America and Revisionist Historiography: A Decade of New Perspectives," *Yivo Annual of Jewish Social Science* 18 (1983), pp. 391–410. Other valuable studies are found in a special issue of *American Jewish History* 71 (December 1981), and in David Berger, *The Legacy of Jewish Immigration: 1881 and Its Impact* (1983). Other significant contributions include Simon Kuznets's statistical study, "Immigration of Russian Jews to the United States: Background and Structure," *Perspectives in American History* 9 (1975), pp. 35–124; Stephan F. Brumberg, *Going to America, Going to School* (1986); Arcadius Kahan, *Essays in Jewish Social and Economic History* (1986); Shelly Tenenbaum, *A Credit to Their Community: Jewish Loan Societies in the United States, 1880–1945* (1993); and Matthew Frye Jacobson, *Special Sorrows: The Diasporic Imagination of Irish, Polish and Jewish Immigrants in the United States* (1995).

The relationship between German Jews and Russian Jews in America is still a passionately debated subject in some circles. Ande Manners, in *Poor Cousins* (1972), offers a highly readable account. Zosa Szajkowski, "The Yahudi and the Immigrant: A Reappraisal," *American Jewish Historical Quarterly* 63 (September 1973), pp. 13–45, is a major revisionist statement that seeks to understand the conflict more objectively and in context. For Moses Rischin's later thoughts on this subject, see *American Jewish History* 73 (December 1983), pp. 194–198.

Paula Hyman has pioneered the study of East European immigrant Jewish women. In addition to her article in this volume, see her "Culture and Gender: Women in the Immigrant Jewish Community," in D. Berger's *The Legacy of Jewish Immigration*, and her "Gender and the Immigrant Experience in the United States," in Judith R. Baskin, *Jewish Women in Historical Perspective* (1991). Jacob R. Marcus, *The American Jewish Woman: A Documentary History* (1981), makes available a bounty of primary sources on this and other aspects of Jewish women's history. Susan L. Braunstein and Jenna Weissman Joselit (eds.), *Getting Comfortable in New York: The American Jewish Home, 1880–1950* (1990), originally a museum catalog, contains both important articles and invaluable photographs bearing on Jewish home life in the immigrant period and beyond. Andrew Heinze, *Adapting to Abundance: Jewish Immigrants, Mass Consumption, and the Search for American Identity* (1990), examines some of these same issues from a different perspective.

No definitive study of the Jewish labor movement in America exists. Special issues of *Yivo Annual* 16 (1976) and *American Jewish Historical Quarterly* 65 (March 1976) contain invaluable articles, including in the latter a fine historiographical review-essay by Irwin Yellowitz. These supplement Elias Tcherikower's pathbreaking *The Early Jewish Labor Movement in the United States* (1961) and Melech Epstein's *Jewish Labor in U.S.A.* (1969). Will Herberg's "The Jewish Labor Movement in the United States," *American Jewish Year Book* 53 (1952) is a penetrating survey, and Moses Rischin, "The Jewish Labor Movement in America: A Social Interpretation," *Labor History* 4 (1963), underscores the wider significance of the subject. Finally, Irwin Yellowitz, "Jewish Immigrants and the American Labor Movement, 1900–1920," *American Jewish History* 71 (December 1981), pp. 188–217, recounts the often stormy relationship between Jewish labor and the labor movement at large.

PART FOUR

COMING TO TERMS WITH AMERICA

The era of mass Jewish immigration into the United States ended with World War I, as wartime conditions and then restrictive quotas stemmed the human tide. Soon, for the first time in many decades, the majority of American Jews would be native born. Where the central focus of American Jewish life had been concentrated on problems of immigration and absorption, American Jewry now entered a period of stable consolidation. The "second generation" moved up into the middle class and out to more fashionable neighborhoods, creating new institutions—synagogue-centers, progressive Hebrew schools, and the like—as they went. "Americanization" stopped being a serious community concern at this point; history had proved that East European Jews would become Americans with a vengeance. The question now was whether, as Americans, they would still remain Jews. Programs designed to ensure that they would do so became high community priorities.

With stability and the rise of a new generation came a growing commitment to communal unity. Germans and East Europeans in America had been drawing closer together even before World War I. After the war, given the growth of external threats directed against all Jews, and the increasing internal pressure for unity coming from young ones, the process of ethnicization speeded up. Leaving old world divisions behind, Jews began to coalesce into an avowedly *American* Jewish community—a community that could attempt, at least on some issues, to speak with a single voice.

Even as the community was uniting, however, it was being rent asunder in new ways. The three-part division among Orthodox, Conservative, and Reform Jews, firmly institutionalized in this period, gave expression to long-standing intracommunal conflicts over rituals, beliefs, and attitudes toward tradition and change. The issue of Zionism proved even more divisive, since it raised fundamental questions about the meaning of American Jewish life, the obligations of Jews to the country in which they lived, and the relationship of American Jews to the Jewish people as a whole.

By the eve of World War II, then, American Jewry presented a mixed picture: united in some respects, divided in others. It was a community at home in America and proud of its achievements, but still uncertain of its identity or its position vis-à-vis other Jewish communities in the world. Many anticipated a long period of transition, during which time Jews in America would organize and gradually assume new responsibilities for their brethren worldwide. But as Hitler's armies began to reduce European centers of Jewry to ashes, it became clear that that was not to be. Instead, given the crisis in Europe, the mantle of Jewish leadership fell to American Jewry at once.

CHAPTER 13

The passions engendered by World War I set off a period of intense social tension in America. The civil rights of many were violated, and innocent people fell prey to hysteria-driven mobs. At first, most hostility focused upon German-Americans and those deemed for one reason or another insufficiently patriotic. Before long, however, Catholics, "radicals," and Jews also felt the sting of popular animus. Anti-Semitism became an increasingly serious problem.

Anti-Jewish hatred was not a new phenomenon in America; it had waxed and waned periodically, and, as we have seen, rose to a particular peak during the Civil War. During the late nineteenth century, America witnessed an unprecedented increase in social anti-Semitism, mostly directed at upwardly mobile German Jews, who found themselves denied membership in certain clubs and refused admittance to certain resorts. Public and private expressions of anti-Semitism, particularly directed against immigrants, also increased during this period, as did the appearance of anti-Semitic images in print.

To be sure, anti-Semitism formed only one side—the dark side—of Jewish-Christian relations in America; on the bright side lay many examples of warm interreligious friendship coupled with severe condemnations of religious prejudice of every sort. Furthermore, the American strain of anti-Semitism proved less virulent than the European variety, given America's constitutional ideals and liberal traditions, its pluralism (pluralism also meant that Jews were far from the only group facing prejudice), its two-party system (that saw both parties vie for Jewish votes), and the fact that Jews could fight back freely against anti-Semitism, without fearing—as some did in countries where Jews had only recently been emancipated—that their rights would be taken away. Still, unpleasant anti-Semitic incidents did occur, and with increasing frequency. They caused Jews considerable anguish and raised disquieting fears about the future.

The first significant incident to arouse the Jewish community in the twentieth century was the Leo Frank case in Atlanta. Frank, a twenty-nine-year-old Jewish factory superintendent, was convicted in 1913 of murdering one of his employees, fourteen-year-old Mary Phagan, and dumping her body in the basement of the pencil factory where they both worked. The case attracted widespread publicity, and much attention centered on Frank's religion. Crowds outside the courthouse chanted "Hang the Jew!" The Jewish community's efforts to help Frank resulted in religious polarization. When Georgia governor John Slaton, unpersuaded that Frank was the murderer, commuted his sentence in 1915 from death to life in prison, a mob broke into the jail, kidnapped Frank, and lynched him: the first known lynching of a Jew in American history. Only recently, an eyewitness has confirmed what many for so long believed: Mary Phagan was murdered by the janitor of the pencil factory, the "star witness" against Frank. Frank himself was innocent.

The Frank case, in spite of its notoriety, was an isolated incident. Its effects were felt mainly in the South, and outside Atlanta the case was soon forgotten. By contrast, Henry Ford's virulent and well-financed anti-Semitic campaign, discussed in the article that follows, had a nationwide impact. It pitted Jews against a genuine American hero, the manufacturer of the Model T car, and lasted for seven long years, reaching millions of people worldwide before Ford retracted and apologized in 1927. Rooted in traditional European Christian thought and modern Progressive-era American fears, Ford's anti-Semitism, as Leo Ribuffo, a leading student of American extremism, demonstrates, was a complex phenomenon related to social, cultural, economic, and psychological aspects of Ford's life. Ford used "the international Jew" as an organizing principle; it "explained" whatever he found wrong with the modern world. Neither logic nor contrary facts fazed him.

Sigmund Freud once observed that "when a delusion cannot be dissipated by the facts of reality, it probably does not spring from reality," and such was certainly the case with Ford. Yet to view him and other anti-Semites of his day merely in narrow pathological terms is not enough. Ribuffo's broader perspective, set against a wide canvas, discloses much more—both about American anti-Semitism and about the culture that nourished it.

Henry Ford and *The International Jew*

Leo P. Ribuffo

Although historians still disagree about the extent of anti-Semitism during the late nineteenth century, the dominant attitude among Christian Americans, as Leonard Dinnerstein rightly concludes, was an amalgam of "affection, curiosity, suspicion and rejection." Comparing Americans and Europeans, we can say that anti-Semitism in the United States was relatively less violent, less racist, and less central to the worldviews of those who accepted it.

The first two decades of the twentieth century witnessed a shift toward greater suspicion and rejection. The lynching of Leo Frank in 1915 was only the most dramatic incident in an era that marked, according to George Fredrickson, a peak of "formalized racism." After World War I, hostility toward Jews escalated, operating in three overlapping areas. First, "polite" anti-Semites, including President A. Lawrence Lowell of Harvard, restricted admissions to clubs, resorts, universities, and the professions. Second, supported by many leading psychologists, such popularizers as Lothrop Stoddard and Kenneth Roberts spread the Anglo-Saxon cult to a wide audience. Third, commentators and members of Congress increasingly associated Jews with radicalism in general and communism in particular. For example, Dr. George A. Simons, a former missionary in Russia, told a Senate committee that the "so-called Bolshevik movement" was "Yiddish." Simons's allegations, which particularly impressed Senator Knute Nelson, were largely endorsed by other witnesses, including a Northwestern University professor, a Commerce Department agent, two representatives of National City Bank, a YMCA official and vice counsel in Petrograd, and several Russian émigrés.

To Simons, "Yiddish" Bolshevism seemed to "dovetail" with the plot outlined in *The Protocols of the Learned Elders of Zion*. In this notorious forgery created by Russian royalists at the turn of the century, a leader of a secret Jewish world government allegedly explained the plot to destroy Christian civilization. For almost two thousand years, the Elders had been "splitting society by ideas" while manipulating economic and political power. Currently they popularized Darwinism, Marxism, "Nietzche-ism" and other anti-Christian doctrines, undermined clergy, corrupted governments, and arranged wars that would profit Jews while killing Gentiles. Above all, the conspirators controlled both the mechanisms of capitalism and the radical movements pretending to offer alternatives. The *Protocols'* generality left room for interpolations to fit local circumstances. Eventually, their basic charges were "Americanized" and disseminated under the imprimatur of a national hero, Henry Ford.

Along with the nation as a whole, Henry Ford faced a series of crises during the years 1915 to 1920. With the introduction of the Model T in 1908, he had begun to achieve his great goal, mass production of a reliable, inexpensive automobile. By the mid-1910s, his decision to freeze auto design and expand production instead of paying dividends alienated subordinates and minority stockholders. Undaunted, he fired employees who disagreed with him, bought out dissatisfied shareholders, and gained full control of the Ford Motor Company in 1920. Thereafter, except for his able son Edsel, he rarely encountered anyone who openly disagreed with him.

Ford became, in Keith Sward's words, "as inaccessible as the Grand Lama." He remained eager to offer wide-ranging advice, but now usually filtered opinions through Ernest G. Liebold, his secretary since 1911. An ambitious martinet, Liebold expanded his authority by exploiting Ford's quirks, such as his dislike of paperwork and refusal to read most correspondence. The secretary gladly managed public relations, issued statements or answered letters in Ford's name, and exercised power of attorney after 1918. Indeed, he substantially controlled Ford's access to the world outside Dearborn.

To promote the views that he developed in virtual seclusion, Ford in 1919 purchased a weekly newspaper. The *Dearborn Independent* was designed to disseminate practical "ideas and ideals" without distortion by the "world's channels of information." The Dearborn Publishing Company, moreover, looked like a family enterprise. Henry Ford, his wife Clara, and his son Edsel were respectively president, vice president, and treasurer. Editorship of the *Independent* was bestowed on E. G. Pipp, a friend of Ford who had edited the *Detroit News*. William J. Cameron, an intelligent but hard-drinking veteran of the *News*, listened to Ford's ruminations and then wrote "Mr. Ford's Page." Both men operated under the watchful eye of Liebold, who detested Pipp and barely tolerated Cameron.

Despite a promise on the masthead to chronicle "neglected truth," the *Independent* at first printed nothing extraordinary. It supported Prohibition, prison reform, the Versailles Treaty, and the League of Nations; yet, these serious issues often received less attention than light stories about prominent persons, cities, or colleges. For sixteen months, the newspaper did not mention an alleged Jewish conspiracy. The owner, however, had been contemplating the issue for several years, and had considered raising it during the 1918 senatorial campaign. After the election, Pipp recalled, Ford began to talk about Jews "frequently, almost continuously."

The source of Ford's animus remains obscure. Ford himself told Liebold and Fred Black, the *Independent* business manager, that Herman Bernstein, editor of the *Jewish Tribune*, and other passengers on Oscar II (the "peace ship" Ford charted in World War I) had blamed Jewish financiers for the war. Liebold, who said that unspecified behavior by Jewish journalists in Norway "confirmed" Ford's suspicions, obviously shared and encouraged the automaker's bias. Indeed, Ford's secretary suspected Jewish automobile dealers of thwarting company policy and, a generation later, still recalled *The International Jew* as a worthwhile enterprise. Closer to home, Clara Ford may have promoted her husband's bigotry. At least she opposed Jewish membership in the country club and urged Ford to fire an executive whose wife was half-Jewish.

Pipp acted briefly as a countervailing influence. Six months after buying the *Independent* in 1919, Ford wanted to run a series on Jewish subversion. The editor held out for almost a year. In April, 1920, he quit instead of sanctioning the articles. The imminent anti-Semitic campaign was probably not the only reason for Pipp's departure. Liebold had been undermining his authority and restricting access to Ford. When he resigned, Pipp joined a formidable list of former employees who had refused to be sycophants.

Because the office files of the *Dearborn Independent* were destroyed in 1963, and because other records for 1920 have disappeared, we must rely on scattered correspondence, self-serving reminiscences, and conjecture to trace the composition of *The International Jew*. Apparently research and writing began toward the end of Pipp's tenure. Investigators directed by Liebold forwarded anti-Semitic information to Dearborn where, Pipp recalled, Ford swallowed "all . . . that was dished out." William J. Cameron, who succeeded Pipp as editor, did most of the writing. Initially unaware of the *Protocols*, Cameron did little "preliminary work" for the first article. He read "whatever was around," including Werner Sombart's *The Jews and Modern Capitalism*. But Cameron's later protests that he considered the articles "useless" must not be taken at face value. Fred Black recalled that Cameron "walked the floor" for three months before agreeing to write *The International Jew*. Within a year or two, however, he came to believe most of what he wrote. In the meantime, along with other Ford employees, he followed orders.

The first article, "The International Jew: The World's Problem," appeared on May 20, 1920. Liebold had suggested the title and date of publication in order to coincide with an attack on "greedy" Jews by Leo Franklin, a prominent Detroit rabbi and Ford's former neighbor. Although the *Independent* promised further revelations, the staff seems not to have planned more than a month ahead. Indeed, Black thought that Ford himself did not anticipate a sustained campaign.

Yet several developments kept the series alive until January 14, 1922. Ford, Liebold, and—eventually—Cameron got wrapped up in their project. Ford visited the *Independent* almost every day, concerning himself only with "Mr. Ford's Page" and *The International Jew.* Despite their mutual hostility, Liebold and Cameron consulted often on the series, sometimes poring over articles together until three o'clock in the morning. Critics provided grist for the mill. When former President Taft or columnist Arthur Brisbane attacked *The International Jew,* they were denounced in subsequent articles as "gentile fronts." Moreover, Liebold's agents regularly supplied rumors, clippings, and forged documents.

The main detective operation, located on Broad Street in New York City, was managed by C. C. Daniels, a former lawyer for the Justice Department, whose aides, including several veterans of military intelligence, used secret identification numbers when contacting Dearborn. Norman Hapgood exaggerated only slightly when he said that the group "muckraked everybody who was a Jew or was suspected of being a Jew." It attracted "adventurers, detectives, and criminals" and gave credence to their stories. For example, though Daniels's brother Josephus, the secretary of the navy, might have told them otherwise, Ford investigators thought that President Wilson took orders from Justice Brandeis over a private telephone line. Daniels's special concerns included Eugene Meyer, Jr., of the Federal Reserve Board, whom he accused of blocking Ford's acquisition of the nitrate plants at Muscle Shoals, Alabama. "As you know," he wrote to Liebold in 1922, "locks and bars make no difference to that portion of God's chosen people seeking to displace the stars and stripes with the Jewish national flag and that calls Lenine [sic] the greatest Statesman alive."

Liebold recalled that he needed few European agents because "people came over here and revealed their stories to us." Russian émigrés ultimately provided a copy of the *Protocols*. Here, too, slight surviving evidence obscures the story. Sometime before the summer of 1920, Liebold apparently met Paquita de Shishmareff, a Russian émigré married to an American soldier. Liebold told Ford that Shishmareff, who is better known as Mrs. Leslie Fry, possessed "full and thorough knowledge of all Jewish operations in Europe." According to Liebold's reminiscences, she provided his "first knowledge" of the *Protocols* as well as a copy of the forgery. Whatever the original source, the *Independent* staff was studying the *Protocols* in the middle of June, 1920. On June 10, W. G. Enyon, a company employee in Delaware, dispatched several copies to Dearborn.

Starting with the July 24 article, the *Protocols* description of an international Jewish conspiracy provided the central thread of *The International Jew.*

For the next three years, Liebold expanded his contacts with Russian royalists and their dubious documents. In addition to Mrs. Fry, he consulted Boris Brasol, an erstwhile member of the Black Hundreds, and several of their friends. A Ford agent in Paris paid seven thousand francs for a report by former Russian Judge Nicholas Sokoloff purporting to show that Jewish conspirators had murdered the Romanovs. Liebold was impressed and invited Sokoloff to Dearborn. The émigrés soon discovered that they were treated as capriciously as other Ford employees. When Sokoloff fell ill, Liebold "hustled" him out of Michigan, and later refused to support his widow and orphans.

Although the *Dearborn Independent* was indebted to émigrés for the *Protocols*, *The International Jew* was not, as Norman Cohn contends, "far more a Russo-German than an American product." The alleged manifestations of the "world's foremost problem" coincided with issues that had unsettled the United States since the Civil War.

First, the *Independent* complained that both the monopolistic activities of large corporations and the countervailing actions of government had produced a "steady curtailment" of freedom.

Second, joining the search for moral order that intensified after World War I, the *Independent* condemned new styles in dress and music, changing sexual mores, Hollywood "lasciviousness," and the "filthy tide" sweeping over the theater. Sensitive to unraveling family bonds, the newspaper warned that children were drawn from "natural leaders in the home, church, and school to institutionalized 'centers' and scientific 'play spots.' "

Third, the *Independent* addressed the issue that had grown in importance since the "endless stream" of immigrants had begun to arrive in the 1880s: What was Americanism? These strangers, especially residents of the "unassimilated province" known as New York City, were responsible for the "mad confusion that passes in some quarters as a picture" of the United States.

Fourth, the *Independent* worried about the problem of determining truth in the modern world. Even before the anti-Semitic campaign, the newspaper had shared the prevailing fear of deception by propaganda. People were "born believers" who needed "deeply" to affirm something. But it was hard to know what to believe. *The International Jew* protested that man was ruled "by a whole company of ideas into whose authority he has not inquired at all." Not only did he live by the "say of others," but "terrific social pressures" on behalf of "broadmindedness" discouraged probes beneath conventional wisdom. Sounding like Walter Lippmann or Harold Lasswell, the newspaper warned that credulity was especially dangerous in the current "era of false labels."

The *Protocols* offered a "clue to the modern maze." Hedging on the question of authenticity, as Liebold did in correspondence, the *Independent* said that the documents themselves were "comparatively unimportant." They gave "meaning to certain previously observed facts." Whether or not an Elder of Zion actually gave these lectures, it was clear that Jews used ideas to "corrupt Collective Opinion," controlled finance, sponsored revolution, and were "everywhere" exercising power.

Following a "historical" survey, *The International Jew* purported to document the current activities of Hebrew capitalists, radicals, and propagandists. In the economic sphere, the *Independent* distinguished between Jewish "finance" and the "creative industry" dominated by Gentiles. From the Rothschild family on down, Jews were "essentially money-lenders" who rarely had a "permanent interest" in production. Rather, they seized a commodity "at just the point in its passage from producer to consumer where the heaviest profit can be extracted." Squeezing the "neck of the bottle" in this way, they dominated the grain, copper, fur, and cotton markets. The rising national debt was another "measure of our enslavement." Furthermore, in 1913, Paul Warburg, a German Jew who had emigrated "for the express purpose of changing our financial system," convinced Congress to pass the Federal Reserve Act. The Reserve Board helped the "banking aristocracy" to contact currency and centralize funds for speculation.

Through four volumes, Jewish vices appeared as the reverse of any "American view." The dichotomies between making and getting, morality and sensuality, fair trade and chicanery, "creative labor" and exploitation, heroism and cowardice, were only the beginning. Some of the most important differences impinged on politics. Anglo-Saxons had created the press to prevent secret domination by any minority, but Jews twisted news for their own advantage. Democratic procedures were another Anglo-Saxon inheritance; Jews "instinctively" favored autocracy. One of the "higher traits" of "our race" fostered obliviousness to Hebrew machinations. Eschewing conspiracies themselves, Anglo-Saxons neither expected them among other groups nor followed the available clues "through long and devious and darkened channels."

Above all, Gentiles advanced "by individual initiative," while Jews took advantage of unprecedented "racial loyalty and solidarity." Because success—a preeminent American and "Fordian" value—could "not be attacked nor condemned [*sic*]," the *Independent* hesitated to criticize Jews for doing "extraordinarily" well. Neither could it concede superiority to another "race." In essence, therefore, the newspaper cried foul. Because Jews took advantage of their position as an "international nation," it was "difficult to measure gentile and Jewish achievement by the same standard." Jews captured the "highest places" only because they began with an unfair advantage.

The *Independent* said that Jewish solidarity required "one rule for the Gentile and one for the Jews." In fact, the newspaper itself not surprisingly held to the double standard. It condemned acts by Jews which, if done by Christians, would have been considered innocuous, legitimate, or admirable. The wartime ban on German and the fundamentalist effort to drive Darwin from the classroom were acceptable; Jewish objections to *The Merchant of Venice* violated "American principles." George Creel's chairmanship of the Committee on Public Information did not prompt a discussion of Protestant traits; Carl Laemmle's production of *The Beast of Berlin* for the same committee was a "lurid" attempt to profit from war. Jacob Schiff's use of dollar diplomacy on behalf of Russian Jews seemed sinister; efforts by E. H. Harriman to squeeze concessions from the Czar passed without comment. Similarly, Irish-American agitation about the Versailles Treaty went unremarked; Jewish concern elicited complaints about the "kosher conference." The immigrant's willingness to change his name was seen as evidence of duplicity, not of a desire to assimilate.

In addition to assuming the worst, the *Independent* singled out Jewish participants in any endeavor and concluded that they were *acting as Jews*. But while Paul Warburg did play a major role in the passage of the Federal Reserve Act, he acted on behalf of major bankers of all faiths. Although the War Industries Board did create a "system of control such as the United States government never possessed," Chairman Baruch believed that the general welfare was synonymous with capitalism, not Judaism. Jews may have been represented disproportionately in the Soviet hierarchy, but they used their positions to further Marxist ends, including the secularization of Russian Jewry; almost none of the "Yiddish" Bolsheviks spoke Yiddish. In 1911 Jacob Schiff's objections to the Russian-American commercial treaty would have meant little if outrage among grass-roots and elite Gentiles had not moved three hundred Representatives to agree with him.

The disposition to single out Jews and to create a separate standard for them derived from three circumstances. First, as Irving Howe notes, Jewish immigrants from Eastern Europe were "radically different from the dominant Protestant culture." The *Independent* was incensed by this lack of "conformity" to the nation's "determining ideals and ideas"; the recent arrivals seemed to think that the United States was "not any definite thing yet." Second, as John Higham argues, Jews attracted special attention because they were relatively more successful—and more visible—than other groups in the "new immigration." Third, despite professed indifference to Jewish religious practices, the *Independent* supposed that acceptance of the nation's ideals meant acquiesence in its "predominant Christian character." Jews, however, were determined "to wipe out of public life" every Christian reference. Their "impertinent interferences" included contempt for Sunday blue laws and protests against Christmas celebrations and Bible reading in public schools. Louis Marshall, president of the American Jewish Committee, even said that the United States was "not a Christian country." Such actions by a race that had had "no hand" in building the nation naturally stirred a "whirlwind of resentment."

From this matter-of-fact amalgamation of Christianity and "100 percent Americanism," the *Independent* moved to theology. The transition was easy for

William J. Cameron, who had preached occasionally, without benefit of ordination, to a "people's church" in Brooklyn, Michigan. Accepting the mangled history and biblical exegesis of the Anglo-Israelite Federation, Cameron believed that contemporary Anglo-Saxons had descended from the lost tribes of Israel. Hence they were "chosen" to receive the blessings that God had promised to Abraham's progeny. But this divine choice of Israel did not extend to Judea, or to the Jewish offspring of the two southern tribes. On the contrary, Anglo-Israelites were often hostile to contemporary Jews.

Fred Black speculated that Cameron's Anglo-Israelism had prepared him to accept conspiratorial anti-Semitism. Certainly the editor's faith gave a peculiar twist to the discussion of religion in *The International Jew.* Citing the *Protocols'* injunction to undermine clergy, the *Independent* blamed Jews for biblical criticism and "liberal" Protestantism, a typically mislabeled doctrine that reduced Jesus to a "well-meaning but wholly mistaken Jewish prophet." Discriminating between Israel and the rebellious Judeans, the weekly said that Jesus was not Jewish in the modern sense of the word. Neither was Moses nor any disciple—except Judas. Fundamentalists also read the Bible through "Jewish spectacles" when they confused modern Hebrews with God's chosen people. Not only did Jews reject Christ, but they abandoned the Old Testament in favor of the Talmud's "rabbinical speculation." Instead of fulfilling the prophetic promise of a return to Jerusalem, as many fundamentalists supposed, Zionism represented the "Bolshevist spirit all over again."

In the broadest sense, then, the *Independent* presented the "Jewish question" as a contest between two peoples, each supposing that God was on its side. There was "no idea deeper in Judaism" than the belief in divine election. But, the newspaper protested, the "Anglo-Saxon Celtic race" was the "Ruling People, chosen throughout the centuries to Master the world." Beneath the bragging, however, there lay a hint of the insecurity that fueled nativism in the 1920s. On the one hand, Yankees could beat Jews "any time" in a fair fight. Still the Kehillah's "extraordinary unity" was impressive. Unpatriotic American "mongrels" and "lick spittle Gentile Fronts who have no tribe . . . would be better off if they had one-thousandth the racial sense which the Jew possesses."

The *Independent* maintained that its pages contained "NO ATTACK . . . ON THE JEWS AS JEWS" (though it was not always possible to "distinguish the group" deserving censure). Occasionally the weekly made ostentatious efforts to sound fair. It quoted admirable (meaning unobtrusive) Jews, admitted that Paul Warburg's Federal Reserve Act contained "important improvements," and recognized Bernard Baruch's intelligence and energy. On January 17, 1922, a "candid address" to Jews urged them to recover Old Testament morality and practice "social responsibility." If Jews stopped trying "to twist Americanism into something else," they could participate without objection in finance, entertainment, and government.

The newspaper's remedies for the "world's foremost problem" combined faith in expertise, national unity, and publicity. A "scientific study of the Jewish Question" would forestall prejudice by transforming gentile assailants and Jewish defenders "both into investigators." Research by "qualified persons" would yield "society's point of view" which, the *Independent* claimed, was the perspective taken in its pages. In the interim, to combat Jewish adulteration of products, a consumer movement should "educate people in the art of buying." Most important, "clear publicity" must be the "chief weapon" against the Hebrew cabal. Their program would then be "checked the moment it is perceived and identified." Russia, Germany, and England had failed to solve the "Jewish Question," but the United States would succeed—without violence.

While new installments of *The International Jew* continued to unroll in its pages, the *Independent* collected in book form articles that had already appeared; sometimes two hundred thousand copies were printed in a single edition. The staff sent complimentary volumes to locally influential citizens, especially clergymen, bankers, and stockbrokers.

To supplement *The International Jew,* the *Independent* ran "Jewish World Notes." This regular feature charged that Madame Curie was treated less well in New York than the spurious Jewish scientist Albert Einstein, chided Billy Sunday for ignorance of the Elders' conspiracy, derided Zionist immigration to Palestine, and feared that President-elect Harding, like his predecessors, was falling under Jewish influence. The *Independent* also kept up persistent attacks on alcohol, tobacco, movies, comic books, jazz, Wobblies, Soviets, and immigration. Simultaneously looking to Ford's financial interests, editor Cameron promoted highway construction, opposed federal aid to railroads, and looked greedily toward Muscle Shoals. In 1922, as Ford began to covet the presidency, his newspaper dutifully emphasized the inadequacy of other possible nominees.

If the *Independent* had offered only a perverse mixture of reform, eccentricity, internationalism, and nativism, it would have attracted relatively little attention. But *The International Jew* was extraordinary even for the "tribal twenties." Opponents mobilized quickly. The Federal Council of Churches condemned the articles in December, 1920. A month later, without specifically mentioning Ford, 119 prominent Christians, including William Howard Taft, Woodrow Wilson, and William Cardinal O'Connell, signed "The Perils of Racial Prejudice," a statement asking Gentiles to halt the "vicious propaganda" against Jews. Officials in several cities considered censoring the *Independent* or removed it from public libraries.

At first many Jews wondered, as Louis Marshall asked, if *The International Jew* had Ford's personal "sanction." Returning Ford's annual gift, a new sedan, his former neighbor Rabbi Leo Franklin warned Ford that he was inflicting harm on innocent people. Similarly, Herman Bernstein, a voyager on *Oscar II*, appealed to the automaker's "humanitarian" nature. Even after Jewish spokesmen recognized the depth of Ford's commitment to the anti-Semitic campaign, they disagreed on countermeasures. Following an initial protest, Marshall worked behind the scenes, sponsoring Bernstein's rebuttal, *The History of a Lie*, recruiting signers for "The Perils of Radical Prejudice," and in mid-1921 urging President Harding to intervene. Others preferred more militant tactics. The *American Hebrew* challenged Ford to abide by an impartial investigation, attorneys for the B'nai B'rith Anti-Defamation League advocated laws against the libel of groups, Yiddish newspapers rejected advertisements for Ford cars, and individual Jews refused to buy them.

The International Jew elicited support as well as opposition. Colonel Charles S. Bryan of the War Department appreciated particularly the attack on "East Side Scum." The journalist W. J. Abbot expressed "sympathy" with Ford's views and critic John J. Chapman hailed the "lucidity and good temper" of Volume II. C. Mobray White, an "authority" on revolution for the National Civic Federation, urged supplementary publication of the *Protocols*. According to Liebold, J. P. Morgan, Jr., liked the series. The number of *Independent* readers fluctuated widely over short periods because Ford dealers, who were ordered to sell the paper, showed little enthusiasm for the task. It appears, however, that *The International Jew* temporarily attracted new subscribers.

Liebold responded to protests and praise. Agreeing with the *Independent* that good Jews had "nothing to fear," he urged them to join Ford's crusade against the worldwide peril. But his supercilious tone was hardly reassuring. He accused Marshall of sounding like a "Bolshevik orator," lectured Rabbi Franklin on the importance of principles, and generally praised the newspaper's reliance on "actual facts." Conversely, he thanked friends of *The International Jew* and encouraged their efforts, telling C. Mobray White, for example, that there was "quite a field" for distribution of the *Protocols*. Occasionally he was forced to retreat. "Amazed" by the accusation that he had been Wilson's Jewish "mouthpiece," columnist David Lawrence wrote to Ford, whom he considered a friend. A testy exchange followed with Liebold, the perennial shield, who finally said that the automaker had had "no knowledge" of the articles relating to Lawrence.

Indeed, consistently distancing his employer from *The International Jew*, Liebold answered protests in his own name and testified in 1924 that Ford devoted his time to the company's "numerous and complex" operations. The *Independent* promoted the same fiction. Because Cameron explicitly attacked Jews on every page except "Mr. Ford's Page," devoted followers could believe that Ford was too busy making cars to supervise his own newspaper. The strategy was transparent, but it laid the groundwork for his face-saving retraction in 1927. The pause did not mean that Ford had begun to doubt the existence of a Jewish conspiracy. He still raised the matter in interviews. In addition, Liebold's agents collected fresh material which, Pipp warned, Ford would order into print "whenever the whim may strike him again." Apparently the whim struck within a year. In November, 1922, anti-Semitic references resurfaced in the *Independent*.

Starting in April, 1924, the *Independent* focused on "Jewish Exploitation of Farmers' Organizations," and on Aaron Sapiro, the alleged chief exploiter. After serving as counsel to the California marketing bureau, Sapiro began in 1919 to organize farm cooperatives in other states. Within four years, he created the National Council of Farmer's Cooperative Marketing Associations, whose constituent groups represented 700,000 farmers. Presidents Harding and Coolidge, Secretary of Commerce Herbert Hoover, former Governor Frank O. Lowden of Illinois, and Senator Arthur Capper, leader of the congressional farm bloc, encouraged Sapiro and sometimes provided substantial assistance. By 1923, however, many cooperative associations collapsed and enthusiasm began to ebb among farmers. In 1926 the National Council quietly disbanded.

Sapiro was a natural target. Cherishing the myth of the sturdy Christian farmer, the *Independent* and its publisher assumed that Jews entered agriculture only as greedy middlemen. Ford joked that he would pay one thousand dollars to anyone who brought in a Jewish farmer "dead or alive." Moreover, farm cooperatives fostered the "steady trend toward systematization" deplored in *The International Jew.* And Sapiro's financial backers included two of *The International Jew's* foremost villains, Bernard Baruch and Eugene Meyer, Jr.

Still, the *Independent*'s assault had an ironic aspect because Ford and Sapiro shared more common ground that either realized. Like Ford, Sapiro cherished farming as a virtuous way of life untainted by radicalism or federal planning. Furthermore, he too was a proud man who resented attacks on his character. In January, 1925, therefore, Sapiro sent a thirty-one-page letter to Ford and his associates, demanding a retraction of "Jewish Exploitation." When the *Independent* refused to comply, Sapiro sued Ford and the Dearborn Publishing Company for a million dollars in order to vindicate "myself and my race."

Sapiro's was the third suit provoked by Ford's anti-Semitism. In January, 1921, Morris Gest had sought five million dollars in damages because the *Independent* accused him of producing lewd plays. Two years later Herman Bernstein had filed a complaint denying that he had told Ford of an international Jewish conspiracy. Neither case came to trial. Nor did they alter the newspaper's course.

The *Independent* repudiated *The International Jew* only after Sapiro pressed the issue. In March, 1927, his suit alleging 141 libels by Ford and the Dearborn Publishing Company began in Federal District Court in Detroit. Opening for the plaintiff, attorney William Henry Gallagher called the *Independent* Ford's "mouthpiece" and held him responsible for malicious attacks on "Sapiro and his race." The defense, led by Senator James A. Reed (Democrat, Missouri), responded that the weekly had had a "moral duty" to expose Sapiro as a "grafter, faker, fraud, and cheat." The *Independent*'s discussion of Jews was irrelevant, Reed added, because the law did not recognize libel of a "race"; Sapiro raised the religious issue merely to "capitalize" on sympathy. Finally, making the familiar distinction between Ford and his newspaper, Reed said that the automaker had not read the series on Sapiro "to this blessed day."

The rival attorneys were skilled and well matched. Gallagher raised doubts about Cameron's sobriety and Ford's intelligence. On the other hand, defense objections excluded from evidence letters to Ford protesting inaccuracies in "Jewish Exploitation of Farmers' Organizations." Gallagher called James Martin Miller, a former *Independent* employee, to testify that Ford personally had charged Sapiro with manipulating agriculture for a "bunch of Jews." Asking one question to reveal that Miller had sued for back pay, Reed dismissed him, "*That's* all." The two sides persistently clashed over Gallagher's effort to broaden the discussion of anti-Semitism. Poking fun at the defense's "extraordinary sensitiveness" to the word "Jew," Gallagher said that comparable "apprehension" three years earlier would have prevented the suit.

The most famous figure in the case avoided an appearance. At first, Ford planned to take the stand. Then he changed his mind and walled himself off from process servers. Company officials claimed that a subpoena intended for Ford was mistakenly presented to his brother. After Gallagher threatened to begin contempt proceedings, Ford's lawyers said that he would speak voluntarily. On March 31, however, he was the victim of a strange accident. A Studebaker sedan forced Ford's car off the road and down a fifteen-foot embankment. The automaker was taken to Henry Ford Hospital where he was treated and shielded by friendly physicians.

Sapiro suggested that Ford "faked" the accident, which has never been fully explained, because his "vanity was punctured at the collapse of his case." Indeed, sensing the jury's skepticism, defense lawyers did fear the verdict. On April 11, using reports from some of the fifty Ford service agents who prowled through the courthouse, they told Judge Raymond that a juror, Mrs. Cora Hoffman, had lied during the venire and later was offered a bribe by a Jew who wanted to convict Ford. Because Mrs. Hoffman's vehement denials appeared in the press, Raymond granted a defense motion of mistrial on April 21. The Court scheduled a retrial for September 12 as lawyers continued to spar. Valuing Raymond's restrictions on discussion of the "Jewish Question," Reed blocked Gallagher's attempt to change judges.

Judge Raymond adhered to the legal fiction that the *Independent*'s attack on Jews was largely irrelevant to the suit, but Ford knew better. By repudiating *The International Jew,* he could open the way to an out-of-court settlement and avoid testifying. During a May 11 meeting with Arthur Brisbane, who remained friendly even though the *Independent* labeled him a "gentile front," Ford mentioned his decision to close the newspaper. At roughly the same time, he told Joseph Palma, head of the United States Secret Service field office in New York City, that he had underestimated the impact of the Jewish series; he wanted the "wrong righted." Serving as Ford's emissaries, Palma and Earl J. David, a former assistant attorney general, met secretly with Louis Marshall of the American Jewish Committee. On July 9, Ford announced through Brisbane that "articles reflecting upon Jews" would "never again" appear in the *Independent*. Liebold, Cameron, and Edsel Ford had known nothing of the negotiations.

The retraction, written by Marshall, allowed Ford to slip through the loophole held open since 1920 by Liebold, Cameron, and a formidable array of lawyers. Ford said that he had failed to "keep informed" about the actions of his newspaper. Thus he was "deeply mortified" to learn that the *Independent* had reprinted a series based on the "gross forgeries," the *Protocols of Zion*. "Fully aware of the virtues of the Jewish people," he begged their forgiveness, promised to withdraw *The International Jew* from circulation, and pledged "future friendship and good will." Marshall considered the statement "humiliating" and was surprised that Ford accepted it.

Sapiro and Bernstein quickly dropped their suits in return for apologies and reimbursement of legal expenses. On July 30, the charge that Sapiro had belonged to an international conspiracy was formally "withdrawn" by the *Independent*. Sapiro pronounced himself "entirely satisfied," embraced the illusion that Ford had been "misled," and claimed credit for helping a "great man get right."

Unfortunately the apologies of 1927, like the remission of 1922, did not mean that Ford had "got right." He closed the *Independent* on December 30, 1927 but—contrary to his lawyers' promise to Marshal—kept Liebold and Cameron, both unrepentant, in his employ. He ordered destruction of thousands of copies of *The International Jew;* yet, despite entreaties by Marshall and Bernstein, barely publicized his retraction in Europe. His subordinates intervened to halt circulation abroad only when pressed by Jewish leaders. Furthermore, Ford informed the *Manchester Guardian* in 1940 that "international Jewish bankers" caused World War II. At roughly the same time, he told the nativist Gerald L. K. Smith that he had allowed Bennett to forge his signature on the retraction, hoped to someday reissue *The International Jew* and urged Smith to do so if he could not.

Partly due to Ford's laxity, the series continued to circulate among the "rabid Jew-baiters" whom the *Independent* professed to disdain. Norman Cohn estimates that *The International Jew* "probably did more than any other work to make the *Protocols* world-famous." The Nazi youth leader Baldur von Schirach recalled the "great influence" of the books on young Germans of his generation. In *Mein Kampf*, Hitler applauded Ford's efforts. Within the United States,

The International Jew provided a "usable past" for anti-Semites like Smith, who ultimately published an abridgement. As early as 1922, Norman Hapgood angrily held Ford responsible for letting "loose a malicious force that added fury to similar forces already in existence."

Detached analysis of *The International Jew* and its supplements illuminates attitudes toward Jews as well as broader aspects of our culture. First, the text undermines the assumption that Christian belief and practice hardly influenced anti-Semitism in the United States. *The International Jew* was imbued with Ford's faith that the national "genius" was "Christian in the broadest sense" and destined to remain so. The series portrayed a clash between two "chosen" peoples, and William J. Cameron, the chief compiler, sometimes cast the conflict in terms of Anglo-Israelite theology. Although we cannot infer the attitudes of a complex society from motifs in a single literary source, there is warrant for paying closer attention to the Christian roots of American anti-Semitism.

Second, a reading of *The International Jew* prompts yet another consideration of the relationship between "populism," "progressivism," and anti-Semitism. While Ford and *Independent* editor Cameron remained aloof from populism, their weekly explicitly endorsed "sane progressivism." The adjective may seem inappropriate, but the general identification makes sense. Ford contributed $36,000 to Woodrow Wilson's campaign in 1916 and was convinced by the president to run for senator two years later. Throughout the 1920s he was hailed as the preeminent business statesman whose commitment to efficiency, social service, and paternal labor relations promised industrial peace. Certainly *The International Jew* contained characteristic progressive themes. For example, adapting a growing consumer movement to its anti-Semitic ends, the *Independent* urged a boycott of Jewish merchants. Furthermore, the "Jewish question" must be subjected to "scientific study" by experts.

The most striking progressive legacy was *The International Jew*'s assertion that "clear publicity" was an American alternative to Jewish disfranchisement or pogroms. Richard Hofstadter observed that progressive intellectuals, scholars, and journalists alike "confirmed, if they did not create a fresh mode of criticism" that purported to uncover "reality." They believed that "reality" was "hidden, neglected, and offstage," something to be dug out from under superficial explanations. Norman Hapgood shrewdly saw that Ford's detectives "muckraked" Jews and suspected Jews. Ford apparently shared the *Independent*'s faith in publicity. In *My Life and Work,* he maintained that the Jewish threat could be "controlled by mere exposure."

Third, an interpretation of *The International Jew* helps to sort out "crucial differences in the variety of things called anti-Semitism." The *Independent* distinguished its answers to the "Jewish Question"—consumer protection, scientific study, and publicity—from violent European solutions. Ford himself claimed only to oppose "false ideas," called hatred of individuals "neither American nor Christian," and remained personally fond of several Jews, including the architect Albert Kahn, baseball player Hank Greenberg, and Rabbi Leo Franklin; he was perplexed by Franklin's refusal of a sedan in 1920 to protest *The International Jew.* These actions by Ford and his newspaper, though eccentric or self-serving, nevertheless point to complexities within nativism during the "tribal twenties."

A venerable nativist position, presented eloquently in Josiah Strong's 1885 polemic, *Our Country,* held that the "new immigration," including Jews, was *culturally* regressive and therefore must be taught superior Anglo-Saxon ways. The racial theorists who gained prominence after 1900 held that the "new immigration," including those whom Kenneth Roberts called "mongoloid" Jews, was *innately* inferior and therefore incapable of learning Anglo-Saxon ways. Whereas Strong suggested that "our country" might benefit from a blend of "races" under Anglo-Saxon guidance, Madison Grant, the premier "Nordic" ideologue in 1915, insisted that assimilation would backfire, producing a "mongrel" nation. Although the doctrine of inherent racial inferiority never fully superseded the earlier tradition, by the 1920s most nativists mixed the two attitudes in varying proportions. For example, Ford and the *Independent* sometimes ascribed behavior by Eastern European immigrants to "nasty Orientalism" or "Tartar" origins. More often, however, they complained that these Jews refused to be like Anglo-Saxons. In the final analysis, *The International Jew,* the major nativist tract of the 1920s, was closer to Strong's assimilationist ethnocentrism than to Grant's biological determinism.

The distinction may provide little comfort to victims of discrimination (though in the long run they gain from it), but it does suggest that the nation's liberal tradition even affects our nativists. Hence, they are more likely than counterparts in Germany or France to judge ethnic targets, in this case Jews, on the basis of individual behavior instead of putative genetic traits. Significantly, the *Independent* did not concur in the basic premise of *Mein Kampf,* that all Jews betrayed "definite racial characteristics."

Fourth, we must ask how thousands, perhaps hundreds of thousands of readers could believe *The International Jew*'s farfetched thesis that a worldwide Jewish network threatened their way of life. Richard Hofstadter maintains that adherents to such conspiracy theories betray a "paranoid style," a frame of mind qualitatively different from normal thinking. Indeed, the notion that bigots make up a psychologically abnormal fringe is popular. It is nonetheless misleading. Much as they exaggerate the tolerance of the dominant culture, leading scholars also mistakenly assume that it was imbued with their own version of liberal rationalism. During the 1920s, however, following a government-sponsored war scare and Red Scare, belief in some sort of conspiracy theory may have been the norm instead of an aberration. In this context, *The*

International Jew's perverse accomplishment was to combine the inchoate anti-Semitism of the Progressive era with the postwar fear of hidden forces.

To be sure, belief in a cabal of Zionist Elders (as opposed to conspiracies by Huns and Bolsheviks) was not endorsed by the government or by a majority of the population. Still we cannot assume that conspiratorial anti-Semites were pathological. The sociologists Peter Berger and Thomas Luckmann recently stressed an old insight, that our knowledge rests on the authority of others and remains plausible only as long as they confirm it. But these significant "others" need not represent the whole society. In the United States, semiautonomous cultures have often nurtured unconventional worldviews in the face of sensible objections by outsiders.

Finally, what disposed Ford to agree with Liebold that there was a Jewish conspiracy instead of accepting counterarguments? As we have seen, Ford's animosity toward Jews grew during the personal crisis after 1915. Seeking to make restitution to the farmer, he was drawn to the convention that Jews were, as Edward Ross wrote, "slovenly" agriculturalists. Moreover, whether or not the process is called projection, Ford attributed to Jews traits that he refused to recognize in himself. For example, in 1920–1921, shortly after Ford had tricked stockholders and exploited his dealers to gain full control of the company, his newspaper accused Jews of violating business ethics. Ford thought that Sapiro inflicted "systematization" on the farmer, but his own machines did more to alter rural mores.

In 1923, more than one-third of 260,000 voters polled by *Collier's* favored Ford for president. They overlooked, if they did not endorse, his personal peculiarities, repression of labor, and sponsorship of anti-Semitism. Ford's reputation thrived partly because it was protected by Liebold and the public-relations experts who followed. But they built on a popular craving to esteem an unspoiled country mechanic whose ingenuity and effort made a contribution to the general welfare as well as a fortune. Samuel Marquis reported that many workers on the assembly line denied that Ford knew of their misery. Similarly, Jews initially doubted that he sanctioned the *Independent*'s attack; their praise of Ford in 1927 moved Louis Marshall to warn against excess. Like their gentile neighbors, Jews wanted to believe in self-made men, benevolent capitalists, and a just system that produced them. In ways that Ford failed to comprehend, these immigrants and their children were embracing American dreams and illusions.

CHAPTER 14

Even before mass Jewish immigration to America ended, American Jewish leaders began to turn their attention to the children of immigrants, "the second generation." Being American born, these children had no difficulty Americanizing; the problem was how to prevent them from Americanizing so much that they left their Judaism behind. Several prominent second-generation Jews spurned Judaism entirely; others intermarried. Fears for the future were widespread.

The Young Men's and Young Women's Hebrew Associations—forerunners of today's Jewish Community Centers—suggested one alternative. They offered social and cultural activities in a secular Jewish setting, and welcomed those who sought to be Jewish without being religious. Many, however, doubted that secular Judaism—whether this kind or that preached by the Jewish labor movement—would actually be strong enough to counteract fierce outside pressures to assimilate and intermarry. The synagogue, they warned, offered the only guarantee that Judaism would survive at all.

The synagogue, however, had to change. Young Jewish religious leaders, trained in America, talked of transforming it into a bustling, full-time "synagogue center," a hub of Jewish religious, educational, cultural, and social activities. They also advocated a new Americanized version of Judaism—not Reform Judaism, but a modern, decorous, and aesthetically pleasing traditional ritual, far removed from the "old fashioned" norm.

As early as 1886, advocates of an Americanized traditional Judaism established the Jewish Theological Seminary of America in New York. Reorganized in 1902 along somewhat more liberal lines, it became the training ground for Conservative rabbis committed to an historically evolving religious faith. Those with a more Orthodox bent often studied at Rabbi Isaac Elchanan Theological Seminary, founded in 1897. It merged in 1915 into what would later be known as Yeshiva University, and became the training ground for Modern Orthodox rabbis seeking to synthesize tradition with secular culture. Graduates of these two schools, much as they may have differed over theology and ritual, resembled one another in their determination to shape a distinctively American Judaism. Both sought to win second-generation Jews back to the synagogue.

Jeffrey Gurock, a leading student of Orthodox Judaism, traces these developments from where they began, in the Jewish community of Harlem in New York. He shows how the first synagogue centers—the work of young, American-trained rabbis, many of whom went on to distinguished careers—succeeded, and how synagogue centers spread, particularly through the Conservative movement. Within one generation, synagogues crowded with activities all through the week—sometimes more then than at Sabbath services—became common. The American synagogue had emerged.

The Emergence of the American Synagogue

Jeffrey S. Gurock

The earliest adumbrations of the Jewish center movement date back to the turn of the century and to a group of Harlem synagogues expressedly constituted to serve the needs of American-born Jewish young adults. The first, Beth Ha-Knesset Ha-Gadol, was organized in December 1896 by fifty men, all of whom, according to newspaper reports, were thirty-seven or younger, who had been born in New York City and had recently migrated from the Lower East Side. They held their first meeting at the Harlem Lyceum (107th Street and Third Avenue), soon purchasing a church at the corner of 109th Street and Madison Avenue, which they converted to a synagogue.

Six years later, responding to what was perceived to be a need for a "large well constructed Orthodox synagogue," Rabbi H. P. Mendes of the Spanish and Portuguese Synagogue and Rabbi Bernard Drachman of Congregation Zichron Ephraim joined with local Harlemites in establishing Congregation Shomre Emunah at 121st Street and Madison Avenue. The organizers of this synagogue promised services conducted according to "Orthodox ritual in an impressive decorous manner." They pledged to their prospective Americanized constituency that the unsightly noise, commotion, and blatant commercialism that attended the immigrant landsmanshaft congregation would find no place in the up-to-date Orthodox synagogue. In 1904 a second modern congregation, Congregation Mount Sinai, was established in central Harlem at 118th Street and Lenox Avenue. This congregation was organized along lines similar to the German Conservative-Orthodox synagogues of the late nineteenth century, offering to its members Orthodox ritual, mixed seating, and a weekly "sermon in the vernacular." These two congregations hoped to attract acculturated, English-speaking East European Jews who wanted to retain a modified traditional form of prayer, while eliminating some of the obvious immigrant trappings of worship.

The first Harlem congregation specifically organized to attract what its leadership called "the rising generation in Israel" was Congregation Mikveh Israel, founded in 1905. This synagogue offered uptown young people decorous Orthodox Sabbath and Holiday services conducted by two English-speaking, university-trained ministers. Both Henry S. Morais and his assistant, Jacob Dolgenas, emphasized the importance of active congregational participation in the prayers and encouraged congregational singing. Recognizing that many young people were uncomfortable in synagogues where cantors droned on in solo recitations of the prayers, Morais instructed his cantor to be a true "servant of the community" by singing simple melodious prayers which could be easily followed by worshippers. Lay people were encouraged to join in singing the prayers, thereby making traditional forms of prayers more meaningful for all those drawn into the synagogue. Congregational singing also helped synagogue leaders to maintain decorum during services; lay people actively participating in the services had little time for idle gossip.

Congregation Mikveh Israel was also ahead of its time in the admission of two women to its original twelve-member congregational board of directors. Most congregations barred women from synagogue office, relegating them to the leadership of a women's auxiliary or sisterhood. Although services were conducted according to Orthodox ritual, which precluded females from leadership in prayer, Mikveh Israel's women had an important voice in all other synagogue affairs. Contemporary observers applauded Morais's efforts both here and as head of the Young Folks' League of the Uptown Talmud Torah. One writer declared him to be the "only Rabbi in Harlem who stands for principle" and his young supporters to be "Harlem's only hope for the future."

Despite this enthusiastic endorsement, Morais and his followers failed in their ambitious undertaking. Morais's synagogue, like all these early youth-oriented congregations, was plagued by persistent financial woes arising from having overestimated the numerical and economic strength of that "rising generation of Israel" which it hoped to influence. The majority of Harlem's second-generation Jews had yet to reach young adulthood, leaving Morais's group with a constituency too narrow from which to draw financial support. Congregation Mikveh Israel was consequently never able to raise sufficient funds to move out of rented quarters. Congregation Shomre Emunah likewise saw its dream of erecting a synagogue shattered when a temporary financial recession in 1908 caused its few financial supporters to withdraw their promised monetary assistance from the institution. The uptown youth-synagogue movement first appeared in Harlem about half a generation too early. None of these early forward-looking congregations lasted more than a very few years.

Several of the community's largest congregations more effectively serviced the spiritual needs of Harlem's small but ever-expanding group of

American-born young. By 1910, at least four Harlem congregations had appointed American-born university-educated and Jewish Theological Seminary–trained rabbis to uptown pulpits and charged them with inspiring the new generation. These young rabbis served either as associates of or as replacements for incumbent German or Yiddish speaking rabbis. Jacob Kohn became rabbi of Congregation Ansche Chesed in May 1910, replacing German-born Gustav Hausman who was dismissed for "not possessing the spiritual uplift which a spiritual leader and religious teacher must have" to lead his laity successfully. The new dynamic rabbi soon inspired "a new religious awakening" in the synagogue. He popularized the study of Hebrew by children and adults alike. Kohn's classmate, Benjamin A. Tintner, son of Moritz Tintner, one of Harlem's earliest German reform rabbis, became rabbi of neighboring Temple Mount Zion in 1911. Tintner came to this prestigious uptown pulpit after a three-year tenure as assistant rabbi of the West Side Congregation B'nai Jeshurun. His appointment sparked an immediate upsurge in synagogue membership as many of Tintner's former young West Side congregants followed their spiritual leader and began attending services in Harlem. Bernard Drachman attracted a similar youthful following when he became English-speaking rabbi of uptown Congregation Ohab Zedek in 1909. Drachman worked in close partnership with Rabbi Philip Klein, whose own sermons were most meaningful to the less-Americanized segment of the congregation.

Congregation Anshe Emeth of West Harlem hired on a part-time basis an English-speaking graduate of the Jewish Theological Seminary, Rabbi Julius J. Price. He was given the primary responsibility of preaching to the American-born children of immigrants on the High Holidays, when these young people would be most likely to join their parents in attending services. These several well-conceived personnel moves, which were designed primarily to attract children of immigrants to services, undoubtedly also helped these congregations retain the continued allegiance of their Americanized immigrant members to synagogue life.

The opportunities to minister to the spiritual needs of American Jewish young adults marked a turning point in the fortunes of the American-born, Conservative-Orthodox rabbi. Earlier, few Jews residing in America identified with the spiritual messages preached by native-born, English-speaking traditional rabbis. Most German Jews had supported the Reform rabbinate, which was certainly American and English-speaking but decidedly not traditional. Their late-arriving German immigrant brethren of both the traditional and Reform persuasions preferred their own imported European-born spiritual leadership. Immigrant East European Jews were similarly content with their own "landsmanshaft synagogue" Orthodoxy and were suspicious of an "Orthodoxy" preached by clean-shaven, university-educated American rabbis. They looked to their transplanted East European rabbinic leadership to serve their religious needs. American Conservative-Orthodox rabbis of the late nineteenth and early twentieth centuries found that they had almost no one to preach to. One such rabbi recalled his frustrations when "it seemed for a time that I had mistaken my vocation, that there was no room, no demand in America for an American-born, English-speaking rabbi who insisted on maintaining the laws and usages of traditional Judaism. . . . There were considerable groups of East European, Polish, and Russian Jews in the East Side or Ghetto districts of the great cities, who adhered to the Orthodox traditions of their native lands, but they were Yiddish-speaking and wanted rabbis of that type. They were strange to me and I was stranger to them." The creation of several pulpit positions for American-born traditional rabbis in Harlem promised a more rewarding future for graduates of America's traditional religious seminaries.

The adoption by both German and East European congregations of almost identical policies in attempting to reach a similar Americanized constituency also foreshadowed future American Jewish communal structure. The acceptance of Seminary rabbis in synagogues ranging from the strictly East European Orthodox Ohab Zedek to the formerly staunchly German Reform Temple Mount Zion indicated that, at least in Harlem, forward-looking representatives of all Jewish denominations recognized the need to readjust Judaism to the impact of Americanization. Congregation Ohab Zedek's leaders understood, for example, that a homiletic discourse delivered in the vernacular German or Yiddish had no greater intrinsic holiness than one spoken in English, and Temple Mount Zion's people recognized that nineteenth-century Radical Reform principles might be too extreme for formerly Orthodox children of immigrants who desired membership in an American synagogue but who were repulsed by the totally nontraditional forms of Reform worship. And although each denomination would remain, to a great extent, theologically separated, they would be, from this point on, similarly engaged in the fight to construct new, enduring forms of Jewish life acceptable to a native-born Jewry.

These early efforts on behalf of Americanized Jewish young adults reached, however, only that limited segment of the next generation which was still more or less committed to religious life. None of these synagogues ever considered Jewish "missionary" work programs to reach those totally alienated from all forms of Jewish life. And as the numbers of American Jews began to grow during the second decade of the twentieth century, there were thousands of Harlem Jewish young people, whom the talmud torahs were never able to reach or failed to influence, who were growing up with no attachment to Judaism. One contemporary Christian student of American Jewish life described these young people as "the ones who, finding themselves unwilling to maintain the forms of Judaism and having a sort of instinctive dread of other religions are going without any religious expression or experience whatsoever." More ambitious rescue plans had to be drawn up to influence those falling away from Judaism.

The middle of the 1920s saw several similarly constituted rescue organizations established both in Harlem and in the other major Jewish sections of New York. Harlem's Young Men's Hebrew Orthodox League and Hebrew League, downtown's Young Israel synagogue, and Brownsville's Young Men's Hebrew League established synagogues and sponsored social activities on lines similar to Morais's early efforts.

The Harlem Young Men's Hebrew Orthodox League was founded in April 1915 by ten members of the Harry Fischel West Side Annex of the Uptown Talmud Torah, to provide the young adults of the community with an "institution which would create an Orthodox environment and teach the great principles of Orthodoxy." They perceived that even talmud-torah-educated young adults experienced a certain disaffection from Judaism "upon entering academic, professional, or business careers." And they understood that once on their own, few Jewish young adults continued to come in contact "during their spare time with a circle that reminds him of his obligations to his faith and people." The leaders of this league believed that they had the intellectual acumen to convince the second generation "that by study, Orthodox Judaism will be found to be entirely compatible with modern ideas."

They inaugurated their program by establishing model youth synagogues at the West Side Annex emphasizing decorum and congregational singing in services conducted by the young people themselves. In the fall of 1914, the new Harlem League conducted a Kehillah-sponsored "provisional synagogue." These provisional synagogues were organized throughout the city to combat the abuses of the "mushroom synagogues" established by private entrepreneurs in public halls and saloons to provide a place for unaffiliated Jews to attend High Holiday services. Many of these entrepreneurs were unscrupulous individuals who hired imposters as rabbis and generally exploited the public for commercial purposes. The provisional synagogues were designed to undercut the market served by "mushroom synagogues" by providing services at reasonable rates under reputable leadership to serve the High Holiday overflow crowd. The selection of the Young Men's Hebrew Orthodox League to serve the Lenox Avenue district of New York represented an early recognition by citywide authorities of the league's usefulness to the uptown community.

Thus established within the community, the Harlem Young Men's Hebrew Orthodox League quickly inaugurated numerous social and cultural activities and planned to maintain its own clubrooms, library, and gymnasium and to hold classes on Jewish topics. Among the lecturers in its early years were Rabbis Jacob Dolgenas, Bernard Drachman, and Herbert S. Goldstein. Goldstein, then associate rabbi at Yorkville's Congregation Kehilath Jeshurun, was elected honorary president of the league in recognition of his constant encouragement of its activities.

A second Harlem-based cultural institution created to attract Jewish young adults back to their faith was organized in September 1915. The Harlem Hebrew League was founded to "make known the ideals of Judaism" to uptown youths. League organizers established a headquarters for "Jewish men under Jewish refining influences" on Lenox Avenue where social and educational programs were held every weekday evening and on the Sabbath. This league offered its members lectures and debates in addition to its dignified modern Orthodox services. Rabbis Drachman, Goldstein, and Morais headed the list of speakers who addressed this youth organization as it began to gain support in the local community.

Uptown efforts to expand the scope of American synagogue life to include social, cultural, and recreational activities in the hope of making Judaism more relevant to neighborhood young people were paralleled on the Lower East Side by the activities of the founders of the Young Israel Synagogue. These advocates of traditional Judaism created in 1915 a model synagogue on East Broadway run according to the same principles as Morais's 1905 Harlem effort. Harry G. Fromberg, one of the founders of the movement, described their synagogue as a place "where every atom of our time-honored tradition could be observed and at the same time prove an attraction, particularly to young men and women: a synagogue where, with the exception of prayer, English would be used in the delivery of sermons and otherwise." The Young Israel synagogue emphasized congregational singing and decorum, outlawed all forms of commercialism in services, and sponsored a variety of social and cultural activities designed to keep the young people in the synagogue. Late in 1915, a federation of "organizations of young Jewry" composed of Harlem, downtown, and Brownsville youth leagues and synagogues was organized "to promote the welfare of Judaism" on a citywide basis.

For all the energy in this movement the founders of the Harlem Young Men's Hebrew Association still perceived them as too limited in scope and parochial in outlook to serve the majority of its community's young adults. These leaders argued that "Orthodox" Jews represented a relatively inconsequential proportion of the total population. They argued that there were thousands of young people whom the talmud torah never reached. These were young people "who never enter a synagogue and for them there must be some kind of training school" in Judaism. Yorkville's Ninety-Second Street Y, which many East Harlemites did attend, was nevertheless considered geographically inaccessible for the majority of uptown residents. And Yorkville leaders, for their part, were unwilling to expand their own activities to Harlem, describing themselves as an exclusively Yorkville institution. They preferred to support the establishment of a separate Harlem branch of their National Y.M.H.A. movement. Just such an institution, emphasizing social, cultural, and recreational activities and offering Jewish religious activities on a limited nondenominational basis was founded at an organizational meeting held at Temple Mount Zion in 1915. The Harlem Y received the support of several important local rabbinic and lay leaders including Rabbis Benjamin A. Tintner, Philip Klein, and Bernard Drachman, and Representative Isaac Siegel.

Rabbi Mordecai Kaplan failed to share his uptown colleagues' enthusiasm for the new Harlem Y. This former religious director of the Ninety-Second Street Y now argued that as presently organized, the YMHAs were no different from nonsectarian settlement houses, providing social and recreational activities for the youth of their communities in the hope of "keeping them off the streets." Kaplan charged that there was little that was "distinctly Jewish" in the content of YMHA programs which would set them off from other community-service organizations as a bulwark against "the possibility of Jews becoming assimilated." He characterized the YMHAs as "secular organizations" financed by Jewish money, and called upon the national movement to either drop the word "Hebrew" from its title and to openly declare itself a nonreligious organization or to immediately reconstitute itself as a "distinctly Jewish organization" committing itself wholeheartedly to the battle against assimilation.

Although he doubted that the YMHA would respond affirmatively to his criticism, Kaplan was not discouraged. For him, the future of Jewish life in America lay outside the hands of both the secular YMHA and the religious Orthodox and Hebrew leagues. Kaplan was convinced that the reconstructed synagogue was destined to play the crucial role in preserving Judaism in America. He believed that the primarily secular, social, cultural, and recreational activities of the Y could be effectively merged with modern religious-oriented programs of the leagues. The resulting synagogue-center movement would effectively influence the American Jewish young adult, who had graduated from the settlements and had outgrown his or her parents' immigrant synagogue culture, to identify with things Jewish. The synagogue center's social attractions would lure the unaffiliated into a religious surrounding, where they would be exposed to or reacquainted with the beauties, and ultimately, the values, of their ancestral faith. It was Kaplan's hope that with time and the proper programs, many Jews would eventually be drawn to the specifically religious activities of the institution and might ultimately attend their services conducted along the most modern Orthodox lines. Such an institution was to produce committed Jews from among the many religiously estranged young adults.

In fashioning his dream of a reconstructed synagogue, Kaplan drew heavily upon the educational philosophy espoused by his colleague Professor

John Dewey of Columbia University. Dewey believed that contemporary modern industrial society had thrust the school, in place of the home and neighborhood, into the role of society's major educative and socializing agent. It was, consequently, the job of modern educators not only to teach the traditional subject matter normally associated with the school but to create within the school an atmosphere conducive both to continued learning and to the personality development of each child/student. For Dewey—and the generation of progressive Jewish educators he trained and inspired—the final judgment on the usefulness of an educational program rested on its success in creating "a desire for continued growth" among its students. Adapting these principles to his proposed synagogue center, Kaplan argued that his new social and recreational activities would create the desired atmosphere conducive to continued identification with synagogue life and would eventually lead to greater interest in studying Judaism.

Kaplan first attempted to put these theories into practice in 1916 when he helped found the Central Jewish Institute organized by leaders of Yorkville's Congregation Kehilath Jeshurun, where he had earlier served as associate rabbi. This congregation and the community it served provided an exceptionally good testing ground for his programs to save affluent, Americanized second-generation Jews from assimilation. Kehilath Jeshurun members were drawn from among the most affluent element in the East European community: individuals who had succeeded in less than a generation in achieving a degree of economic advancement comparable to that of the Jews of Lenox Avenue. These Yorkville Jews were described by one official of the Central Jewish Institute as "bourgeois, well-to-do and distinctly conservative in contradistinction to the new Russian immigration which has a strong element of Radicalism and Yiddishism." Religiously, they were depicted as "Orthodox, which implies adherence to Jewish ceremonies and customs and an allegiance to Jewish life." Many were described as the scions of "families which were respected in the social life of the Eastern European ghetto, where learning was the distinguishing class mark."

Their affluent American-born children and their fellow Yorkville friends showed little of their ancestors' commitment to Jewish learning. On the contrary, these young people were observed by the same official to be a "half-baked second generation who knew little of Jewish life, tending to associate it merely with the ceremonies and especially with the prohibitions observed in the home. They are generally indifferent to, if not ashamed of Jewish life." The recipients of a public school education, these proficient English-speakers were also quick to regard themselves "as superior to their parents and everything associated with them." This same student of the community feared that these Yorkville Jews were representative of the disintegration of the ethnic and religious culture in the second generation and recognized the need for an "adequate agency to bridge the gap between the generations, to interpret the old traditions in terms of the new." Yorkville provided Rabbi Kaplan with a ready constituency for his Jewish "rescue" plans.

The Central Jewish Institute represented the first major attempt at amalgamating Jewish social, cultural, and recreational programs with religious educational activities under the auspices of an established Orthodox congregation. Institutional leadership emphasized the "harmonization of Jewish purpose with American life" as its *raison d'être*. It promoted with equal vigor its program of Jewish studies through a talmud torah and an extension school for "those who cannot be induced to enroll in the intensive work" and a center program whose activities "make for the physical and social well-being of the people who live in the neighborhood." Health and citizenship, it was declared, "are a part of, and not opposed to Judaism."

The Central Jewish Institute was not, however, the truly complete synagogue center envisioned by Kaplan. The single major component missing from its multifaceted program was, ironically, the synagogue itself. Although supported by the leadership of Kehilath Jeshurun and housed in an adjoining building, the C.J.I. lived an almost separate existence from its sponsoring institution. The synagogue failed to coordinate or update its traditional religious practices and rituals with the social and educational activities of the Institute. One critic of this Yorkville movement claimed that it possessed all the elements of a synagogue center "but only externally so. The three departments have no close contact because the synagogue element is not bold enough. The synagogue has not developed its full capacity and its influence is small." In 1918, Rabbi Kaplan, undoubtedly frustrated with the incompleteness of the C.J.I. program, severed his remaining ties with Yorkville's institutions and with the financial assistance of several of Kehilath Jeshurun's most affluent members, who had migrated to the elegant newly developed West Side neighborhood, established the Jewish Center Synagogue at 86th Street between Columbus and Amsterdam avenues. Now on his own, he was free to create a true synagogue-center program under Orthodox auspices which would serve as a model for hundreds of Jewish center–synagogues organized over the next several decades.

Rabbi Herbert S. Goldstein, founder of Harlem's Institutional Synagogue, shared Kaplan's critique of existing youth organizations and advocated an almost identical synagogue-centered program for attracting young people back to their faith. Goldstein was first directly exposed to Kaplan's philosophy in 1913, when as a senior at the Jewish Theological Seminary he was elected to succeed his teacher as English-speaking minister at Kehilath Jeshurun. He worked in close concert there with Kaplan in the founding and direction of the Central Jewish Institute and learned first-hand of the problems facing those committed to this new form of Jewish communal work. Goldstein first expressed his own dedication to meeting the challenges posed by the new generation of American Jews in June 1915, when he declared that the salvation of "the Judaism of the future" lay solely in the hands of the "young university-trained Orthodox Rabbis" like himself. In a public charge to his American-born, English-speaking colleagues, Goldstein argued that only they could help, for example, the "scientifically-trained, skeptical young Jew, reconcile what he learned in public school and college with the ancient doctrines of his faith." Goldstein believed that only those "reared on American soil, who have breathed the ideals of American democracy, who have been born and bred like other Americans, who have received a systematic scientific, secular education, and who are at the same time deeply saturated with a knowledge and desire of practicing the tenets of our faith" can understand the needs and desires of those eager "to break down ghetto walls . . . to live as their neighbors, their fellow citizens—the Americans." They alone "who have gone through this kind of youth" and remained true to Judaism can meet American Jewish men or women on their own level.

Goldstein called upon all Orthodox Jews to rally around these young zealots and directed established congregations to hire young men to their pulpits who would engage in missionary work among those "who have gone astray, to bring them back to Orthodox Judaism and keep and sustain those who are in the fold."

Goldstein outlined a concrete plan for what he called Jewish missionary work some fifteen months later when he called for the establishment of an Institutional Synagogue to serve second-generation American Jews. In a public letter to New York Jewry published in several local periodicals, Goldstein argued that all existing Jewish institutions were failing to influence young people toward Jewish observance. The relatively few modern educational institutes in existence reached, according to Goldstein, only 15 percent of Jewish youth. The religio-social landsmanshaft synagogues (the so-called "provincial synagogues," that expressed "local European mannerisms") were characterized as "un-American, antiquated and largely responsible for the great gap which now exists between the sons of the founders of the synagogues and the founders." The cheder education system, he declared, was a complete failure for its total inability "to impart to students the true meaning of the Jewish religion, nor inspire in them the proper love of their faith." The talmud torah movement, with which his father-in-law, Harry Fischel, and some of his own closest associates were intimately involved, Goldstein described as a worthy improvement over the earlier system. But he declared it too suffered from some important defects. The talmud torah movement had, he said, failed to overcome its East European roots. As a pauper's school, it failed to attract children of parents who could afford to pay tuition. In addition, the talmud torah movement's approach to Jewish youth was itself not ideal because "it is fractional in its work and divorces the child from the synagogue."

Goldstein expressed similar objection to the Y.M.H.A. movement, characterizing its efforts in the Jewish social field as "partial" because "it only takes the boy off the street and does not give him the education of a Jewish religious environment." Paralleling Kaplan's criticisms published a year earlier, Goldstein also stated that the YMHA's work was "negative" because it "failed to impart positive religion in the minds of the youth. It does not stand for positive religious conviction."

For Goldstein, just as for Kaplan, the "Institutional Synagogue–Jewish Center" concept represented Jewry's best chance to save a lost generation from voluntarily surrendering its Jewish identity. Goldstein too argued that historically "the synagogue of old was the center for prayer, study and the social life of the community all in one," and suggested that with the proper program, it could once again assume that traditional role. He envisioned a new multifaceted synagogue which would be "a place for study for adults in the evenings and for children in the afternoons." It would be a social and recreational center for young adults where "after plying their daily cares, they could spend a social hour in an Orthodox environment and in a truly Jewish atmosphere." This synagogue would also offer decorous modern Orthodox religious services designed specifically for an American congregation, while "keeping intact the Jewish ceremonies of our people." Goldstein was convinced that "if we desire to perpetuate the ideal Judaism of the past we must so shape Jewish spiritual activity that it will all find expression in one institution." He offered the Institutional Synagogue as that ideal Jewish social, religious, and cultural organization, embracing the best of the synagogue, talmud torah, and YMHA.

Goldstein submitted that he had both history and practicality on his side. From a purely financial standpoint it would be cheaper for local Jewish communities to build one large Institutional Synagogue, combining all the activities of a large congregation, talmud torah, and YMHA, than to support each separately. He also reasoned that the individual Jew could, for a little higher membership fee in the institutional synagogue, derive the benefits of three Jewish institutions. The three-in-one synagogue centers would have the additional advantage of making it possible for all members of a family to participate in their own age-group activities within the same religious institution and thereby bring back to family life "that religious unity and enthusiasm which is sorely lacking today."

Rabbi Goldstein's ambitious proposals for reviving Jewish youth were well received by the leaders of both the Harlem Young Men's Hebrew Orthodox League and the Harlem YMHA. Late in 1916, these men considered amalgamating their organizations to reach the youth of their neighborhood. The Harlem League, the smaller of the two organizations, with only thirty-five members on its rolls, was almost immediately taken by Goldstein's concepts; it decided several weeks after this published pronouncement to reorganize the organization and to "push with vigor its campaign for the establishment of a real Jewish center in Harlem." The League, which previously sponsored only religious and cultural activities, now announced its intention to construct a gymnasium and organize a library to attract a wider segment of uptown Jewry to its organization. The Harlem YMHA, seventy-five members strong, expressed its support of Goldstein's idea in April 1917, when it agreed under the leadership of its new president, Representative Isaac Siegel, to join Harlem League officials in inviting Rabbi Goldstein to coordinate uptown youth work. The rabbi was given the mandate of "bringing the message of Jewish Religious Revival to (Harlem) youth" through existing youth organizations reconstituted as the Institutional Synagogue.

Representative Siegel's leadership in the Harlem YMHA and his subsequent presidency of the Institutional Synagogue was the second instance of his direct involvement in local religious affairs. Almost a decade earlier, in 1908, Siegel had led a group of young protestors against Congregation Ohab Zedek, accusing this leading uptown synagogue of conducting organizational "business" on the Sabbath. Siegel's group claimed that on a given Sabbath several young men had attempted to gain admittance at the 116th Street sanctuary and were told by congregational leaders that only worshippers holding admission "tickets" could enter the synagogue. Siegel's young men were allegedly told that tickets could be purchased at a cigar store located across the street from the synagogue. Siegel publicly condemned this open commercialism and this obvious desecration of the Sabbath practiced by the religious "hypocrites" of Ohab Zedek.

Siegel's charges, which were published in a local Jewish periodical, were answered in print by a Mr. D. Berliner, an officer of the congregation. Berliner counterclaimed that admission tickets were "authorized solely to preseve order and decorum" in the services and vigorously denied that tickets were sold on the Sabbath. According to Berliner, tickets were needed to "keep back the mob of young men struggling to enter and the young dandies who came in merely to ogle women in the balcony."

Berliner's defense failed to move one contemporary editorialist who condemned Ohab Zedek for failing to recognize that a synagogue "has something more to do than to engage a chazan with a beautiful voice." "Where is the Rabbi?" this critic asked. "Where is the Hebrew and Religious School? What is the new Hungarian congregation doing for the community?" The editorialist went on to declare that the "Jewish community expects more" from its synagogues and commended Siegel for bringing this problem to public attention. Ohab Zedek's decision in 1909 to appoint Bernard Drachman to its uptown pulpit may well have been directed, to some extent, by communal pressure to modernize its approach to synagogue life, arising from this incident.

It is interesting, however, to note that Siegel deemed it inappropriate or impolitic to point to this early involvement in communal affairs when attacked by Rosenblatt as a "non-Jewish" representative in the fiercely contested 1916 congressional elections. It is possible that the candidate of the then "respectable element" in uptown Jewry did not want at that point to remind his most consistent supporters that he had once openly criticized the policies of one of Harlem's major religious establishments. By the same token, it is possible that Siegel's reawakened interest in communal activities may be attributed in part to his desire to still critics of his "Jewish" record. Whether the congressman's involvement in the Institutional Synagogue project was pietistic or political, it was Siegel who assumed the presidency of the merged organizations and who accepted the responsibility of contacting Rabbi Goldstein to invite him to assume the new Harlem pulpit.

Rabbi Goldstein accepted the call of uptown Jewry in April 1917 as an exciting challenge, making only two major requests of Harlem leaders: that he be granted life tenure as rabbi and leader of the Institutional Synagogue, and that the synagogue's constitution indicate that "no innovation in traditional Judaism may be inaugurated" into the synagogue's ritual "if there be one dissenting vote at a meeting of the corporation." His position thus secured, Goldstein immediately made plans for creating what he described as a "Jewish revival movement" in Harlem.

The new synagogue leased a private house near 116th Street and Lenox Avenue, described by Goldstein as the "heart of the most distressing Jewish conditions in the United States," for a synagogue, club, and schoolhouse. Goldstein announced plans for conducting "monster rallies" throughout Harlem to attract thousands of young people to his movement. He proposed the leasing of local theaters on Sunday mornings for services and lectures to reach "the large mass of young men and women who cannot be reached on Sabbath." In a related move, Goldstein suggested that Institutional Synagogue leaders approach leading Orthodox Jewish merchants in Harlem to solicit jobs for Jewish young people who themselves wished to keep the Sabbath.

Goldstein's Institutional Synagogue received an early spiritual boost in May 1917, when Henry S. Morais voiced his public support for this contemporary "youth synagogue." That same week saw the new project obtain its greatest financial assist when an anonymous supporter donated a five-story building at 116th Street between Lenox and Seventh avenues as a home for Goldstein's Jewish center-synagogue-school complex.

The new movement, through its Sunday revival meetings and its diversified program of youth activities, quickly gained the support of neighborhood people. By September 1917, after only five months of existence, the Institutional Synagogue attracted some 1,200 people to its Rosh Hashanah services, held at a public hall in Central Harlem. In January 1918, the synagogue reported a membership of 2,000 dues-paying members supporting thirty-one clubs and eight religious classes housed at the 116th Street building. A month later, the Institutional Synagogue, in conjunction with the Jewish Sabbath Association, opened a Harlem branch of the Association's employment bureau. Goldstein subsequently attempted to convince all Jewish shopkeepers in Harlem to close their stores on Saturday, in order to "arouse a Jewish spirit" in the neighborhood.

The Institutional Synagogue's most ambitious program remained its Jewish "missionary" work expressed through frequent "monster rallies." Mount Morris Theater, located only one-half block away from the synagogue, was the usual location for these meetings which often featured lectures by United States senators, congressmen and well-known local and national Jewish figures. Rabbi Goldstein explained the underlying purpose of these revival meetings when he declared that "every community needs an occasional soul-stirring reawakening and a revival of a religious interest from time to time. At our regular religious services we attract only those who are habitual synagogue-goers, but we must reach the wavering as well. This can only be done through revival meetings."

The Institutional Synagogue absorbed more than its share of criticism during its early years. The most frequently heard charges contended that this Orthodox institution was "elitist" in nature and was simply a recast, improved Harlem Hebrew League, of use only to those of that particular religious persuasion. The presence of the Harlem YMHA leaders on the board of the Institutional Synagogue apparently made little impression upon those who opposed Goldstein's efforts. Critics echoed the traditional National YMHA contention that "inasmuch as in a community there are young men of various religious beliefs and some of no religion at all, the problem cannot be solved by a temple or synagogue." While admitting that in theory the synagogue was the ideal, dissenters were quick to observe that "some people are not inspired by that ideal. Shall they come under no influence at all?"

Critics also noted the Institutional Synagogue's higher "three-in-one" membership fee as further proof of its fundamentally "elitist" nature. Goldstein's organization was described by one spokesman for the Yiddish press as "a private institution for the children coming from parents not necessarily wealthy, but from those who can afford to pay for instruction." Membership rates at the Institutional Synagogue, critics contended, "were prohibitive to the wage earner." Those who felt that the mass-oriented revival movement was not within the true spirit of Judaism also censured the new Harlem movement, and those who preferred rabbis to play a less activist role in community social problems deplored Rabbi Goldstein's decision to "resign as a minister of an established congregation to donate his entire time and energy to Billy Sundayism." Rabbi Goldstein was advised to "concentrate on religious education" and leave "sensationalism" to Christian evangelists.

Rabbi Goldstein responded by asserting that his movement was primarily religious and was pointed toward bringing the unaffiliated into the synagogue and leading those ignorant of Judaism toward the house of study. Goldstein also argued that there was nothing novel or radical in the concept of "Jewish revivalism." The prophets of old and the itinerant preachers of the East European settlement were all "revivalists" and all operated within the fabric of Jewish tradition. He asserted that his movement had both Jewish history and modern ministerial techniques on its side.

In considering Rabbi Goldstein's Institutional Synagogue and the other early youth organizations that operated both in Harlem and in the adjoining communities as forerunners of the Jewish Center movement of the 1920s and 1930s, one immediately notes that as early as 1910 or so, religious leaders were aware that rapid, complete Americanization brought with it profound challenges to the continuity of Jewish life in this country. They understood that even young adults who had been exposed as children to some Jewish education were not immune to the pressures imposed by general society to assimilate; to conform totally to majority cultural values. They feared for those Jews but even more so for those children of immigrants who received no training in Judaism and who were growing to maturity as Americans oblivious of the traditions of their people. And although American Jews still constituted but a relatively small proportion of their predominantly immigrant community, they understood that these people were the first wave of a second-generation American Jewish society that would grow to full maturity in later decades.

The Central Jewish Institute, the Jewish Center, and, of course, Harlem's Institutional Synagogue, which operated under Orthodox auspices, represented the first concerted efforts to deal with these problems and served as workable prototypes for later Conservative Jewish synagogue centers established in the soon-to-be constructed outlying neighborhoods by second-generation Jews. The Harlem and Yorkville youth organizations also influenced later communal developments by providing a forum for the emergence of the American-born or -educated, university-trained, traditional rabbi as a dominant force in communal life. Men like Drachman, Morais, Kaplan, and Goldstein represented the vanguard of a new generation of traditional American Jewish rabbis dedicated and equipped to tend to the spiritual needs of the American Jewish community. Jewish Theological Seminary teachers and rabbis who had made so little impact on the immigrant ghetto population found a small but enthusiastic group of followers within the Americanized segment of Harlem's German and East European communities. These rabbis and their successors were destined to become even more important factors in the life of their communities in the years to come. Many of the lessons learned in these uptown Orthodox institutions were readily applied to suburban Conservative congregations.

A high level of cooperation existed between the founders of the Conservative movement and their contemporary modern Orthodox counterparts. Indeed, it is often difficult to differentiate between the two. Both stood for traditional Judaism and preached similar messages to their Americanized congregants. A study of the early careers of Rabbis Herbert S. Goldstein and Mordecai M. Kaplan is highly instructive in this area. Before entering the seminary and earning his rabbinic degree from this American rabbinic institute, Goldstein was ordained as an Orthodox Rabbi by Rabbi S. Jaffee of Beth Ha-Midrash Ha-Gadol of Norfolk Street. Armed with this dual ordination, Goldstein was a logical choice as an English-speaking assistant rabbi under Rabbi Moses Z. Margolies, a leading East European Orthodox Rabbi who was sensitive to American problems and values. Margolies, it will be remembered, was a director of the Uptown Talmud Torah and supported local and Kehillah-sponsored efforts to update Jewish educational practices. Named to his post at Kehilath Jeshurun, Goldstein succeeded Rabbi Kaplan, a fellow seminary graduate, who had not earned Orthodox ordination prior to his rabbinic appointment but who nevertheless was deemed qualified to minister to an important traditional congregation. Margolies and Kaplan and, later, Margolies and Goldstein apparently worked harmoniously in the Yorkville pulpit. And they all seem to have cooperated successfully in the founding of the Central Jewish Institute, as the senior rabbi undoubtedly regarded both men as traditional rabbis and as skilled communal workers. The differences in their rabbinic training do not seem to have been a point of conflict among the three.

Both Goldstein and Kaplan severed their ties with the Kehilath Jeshurun community to establish similarly constituted youth-oriented synagogues in Harlem and on the West Side. Both institutions were organized and maintained according to traditional Orthodox guidelines. It is therefore interesting to observe, in retrospect, that the "Jewish Center–Institutional Synagogue" concept, which found its first expression within an Orthodox context controlled by seminary-trained rabbis, ultimately gained its greatest acceptance within the Conservative movement.

A final, enduring similarity between early modern Orthodoxy and Conservative Judaism may be seen from an examination of Rabbis Goldstein and Kaplan's later careers. Although Goldstein and Kaplan would ultimately go their separate theological and denominational ways, the former as a leader of both the Union of Orthodox Jewish Congregations of America and Yeshiva University, the latter as the founder and leader of the left-wing Conservative Jewish Reconstructionist movement, both remained united in their continued commitment to leading and inspiring that emerging heterogeneous group of modern Jewish religious leaders who sought, through similar homiletics and almost identically constituted socio-religious institutions, to serve the spiritual needs of a truly American Jewish community.

CHAPTER 15

Just as the synagogue underwent a transformation during the interwar years, so too did the Jewish home. Traditionally viewed as part of "women's sphere," the home in its size, arrangement, and furnishings actually evidenced the shifting values and mores of both sexes of Americanized Jews. Economically, these Jews were moving up the ladder of success; geographically, they were moving out to fancier neighborhoods; religiously, they were moving away from traditional Judaism; and culturally, they were moving into step with their non-Jewish neighbors. Each of these developments left its distinctive mark on the Jewish home and helped to shape the life within it.

Those seeking to revitalize Judaism, believing that religion begins in the home, had long looked to women, "the mistresses of the home," as the faith's potential saviors. Now as evidence mounted that traditional Jewish home life was itself on the wane, particularly among East European Jews (Central European Jews had traversed this course years before), a campaign to enlist women in the "rebuilding" of Jewish homes began in earnest, spearheaded by representatives of Conservative and Modern Orthodox Judaism. This campaign, as Jenna Weissman Joselit, the leading student of American Jewish domestic culture, demonstrates in the selection that follows, sought to blend contemporary American with traditional Jewish values to create the reassuring synthesis symbolized in the phrase "the Jewish home beautiful." Behind it lay one of the most cherished and oft-repeated assumptions of American Jewish life of that time: the belief that Americanism and Judaism were utterly compatible, each reinforcing the other. Being a better Jew meant being a better American woman, proponents insisted, and vice versa.

The Jewish Home Beautiful

Jenna Weissman Joselit

In the years following the Great War Jewish life in the Empire City underwent dramatic changes. For one thing, the common cultural vocabulary and shared experience of being an immigrant—that potent "sense of kinship"—gave way to an increasing heterogeneity in behavior and attitude. Making the Lower East Side look almost consensual by comparison, the Jewish community of the interwar years became highly stratified, marked by differences of class, denomination, and neighborhood. For another, a new kind of Jewish consciousness came into play, superseding the organic, all-embracing *Yiddishkeit* (Jewishness)—"nine parts feeling and one part fact"—of the immigrant era. Ethnicity, a generalized sense of cultural distinctiveness, increasingly characterized members of the second generation of Jews in New York. This brand-new construct did not demand much of its adherents: Jewishness, as one writer recalled, "was taken for granted, accepted; it was unquestioned. . . . " Without being fully articulated or acted upon, Jewish identity became more and more diffuse, segmented, and perhaps even ceremonialized. "Sometimes the family was about all that was left of Jewishness; or, more accurately, all that we had left of Jewishness had come to rest in the family," Irving Howe has written. "Jewishness flickered to life on Friday night . . . it came radiantly to life during Passover. . . . "

Inside the home, there was little to distinguish the household milieu, daily housekeeping rituals, and domestic arrangements of the middle-class Jewish New Yorker from those extolled in the pages of the popular and much-read *Good Housekeeping.* In its physical and social characteristics, its function and composition, the New York Jewish home of the interwar years seemed to approach the American domestic ideal. Conspicuously absent were those features intrinsic to the tenement experience: No longer the site of production, the home functioned as a private retreat for the exclusive use of the immediate family and, increasingly, as the site of consumption, a showcase of increased affluence. In the specialized distribution of space the nuclear family reigned supreme; boarders, those extra-familial staples of the immigrant experience, were seldom seen. Having wholeheartedly internalized the social and behavioral norms of American middle-class culture, Jewish families routinely ate dinner together, set their tables with matched cutlery, and in all things displayed a profound respect for and familiarity with the American culture of domesticity.

In matters of taste and style, no less than in those of behavior, middle-class Jews of this era absorbed prevailing American notions of home decor. The glaring disjunctions between approved style and actual practice that had typified the immigrant household had virtually disappeared. The Jewish woman, manager of the household and arbiter of its appearance, "had read one full year's back issues of *House Beautiful* and *American Home.* She knew what she wanted." Whether following the latest trends reported in women's magazines or, if finances permitted, the dictates of a private decorator, Jewish middle-class women tended to furnish their homes in one of several prevailing styles, among them Chinoiserie, Jacobean, or Spanish Oak. "They cultivate interiors and the principle of display," a resident of the Grand Concourse wrote of her neighbors, noting a seeming predisposition to entire sets of coordinated furniture or what she branded as "the urge to unity."

Amid this welter of styles, one point emerged clearly: the absence of a specifically Jewish style of home furnishing. More a function of class than of ethnicity, the look of one's home was determined by a number of factors, from personal taste to the state of one's exchequer. Jewishness, however broad or narrow its definition, appears to have had nothing to do with such "eccentric fancies" as the choice of color scheme in the living room or the configuration of furniture in the dining room. To be sure, a number of contemporary observers held out the possibility of a distinctive Jewish look; by endowing certain commonplaces of decor with a quality of perceived Jewishness, they conflated class with ethnicity. Writing about the heavily Jewish West Bronx, Ruth Glazer insisted that "undeniably there *is* a Bronx style. . . . Wherever there is an upholstered surface, it is tufted; wherever a wooden one, it is carved into sinuous outlines and adorned with gilded leather." Others seized on the popularity of cut glass to make a similar point. If writers as diverse as Sholom Asch and Delmore Schwartz are to be taken at their word, New York Jews seemed to have a particular affinity for objects fashioned from that medium. "A piece of sparkling cut glass" was bought "to make a grand impression," recalled a character in one of Asch's novels while Schwartz facetiously described the cut-glass candy dishes and fruit bowls favored by his parents' circle of determinedly middle-class friends in Washington Heights as the "works of art of these rising Jews."

Despite the seeming ubiquity of cut-glass dishes, most Jewish homes in the interwar years were essentially devoid of explicitly Jewish markers, especially when compared with earlier tenements. With its prominently displayed rabbinical portraits, *yahrzeit* plaques, *ketubot,* and its highly visible and worn assortment of Old World treasures, there was no mistaking the interior of a Jewish immigrant home for anything else. The middle-class interior, on the other hand, was virtually mute on that score. The requisite print of Theodor Herzl or Moses, observed one student of middle-class Jewish behavior, "has given way to copies of Van Goghs and Renoirs and the usual standard, highly impersonal 'art' of the department store." Where once a gilt-framed picture of a Jewish grandparent had hung prominently in the living room, " . . . after a few years we found it didn't look 'nice' with the new furniture, and so *zeda* was relegated to the bedroom. A Van Gogh print was put in his place." Making do with inherited Judaica, few homes had anything but the barest of Judaica collections: Brass candlesticks and perhaps a menorah and a mezuzah appear to have been the norm. A few scattered Palestinian art objects and tourist souvenirs as well as a modest collection of Jewish books and recordings supplemented these overt indexes of Jewish cultural identity. As a whole, the modern middle-class Jewish home contained "few objects of specific Jewish character." More poignant still was the new identity assigned to artifacts of the immigrant past: As they made the transition from tenement to apartment, functional objects became ornaments. Cherished copper pots formerly used for making gefilte fish now served as planters, while brass candlesticks, no longer in active service as ritual implements, adorned bookshelves. "There is no need for mother's pot in my kitchen," explained one writer; "it has become an emblem of the past, an ornament in my living room."

The absence of an identifiably Jewish atmosphere in most homes during the interwar years greatly alarmed many New York Jewish social and religious arbiters: In their eyes this neutral appearance signaled a diminution in Jewish consciousness and pointed to "disintegration and encyclopedic ignorance" of traditional Jewish culture. It is against this background that a second phase in the development of American Jewish domestic culture unfolded. The realization that Jewish identity could no longer be taken for granted but had instead to be carefully cultivated shaped the domestic agenda of these interwar domestic reformers, who, cutting across denominational lines, included Mordecai M. Kaplan, Mathilde Schechter, and the lay authors of *The Jewish Home Beautiful,* an immensely popular interdenominational compendium of Jewish ritual practice. Unlike the domestic reformers of the prewar era, this second generation was primarily concerned with the spiritual and emotional properties of the home. Moving away from the physical and corrective objectives of the earlier generation, these latter-day architects of American Jewish domestic culture placed the ideology of "home observance" at the center of their thinking, seeking to fashion a positive attitude toward Jewish ritual performance. "Earnest rabbis and teachers are doing their best from pulpit and platform to turn the tide," Mathilde Schechter observed in May 1918, "but they and the Synagogues are helpless, unless the women of Israel create Jewish homes again." Women had to "rebuild our Jewish homes," she insisted.

In calling for the "rebuilding" of the Jewish home, Mathilde Schechter, the wife of the chancellor of the Jewish Theological Seminary and a talented individual in her own right, sought to reestablish its primacy as an agent of Jewish cultural identity. "Home-making, Jewish home-making," remarked Henrietta Szold about her friend's communal career, "that was the fundamental principle." Much like Esther J. Ruskay decades earlier, Schechter hoped to infuse the home with manifestly Jewish qualities by situating Jewish ritual practice squarely within its four walls and by joining the image of the family "together in close and tender companionship" to the celebration of the Sabbath and holidays. At the same time she provided a rationale, a contemporary twist for the continuation of Jewish ritual practice, maintaining that "women of culture and feeling cannot live without traditions, without memories, without sentiment." Through her efforts on behalf of the Women's League of Conservative Judaism, which she helped to establish, and her work on behalf of the Seminary, Mathilde Schechter determinedly promoted a new canon of domestic ideals rooted in Jewish tradition.

One of the earliest and most articulate champions of Jewish "home observance," Schechter was by no means its sole exponent. The idea enjoyed widespread currency throughout the interwar years and gave rise to a new variant of prescriptive literature: guidebooks and manuals on Jewish practices whose audience was the middle-class Jewish housewife, whose language was English, and whose context was the Jewish home. Published throughout the interwar years, texts like *The Three Pillars, The Rites and Symbols of the Jewish Home,* and *The Jewish Woman and Her Home* reacquainted the Jewish woman of that era with the cultural assumptions and practices of Jewish ritual, guiding her through the particularities of kashrut and the rhythms of the Jewish calendar, or, as *The Three Pillars* put it, focusing on "those fundamentals with which every modern Jewish woman should be familiar." "Many will read this book and perhaps become discouraged. So many laws—so many rules to remember!" observed Hyman Goldin, the author of *The Jewish Woman and Her Home.* Ultimately, however, his text and those of his contemporaries became widely consulted household staples, modern analogues to the traditional *Shulchan Aruch*.

Practical compendia to modern Jewish life, these prescriptive texts also contained an ideological component: an idealized portrait of the Jewish home. Sanctifying the very notion of domesticity, *The Three Pillars* and its kindred texts described the home as a "religious domain," or even more explicitly perhaps, as a "miniature temple." As the poetically inclined *Jewish Home Beautiful* put it, "With woman as priestess to tend to its altars, each home is a Temple, each hearth is a shrine." Thanks to the popularity of these notions, the Jewish home by the 1940s had developed into the physical embodiment of Jewish continuity and cultural persistence, and, at the same time, into an "impregnable armor" against assimilation.

Once the Jewish home had been sanctified, or in Mathilde Schechter's words "religionized," the authors of these tracts did much the same thing to the Jewish housewife. The very health of American Judaism, it seemed, rested with her. "In her hands, perhaps more than in any other, lies the future of Jewish life," contemporary readers were told time and again. "She is responsible for keeping alive the Jewish home in which all that is notable in Judaism is bred and fostered." Another text maintained that "under modern conditions, it is the mother who becomes the guardian of the Sabbath and its interpreter." Protecting hearth, home, and family against the blandishments of a hostile and threatening world, the Jewish housewife cum priestess set and defined the ritual pace of her family's existence.

When viewed from this perspective homemaking was less an avocation than a vocation, a spiritual calling and one highly esteemed, at that. In fact, no higher compliment could be paid to a Jewish woman in those years than to extol her domestic abilities; as the *United Synagogue Recorder* succinctly put it, "the ideal Jewess is a homemaker." However tempting it may be to dismiss such statements as patronizing or empty-headed, they carried great cultural weight for those of an earlier generation. Significantly enough, when it came to eulogizing Mathilde Schechter after her death in 1924, every one of her male and female admirers singled out Schechter's devotion to domestic matters as her most salient and praiseworthy characteristic. "For she, with her aestheticism and her sympathy was above all a home-maker," declared Szold, the founder of Hadassah and a close personal friend. "Even when she went beyond her four walls and made her way into the arena of public life . . . [Mathilde Schechter] remained the homemaker." To be sure, Jewish women, especially of the middle class, did not restrict themselves solely to the kitchen or dining room. Throughout the interwar years a variety of women's organizations, from Hadassah and American Mizrachi Women on the national level to synagogue sisterhoods at the grass roots, came into being and multiplied rapidly. As outlets of communal involvement, each of these institutions expanded the Jewish woman's participation in matters "beyond her four walls." Yet the home, that "fountain source of Judaism," remained the lodestar of the American Jewish woman's existence and the source of her moral authority well into the postwar era.

To ensure the "reign of religion," Jewish women were actively encouraged to adorn their homes with Jewish ceremonial objects and realia. It is of the utmost importance that every available aesthetic means of giving Jewish atmosphere to the home be utilized," Mordecai M. Kaplan wrote, even suggesting the design of furniture and bric-a-brac "that would reflect Jewish individuality." Like so many of his pronouncements, Kaplan's advice proved a bit too advanced for his contemporaries, who preferred a more selective and limited approach to Jewish home decor. That approach came to be known as "beautifying" the Jewish home. In order to "reestablish the charm and beauty of Jewish life and piety," the modern Jewish woman's aesthetic sensibility along with her collection of material goods—"snowy linen, sparkling silver, flowers"—was harnessed to the promotion of Jewish ritual life. "Living as a Jewess," explained *The Jewish Home Beautiful,* the fullest expression of this trend, "is more than a matter of faith, knowledge or observance. To live as a Jewess, a woman must have something of the artist in her."

With its explicit appeal to the aesthetic sensibilities of the modem Jewish woman, *The Jewish Home Beautiful* struck an immensely responsive chord. Adding a new dimension to the prescriptive literature, this text joined home decoration, floral design, recipes, coordinated table settings, and notions of elegance and refinement—aspects of contemporary life most likely to engage the upwardly mobile woman—to the promotion of Jewish observance. "The attractive settings offered by our large department stores and women's magazines for Valentine's Day, Hallowe'en, Christmas and other non-Jewish festive days have won the hearts of many of our women," the authors of the guidebook explained. "In the following pages we have offered a few suggestions which we hope will inspire Jewish women to a deeper search of their own treasure house." By adapting the secular patterns of consumption to Jewish ceremonial life, the text not only unwittingly provided an astute assessment of the attractions of a consumer society but purposefully provided the tools with which to mediate between the two. With the avowed purpose of enabling "every mother in Israel to assume her role as artist," *The Jewish Home Beautiful* supplied the rationale and practical know-how so that the Jewish Sabbath and holiday table could become a "thing of beauty as precious and as elevating as anything painted on canvas or chiseled in stone."

American Jewry's domestic culture throughout its history exerted a powerful influence on the way Amercian Jews lived their lives, not only guiding their consumption of food and uses of space but also shaping their relationship to the larger society and to one another. In the final analysis, the tenets of this fluid, adaptive domestic culture enabled three generations of New York Jews over more than eighty years to make themselves confortably at home in America.

CHAPTER 16

No issue so divided the American Jewish community after World War I as did the issue of Zionism, the movement to create a Jewish state in the Land of Israel. On one side stood those who viewed Zionism as a return to tribalism, a negation of Judaism's mission to the world, and a dangerous slap at those countries that had made Jews feel welcome. On the other side stood those who viewed Zionism as a movement of Jewish spiritual uplift, the only solution to the rising problem of anti-Semitism, and a practical response to anti-immigration legislation everywhere.

Although some have seen the Zionist question in America as merely an extension of an older German–East European debate, the situation in fact was far more complicated. German Jews were far from being of one mind on the issue (the Reform Movement remained officially anti-Zionist until the 1930s, although individual Reform rabbis served as Zionist leaders), and prominent native Jews of German descent became Zionism's most ardent advocates. Such in fact was the case with Louis Brandeis, then a noted Boston lawyer with ties to the Brahmin elite, who not only converted to Zionism, but in 1914 agreed to assume the movement's leadership. Why Brandeis converted remains the subject of conjecture. What is clear is that he proceeded to translate Zionism into American terms: He stressed action over ideology, divorced Zionism from any personal commitment to immigrate to a Jewish state, and yoked the Zionist mission to America's mission—the outward spread of democratic ideals.

Can Brandeis's form of Zionism be denominated "American Zionism"? In one sense obviously not, since every permutation of European Zionism had its American counterpart, and a full range of Zionist dignitaries traveled to America in search of supporters. Non-Zionism—composed of people who aided the upbuilding of Palestine as a Jewish refuge but did not otherwise subscribe to any form of Zionist ideology—also claimed to be quintessentially American. Yet Melvin Urofsky, who has written major studies of both Louis Brandeis and American Zionism, argues here that what Brandeis espoused was *American Zionism. Although many American Jews followed other Zion-*

ist doctrines, and many of Brandeis's ideas were derivative, he legitimated Zionism in a new way—one firmly geared to American Jews' special needs.

American Zionism's challenge—similar to many we have seen before—was how to balance independence and interdependence, maintaining a separate American Jewish identity while remaining part of the larger worldwide Zionist movement. Brandeis more successfully than anyone else met this challenge. His writings and ideas, laced with characteristically American rhetoric, continued to dominate Zionist thinking in America long after 1948, when the State of Israel came into being.

Zionism: An American Experience

Melvin I. Urofsky

European Zionism resulted from the interaction of anti-Semitism, the nationalistic mood of the nineteenth century, and the age-old religious yearning for a return to Zion. Arguing that as long as Jews had no home of their own they would continuously be persecuted, Theodore Herzl declared that the only solution to the Jewish problem was the creation of a Jewish homeland. "The Jewish question exists wherever Jews live in perceptible numbers," he wrote. "Where it does not exist, it is carried by Jews in the course of their migrations. We naturally move to those places where we are not persecuted, and there our presence produces persecution. This is the case in every country, and will remain so . . . till the Jewish question finds a solution on a political basis." Although tempered to some extent by an insistence on cultural and religious priorities by theorists like Achad Ha-am, the Zionism of Herzl, Max Nordau, and even Chaim Weizmann was essentially secular. With the help and under the protection of the European powers, a geopolitical entity would be established in which Jews could build an autonomous society. There, all Jews who wanted to could come to live free from persecution.

As Joseph Adler has pointed out, Herzl intuitively heightened his nationalistic appeal by tying it to the ancient Jewish dream of messianic redemption. Although in the beginning he did not care where the Jewish state might be located, he ultimately realized that only Palestine would awaken the hearts of the people. This strain of messianism was particularly attractive to the East Europeans; for all of his scientific rationalism, it runs like a thread through the speeches and writings of Chaim Weizmann.

European Zionism, therefore, primarily addressed itself to the problem of anti-Semitism. "Everything depends on our propelling force," wrote Herzl. "And what is our propelling force? The misery of the Jews." Influenced by cultural and religious forces, especially messianism, Zionism was essentially a secular attempt to resolve that problem through the creation of a political homeland. In crossing the ocean to America, however, Herzlian Zionism ran up against a completely different situation.

Most importantly, there had been no long history of anti-Semitism in the United States. Prior to the American Revolution, the Jewish population of the colonies had been relatively small and had encountered little resistance. In 1740 an act of Parliament permitted the naturalization of Jews in the British colonies; thus Jews in America enjoyed more freedom, legally and in fact, than their brethren any place else in the world. Moreover, Jews were not singled out any more specifically than other dissident religious groups, such as Catholics or Quakers. In the decades following independence, one state after another struck down religious qualifications for suffrage and office-holding. In 1845, David Levy Yulee entered the United States Senate from Florida, soon to be followed by Judah P. Benjamin. In 1859, Attorney General Jeremiah S. Black declared that "In regard to the protection of our citizens in their rights at home and abroad, we have no law which divides them into classes or makes any difference whatever between them." Secretary of State Lewis Cass reemphasized this in regard to protection of American citizens overseas. The object of the United States, according to Cass, was "not merely to protect a Catholic in a Protestant country, a Protestant in a Catholic country, a Jew in a Christian country, but an American in all countries."

The first significant expression of anti-Semitism was General Ulysses S. Grant's infamous Order No. 11, which, however, was quickly rescinded, and appropriate apologies made. But after the Civil War, anti-Jewish feeling seemed to increase perceptibly. The *Social Register* closed its lists to Jews, and fashionable hotels, resorts, and private schools followed suit; in 1892 the Union League Club blackballed Theodore Seligman, son of one of the club's founders. Yet even here, as John Higham and Ellis Rivkin have pointed out, American anti-Semitism was by and large unrelated to religion. Rather, it was part of wider American problems dealing with large-scale immigration and economic mal-distribution. The anti-Semitism of the late nineteenth century bore little relation to the centuries-old Jew-hatred of Europe; it grew out of distinctly American tensions, and affected other immigrant and religious groups as well. As these tensions rose or waned, so did the hostilities. Moreover, at no time were American Jews without defenders against prejudice, and their champions included such distinguished Gentiles as Zebulon B. Vance and Theodore Roosevelt. Modern nationalistic anti-Semitism has just not appeared in the United States. This is not to say that there is not or never has been anti-Semitism in this country, but rather that it has been of very low intensity, and of a much different type than in Europe.

Another condition unique to the United States was a widely held belief that America itself was a new Zion, an attitude dating back to the Puritans, who saw themselves as a seventeenth-century version of biblical Israel, come to build their "city upon a hill" in a wilderness Zion. Throughout American history, there have been continuous references to this country as unique, set apart, even as divinely inspired. This attitude has been shared not only by the dominant Christian society, but by Jews as well. In Europe, prospective emigrants equated the United States with Palestine as a land of hope and redemption, and once here pledged their complete loyalty. In the 1840s, the Jews of Charleston, South Carolina, plainly declared: "This country is our Palestine, this city our Jerusalem," a cry echoed constantly over the next century. Louis Marshall, celebrating 250 years of Jewish life in America, prayed that Jews "never forget . . . the gratitude that we owe to the God of our fathers, Who has led us out of Egypt into this land of freedom."

This concept of America as the new Zion dominated the thinking of the preeminent American Jewish religious and secular organizations, and especially of the American Jewish Committee. Unlike many European Jews who saw their native lands primarily as places of prejudice and repression, American Jews viewed this country as a bastion of freedom, where anti-Semitism was the exception rather than the rule. In Europe, Palestine was viewed as a symbolic and spiritual refuge; American Jews, especially if Reform, dismissed Eretz Yisroel as a barren wasteland, a relic of ancient history. In 1885 the Reform leadership explicitly denounced any desire to return to the land of their forefathers. Even those Orthodox and Conservative Jews who still prayed for redemption and annually chanted "Next year in Jerusalem" did so more out of religious habit and custom than from any real desire to go there. While they did not categorically deny Zion, in practice they too had chosen America as the land of redemption.

In this choice, they deferred, either temporarily or permanently, the personal commitment of "going up to Zion." Herzlian Zionism assumed that persecuted Jews would want to go to a Jewish homeland, choosing it in preference to any other nation, even the United States. (Since Herzl believed that Jews carried the seeds of anti-Semitism with them wherever they went, even America would ultimately oppress its Jews.) This contention became the focal point of anti-Zionist claims that Zionism and Americanism were incompatible. If one was a Zionist, he owed his ultimate loyalty to Palestine and not to America. The United States had up until then welcomed all immigrants, but demanded that once here, the newcomers give all their allegiance to their new home.

In such a setting one would not expect Zionism to flourish, and this indeed was the case prior to 1914. Pre-Herzlian Zionism consisted either of dreamers like Mordecai Noah or Warder Cresson, poets like Emma Lazarus, isolated units of Hoveve Zion or Shave Zion, and equally isolated pockets of Hebraicists. The advent of Herzl and the [Zionist] Congress coalesced many of these people into either the Federation of American Zionists (F.A.Z.) or one of several pro-Zionist fraternal orders, such as the Knights of Zion in the Midwest. None of these groups made much headway in building up large memberships, raising funds for Zionist institutions, or in developing pro-Zionist sentiment in the Jewish or the general communities. On the eve of World War I, with a Jewish population of over 2.5 million, the Federation claimed only 12,000 members and operated on an annual budget of slightly more than $12,000. Zionism, as a force in the American Jewish community, was negligible.

Between 1897 and 1914, however, the United States underwent massive change. The industrialization following the Civil War had altered the nature of the economy and of the society. Millions of immigrants, responding to the demand for cheap factory labor, had poured into the country. But where earlier immigrants had been primarily Protestant, from Northern and Western Europe, and had settled mainly on the land, the newcomers were Jewish and Catholic, from Southern and Eastern Europe, who settled in the cities in ethnic enclaves. Slower to assimilate than the earlier immigrants, they tended to retain their ties to the old country and the old ways. Where the earlier Jewish immigrants had been German and Reform, the new wave came from Russia and Poland, and clung to their Orthodoxy. Moreover, they brought with them a basic sympathy for Zionism. They found themselves too busy earning a living and becoming Americanized to cultivate that sympathy, but when the time came, they would be ready to support a revivified Zionist movement in the United States.

Industrialization also created a number of social and cultural problems, and in the two decades prior to the war, a series of reform movements attempted to deal with those problems. The progressive impulse created new conditions in American society that would make it possible for an Americanized Zionism to flourish. The great achievements of the new leadership between 1914 and 1921 were (1) the reformulation of Zionist philosophy to make it complementary of American as well as Jewish hopes and ideals; (2) the identification of specific practical goals for which the movement and its sympathizers could work; and (3) the revitalization and reorganization of the administrative machinery. The war years marked a critical period for Zionism, both in Europe and in the United States, and the events shaping the movement came primarily from external, non-Jewish forces. The ability of Zionist leaders to respond to these forces determined the success of the cause.

The chief external factor was obviously the war that erupted in August 1914. The disruption and damage of battle affected all civilians, but bore down particularly hard on the Jews in Eastern Europe, the site of heavy fighting, and in Palestine, where the war disrupted normal economic routines. Responding to the distress of their brethren overseas, a number of Jewish organizations, all sympathetic to Zionism, convened in extraordinary session at the Hotel Marseilles in New York on August 30. The delegates formed a Provisional Executive Committee for General Zionist Affairs (P.E.C.), and, at the urging of Jacob de Haas, elected Louis D. Brandeis as chairman. The choice was a happy one, and Brandeis's assumption of the American Zionist leadership marked a turning point in the fortunes of the movement. Within six years a near-moribund movement had become the most powerful Zionist organization in the world.

Brandeis was a singularly gifted man, and undeniably those talents contributed greatly to the growth of American Zionism. Without detracting from his credit, however, it is obvious that conditions over which he had no control made it possible for him to mobilize American Jews and to win over a larger part of public opinion in favor of the cause. Drawing upon his experience as a reformer, and building upon the assumptions and techniques of those reforms, Brandeis molded the movement in the image of other progressive causes. By de-emphasizing the *Yiddishkeit* of Zionism, and enlarging upon its ethical and democratic ideals, he not only paved the way for Zionist acceptance and success in the United States but also set the stage for the later tension and struggle between European and American advocates of the movement.

Brandeis first set out to nullify the argument that Zionism was incompatible with Americanism; indeed, he declared just the opposite, that Zionism and Americanism shared the same basic beliefs in democracy and social justice. His efforts meshed perfectly with a growing reappraisal of the makeup and nature of American society.

The same large-scale immigration which had created a latent pool of pro-Zionist sympathy also called into question earlier assumptions about assimilation and Americanization. Because earlier immigrants seemingly had joined the general population so effortlessly, and also seemingly had shed their old world traits, most Americans subscribed to the so-called "melting pot" philosophy of assimilation. Once here, this theory assumed, every immigrant would want to speak only English, drop all vestiges of prior cultures and loyalties, and work to be as American in appearance and behavior as native-born sons. In a line stretching back to J. Hector St. John de Crèvecoeur, writers argued that Americanization involved homogenization, and that true patriotism demanded a single-minded loyalty to the United States. Theodore Roosevelt's polemics against "hyphenated" Americans was the last anguished cry of a theory that by 1910 was breaking upon the failure of millions of new-wave immigrants to lose their Old World ways and attachments.

The progressives, especially those concerned with education, wrestled mightily with this problem, and gradually a new philosophy emerged that turned necessity into virtue. Led by settlement-house workers like Jane Addams and academics like Horace Kallen, these theorists argued that America's strength lay not in a bland uniformity but in a vibrant heterogeneity of dozens of different cultures. Immigrants should be encouraged to learn English, assume American ways, and be loyal to American institutions, but they should also value the heritage and customs of their ancestral homes. Cultural pluralism undermined the argument that one could or should be loyal to only one country or culture; by doing so it also helped to undercut the anti-Zionists' claim that Zionism contradicted Americanism.

In his appeal for Zionist support, Brandeis rang numerous changes on this theme, even though up until 1910 he had himself vehemently attacked dual loyalties. There was no room in this country for "hyphenated Americans," he had once proclaimed. "Habits of living or of thought which tend to keep alive differences of origin or classify men according to their religious beliefs are inconsistent with the American ideal of brotherhood, and are disloyal." In 1915, he summed up his new beliefs when he argued that dual loyalties were only objectionable if inconsistent; if the objectives of different loyalties were similar, then they supported one another. Zionism and Americanism shared many basic assumptions, and "every American Jew who aids in advancing the Jewish settlement in Palestine . . . will be a better man and a better American for doing so." Assimilation he now denounced as "national suicide," and American Jews owed it to America as well as to themselves to preserve their distinctive identity.

This assertion that Zionism and Americanism shared similar values is the clue both to Brandeis's involvement in the cause and to his success as its leader. Stephen S. Wise, Julian W. Mack, Felix Frankfurter, and other members of the Brandeis group shared a deep commitment to American ideals and culture. What attracted them to Zionism was not just the need for a haven from persecution—since they themselves did not suffer from oppression—but rather the possibility that a Jewish state could be established based on the ethical tenets of Judaism, principles they viewed as closely akin to American ideals. Addressing the 1915 American Zionist convention, Brandeis said: "The highest Jewish ideals are essentially American in a very important particular. It is Democracy that Zionism represents. It is Social Justice which Zionism represents, and every bit of that is the American ideal of the twentieth century." Both in public and in private, Brandeis emphasized the closeness of these two: "Zionism is the Pilgrims' inspiration and impulse over again"; "the ideals for America should prevail likewise in the Jewish State"; "we [Zionists] stand for democracy and social justice. And what have been made fundamentals of American law, namely, life, liberty, and the pursuit of happiness are all essentially Judaistic and have been taught by them for thousands of years."

To those who had been disheartened by the failure of the United States to achieve those ideals, and who believed that industrialization and growing economic giantism undermined democracy, Zionism offered a new opportunity. With their passion for equality, progressive reformers sympathized with the plight of a people unjustly persecuted for nearly two thousand years. The demand for a Jewish homeland meshed not only with the Zeitgeist of nineteenth-century nationalism, but with American reform ideals of self-determination. For those American Jews who believed in the humane ethics of Judaism, rather than in its ritual and theology, the Zionist goals represented a logical union of secular and religious beliefs.

The Brandeisian synthesis also rejected the personal commitment to "go up to Zion," which had been a major weapon in the arsenal of those who claimed that Zionism contradicted patriotism, since if each Zionist was expected to leave for the promised land, then in truth one could not be a good American and a good Zionist at the same time. Moreover, the anti-Zionists worried that the creation of a Jewish state might give rise to anti-Semitic forces demanding the removal of all Jews to the new homeland.

The personal commitment had been integral to European Zionism, but American leaders of the F.A.Z. had immediately rejected it, realizing the difficulties it would raise in the United States. A Richard Gottheil or a Harry Friedenwald, however, lacked the stature and prestige of a Brandeis. Their protestations that no Jew would be forced to go to Palestine had been ignored, and in 1914 the anti-Zionist press still argued that Zionism meant the removal of all Jews from the United States.

Brandeis constantly emphasized that no Jews would be forced to go to Palestine. "The place is made ready; legal right of habitation is secured; and any who wish are free to go. But it is of the essence of Zionism that there shall be no compulsion." Brandeis considered Palestine spiritually necessary for the American Jews, but those being persecuted in Europe, especially in Russia, still had need of a haven; and growing pressure to restrict immigration to the United States made it likely that this country would no longer be a refuge for those seeking to escape oppression in the old world. American Jews had found their Zion, but they still owed it to their less fortunate brethren in Europe to secure a Zion for them. American Jews had the responsibility to build up Palestine, not primarily for themselves, but as an asylum for other Jews.

Yonathan Shapiro has termed this shift of emphasis "Palestinianism," and has condemned the Brandeis group for diverting energy from a commitment to Zionist ideology and principle to a pragmatic and expedient philanthropism. It is true that the American Zionists were more interested in practical work than in ideas, but here again, this is very typical of the entire progressive movement. It is noteworthy that the most important philosophic movement this country has ever produced is pragmatism, and the basic ideas of William James, John Dewey, Charles S. Peirce, and others were receiving wide attention at this time. And pragmatism, we may recall, was once defined less as a philosophy than as a means of doing without one. Americans have always been more interested in specific practical work than in ideas, and the emphasis on building up Palestine appealed to the American need to *do* rather than to *analyze*. By identifying specific tasks, by aiming for concrete accomplishments, Zionism made itself attractive and understandable to those

American Jews in whom the American cultural traits outweighed the European Jewish antecedents. It made it possible for Jacob Schiff and Louis Marshall to join in the upbuilding of Palestine, although each proclaimed to his death that he was not a "Zionist."

At the same time that Brandeis was emphasizing the similarity of Zionist and American beliefs, he reshaped the organizational structure of the movement along lines he had earlier developed in reform battles in New England. Prior to 1914, no single Zionist group had been able to claim primacy in the United States. Although the Federation of American Zionists had continuously proclaimed that it officially represented the World Zionist organization, other American Zionist groups almost totally ignored the F.A.Z. A number of fraternal and religious orders collected monies for various Zionist projects, and the W.Z.O., fearful of losing any funds or alienating any supporters, dealt with them all on a more or less equal basis. Herzl, and Max Nordau after him, consistently refused pleas by F.A.Z. leaders to deal with it as the official American arm, and this refusal undercut periodic attempts to unite all American Zionists into one organization.

The trauma of the war, the obvious need for unified action, and the national prestige of Brandeis and his lieutenants set the stage for the unification of the American movement, a process culminating in 1918 with the creation of the Zionist Organization of America. Brandeis from the start, however, insisted upon organizational reform that would channel Zionist sentiment into one powerful force, and though his actions undeniably created that force, they also alienated some who preferred the autonomy of local clubs and an independence from the interference of national leaders.

Many of the men and women assembled at the Hotel Marseilles assumed that they were merely establishing a fund-raising operation, and saw Brandeis more as a "name" than as a leader. In accepting the chairmanship, he at first seemed to confirm this view. He apologized that he lacked a greater familiarity with American Jewish affairs, emphasized the great need for relief funds, and opened the drive with a personal donation of $1,000. As many of the delegates prepared to leave, they were jolted when Brandeis called upon them to stay and prepare reports on the status of their organizations, how many members they had, their annual budgets, and how much work they were prepared to undertake. In the next two days Brandeis must have been equally as shocked when he learned of the chaotic conditions and disarray among those he was now expected to lead.

The first thing he did was to establish a full-time office staff and impose strict accounting procedures. He expected and demanded almost daily reports on amounts of money raised, new members enrolled, and propaganda produced. Despite his concurrent involvement in national political affairs, Brandeis found time to oversee practically every detail of Zionist activity. No matter how large or small a donation to the relief fund, a personal note of thanks should be sent, and Zionist propaganda enclosed. Had a local branch pledged a specific amount; if so, was the pledge met, and what was being done to raise more money? Even the print size of the Hadassah newsletter came in for his scrutiny, and the format ultimately changed. To prevent conflicts of directions and energies, he made it clear to the Actions Committee of the W.Z.O. that in the future it would have to deal with American Zionists solely through the Provisional Committee.

Within a year after he had assumed the chairmanship, Brandeis had revitalized the movement, and created for the first time an efficient and functioning organizational apparatus. He secured the cooperation and active involvement of a number of prominent American Jews who had previously eschewed Zionist interests, such as Julian W. Mack and Felix Frankfurter, and he brought Stephen Wise back to a central role in the movement. Moreover, he spurred an intense effort to recruit college students and graduates into Zionist organizations like the Menorah Society and the Intercollegiate Zionist groups, emphasizing that this body of educated Americans was the future hope of the cause. While recent European immigrants formed the mass support now, future growth depended on recruiting Americanized Jews to the movement.

Even as the movement grew, some voices questioned what had happened to the problems of ideology. They saw reports on dollars and cents, on numbers of members, on pieces of literature, but who was paying attention to what it all meant? The old-line European Zionists and Socialist Zionists were especially aggrieved at what they considered an abandonment of philosophy. Here again, Brandeis molded the movement to specific American needs and assumptions. Despite their distrust of gigantic corporations, Americans insisted that civic enterprises operate on sound, efficient business principles. The F.A.Z. had been a sloppy organization: literature had been mailed irregularly, collections for shekel stamps haphazard, and stock certificates of the Jewish Colonial Trust mislaid for months. If the principles of European Zionism were unacceptable to many Americans, so were its operating procedures. We do not wish to imply, however, that Brandeis had no interest in philosophy or principles. Like most progressive reformers, he held a deep commitment to a well-defined set of first principles; but these he considered constant and eternal verities, not open to discussion or analysis. Once the progressives determined upon these principles, they acted upon them; no one has ever accused these reformers of being introspective.

To Brandeis, the first principles of Zionism had been well defined by Herzl (with, of course, the American modifications) and to a lesser degree by Achad Ha-am. In the crisis of the war the important thing was not to debate endlessly on minute questions of philosophy, but to work for specific and attainable goals. Brandeis considered one of the most important of these goals to be the development of a well-organized, well-disciplined and influential Zionist movement in America. His motto, repeated time and again, of "Members! Money! Discipline!" emphasized the practical rather than the theoretical, the doing rather than the saying.

This is neither the time nor the place to explore in detail the inner workings of the American Zionist organization during the war years, nor the ensuing conflict with Chaim Weizmann that ultimately erupted at the Cleveland convention in 1921. Research so far confirms the contention that the movement during the whole of the Brandeis leadership faithfully reflected the prevailing ethos of progressivism, the faith in equality and the perfectability of man, the need for identification of specific and attainable goals, the assumption that organization was necessary for action. By recasting American Zionism along these lines, Americanized Jews like Brandeis, Mack, and Frankfurter took a fringe cult and made it part of the mainstream of American reform. One could, in fact, say that they made it respectable.

Many Jews, however, did not view the Americanization of the movement as a blessing. For them, the Brandeisian synthesis weakened Zionism by diverting attention from important ideological considerations toward mundane practical work. The immigrants who had brought their Zionism to America with them were at first thrilled by the advent of "real" Americans as leaders, but they eventually came to fear and resent the dilution of the Jewish component. The Brandeis leadership was frankly American; it lacked *Yiddishkeit*. If it had been more Jewish, however, it is doubtful whether it could have adapted the movement to American circumstances.

By the end of 1918, rebellion was brewing in the immigrant ranks, fanned by the resentment of some of the older F.A.Z. leaders like Louis Lipsky who had been shunted aside by the new men. When Chaim Weizmann made his move to assume the complete leadership of the world movement, he provided a nucleus around which the anti-Brandeis resentment could form. The fight over the Keren Hayesod (Development Fund) in 1921, which led to the resignation of the American leadership, was only in part a power struggle between two strong personalities, neither of whom could play a secondary role. It also marked the divergence in methods and philosophy between two factions, one which saw itself principally as Jewish and one which considered itself primarily as American.

In the 1920s, the Zionist Organization of America fell away drastically from its peak membership and budgets of the war years. Some of this undeniably was the letdown following the war crisis, a letdown shared by all segments of the society. But it also saw the rank-and-file membership demand the return of the "American" leaders, and the adoption by Weizmann and his American lieutenants of practically the entire Brandeis program. With the return of Julian Mack and Robert Szold to leadership in the 1930s, the American Zionists sealed their adherence to a philosophy that gave precedence to American customs and ideals. The shock of the Holocaust confirmed them even further in their devotion to America at the same time it spurred them on to the final practical attainment of the Jewish state.

CHAPTER 17

The nineteen thirties, the decade of the Great Depression, was a period of stress and ferment, with poverty, fear, and hopelessness stalking the American landscape and dark clouds looming on the European horizon. From a Jewish point of view the situation looked especially bleak. Doubly burdened in the depression, Jews faced not only economic privations but anti-Semitism as well.

Just at the moment when the American dream seemed to be failing so painfully, a whole new generation of American Jews—the children of the East European immigrants—came of age. Sometime during the 1930s, as Lloyd P. Gartner, a leading student of British and American Jewish history, points out in his article here, the majority of Jews living in America became American born. Old leaders and old established patterns no longer seemed relevant. Rather than being concerned about natives and immigrants, American Jews now worried far more about economics and ideology.

Two features of the 1930s merit special attention: the emergence of Jews in American public life, and the first flourishing of American Jewish intellectuals and literati. Both signified in different ways Jewish educational achievements. Both also foreshadowed the post–World War II rise of Jews to the crest of American public life and culture. Yet for all their similarities, these two features also evidenced two diametrically opposite trends in American Jewish life. One saw Jews seeking entry into the centers of American power and influence. The other saw them firmly committed to remaining on the outside, as critics, gadflies, and advocates of revolutionary change.

The New Deal, coupled with President Franklin D. Roosevelt's penchant for talent, opened the door for the "best and the brightest" in Jewish life (and those in other minority groups as well) to enter government service for the first time. Felix Frankfurter, Samuel I. Rosenman, Ben Cohen, Bernard Baruch, David Niles, Henry Morgenthau, Sidney Hillman, David Lilienthal, Abe Fortas, and countless other Jews played prominent and behind-the-scenes roles in the Roosevelt administration as policymakers and implementers. Never before had Jews been active in government to such a large extent. In the wake of the New Deal, Roosevelt became a Jewish hero, and Jewish ties to the Democratic party were secured for a generation or more.

At the same time as some Jews were gaining prominence for their work in the nation's capital, other Jews—-more radical in background—were gathering in New York. These New York Jewish intellectuals, as they came to be known, advocated more drastic responses to the social and economic crises of the depression years; many openly espoused communism. Their critical analyses of American life and society—sometimes brilliant, sometimes doctrinaire—marked them as outsiders; they thought "dangerous thoughts" and sometimes acted in dangerous ways.

The most creative and lasting works produced by these figures were novels, volumes such as Henry Roth's Call It Sleep *and Michael Gold's* Jews Without Money. *These books, drawn from the lives of Jewish immigrants and their children, featured elements that would characterize American Jewish fiction for decades afterward, even into the 1980s. "The patterns of Jewish speech, the experiences of Jewish childhood and adolescence, the smells and tastes of the Jewish kitchen, the sounds of the Jewish synagogue"—these, according to Leslie A. Fiedler, have become "staples" of American Jewish literature since the 1930s. Irving Howe has compared American Jewish literature throughout this period to a regional culture breaking through into national consciousness. It is regional, he explains,*

> *in that it derives from and deals overwhelmingly with one locale, usually the streets and tenements of the immigrant Jewish neighborhoods or the "better" neighborhoods to which the children of the immigrants have moved; regional in that it offers exotic or curious local customs for the inspection of native readers; and regional in that it comes to us as an outburst of literary consciousness resulting from an encounter between an immigrant group and the host culture of America.*

American Jewish literature, like so much else, thus harkens back to the experience of those who passed through "the midpassage of American Jewry," the dark years of the depression. From the creative ferment of this period, in all its bleakness, the contemporary American Jewish community arose.

The Midpassage of American Jewry

Lloyd P. Gartner

Zurich, August 1929. The reconstruction of the Jewish world after World War I came to fullness when, after years of negotiation, non-Zionist notables entered into the "Pact of Glory" with the Zionist movement to found the Jewish Agency for Palestine. The agreement was joyously made official at the Zionist Congress, held as usual in Switzerland. Then, after a few heady days, began the rapid, steep, and almost uninterrupted descent. Louis Marshall, the recognized head of American Jewry and main negotiator with Chaim Weizmann, fell ill after the Jewish Agency assembly and was dead in three weeks. As Marshall lay dying, a bloody onslaught by Arabs on the Jewish National Home exposed its physical weakness and made clear a depth of Arab hostility that few had reckoned with. Great Britain started its long retreat from the promise of the Balfour Declaration and the stipulations of the Palestine Mandate. The disturbing summer of 1929 ended with the first massive crack in the United States stock market, and other cracks followed until the securities market lay in ruins. Unemployment and business failures increased monthly, while banks collapsed and the world's financial system came into peril. The international dimensions of the economic crisis gave point to the alarming reports being received from Germany over the rising power of the Nazi movement.

The new agenda of American Jewry was outlined during that summer and autumn of 1929, while the death of Marshall symbolized the weakening of its patrician leadership. Depression in America on a scale never known before had to turn the concerns even of prosperous American Jews to making a living and holding on to what they had. The world depression helped the Nazis into power in 1933, and the hideous twelve years' chronicle of European Jewry began. Where lay hope? It was not a propitious time to wager on America's liberal democracy. Soviet Russia, many urgently argued, was the future and it worked. Depression in America, Nazism in Germany, the Jewish

National Home, and the sinking fortunes of East European Jewry became the agenda of American Jewry after 1929, and a hesitant, uncertain leadership had to cope with it all. Fifteen years earlier, in 1914, it is hard to imagine anyone foreseeing even a small part of this agenda. Fifteen years after it ended, in 1960, did not many sense that their world was so different that what had happened between 1929 and 1945 was a nightmare, or some portion of it a matter decent enough for nostalgia? So different had the times become, and that much had the public affairs of American Jewry changed. Historians generally stress continuity beneath the surface of change, but we had better look upon these years as a time of abrupt and drastic alterations in the regularities and tempo of American Jewish life. It is not only that the events of these years were stark, horrifying, and sometimes thrilling. In 1929, American Jewry was still dominated by its immigrant experience, the end of which had been decreed only four years earlier by the Johnson Act. Yiddish in its varied uses, Jewish trade unions, and *landsmanshaften* all reflected publicly the kind of life led in thousands of Jewish households. Thousands more studiously kept apart from the immigrant milieu in which they had grown up, or rebelled against it. Sixteen years later, in 1945, the immigrant world was shriveled or gone, and so was the complex of attitudes toward it. The years when this happened were American Jewry's eventful, trying midpassage.

How can we recount what happened to the Jewish people between 1929 and 1945 without seeking the wrath of Amos, the grandeur of Isaiah, the despair of Jeremiah? There is no hope I can do this. Let me attempt something modest by comparison: What lay before American Jews in their country? How did they attempt to cope with their public agenda? And how did their domestic affairs influence their foreign activities?

During the first thirty years of the twentieth century American Jews had progressed materially to an astonishing degree. Neither the foreignness of most of them as East European immigrants nor xenophobia nor anti-Semitism kept them from improving their lot with the general prosperity of the age, marked only by brief setbacks. The Jews quit the Lower East Side and its counterparts in practically every city and moved to better neighborhoods. They left proletarian occupations and peddling to become shopkeepers, petty entrepreneurs, and white-collar workers. Those who remained garment workers were fortified in strong unions. There were high hopes for the economic advance of the children. A good many Jews were teachers, accountants, lawyers, and physicians. From 1929 all that changed. As large enterprises laid off their workers en masse and small firms closed down, unemployment rose to levels never imagined: In major industrial cities like Pittsburgh, Cleveland, and Detroit it ranged between 30 percent and 35 percent of the labor force, besides those who could find only part-time work. Unemployment also struck the Jews hard. With the cessation of building in the boom city of Los Angeles, "two hundred Jewish carpenters cannot find work, or to put it in milder terms sixty percent of the Jewish carpenters belonging to this group have been out of employment . . . for many, many months." We learn of a man with a wife and three young children who was "working as a presser irregularly, averaging $3.50 per week." Jewish needleworkers' unions could do nothing against their employers' going out of business or cutting back severely. The old days of sweatshops and piece work seemed to be returning as wages and hours fell back to what they had been twenty-five years before. Voluntary wage cuts and industry-wide strikes accomplished little before the New Deal's programs. Many dispossessed shopkeepers and men out of work took to door-to-door peddling, which underwent a revival owing to the desperate efforts of men to support themselves. Ruined businessmen presented an "insistent and increasing demand" for relief to Jewish agencies:

> Our Jewish people have asked help later because they are tradesmen. They will buy and sell as long as there are those to trade with. Coming to us now in increasing numbers [in 1931] are the small merchant, the builder and real estate dealer. In fact, a new clientele is being created—the so-called "white collar" class.

The Jewish merchant could hold out longer, but to return to business was harder than for the worker, who needed no capital but only a job. Jewish institutions suffered harshly as contributions dwindled. Perhaps the worst off were schools, especially those with ambitious programs whose following was mainly among the Orthodox, then the least prosperous segment of the Jewish community. Tuition could not be collected and other income was scarce. For the unfortunate teachers there were frequent payless paydays, and months of waiting for even partial payment of arrears of salary.

A generation inured to the psychic trials of prosperity might be reminded of those that came from poverty:

> . . . a period such as we are passing through takes its toll in various forms of physical illnesses, particularly that of undernourished children, to say nothing of mental conflict and mental illness, depression and despondency and the increasing number of problems of delinquency.

And a veteran social worker sighed:

> As I observe the young people in this fourth year of the depression [1934] I am appalled by their cynical acceptance of things as they are. They are not avid for tools of understanding: they reject opportunities for vocational preparation, seeing, as they do, that fitness is no guarantee of work. . . .

Young people went to college but with faint prospect of employment. Alfred Kazin's mood was typical: "One hot afternoon, in June, 1934, deep in the depression, I had just completed my college course for the year and was desolately on my way home to Brooklyn." Early in the depression it was possible to declare, as did the director of a Jewish employment bureau, that "We should face our employment situation as a people and solve our problems within the group," in the spirit of the apologetic pride that "Jews take care of their own." However, the dimensions of the problem became so huge that Jews no longer even made the attempt. Until the New Deal made the relief of unemployment a federal responsibility, there were sad and sometimes stormy scenes in Jewish agencies which, like other private charities, were the funnel through which state unemployment relief appropriations were doled out to recipients. The New Deal unemployment burden relieved Jewish and private charities of an impossible burden. Even in 1938 there was heavy Jewish unemployment, said to be 14.7 percent of the Jewish labor force in Pittsburgh, 5.2 percent in Buffalo, and 8.8 percent of experienced Jewish workers in San Francisco; in Detroit, three years before, it had stood at 14.7 percent. In the New York metropolis, the percentage was 12 to 13 percent in 1935–1937. The rapid shifting of Jewish neighborhoods which accompanied upward mobility lessened or ceased.

So shattering was the depression and the wave of economic anti-Semitism it released that the economic future of the Jews in the United States seemed in question:

> Unlike Americans as a whole, the Jewish group does not possess a balanced economic distribution which allows economic gains and losses, strains and tensions, to be spread evenly among their number. Jews are not represented on the farms or in manual jobs. The needle trades have employed large numbers, although even here other nationalities have been supplanting them in recent decades. The heavy industries engage few Jews either among employers or workers. Banking, stock brokering, moving pictures and other forms of amusement, real estate, and the distributive trades account for most of our Jewish wealth. The professions, small business and white-collar occupations yield our large Jewish middle class.

The middle class, and precisely its mercantile and white-collar segment in which Jews sought their place, seemed the most endangered in the long range, although, as it happened, it was rather less afflicted by unemployment than was unskilled and proletarian labor. Thus, unemployment among Jews was proportionately less severe. Perhaps, it was argued, Jews were "overrepresented" in trade and the professions, and their youth should be directed to become farmers, technicians, and skilled craftsmen. By no means was it clear when representation became overrepresentation. More or less it meant fields where there were many Jews or against which anti-Semites complained. These proposals for vocational shifts, in retrospect, were attuned more to public relations than to economic realities. Young Jews disregarded them, and continued along to college with an eye on independent business and the professions, preparing without realizing it for the opportunities which opened wide in the 1940s.

What disturbed Jews deepest was not the high unemployment and economic insecurity they shared with the American population at large, but the dangerously anti-Semitic atmosphere fostered by the depression which might last many more years. Father Charles E. Coughlin broadcast nationally from Detroit, and his anti-Semitism became more explicit with each weekly talk. At street-corner meetings in upper Manhattan hatred of Jews was spewed and in subway stations beneath they could be assaulted. The Nazis of the German-American Bund sought to carry on like their mentors in Germany. There was a plethora of anti-Semitic organizations. All the time American Jews had in mind the ravaging of the Jews in Germany, like themselves educated, acculturated, patriotic, economically successful. *It Can't Happen Here* was the ironic title of Sinclair Lewis's popular novel of 1935 which imagined how "it" did happen. There was reassurance that the American people largely detested Nazism, yet impossible to suggest any easing of restrictions on the immigration of its Jewish or other victims. President Roosevelt did not choose to try. A proposal for freer immigration was likely to generate a popular counterproposal to halt all immigration to the United States during a period of mass unemployment.

All Jews knew of the large areas of the labor market that were practically shut to them. They had almost no chance in banks, insurance firms—except as brokers selling policies to other Jews—large corporations, department stores, as lawyers in large law firms, as scholars in universities or as physicians in hospitals. To make matters look cleaner, some of these enterprises would hire token Jews who would not be advanced. There were Jewish employers who followed the trend and did not hire Jews. But during a time of desperate job-seeking, many employers did not have to bother with excuses—they didn't want Jews working for them. Most private universities, particularly the most distinguished, had quotas on Jewish admissions. Notorious were the medical schools, whose anti-Semitic policies compelled hundreds of Jewish medical students to emigrate to foreign schools, notably Edinburgh in Scotland.

The large cities knew sharp interethnic tensions. In Boston and New York there was friction between Jews and Irish, as the Jews competed hard and often successfully for jobs in which the Irish had long predominated. These included white-collar work, positions in the school system, and a share in the control of the Democratic party machine with its vast job-giving powers, from street cleaners to judges. The dramatic mayoralty of Fiorello H. LaGuardia in New York City meant the decline of Irish municipal power entrenched in Tammany Hall, and the rise of Jews and Italians. Irish anger at the Jewish challenge also had an ideological basis, with the Jews strongly supporting the Spanish Republicans during the Civil War in Spain and the Catholics—meaning mainly Irish, especially at the level of the hierarchy—strong for the insurgents. Jews opposed the Catholic and Irish desire for some religious influence in the public schools. Before Pearl Harbor, the Irish generally opposed aid to their homeland's old oppressor Great Britain, while most Jews advocated aid to Hitler's enemies. Communism rather than Nazism was the great enemy to many Catholics.

Against this bleak setting of economic trouble, anti-Semitism, and concern for Jews overseas, the presidency of Franklin Delano Roosevelt held a meaning which was not only tangible and political. Even today, almost fifty years after he entered the White House for the longest and most dynamic and eventful tenure in American history, Roosevelt appears so much more vivid a figure than any of his successors that it is easy to realize what he meant to the electorate which four times sent him to the White House. As William E. Leuchtenburg observes:

> When Roosevelt took office, the country to a very large degree responded to the will of a single element: the white, Anglo-Saxon, Protestant property-holding class. Under the New Deal, new groups took their place in the sun. It was not merely that they received benefits they had not had before but that they were "recognized" as having a place in the commonwealth.

The New Deal, that vast, quite unplanned aggregation of relief and reform measures, many of which owed something to Jewish economists and social workers, to the Jewish labor movement and the Lower East Side of New York, became part of the fabric of American life. The mass of Jews embraced it enthusiastically. Yet important as they were, these measures were not the reason for the support of Roosevelt which at times surpassed even adoration to become idolatry. This old American Protestant aristocrat, a type Jews have often supported politically, smiling and supremely affable, placed Jews at the political nerve center in his victorious coalition of ethnic urban groups, proletarian workers, Blacks, and deprived farmers. He openly loathed Nazism and Fascism. He appointed Jews to high office, and it was learned with appreciation that he brushed aside the pleas of some prominent Jews not to raise the Jewish political profile in the dangerous year of 1939, and replaced the revered Brandeis on the Supreme Court with Felix Frankfurter. Eighty to 90 percent of the Jews voted for Roosevelt in his four elections, each time in a higher proportion. The lowest was in the 1932 election when many Jews voted Socialist and Communist. The vote for these parties of the left declined with succeeding presidential elections, and the Jews, like most of the other voters, switched to Roosevelt. One might also suggest a kind of Manichean politics. The embodiment of evil, Adolf Hitler, required the embodiment of good against him, and that had to be Franklin Delano Roosevelt, except for those who insisted in seeing the embodiment in Josef Stalin. Roosevelt was supported in New York by such Jewish favorites as Herbert H. Lehman, Robert F. Wagner, and Fiorello H. LaGuardia.

The evident failure of American capitalism in a liberal, democratic state to fulfill the American promise of mass prosperity led to movements leftward and rightward, for abandoning democracy as the right demanded, or for doing away with capitalism as the left demanded. Jews, of course, gravitated to the left, especially because the far right was anti-Semitic. American literature, including the Jewish writers who were beginning to figure prominently in it, was saturated with the social questions of the time. Jewish writing and thinking moved generally to the left along with American thought and letters at large. The numerous novels of Jewish immigrant life were as a rule autobiographical. They were critical, often harshly so, of the immigrant world and of those who rose within it to worldly success. Now their attitude of rejection extended to the inhospitable social order. One scholar has enumerated seventy radical proletarian novels appearing between 1930 and 1940 by fifty-three authors of whom seventeen appear to be Jewish. Jewish prominence in American literature really begins with these novels of radical protest of which few, to be sure, are good literature.

Social problems were conceived by the intellectual consensus of the time in general social and economic terms, and answers to them were provided in the same frame. There were thus no distinct or specific Jewish problems, and it was unscientific and ethnocentric to assume otherwise. Anti-Semitism had to be regarded as a disease of capitalist society, and the Jews were victims on account of their economic stratification and minority status. Two things were required: a drastic change in capitalism or its abolition, and the participation of the Jews in the forces which were to bring this about, whether these were Socialists or Communists or the new industrial union movement. It was a specious universalism, for it denied that the Jews constituted a group which, whatever else they were part of, was also whole in itself and merited serious attention as such; whatever society did to solve its problems as a whole would not as an automatic consequence solve the problems of the Jews. The universalist Jews naturally sought their place in universalist social and political movements where they frequently found that quite a high proportion of their fellow universalists were also Jews. Many were writers and teachers, as well as social workers who were often employed by institutions within the Jewish community.

It was during the 1930s, at a point in time which cannot be determined, that the majority of Jews became American born. Moreover, American Jews became an older group as their birthrate continued to decline. The immigrant world and its Yiddish press, speech, synagogues, theatre, and literature was passing, and so was the Jewish character of the trade unions they had built. *Landsmanshaften* were shriveling, while "Americanization" activities lost their point except to serve the limited number of refugees from Germany. Religious and cultural life was dominated by the quest for an American form of religious tradition and by the effort to maintain institutions unaided by government or federations of Jewish philanthropies. The characteristic face of Orthodoxy was the postimmigrant neighborhood synagogue, most of whose members were but superficially observant. Major Orthodox leaders arrived from Europe during this time—Rabbis Soloveitchik, Feinstein, Breuer, and Schneerson in chronological order—but their impact was felt only in later years. Reform Judaism, financially better established and long past its adaptation to the American scene, began very tentatively to examine the possibilities of a renewal of religious tradition. It adopted a pro-Zionist policy, but with a forceful anti-Zionist minority in opposition, and also devoted much attention to general social questions. Conservative Judaism was not yet a powerful third force on the religious scene. Yet its Reconstructionist wing, led by Mordecai M. Kaplan, combined theological radicalism with traditional ritual practice, Zionism with the social gospel, and obtained much attention and some influence among rabbis and Jewish communal intelligentsia.

At the level of the organized Jewish community as a whole, except for local Jewish charities, fund-raising faded into the background because so little could be raised for overseas needs. The antiseptic words of the *American Jewish Year Book* for 1931–1932 described the situation:

> Economic conditions in the United States during the past year were such as to compel the Jewish community to apply by far the greater part of its energies to the solution of its own domestic problems, including those of continuing the activities and, in some cases, preventing the dissolution of institutions and agencies which had been created by the community in previous years. American Jewry was prevented therefore from taking as active an interest in its sister communities overseas as in former years, especially as far as material aid was concerned.

The Joint Distribution Committee, supported by the older German-Jewish wealth, saw its income shrink from $4,583,000 in 1927 to $1,632,000 in 1929 and to $385,000 in 1932. The disaster of German Jewry brought a great increase, to $1,151,000 in 1933 and to $1,402,000 in 1934. From 1936 the income of the JDC went up steadily, but still lagged far behind the needs. The combined income of the two main funds for Palestine, the Jewish National Fund and the Palestine Foundation Fund, fell even lower than the JDC. From a mere $723,000 in 1930 it sagged to $339,000 in 1933, and then climbed gradually to $3,489,000 in 1939. Hadassah, however, managed to maintain its income fairly well. During the depressed 1930s the permanent overseas aid structure was built. The Jewish National Fund, the Palestine Foundation Fund, and a few smaller bodies joined to form the United Palestine Appeal in 1935. Four year later the financially successful UPA entered into an agreement with the Joint Distribution Committee and the National Refugee Service, renewable annually, to establish the United Jewish Appeal. There was little about the United Jewish Appeal's early years to foretell that after World War II it would become the largest voluntary philanthropy in history. The partners fought one another constantly over the proportionate distribution of UJA funds. The leaders of the Joint insisted that European Jewry required assistance for physical survival, while the Zionists argued that only by developing Palestine could there be a sure and certain solution to Jewish persecution and homelessness which philanthropy could never provide. Individual communities that conducted combined campaigns were vexed by debates over the proportions to be retained for local needs and those to be sent for overseas requirements.

The time appeared ripe during the 1930s for power within American Jewry to pass into the hands of the East European stock. Numerically, they constituted the vast majority. They were rising fast in political recognition, thanks especially to the New Deal and its local counterparts. The disillusion with America's political and economic leaders of the 1920s included the affluent stockbrokers, bankers, merchants, and lawyers, mainly Republicans of the German-Jewish stock who had controlled the American Jewish community. Louis Marshall, had he lived, would have been out of his element in the 1930s. The old patriciate was vulnerable on other scores. Some of them lost their wealth or much of it, while many patrician heirs were but faintly Jewish when they were Jewish at all. The patriciate had placed its faith in emancipation as the full and sufficient cure for Jewish needs, and in philanthropy, preferably nonsectarian, as their highest expression as Jews. Nazism shattered the first article, while the New Deal made the second expendable. Shorn of their prestige, and in some cases of their wealth and Judaism, their deepest beliefs challenged, it is no surprise that the old leaders hardly led. Their circumspection in Jewish matters domestic and foreign, and their fear and dislike of public agitation ran counter to the eagerness of American Jewry for forceful, passionate demonstration and protest. These were the tactics of the pro-Zionist, pro-New Deal American Jewish Congress, revived in 1930 by Rabbi Stephen S. Wise, and they were deplored by the American Jewish Committee, spokesman of the diminished patriciate. In most local communities Jewish Community Councils were established, functioning as a council of local organizations with a degree of moral suasion but little real power.

Yet the East European stock failed to take over the American Jewish community nationally during the 1930s. They had the numbers but not the money, and men of means are always indispensable in a voluntarily organized community. Perhaps the East Europeans lacked the confidence and the men. Behind the veteran Wise, not an East European himself, one does not find a cadre of potential national leaders of note waiting in the wings, except a few rabbis of whom the most notable was acknowledged to be the brilliant, dominating Abba Hillel Silver of Cleveland. Thus, the old order of the patriciate was gravely weakened during the 1930s, but the newer stock was unable to take over. There was a vacuum of national Jewish leadership at the most critical moment. It was upon this troubled, hesitant Jewish community of some five million souls that war descended in December 1941.

FOR FURTHER READING

The best surveys of American Jewish history between the world wars are Henry Feingold, *A Time for Searching: Entering the Mainstream, 1920–1945* (1992), Judd L. Teller, *Strangers and Natives* (1968), which describes "the evolution of the American Jew from 1921 to the present," and Lucy S. Dawidowicz's *On Equal Terms* (1982), which covers American Jewish life during the past century. Oscar Janowsky (ed.), *The American Jew: A Composite Portrait* (1942), contains insightful articles on the period by contemporaries. For in-depth study, the annual volumes of the *American Jewish Year Book* are indispensable.

Leonard Dinnerstein has surveyed American anti-Semitism, including the twentieth century, in his *Antisemitism in America* (1994); see also his "The Historiography of American Antisemitism," in L. Dinnerstein (ed.), *Antisemitism and the American Jewish Experience* (1987), and John Higham's pathbreaking essays collected in his *Send These To Me* (1975). The most thoroughly documented incident of twentieth-century American anti-Semitism is the subject of Leonard Dinnerstein's *The Leo Frank Case* (1966). Anti-Semitic quotas against Jews at American universities are treated in Henry L. Feingold, "Investing in Themselves: The Harvard Case and the Origins of the Third American Jewish Commercial Elite," *American Jewish History* 77 (1988), pp. 530–553; Harold Wechsler, *The Qualified Student* (1977); and Marcia Synnott, *The Half-Opened Door* (1979). Concerning other manifestations of anti-Semitism during this period, see Robert Singerman, *Antisemitic Propaganda: An Annotated Bibliography and Research Guide* (1982), which covers primary and secondary sources.

Jewish religious developments in twentieth-century America are treated broadly in Nathan Glazer's *American Judaism* (1972), Marc Lee Raphael's *Profiles in Judaism* (1984), and the articles in Jack Wertheimer (ed.), *The American Synagogue* (1987). Various important articles are also gathered in Jacob Neusner (ed.), *Understanding American Judaism* (2 vols., 1975). The emergence of the American rabbinate is analyzed from three Jewish religious perspectives in a special issue of *American Jewish Archives* 35 (November 1983). For other religious developments, see Deborah Dash Moore's *At Home in America: Second Generation New York Jews* (1981); and Arnold M. Eisen's *The Chosen People in America* (1983), the first serious study of American Jewish religious ideology. Specific developments in Judaism's different movements can be traced through three excellent volumes published in the "Jewish Denominations in America" series, each a biographical dictionary and sourcebook with an extensive bibliography: Pamela Nadell, *Conservative Judaism in America* (1988); Kerry Olitzky, Lance Sussman, and Malcolm Stern, *Reform Judaism in America* (1993); and Moshe D. Sherman, *Orthodox Judaism in America* (1996). Mel Scult's *Judaism Faces the Twentieth Century: A Biography of Mordecai Kaplan* (1993) and Emanuel S. Goldsmith et al. (eds.), *The American Judaism of Mordecai M. Kaplan* (1990) treat one of the most significant figures in American Judaism, who was also the founder of Reconstructionism. Jenna Weissman Joselit, *New York's Jewish Jews* (1990) treats the "Orthodox community in the interwar years," and her *The Wonders of America* (1994) looks at the Americanization of Judaism through the prism of domesticity.

The Zionist movement in America has spawned a vast literature. Melvin I. Urofsky, *American Zionism from Herzl to the Holocaust* (1976) and Naomi W. Cohen, *American Jews and the Zionist Idea* (1975) are the best synthetic treatments, both with extensive references to other sources. Philippa Strum, *Louis Brandeis: Justice for the People* (1984) and Urofsky's *A Voice That Spoke for Justice* (1982), a biography of Stephen S. Wise, also contain much on Zionism during this period. Benjamin Halpern, "The Americanization of Zionism, 1880–1930," *American Jewish History* 69 (1979), pp. 15–33 and Jehuda Reinharz, "Zionism in the USA on the Eve of the Balfour Declaration," *Studies in Zionism* 9 (1988), pp. 131–145 reinterpret American Zionism's early history. Yonathan Shapiro, *Leadership of the American Zionist Organization* (1971); Samuel Halperin, *The Political World of American Zionism* (1961); Benjamin Halpern, *A Clash of Heroes* (1987), and Allon Gal, *David Ben-Gurion and the American Alignment for a Jewish State* (1991) deal more broadly with the American Zionist leadership. *American Jewish History* 75 (1985), pp. 130–183, contains assessments by Israeli and American historians of "the influence of Zionism on the American Jewish community"; see also Evyatar Friesel, "American Zionism and American Jewry: An Ideological and Communal Encounter," *American Jewish Archives* 40 (1988), pp. 5–23. Stuart Knee, *The Concept of Zionist Dissent in the American Mind* (1979), Thomas A. Kolsky, *Jews Against Zionism: The American Council for Judaism, 1942–1948* (1990), and Menahem Kaufman, *An Ambiguous Partnership: Non-Zionists and Zionists in America, 1939–1948* (1991) look at a range of American Zionism's allies and critics. For articles on other specialized themes see the *Herzl Year Book* and the journal *Studies in Zionism* (now *Journal of Israel Studies*).

The relationship between American Reform Judaism and Zionism has attracted particular attention in recent years: see David Polish, *Renew Our Days: The Zionist Issue in Reform Judaism* (1976); Howard

R. Greenstein, *Turning Point: Zionism and Reform Judaism* (1981); Michael A. Meyer, "American Reform Judaism and Zionism: Early Efforts at Ideological Rapprochement," *Studies in Zionism* 7 (1983), pp. 49–64; and Gary P. Zola, "Reform Judaism's Pioneer Zionist: Maximilian Heller," *American Jewish History* 73 (June 1984), pp. 375–397. For the American government's attitude toward the Zionist movement, see Peter Grose, *Israel in the Mind of America* (1983); Zvi Ganin, *Truman, American Jewry and Israel* (1979); Michael Cohen, *Truman and Israel* (1990); and the review essay by Ian Bickerton in *American Jewish Archives* 33 (April 1981), pp. 141–152.

Beth Wenger, *New York Jews and the Great Depression* (1996), offers the first book-length study of this subject. See also Leonard Dinnerstein's study of "Jews in the New Deal" in the special issue of *American Jewish History* 72 (June 1983) devoted to "The Centennial of Roosevelt's Birth." Years ago, Abraham Cronbach argued that Jews' pioneering role in American social welfare influenced New Deal legislation: see his "Jewish Pioneering in American Social Welfare," *American Jewish Archives* 3 (June 1951), pp. 51–78.

American Jewish literature has a large bibliography of its own. See Lewis Fried et al., *Handbook of American-Jewish Literature* (1988); Daniel Walden, *Twentieth-Century American Jewish Fiction Writers* (1984); Ann R. Shapiro et al., *Jewish American Women Writers: A Bio-Bibliographical and Critical Sourcebook* (1994); and Ira B. Nadel, *Jewish Writers of North America: A Guide to Information Sources* (1981). Book-length surveys include Louis Harap, *The Image of the Jew in American Literature: From Early Republic to Mass Immigration* (1974), which covers the early literature, and its sequels: *Dramatic Encounters* (1987), *Critical Awakening* (1987), and *In the Mainstream* (1987). For Irving Howe's stimulating interpretation, see the introduction to his *Jewish-American Stories* (1977). Recent developments are surveyed in Sylvia B. Fishman, "American Jewish Fiction Turns Inward," *American Jewish Year Book* 91 (1991), pp. 35–69.

PART FIVE
THE HOLOCAUST AND BEYOND

Three major developments shaped American Jewish life in the decades following World War II. The first, the Holocaust—the mass murder of six million Jews by the Nazis—had the most immediate effect. With European centers of Judaism destroyed, America remained the only major culturally vibrant Jewish center left in the Diaspora. As a result, smaller Jewish communities in Europe and around the world turned increasingly to American Jewry for guidance and support. Thousands of Jewish refugees likewise turned to America, and under more liberal immigration procedures many gained admission. Within a few years, some had contributed in vital ways to American cultural, scientific, and intellectual life. Others, especially Hungarian and Hassidic Jews, added fresh dimensions to American Judaism, and helped to promote Orthodoxy's postwar revitalization.

The second major development to have an impact on American Jewish life came in 1948 with the creation of the State of Israel. Before long, support for Israel became a fundamental tenet of American Jewish life, the main focus of American Jewish charities, and a basic standard by which American Jews judged their political allies. The precise relationship between American Jews and Israel remained ill-defined, particularly as Israel emerged as an independent center of worldwide Jewish life. Still, the two Jewish communities came to share and experience a growing emotional feeling of interdependence—perennial disagreements notwithstanding.

The final development that changed postwar Jewish life was the spectacular rise of American Jews to positions of authority and respect within the general American community. Burgeoning economic growth, the postwar decline of anti-Semitism, increasing popular acceptance of religious and cultural pluralism, the high educational achievements of native-born Jews, and an overpowering desire on the part of many Jews to "make it" in America all contributed to this extraordinary success. The result was a community more at home in America than ever before: more self-assured, more confident about expressing its Judaism in public, more willing to use the political arena to fight for issues of communal concern. Jews did, to be sure, still continue to monitor anti-Semitism and to express concern whenever it arose. But they worried far more about assimilation, for as anti-Semitism declined intermarriage rates rose. The question Jews faced as they entered their fourth century on American soil—a perennial question, as we have seen—was how to *balance* assimilation and identity; how to be at home in two worlds, American and Jewish, without having to forsake one for the other.

CHAPTER 18

The word "Holocaust" came to refer to the mass Nazi extermination of six million Jews only in the early 1960s. It was then that the trial of Adolf Eichmann, the writings of Elie Wiesel, and, slightly later, Arthur Morse's best-seller, While Six Million Died, *brought home to many just how awesome the effects of the catastrophe had been, and how many unresolved questions it left in its wake. Since that time, the Holocaust in all its dimensions has been closely studied, and volumes concerned with the subject have multiplied. But some of the most sensitive questions relating to the Holocaust remain unanswered. They are still passionately debated today.*

From the point of view of American Jewish history one critical question stands out: Could American Jewry have done more to save their brethren in need? Many say yes. They blame Jewish leaders for doing too little too late, argue that American Jews generally should have applied greater pressure on the government, and point accusingly at missed opportunities—actions that if taken might have made a difference. Their bill of indictment is a long one, and includes some of American Jewry's best respected leaders.

But there is also another side to the question, ably argued here by Henry L. Feingold, one of the foremost scholars in the Holocaust field. He concludes—-sadly—that given the realities of the day much more could not *have been done. America's highest priority was to win the war; that, President Roosevelt argued, was the best way to rescue Jews. As for admitting Jewish refugees outside the normal quota, nativist feelings ran so high that even a bill to admit refugee children failed to pass the Congress. Efforts to admit hundreds of thousands of Jews were foredoomed. Of course, Americans failed to fully appreciate what the Final Solution meant. Even those who did read about it in their newspapers could not have comprehended it; nothing on such a scale had ever happened before. While Feingold agrees that Jewish leaders might have been more united, and probably put too much faith in the President's goodwill, he points out that they could hardly have opposed the President in wartime even if they had wanted to. The lesson he draws is clear: American Jews, indeed Jews everywhere in the Diaspora, were far less powerful than they or their enemies believed.*

Who Shall Bear Guilt for the Holocaust? The Human Dilemma

Henry L. Feingold

A simple searing truth emerges from the vast body of research and writing on the Holocaust. It is that European Jewry was ground to dust between the twin millstones of a murderous Nazi intent and a callous Allied indifference. It is a truth with which the living seem unable to come to terms. Historians expect that as time moves us away from a cataclysmic event our passions will subside and our historical judgment of it will mellow. But that tempered judgment is hardly in evidence in the historical examination of the Holocaust. Instead, time has merely produced a longer list of what might have been done and an indictment that grows more damning. There are after all six million pieces of evidence to demonstrate that the world did not do enough. Can anything more be said?

Given that emotionally charged context, it seems at the least foolhardy and at the most blasphemous to question whether the characterization of the Holocaust's witnesses as callously indifferent does full justice to the historical reality of their posture during those bitter years. There is a strange disjuncture in the emerging history of the witnesses. Researchers pile fact upon fact to show that they did almost nothing to save Jewish lives. And yet if the key decision makers could speak today they would be puzzled by the indictment, since they rarely thought about Jews at all. Roosevelt might admit to some weakness at Yalta, and Churchill might admit that the Italian campaign was a mistake. But if they recalled Auschwitz at all it would probably be vague in their memories.

Historical research in the area of the Holocaust is beset with problems of no ordinary kind. It seems as if the memory of that man-made catastrophe is as deadly to the spirit of scholarship as was the actual experience to those who underwent its agony. The answers we are receiving are so muddled. The perpetrators have been found to be at once incredibly demonic but also banal. The suspicion that the victims were less than courageous, that they supposedly went "like sheep to the slaughter," has produced a minor myth about heroic resistance in the Warsaw ghetto and the forests of eastern Europe to prove that it wasn't so. Like the resistance apologetic, the indictment against the witnesses is as predictable as it is irresistible.

That is so because in theory, at least, witnessing nations and agencies had choices, and there is ample evidence that the choices made were not dictated by human concern as we think they should have been. In the case of America the charge of indifference is heard most clearly in the work of Arthur Morse, who found the rescue activities of the Roosevelt administration insufficient and filled with duplicity, and Saul Friedman, who allowed his anger to pour over into an indictment of American Jewry and its leadership. One ought not to dismiss such works out of hand. And yet it is necessary to recognize that they are as much cries of pain as they are serious history.

The list of grievances is well known. The Roosevelt administration could have offered a haven between the years 1938 and 1941. Had that been done, had there been more largess, there is some reason to believe that the decision for systematic slaughter taken in Berlin might not have been made or at least might have been delayed. There could have been threats of retribution and other forms of psychological warfare which would have signaled to those in Berlin and in the Nazi satellites that the Final Solution entailed punishment. Recently the question of bombing the concentration camps and the rail lines leading to them has received special attention. The assumption is that physical intercession from the air might have slowed the killing process. American Jewry has been subject to particularly serious charges of not having done enough, of not using its considerable political leverage during the New Deal to help its brethren. Other witnesses also have been judged wanting. Britain imposed a White Paper limiting migration to Palestine in the worst of the refugee crisis, the Pope failed to use his great moral power against the Nazis, the International Red Cross showed little daring in interpreting its role vis-à-vis the persecution of the Jews. The list documenting the witnesses' failure of spirit and mind could be extended; but that would take us away from the core problem faced by the historian dealing with the subject.

He must determine what the possibilities of rescue actually were. Failure cannot be determined until we have some agreement on what was realistically possible. There is little agreement among historians on what these possibilities were, given Nazi fanaticism on the Jewish question. Lucy Dawidowicz, for example, argues compellingly that once the ideological and physical war were merged in the Nazi invasion of Russia in June 1941, the possibilities for rescue were minimal. That, incidentally, was the position also taken by Earl Winterton, who for a time represented Britain on the Intergovernmental Committee, and Breckinridge Long, the undersecretary of state responsible for the potpourri of programs that made up the American rescue effort during the crisis. Other historians, including myself, have pointed out that the Nazi *Gleichshaltung* on the Jewish question was nowhere near so efficient as generally assumed. The war mobilization of their economy, for example, was not achieved until 1944. Opportunities for rescue were present especially during the refugee phase, when the Final Solution had not yet been decided upon and possibilities of bribery and ransom existed. It was the momentum of this initial failure during the refugee phase that carried over into the killing phase.

The point is that in the absence of agreement on possibilities, historians are merely repeating the debate between power holders and rescue advocates which took place during the crisis. The latter group insisted that not enough was being done and the former insisted that the best way to save the Jews was to win the war as quickly as possible. Nothing could be done to interfere with that objective—including, ironically, the rescue of the Jews. When Stephen Wise pointed out that by the time victory came there would be no Jews left in Europe, he exposed what the argument between rescue advocates and their opponents in fact was about. It concerned priorities, and beyond that, the war aims that ordered those priorities. What rescue advocates were asking then, and what the historians of the role of witness are asking today, is: Why was not the Jewish question central to the concern of the witnesses as it was to the Nazis who spoke about it incessantly? But we cannot solve that question of priorities until we have some answer to the question of what World War II was all about, and what role the so-called "Jewish question" played in it.

Clearly, Allied war leaders were wary of accepting the Nazi priority on the Jewish question. The war was not one to save the Jews, and they would not allow war strategy and propaganda to be aimed in that direction. None of the conferences that worked out war aims and strategy—the Argentina meeting which produced the Atlantic Charter (August 1941), the several visits of Churchill to Washington, the Casablanca Conference (January 1943), the Quebec Conference (August 1943), the Moscow Conference (October 1943), the Teheran Conference in November, and finally the Yalta and Potsdam conferences in 1945—had anything to say about the fate of the Jews. The silence was not solely a consequence of the fact that Allied leaders did not remotely fathom the special significance of what was happening to Jews in Nazi concentration camps. Even had they understood, it is doubtful that they would have acknowledged the centrality of the Final Solution. To have done so would have played into Nazi hands and perhaps interfered with a full mobilization for war. Hence Roosevelt's insistence on using a euphemistic vocabulary to handle what Berlin called the Jewish problem. There was distress in the Oval Office when George Rublee, who had unexpectedly negotiated a "Statement of Agreement" with Hjalmar Schacht and Helmut Wohlthat in the spring of 1939, spoke of Jews rather than the "political refugees," the preferred euphemism. The two agencies concerned with Jews, the Intergovernmental Committee for Political Refugees which grew out of the Evian Conference, and the War Refugee Board, carefully avoided the use of the word Jew in their titles. When the American restrictive immigration law was finally circumvented in the spring of 1944 and a handful of refugees were to be interned in Oswego outside the quota system, just as had been done for thousands of suspected Axis agents active in Latin America, Robert Murphy was cautioned to be certain to select a "good mix" from the refugees who had found a precarious haven in North Africa. Undoubtedly what Roosevelt meant was not too many Jews. The crucible of the Jews under the Nazi yoke was effectively concealed behind the camouflage terminology conceived by the Nazi bureaucracy and the Allies. Even today in eastern Europe unwillingness persists to recognize the special furor the Nazis reserved for the Jews and the relationship of the Jews to the Holocaust. The Soviet government does not acknowledge that it was Jews who were slaughtered at Babi Yar; and in Poland the Jewish victims have become in death what they were never in life, honored citizens of that nation. In the East it became the Great Patriotic War and in the West it was ultimately dubbed the Great Crusade, never a war to save the Jews. Those who examine the history textbooks continually note with despair that the Holocaust is barely mentioned at all.

The low level of concern about the fate of the Jews had a direct effect in strengthening the hands of those in Berlin responsible for implementing the Final Solution. They became convinced that the democracies secretly agreed with their plan to rid the world of the Jewish scourge. "At bottom," Goebbels wrote in his diary on December 13, 1942, "I believe both the English and the Americans are happy that we are exterminating the Jewish riff-raff." It was not difficult even for those less imaginative than Goebbels to entertain such a fantasy. Each Jew sent to the East meant, in effect, one fewer refugee in need of a haven and succor. Inadvertently the Final Solution was solving a problem for the Allies as well. Nazi propaganda frequently took note in the early years of the war of the reluctance of the receiving nations to welcome Jews. They watched London's policy of curtailing immigration to Palestine, American refusal to receive the number of refugees that might have been legally admitted under the quota system, the Pope's silence. Goebbels' impression was after all not so far from the truth. Smull Zygelbojm, the Bundist representative to the Polish Government-in-Exile, came to much the same conclusion shortly before his suicide.

Yet Zygelbojm, who was very close to the crisis, was bedeviled by the dilemma of what to do. He was dismayed by the assumption underlying a request for action that he received from Warsaw in the spring of 1943. The message demanded that Jewish leaders "go to all important English and American agencies. Tell them not to leave until they have obtained guarantees that a way has been decided upon to save the Jews. Let them accept no food or drink, let them die a slow death while the world looks on. This may shake the conscience of the world." "It is utterly impossible," Zygelbojm wrote to a friend, "they would never let me die a slow lingering death. They would simply bring in two policemen and have me dragged away to an institution." The bitter irony was that while Zygelbojm had come to have grave doubts about the existence of a "conscience of the world," his former colleagues in Warsaw, who were aware of the fate that awaited Jews at Treblinka, could still speak of it as if it were a reality.

Once such priorities were in place it proved relatively easy for State Department officers like Breckinridge Long to build what one historian has called a "paper wall"—a series of all but insurmountable administrative regulations to keep Jewish refugees out of America. "We can delay and effectively stop for a temporary period of indefinite length," he informed Adolf A. Berle and James C. Dunn on June 26, 1940, "the number of immigrants into the U.S. We could do this by simply advising our consuls to put every obstacle in the way and resort to various administrative advices [*sic*] which would postpone and postpone." That is precisely what was done; only in the year 1939 were the relevant quotas filled. During the initial phase the mere existence of strong restrictionist sentiment reinforced by the depression proved sufficient. After the war started, the notion that the Nazis had infiltrated spies into the refugee stream was used. The creation of a veritable security psychosis concerning refugees triggered the creation of a screening procedure so rigid that after June 1940 it was more difficult for a refugee to gain entrance to the neutral United States than to wartime Britain. During the war a similar low priority for the rescue of Jews might be noted in the neutral nations of Latin America and Europe, the Vatican and the International Red Cross. There was no agency of international standing which could press the Jewish case specifically. But that is a well-known story that need not be retold here.

The question is, why did not the witnessing nations and agencies sense that the systematic killing in the death camps by means of production processes developed in the West was at the ideological heart of World War II, and therefore required a response? Why were they unable to fathom that Auschwitz meant more than the mass destruction of European Jewry? It perverted the values at the heart of their own civilization; if allowed to proceed unhampered, it meant that their world would never be the same again. Roosevelt, Churchill, and Pius XII understood that they were locked in mortal combat with an incredibly demonic foe. But as the leaders of World War I sent millions to their death with little idea of the long-range consequences, these leaders never had the moral insight to understand that the destruction of the Jews would also destroy something central to their way of life. Even today few thinkers have made the link between the demoralization and loss of confidence in the West and the chimneys of the death camps. The Holocaust has a relatively low priority in the history texts used in our schools. It is merely another in a long litany of atrocities. Today as yesterday, few understand that a new order of events occurred in Auschwitz, and that our lives can never be the same again.

Yet how could it have been different? If the key decision makers at the time were told what Auschwitz really meant, would it have made a difference? They would have dismissed the notion that they could make decisions on the basis of abstract philosophy even if the long-range continuance of their own nations were at stake. They were concerned with concrete reality, with survival for another day. Until the early months of 1943 it looked to them as if their enterprise would surely fail. And if that happened, what matter abstract notions about the sanctity of life? The sense that *all* life, not merely Jewish life, was in jeopardy may have been less urgently felt in America, which even after Pearl Harbor was geographically removed from the physical destruction wrought by war. In America it was business as usual. What was being done to Jews was a European affair. Roosevelt viewed the admission of refugees in the domestic political context, the only one he really knew and could control to some extent. He understood that the American people would never understand the admission of thousands, perhaps millions, of refugees while "one third of the nation was ill housed, ill fed and ill clad." In case he dared forget, Senator Reynolds, a Democrat from North Carolina in the forefront of the struggle to keep refugees out, was there to remind him, and did so by using the President's own ringing phrases.

That brings us to the most bitter ironies of all concerning the role of America. The Roosevelt administration's inability to move on the refugee front was a classic case of democracy at work, the democracy which American Jewry revered so highly. The American people, including its Jewish component before 1938, did not welcome refugees. So strong was this sentiment that it would have taken an act of extraordinary political courage to thwart the popular will. Had Roosevelt done so there was a good chance, as Rep. Samuel Dickstein, the Jewish chairman of the House Committee on Immigration and Naturalization pointed out, that there would have occurred a congressional reaction of even more restrictive laws in the face of the crisis. Roosevelt was occasionally capable of such political courage, especially on a major issue. Witness his action on the destroyer-bases deal which he implemented by executive order in September 1940. But in the case of refugees, even Jewish refugee children, he chose to be more the fox than the lion. He settled first for a politics of gestures. That is perhaps the key to the mystery of the invitation of thirty-two nations to Evian extended in March 1938 to consider the refugee problem. The invitation was carefully hedged. It stated that the United States would not alter its immigration regulations and did not expect other states to do so. That of course consigned the Evian conference to failure.

Soon the "politics of gestures" became more elaborate. It featured among other things an enthusiasm for mass resettlement schemes. That usually amounted to tucking away a highly urbanized Jewish minority in some tropical equatorial rain forest or desert to "pioneer." The Jews predictably could not muster much passion for it. Resettlement imposed on Jews, whether conceived in Berlin or Washington, they understood as a concealed form of group dissolution, and they would have little to do with it. Thus it was doomed to failure.

By the time Henry Morgenthau, Jr., Roosevelt's secretary of the treasury and perhaps his closest Jewish friend, was enlisted in the rescue effort, it was already late in the game. Morgenthau did succeed in convincing the President to establish the War Refugee Board in January 1944. He prepared a highly secret brief which demonstrated that the State Department had deliberately and consistently sabotaged efforts to rescue Jews. It was a devastating document, and the WRB which it brought into existence did play an important role in saving those Hungarian Jews in Budapest who survived the war. But it was created too late to save the millions.

Similar practical concerns dictated the response of other witnessing nations and agencies. Pressed unwillingly into a life-and-death struggle for survival, British leaders predictably viewed German anti-Jewish depredations within the context of their own national survival. It was a foregone conclusion that in balancing the needs of the Jews against their own need for Arab loyalty and oil should there be a war, the latter would win out. Within that context they were, according to one researcher, more generous to Jewish refugees than the United States. Apparently moral considerations did bother some British leaders after the betrayal of the White Paper. It was partly that which led to the hedged offer of British Guiana for a small resettlement scheme. That colony had been the scene of two prior resettlement failures, and posed many other problems, so that except for some territorialists like Josef Rosen, Jews did not welcome it with enthusiasm and Zionists certainly did not see it as a substitute for Palestine. The indifferent response of Jewish leaders exasperated Sir Herbert Emerson, chairman of the Intergovernmental Refugee Committee. The subtle anti-Semitism in his reaction was not uncommon among middle-echelon bureaucrats in London and Washington: "The trouble with the refugee affair was the trouble with the Jews and most eastern people," he complained in Washington in October 1939. "There was always some other scheme in the background for which they were prepared to sacrifice schemes already in hand."

The problem with assessing the role of the Vatican as witness is made complex by the fact that such power as it had was in the spiritual rather than the temporal realm; and yet the Pope faced a problem of survival which was physical, involving as it did the institution of the Church. Just as we expected the leader who introduced the welfare state in America to demonstrate a special sensitivity to the plight of the Jews, so the Pope, who ostensibly embodied in his person the moral conscience of a good part of the Christian world, was expected to speak out, to use his power. He did not, and it does not require a special study of Church politics to realize that its priorities were ordered by crucial requirements in the temporal rather than the spiritual sphere. During World War II it also sensed that it faced a struggle for mere survival. The Vatican probably possessed more precise information on the actual workings of the Final Solution than did any other state. And while the Pope had none of the divisions Stalin later sought, he had an extensive, brilliantly organized infrastructure which might have been brought into play for rescue work and a voice that had a profound influence with millions in occupied Europe. Yet the Pope remained silent, even while the Jews of Rome were deported "from under his window." That posture contrasted sharply with the activities of certain Dutch and French bishops and some lesser officials like Cardinal Roncalli, later Pope John, who were active in the rescue effort. But these did not bear the responsibility for the survival of the institution of the Church itself.

One need not search out the reason for the Pope's silence in his Germanophilia or in his oversensitivity to the threat the Church faced from the Left. The latter had been demonstrated under the Calles and Cardenas regime in Mexico and during the Civil War in Spain. But observing that the Church genuinely felt the threat of "Godless Communism" is a long way from concluding that therefore Pius XII accepted the Nazis' line that they were the staunchest opponents of a Communist conspiracy which was somehow Jewish in nature. The immediate threat to the Church during the years of the Holocaust emanated from Berlin, and we know today that Hitler did indeed intend to settle matters with the Church after hostilities were over.

The Nazi ideology not only posed a physical threat, but also divided the Catholic flock. Over 42 percent of the SS were Catholic, and many top-ranking Nazi leaders, including Hitler, Himmler, Heydrich, and Eichmann, were at least nominally so. The war itself had placed the Vatican in a delicate position since Catholics fought on both sides. The Pope's primary problem was how to walk that delicate tightrope. The determination not to speak out on Jews, which was at the very center of Nazi cosmology, should be viewed in that light. His choice was not basically different from that of the British in the Middle East or of Roosevelt on refugee policy.

The International Red Cross also thought in terms of its viability as an agency whose effectiveness was based on its ability to maintain a strict neutrality. It faced a legal dilemma, for although the Nazis spoke endlessly about the threat of "international Jewry" the Jews of Germany were legally an "internal" problem during the refugee phase. After the deportation and internment in camps began, their status became even more difficult to define. When Denmark requested the Red Cross to investigate the fate of Danish Jews deported to Theresienstadt, it could do so since the request indicated that Denmark continued to recognize them as Danish citizens. But such requests were not forthcoming from other occupied countries. And the

Danish request set the stage for one of the cruelest hoaxes of the war. The Red Cross delegation which visited Theresienstadt to carry out that charge apparently was totally taken in by the Potemkin village techniques, and gave the "model" camp a clean bill of health even while inmates were starving to death and being deported to Auschwitz behind the facade. Overly sensitive to the fact that it was a voluntary agency whose operation depended on the goodwill of all parties, it did not press with determination the case concerning Jews. Food parcels were not delivered to camps until 1944, nor did it press for a change of classification of certain Jewish inmates to prisoners of war. That tactic, suggested by the World Jewish Congress, might have saved many lives. It was for that reason that Leon Kubowitzki, the leading rescue proponent of the World Jewish Congress, found that "the persistent silence of the Red Cross in the face of various stages of the extermination policy, of which it was well informed, will remain one of the troubling and distressing riddles of the Second World War." Yet here too one can observe how the integrity and well-being of the agency took precedence over the rescue of the Jews. It may well be that the priorities of nations and international agencies are directed first and foremost to their own well-being and cannot readily be transferred for altruistic reasons to a vulnerable minority facing the threat of mass murder.

We come next to a question which embodies at once all the frustrations we feel at the failure of the witnesses and which is for that reason posed with increasing frequency in Holocaust symposia and in publications on the catastrophe. The question of bombing Auschwitz and the rail lines leading to the camp raises the twin problems of assessing the failure of the witnesses and of determining the range of possibilities and their relationship to strategic priorities. The assumption is that interdiction from the air was, in the absence of physical control of the death camps, the best practical way to interrupt the killing process.

A recent article in *Commentary* by Professor David Wyman and another by Roger M. Williams in *Commonweal* demonstrate beyond doubt that by the spring of 1944 the bombing of Auschwitz was feasible. Thousands of Hungarian and Slovakian Jews might have been saved had the American 15th Air Force, stationed in Italy and already bombing the synthetic oil and rubber works not five miles from the gas chambers, been allowed to do so. Moreover, by the fall of 1944 Auschwitz was well within the range of Russian dive bombers. Given that context, the note by Assistant Secretary of the Army John J. McCloy that bombing was of "doubtful efficacy" and the Soviet rejection of the idea are the most horrendously inhuman acts by witnesses during the years of the Holocaust. All that was required was a relatively minor change in the priority assigned to the rescue of Jews.

Yet a perceptive historian cannot long remain unaware of the seductive element in the bombing alternative. All one had to do, it seems, was to destroy the death chambers or the railroad lines leading to them, and the "production" of death would cease or at least be delayed. Things were not that simple. Jewish rescue advocates were late in picking up the signals emanating from Hungary for bombing, and even then there was little unanimity on its effectiveness. It was the World Jewish Congress which transmitted the request for bombing to the Roosevelt administration; but its own agent, A. Leon Kubowitzki, held strong reservations about bombing since he did not want the Jewish inmates of the camps to be the first victims of Allied intercession from the air. There were then and continue to be today genuine doubts that, given German fanaticism on the Jewish question and the technical difficulties involved in precision bombing, bombing the camps could have stopped the killing. The *Einzatsgruppen*, the special killing squads which followed behind German lines after the invasion of Russia, killed greater numbers in shorter order than the camps. The Germans were able to repair rail lines and bridges with remarkable speed. And, of course, Auschwitz was only one of the several camps where organized killing took place.

Most important, the bombing-of-Auschwitz alternative, so highly touted today, does not come to grips with the question of the fear that the Germans would escalate the terror and involve the Allies in a contest in which the Germans held all the cards. In a recent interview, McCloy cited this reason rather than the unwillingness to assign war resources to missions that were not directly involved in winning the war as the reason uppermost in Roosevelt's mind when the bombing alternative was rejected. An almost unnoticed sub-theme in McCloy's August 14 note spoke of the fear that bombing might "provoke even more vindictive action by the Germans." Survivors and rescue advocates might well wonder what "more vindictive action" than Auschwitz was possible. But that views the bombing alternative from the vantage of the Jewish victims—which, as we have seen, is precisely what non-Jewish decision makers could not do, given their different order of priorities and sense of what was possible. The people who conceived of the Final Solution could in fact have escalated terror. They could have staged mass executions of prisoners of war or of hostages in occupied countries or the summary execution of shot-down bomber crews for "war crimes." Their imagination rarely failed when it came to conceiving new forms of terror, nor did they seem to possess such normal moral restraints as one might find in the Allied camp. That was one of the reasons that the Final Solution could be implemented by them.

Nevertheless, one can hardly escape the conclusion that bombing deserved to be tried and might conceivably have saved lives. The failure to do so, however, is best viewed in the larger framework of the bombing question. It began with a collective *démarche* delivered by the governments-in-exile to the Allied high command in December 1942. That request did not ask for the bombing of the camps, but for something called "retaliatory bombing." That notion too was rejected because of the fear of an escalation of terror, and rescue advocates did not pick up the idea until it was all but too late. There is good reason to believe that retaliatory bombing offered even greater hope for rescue than the bombing of the camps themselves.

In 1943, when the death mills of Auschwitz and other death camps ground on relentlessly, bombing was in fact not feasible but retaliatory bombing was. That was the year when the heavy saturation bombing of German cities was in full swing. In one sense the bombing of Hamburg in July 1943 and the savaging of other German cities, including the bombing of Dresden, which many Germans consider a separate war atrocity, make sense today only when considered in the context of the death camps. Albert Speer and our own postwar evaluation of saturation bombing inform us that it had almost no effect on curtailing German war production. Not until one industry, fuel or ball bearings, was target-centered did the Nazi war machine feel the pinch. Yet it might have furnished rescue advocates with an instrument to break through the "wall of silence" which surrounded what was happening to Jews. Even bombing interpreted as retaliatory could have remarkable effects, especially in the satellites. When Miklos Horthy, the Hungarian regent, called a halt to the deportations on July 7, 1944, he did so in part out of fear that Budapest would be subject to more heavy raids, as it had been on June 2. It was the bombing of Budapest, not Auschwitz, that had the desired effect. We know that Goebbels in his perverse way fully expected such a *quid pro quo* and had even taken the precaution of planning a massive counter-atrocity campaign should the Allies make a connection between bombing and the death camps. Himmler also had already made the link. We find him addressing his officers on June 21, 1944, on the great difficulties encountered in implementing the Final Solution. He told the gathered group that if their hearts were ever softened by pity, let them remember that the savage bombing of German cities "was after all organized in the last analysis by the Jews."

Yet the natural link between bombing and the Final Solution made by Nazi leaders was not shared by Allied leadership or by Jewish rescue advocates. Had they done so, it is not inconceivable that the fear of disaffection and the terrible price the Reich was paying might have led more rational-minded leaders in the Nazi hierarchy to a reevaluation of the Final Solution, which was after all a purely ideological goal. Not all Nazis were convinced that the murder of the Jews was worth the ruin of a single German city. We do not know if such a rearrangement of Nazi priorities was possible; the theme of retaliatory bombing was not fully picked up by rescue advocates, and by the time the notion of bombing the camps came to the fore in March 1944, millions of Jews already were in ashes. That is why the twelve-point rescue program which came out of the giant Madison Square Garden protest rally in March 1943 is as startling in its own way as McCloy's later response to the plea to bomb Auschwitz. It was silent on the question of bombing. It seems clear that the researchers into the role of the witnesses in the future will have to place failure of mind next to failure of spirit to account for their inaction during the Holocaust.

I have saved the discussion of the role of American Jewry for the end because it is the most problematic of all. For those who remain convinced that American Jewry failed, how the problem is posed does not really matter, since the answer is always the same. Still, how did it happen that American Jewry—possessing what was perhaps the richest organizational infrastructure of any hyphenate group in America, experienced in projecting pressure on government on behalf of their coreligionists since the Damascus blood libel of 1840, emerging from the depression faster than any other ethnic group, boasting a disproportionate number of influential Jews in Roosevelt's inner circle, and chairing the three major committees in Congress concerned with rescue—despite all this was unable to appreciably move the Roosevelt administration on the rescue question?

Stated in this way, the question provides not the slightest suggestion of the real problem which must be addressed if an adequate history of the role of American Jewry during the Holocaust is ever to emerge. For even if all these assets in the possession of American Jewry were present, one still cannot avoid the conclusion that American Jewry's political power did not match the responsibilities assigned to it by yesterday's rescue advocates and today's historians. We need to know much more about the character and structure of American Jewry during the thirties, the political context of the host culture in which it was compelled to act, and the ability of hyphenate or ethnic groups to influence public policy.

The political and organizational weaknesses of American Jewry during the thirties have been amply documented. It seems clear that the precipitous shift of the mantle of leadership of world Jewry found American Jewry unprepared. A communal base for unified action did not exist. Instead there was fragmentation, lack of coherence in the message projected to policy makers, profound disagreement on what might be done in the face of the crisis, and strife among the leaders of the myriad political and religious factions that constituted the community. It may well be that the assumption of contemporary historians that there existed a single Jewish community held together by a common sense of its history and a desire for joint enterprise is the product of a messianic imagination.

One is hard-pressed to find such a community on the American scene during the thirties. Even those delicate strands that sometimes did allow the "uptown" and "downtown" divisions to act together vanished during the crisis. The issues that caused the disruption stemmed from the crisis and seem appallingly irrelevant today. There was disagreement on the actual nature of the Nazi threat, the efficacy of the anti-Nazi boycott, the creation of a Jewish army, the commonwealth resolution of the Biltmore Conference, the activities of the Peter Bergson group, and the way rescue activities were actually carried out around the periphery of occupied Europe. There was something tragic in the way each separate Jewish constituency was compelled in the absence of a unified front to go to Washington to plead separately for its particular refugee clientele. In 1944 Rabbi Jacob Rosenheim, director of the Vaad Ha-Hatzala, the rescue committee of the Orthodox wing, explained why he found it better to act alone. He observed that the rescue scene "was a dog eat dog world [in which] the interest of religious Jews [is] always menaced by the preponderance of the wealthy and privileged Jewish organizations especially the Agency and the Joint." Clearly for Rosenheim the Nazis were not the only enemy. It did not take long for the unfriendly officials in the State Department to learn about the strife within the community. In 1944 we find Breckinridge Long writing in his diary: "The Jewish organizations are all divided amidst controversies. . . .there is no cohesion nor any sympathetic collaboration [but] . . . rather rivalry, jealousy and antagonism." It was a fairly accurate observation.

Yet one can have doubts whether the administration's rescue policy would have been appreciably changed had the Jews had a Pope, as Roosevelt once wished in a moment of exasperation. In the American historical experience the ability of pressure groups to reorder policy priorities has been fairly circumscribed. The Irish-Americans, perhaps the most politically astute of all hyphenate groups, tried to use American power to "twist the lion's tail" in the nineteenth and twentieth centuries. Yet with all their political talent they were unable to prevent the Anglo-American rapprochement which developed gradually after 1895. During the years before World War I the German-Americans were a larger and more cohesive group than American Jewry during the thirties. Yet they failed to prevent the entrance of America into war against their former fatherland. And adamant opposition of Polish-Americans did not prevent the "Crime of Crimea," the surrender of part of Poland to the Soviet Union at Yalta.

More examples could be cited to establish the fact that hyphenate pressure has not been distinctly successful in pulling foreign policy out of its channels once it has been firmly established that a given policy serves the national interest. Despite the rantings of the former head of the Joint Chiefs of Staff and others, Jews have done no better than other groups in this regard. That it is thought to be otherwise is part of the anti-Semitic imagination, which has always assigned Jews far more power and importance behind the scenes than they possessed. It is one of the great ironies of our time that many Jews share the belief that they possess such secret power. It is a comforting thought for a weak and vulnerable people. It should be apparent to any Jew living in the time-space between Kishinev and Auschwitz that such can hardly be the case. A powerful people does not lose one third of its adherents while the rest of the world looks on.

The charge that American Jewry was indifferent to the survival of its brethren during the Holocaust is not only untrue, but would have been highly uncharacteristic from a historical perspective. Much of American Jewry's organizational resources in the nineteenth and twentieth centuries—the Board of Delegates of American Israelites, the American Jewish Committee, the Joint Distribution Committee and the various philanthropic organizations which preceded it, the American Jewish Congress, the various Zionist organizations and appeals—were structured in relation to Jewish communities and problems abroad. From its colonial beginnings, when American Jewry welcomed "messengers" from Palestine, it has consistently demonstrated a strong attachment to Jewish communities overseas. The Holocaust years did not mark a sudden change in that pattern. A close perusal would indicate that virtually every means of public pressure, from delegations to the White House to giant public demonstrations—techniques later adopted by the civil rights movement—were initially used by American Jewry during the war years to bring their message to American political leaders. They were not terribly effective because leaders were not fully attuned to Jewish objectives, and because the war itself tended to mute the cry of pain of a group trying vainly to convince America that its suffering was inordinate and required special attention.

Given the circumstances, American Jewry seemed bound to fail. Sometimes one is tempted to believe that such was the case with everything related to the Holocaust, including the writing of its history. Those who despair of the role of American Jewry forget that throughout the war years the actual physical control of the scene of the slaughter remained in Nazi hands. Wresting that physical control from them, the most certain means of rescue, required a basic redirecting of war strategy to save the Jews. Even under the best of circumstances, military strategists never would have accepted such restrictions. British historian Bernard Wasserstein, searching through recently declassified British documents, discovered that at one point, as the war drew to a close, Churchill and Eden actually favored a direct military effort to save the Jews. But they did not succeed in breaking through the middle echelons of the bureaucracy and the military command to effect it. That is the reason why the American failure during the refugee phase (1938–1941), and the failure to support the notion of retaliatory bombing and the bombing of the camps and rail lines leading to them looms so large today. Such steps were impossible without a massive redirecting of strategy and without great sacrifice of lives and material. Aside from the possibility of ransoming proposals, which came at the beginning and end of the Holocaust, there seemed to be no other way to rescue appreciable numbers.

Besides the lack of precedent for responding to such a situation, American Jewry was plagued by its inability to get the fact of systematized mass murder believed. Few could fathom that a modern nation with a culture that had produced Goethe, Heine, Bach, and Beethoven, the German *Kulturgebiet* which Jews especially linked to progress and enlightenment, had embarked on such a program. It beggared the imagination. The immense problem of gaining credibility was never solved during the crisis and contributed notably to the failure to activate decision makers to mount a more strenuous rescue effort. The role of the State Department in deliberately attempting to suppress the story of the Final Solution, a now well-known and separate tragedy, made breaking through the credibility barrier even more difficult.

It is in that context that the role of Rabbi Stephen Wise in asking Sumner Welles to confirm the Riegner cable, which contained the first details of the operation of the Final Solution, is best viewed. American Jewish leadership might be accused of ignorance, ineffectiveness, or just sheer lack of stature, as Nahum Goldmann recently observed, but the charge of betrayal is unwarranted and unfair. The contents of the Riegner cable, which spoke of the use of prussic acid and the production of soap from the fat of the cadavers, was so horrendous that to have publicized it without confirmation would have resulted in widening the credibility gap. Middle-echelon State Department officials were not remiss in accusing Jewish leaders of atrocity mongering. In the context of the history of the thirties that charge was far from innocent. The notion that Americans had been skillfully manipulated by British propaganda into entering World War I was common fare in the revisionist history that made its debut in the thirties. A warning that British and Jewish interests were plotting to bring America into World War II had been a major theme in a speech delivered in September 1941 in Des Moines by Charles Lindbergh, a greatly esteemed national folk hero. It was but a small jump for the isolationist-minded American public to believe that it was happening all over again. The neutrality laws passed by Congress in the thirties were based on the same supposition.

Although the delay of several months in publicizing the Riegner report was probably costly, it was necessary to gain credibility. Moreover, a duplicate cable had been forwarded to the British branch of the World Jewish Congress, so that there was little danger that the story could have been permanently suppressed by the State Department. Eventually even the department's attempt to cut off the flow of information at the source was discovered and used to remove its hand from the rescue levers.

The inability to believe the unbelievable was not confined to Washington policymakers. It plagued Jewish leaders who were right on top of the operation and had every reason to believe it. The strategies developed by the Jewish councils in eastern Europe, "rescue through work" and "rescue through bribery," and eventually the surrender of the aged and the infirm in the hope that the Nazis did not intend to liquidate useful Jews, was based on the assumption that the Nazis did not intend to kill *all* the Jews.

Even after the press made public news of the Final Solution, most

Americans, including many Jews, simply did not absorb the fact of what was happening. A poll of Americans in January 1943, when an estimated one million Jews already had been killed, indicated that less than half the population believed that mass murder was occurring. Most thought it was just a rumor. By December 1944, when much more detail was available, the picture had not drastically altered. Seventy-five percent now believed that the Germans had murdered many people in concentration camps. But when asked to estimate how many, most answered one hundred thousand or less. By May 1945, when Americans already had seen pictures of the camps, the median estimate rose to one million, and 85 percent were now able to acknowledge that systematic mass murder had taken place. But the public was oblivious to the fact that the victims were largely Jewish. The inability to understand the immensity of the crime extended to the Jewish observers around the periphery of occupied Europe. They underestimated the number who had lost their lives by a million and a half. The figure of six million was not fully established until the early months of 1946.

The credibility problem was at the very core of the reaction of the witnesses: they could not react to something they did not know or believe. The problem of credibility takes us out of the realm of history. We need to know much more about how such facts enter the public conscience. How does one get people to believe the unbelievable? Rescue advocates did not succeed in solving that problem during those bitter years; and that, in some measure, is at the root of their failure to move governments and rescue agencies. In democracies it requires an aroused public opinion to move governments to action. Without that there is little hope that governments who are naturally reluctant to act would do so.

Thus far no historians have probed the role of Jewish political culture, those assumptions and qualities of style and habit that shape relationships to power and power holders, in accounting for the Jewish response. To be sure there are some untested observations in Raul Hilberg's *The Destruction of European Jewry* and Lucy Dawidowicz's *The War Against the Jews.* But no systematic study of its workings during the Holocaust years has been published. It is such an elusive subject that one can seriously wonder if it can be examined by modern scholarship. Yet it is precisely in that area that one of the keys to our conundrum regarding the Jewish response may lie.

Underlying the response of Jewish victims and witnesses at the time is an assumption about the world order so pervasive that we tend to forget that it is there at all. Jews believed then that there existed somewhere in the world, whether in the Oval Office or the Vatican or Downing Street, a spirit of civilization whose moral concern could be mobilized to save the Jews. The failure to arouse and mobilize that concern is the cause of the current despair regarding the role of the Jewish witness, and which leads to the search for betrayers. It is an assumption that continues to hold sway in Jewish political culture, despite the fact that there is little in recent Jewish experience that might confirm the existence of such a force in human affairs.

To some extent that despair is present in most literary works dealing with the Holocaust, especially in the speeches and works of one of the leading spokesmen for the victims, Elie Wiesel. It is a contemporary echo of what the Jewish victims felt before they were forced to enter the gas chambers. Emmanuel Ringelblum and others recorded it in their diaries. They wondered why no one came to their rescue and often assumed that the civilized world would not allow such a thing to happen. It can be heard most clearly in the message sent to Smull Zygelbojm which asked Jewish leaders to starve themselves to death if necessary in order to "shake the conscience of the world." The assumption was and continues to be that there is a "conscience of the world."

American Jewry, no less than others, shared that belief. Most of them were convinced that Roosevelt's welfare state, which reflected their own humanitarian proclivities, was a manifestation of that spirit of concern. That is why they loved him so; after 1936, even while other hyphenates began to decline in their political support, American Jewry raised the proportion of its pro-FDR vote to over 90 percent. Yet if they searched for deeds which actually helped their coreligionists, they would have found only rhetoric. That and their support of FDR's domestic program proved sufficient to hold them even after he had passed from the scene.

It may be that the Jewish voter had not resolved in his own mind the problem of possibilities of rescue or even the need for it. He assumed in his private way that the "authorities" were doing all that could be done. American Jewish leaders who were aware of the previous dismal record of government intercession in the Jewish interest nevertheless were hard-pressed for an alternative. They might have recalled how hard Jews had fought for an equal-rights clause in the Roumanian Constitution at the Congress of Berlin in 1878, only to see it almost immediately thwarted by the Roumanian government. They surely were aware that dozens of diplomatic intercessions on behalf of Russian Jews at the turn of the century had come to nothing. Surely they knew that the most successful single effort to bring better treatment for their coreligionists, the abrogation of the Treaty of 1832 with Czarist Russia in 1911, had come to nothing. They might have recalled that when Louis Marshall turned to the Vatican in 1915 with a request that it use its influence to halt the anti-Jewish depredations in Poland, the response had been indifferent. The League of Nations, which many Jews imagined would house the spirit of humanity and even amplify it, had become a dismal failure by the thirties. They must have noted Roosevelt's niggardly response to the refugee crisis and Britain's reneging on the promise contained in the Balfour Declaration. They must have seen how drastically the situation had deteriorated even since World War I. At that time one could at least hint that Berlin would do for Jews what London would not and gain concessions. In short, they could not have failed to understand that for Jews living in the thirties the world had become less secure and benevolent than ever. But living with the knowledge of total vulnerability in an increasingly atavistic world is a reality almost too painful to face. One had to choose sides, and clearly Roosevelt with all his shortcomings was still better than the alternatives. There were in fact no alternatives, not on the domestic political scene and not in the international arena. The truth was that during the years of the Holocaust Jewish communities were caught in the classic condition of powerlessness which by definition means lack of options. That was true of American Jewry as well.

In that context the central assumption of pre-Holocaust Jewish political culture becomes understandable. It was based as much on powerlessness as on residual messianic fervor, or the universalism of democratic socialism which large numbers in the community adhered to. As a general rule it is precisely the weak and vulnerable who call for justice and righteousness in the world. The powerful are more inclined to speak of order and harmony. It is in the interest of the weak to have a caring spirit of civilization intercede for them. That may explain why Jews especially called on a threatened world to be better than it wanted to be.

For American Jewry the notion of benevolence and concern in the world was not totally out of touch with reality. Bereft of specific power, they did in fact make astounding economic and political advances in the eighteenth, nineteenth, and twentieth centuries. Despite occasional setbacks, the idea that progress was possible, even inevitable, was deeply ingrained in American Jewry's historical experience. More than other Jewries who lived in the West, they had to some degree been disarmed by their history so that they never fully understood the signs that all was not well in the secular nation-state system. The most important of these signs was the relative ease with which the nations ordered and accepted the incredible carnage of World War I. That experience contained many of the portents of the Holocaust, including the use of gas and the cheapening of human life. The rise of totalitarian systems in the interwar period which extended further the demeaning of individual human dignity was not part of their experience, so they did not understand what the massive bloodletting in the Soviet Union and the transferring of populations like so many herds of cattle signified. They did not understand that the nation-state was dangerously out of control, that all moral and ethical restraints had vanished and only countervailing power held it in check.

Many Jews still looked to the nations for succor; they sought restraints. "We fell victims to our faith in mankind," writes Alexander Donat, "our belief that humanity had set limits to the degradation and persecution of one's fellow man." The countering facts were of too recent a vintage to seep into their historical consciousness and alter their visions and assumptions about the world in which they lived. Jewish leaders and rank and file blithely disregarded the mounting evidence that states and other forms of human organization, even those like the Holy See, which professed to a humanizing mission through Christian love, were less than ever able to fulfill such a role. The behavioral cues of states came from within and were determined by the need of the organization to survive at all costs. With a few notable exceptions the rescue of Jews during the years of the Holocaust did not fit in with such objectives, and they were allowed to perish like so much excess human cargo on a lifeboat.

The indictment of the witnesses is based on the old assumption that there exists such a spirit of civilization, a sense of humanitarian concern in the world, which could have been mobilized to save Jewish lives during the Holocaust. It indicts the Roosevelt administration, the Vatican, the British government, and all other witnessing nations and agencies for not acting, for not caring, and it reserves a special indignation for American Jewry's failure to mobilize a spirit that did not in fact exist. It is an indictment which cannot produce authentic history. Perhaps that cannot really be written until the pain subsides.

CHAPTER 19

With the terrible destruction of the major European centers of Judaism, America assumed the mantle of Diaspora Jewish leadership. It now stood unrivaled as the largest, richest, and politically most important Jewish community in the world. The State of Israel, created in 1948, served as world Jewry's spiritual homeland. It became the focal point of American Jewish life and philanthropy, and the symbol around which American Jews united. But for years it remained dependent on American Jewry's massive economic and political support. For leadership, American Jews continued to rely on their own resources.

Taking their new responsibilities seriously, and shaken by the mass destruction of Jewish life in Europe, American Jews worked in the years following World War II to reinvigorate American Jewish life. During this "golden decade" (1945–1955), historian Arthur Goren argues here, the foundations of the postwar American Jewish community were laid. Goren points to three themes that defined this critical period: suburbanization, the reconstruction of the communal order to emphasize Israel and political liberalism, and glowing optimism concerning the American Jewish community and its future. Debates over class, ideology, and religion, a staple of prewar American Jewish life, largely vanished in this new consensus-oriented era. The celebration of the tercentenary of American Jewish life in 1954 reinforced what Goren describes as the "intensified group consciousness and pride" that characterized the decade as a whole.

A "Golden Decade" for American Jews: 1945–1955

Arthur A. Goren

Few would deny the proposition that American Jewish life has undergone a radical transformation in the half century since the end of the Second World War. Lucy Dawidowicz, in a synoptic review of American Jewish history, captured this sense of major change in two chapter titles. She designated the years 1920 to 1939, "Decades of Anxiety," and the years 1945 to 1967, "The Golden Age in America." "Recovery and Renewal" is how Dawidowicz conceived of the postwar period as a whole.

Remarkably, the essential features of that transformation—the suburbanization of the Jews, the fashioning of a new communal order, and the emergence of a collective self-confidence and sense of well-being—were already in place by the mid-1950s. At that point, American Jewry seemed to pause to take stock. The occasion was the year-long celebration, beginning in the fall of 1954, of three hundred years since the first group of Jews settled on the shores of North America. The flood of tercentenary events intensified group consciousness and pride. The celebrations also encouraged the search for self-definition and self-understanding. Alongside the official and dominant theme of achievement and thanksgiving, a contrapuntal note of disquiet and discontent with the state of American Jewish life was sounded. In this respect, too, the culminating event of the decade set the terms for the years to come. Important publicists and ideologues recognized and debated what Charles Liebman would later pose as the tensions between "two sets of values." In Liebman's formulation, the "ambivalent American Jew" is torn between "integration and acceptance into American society" and "Jewish group survival." Precisely because Jews were fulfilling, at last, their aspiration to integrate into the society at large, identifying with the group and maintaining it were becoming increasingly matters of personal choice. For the most part, Jews responded to their new condition by instinctively adopting a dual construct of identity that aided them in locating and relocating themselves in the volatile pluralism that characterized the nation as well as the Jewish community. This essay seeks to place the first decade of our times, with its new conditions and new perceptions, in historical perspective. It also examines the Jewish community's endeavors to fix its place on the map of the new era and set its future course.

Surely, the subject most discussed among observers of the American Jewish scene in the late 1940s and early 1950s was the exodus of Jews from city to suburb. This was the most concrete expression of the new affluence of the rising Jewish middle class. Entering the professions and the higher levels of entrepreneurship on the wave of postwar prosperity, benefiting from the decline in occupational and social discrimination, integrating culturally both in the workplace and in the classroom and pursuing leisure-time activities similar to those of their social class, the new Jewish suburbanites embraced the tolerant, cosmopolitan image of the suburbs. For the majority of Jews, the creation of an amiable and lenient communal order, religious by definition, went hand in hand with the suburban ethos.

The suburban setting was a far cry from the compact, big-city, middle- and working-class neighborhoods where they had grown up and where some had started their own families during the interwar decades. The Jewish group life in those urban neighborhoods as recalled by the newly arrived suburbanites had contained a multiplicity of synagogues, Jewish secular societies, informal social street settings, and "neutral" public institutions that possessed a Jewish ethnic coloration merely by virtue of the high ratio of Jews attending. Less by design than geography, the Jewish neighborhoods had served the broad spectrum of interests, convictions, and degrees of Jewish identification both of second-generation Jews and of acculturated immigrant Jews.

The communal order reconstructed during the 1945–1955 decade reflected the new affluence and the rapid pace of social and cultural integration. The synagogue, now including educational and recreational facilities, became the primary guardian of ethnic identity and continuity. The social and educational services of the suburban synagogue expanded enormously when compared with the synagogues of the urban neighborhoods, at the same time as its ritual functions contracted. The years from 1945 through the 1950s witnessed the construction of some six hundred synagogues and temples. In their imposing size and sumptuous architectural design, they reflected their preeminent place in the suburban landscape as the accepted presence of a Jewish community. At the same time, the secular ideologies and particularistic interests that had existed in the urban neighborhoods faded away or were absorbed by the synagogue centers or by the broad-based federations of philanthropies.

This blurring of differences during the early postwar years enabled the national coordinating agencies of American Jewry to flourish, particularly those agencies that guided fund-raising campaigns and the policy-making implicit in allocating the funds. The local communities channeled vast sums of money and political influence to these bodies through their federations. They, in turn, dispersed overseas relief, aid to Israel, support for the community relations organizations and help for the national denominational and cultural institutions. There is a striking correlation between the enormous increase in the sums raised to aid Jewish displaced persons in Europe and their resettlement in Israel, which peaked between 1946 and 1948, and the decline in such revenue in the 1950s when the overseas crises seemed to have abated and synagogue building and domestic concerns were high on the community's agenda. Nevertheless, American Jewry was sufficiently affluent and committed enough to Israel to give more aid to the young state than to any other nonlocal cause.

Two compelling experiences during the first few years following the end of the Second World War gave coherence to these developments and provided the basis for the collective behavior of American Jews that has persisted ever since. The first, the establishment of Israel, has defined the one arena of greatest concern to the Jews. The second, the emergence of an aggressive liberalism, has directed the political energies of the Jewish community into the general American domain. This parity of interests and commitments, which has been at the heart of the Jewish communal consensus for nearly half a century, was firmly in place by the mid-1950s.

In the first instance, at the war's end, American Jews confronted the enormity of the destruction of European Jewry and the urgent need to resettle and rehabilitate the one-third that had survived. This task merged almost immediately with the struggle for Jewish sovereignty in Palestine. Linking the solution of the problem of the survivors with the attainment of statehood created a unity of purpose on a scale unprecedented in the modern history of the Jews.

The American Jewish community mobilized its communal, financial, and political resources in a massive outpouring of support. One gauge of this response was the dramatic rise in the contributions to the central communal campaigns. These soared from $57.3 million in 1945 to $131.7 million in 1946 and to $205 million in 1948, when 80 percent of the monies raised went for settling immigrants in Israel. There were other indications of momentous change. Eminent Jews who had taken little part in Jewish affairs now assumed crucial leadership roles, while others who until then had rejected all affirmations of Jewish nationalism rallied their organizations to the common endeavor. Henry Morgenthau, Jr.'s acceptance of the general chairmanship of the United Jewish Appeal in 1946 is one striking case; the collaboration of Joseph Proskauer, president of the American Jewish Committee, with the Jewish Agency in the final diplomatic push for statehood is another. Political figures and presidential advisers such as Herbert Lehman, Felix Frankfurter,

David Niles, Samuel Rosenman, and Bernard Baruch overtly or covertly aided the Zionist cause, which they now considered to be the sole means of saving Jews.

The three years between the surrender of the German armies and the declaration of Israel's independence also saw many rank-and-file American Jews take part in European rescue work at considerable personal risk. Soldiers, chaplains, and merchant mariners participated in the clandestine operations directed by the Jewish Agency and the Yishuv to transport refugees from the Allied-occupied zones in Germany to Mediterranean ports and from there in ships (purchased in the United States) to Palestine. Arms, too, were acquired surreptitiously in the United States with funds given by wealthy American Jews and shipped illegally to the Jewish underground in Palestine. At the same time, Jewish war veterans were recruited for the fledgling Israeli army.

Pockets of animosity or indifference remained. The small but vocal American Council for Judaism opposed the widespread support for a Jewish state with singular passion. Denouncing Jewish nationalism as an aberration of Judaism and support of a Jewish state as a violation of American loyalty, the council was soon swept to the fringes of the community. Some left-wing circles remained outside the consensus. Pro-Soviet Jewish radicals, except for the brief period when the Soviet Union supported the partitioning of Palestine, opposed the Jewish state; and a number of ex-socialist writers, the children of Jewish immigrants who were beginning to make their mark in intellectual circles, simply took no notice. However, mainstream Jewish America from the very beginning accepted the State of Israel as haven and protector of the Jews. Sovereignty was recognized as the guarantee of security for the dispossessed.

The alacrity with which statehood was embraced was in fact quite extraordinary. The specter of charges of divided loyalties, and the fear of providing grist for the mills of anti-Semites, had long haunted the Zionist movement in America. Even after the Biltmore Conference in May 1942 declared a Jewish commonwealth to be the immediate postwar goal of Zionism, the American Jewish leadership (including some Zionists) viewed the demand for a sovereign state as being at best an opening gambit for later bargaining and compromise, or at worst an unrealistic if not perilous political program. Yet four years later, nearly the entire American Jewish community joined in the political battle for a Jewish state. To take one symbolic act, in May 1947, in the absence of David Ben-Gurion, Rabbi Abba Hillel Silver of Cleveland, representing the Jewish Agency (then the shadow government of the state-to-be), presented the case for a Jewish state before the United Nations General Assembly.

Today it is a truism that the security and welfare of Israel have literally become articles of faith in the belief system of American Jews. Nurtured by the writings of publicists and theologians, encapsulated in the slogans of communal leaders and celebrated in commemorative and fund-raising events, Israel, as nearly every observer of Jewish life has suggested, has become "*the* religion for American Jews." One must stress, however, that *the conjunction of circumstances*—the crying need, on the one hand, to resettle the surviving remnant somewhere, and the growing recognition, on the other hand, that establishment of a Jewish state in Palestine was the only feasible means of saving the remnant—was the nexus at the heart of the overwhelming support for statehood between 1945 and 1948.

This coupling of circumstances molded the sentiments and attitudes of American Jews. At its birth, Israel's survival became inextricably bound to that other primal remembrance of our times, the destruction of European Jewry. Later events, such as the alarm for Israel's survival in the weeks preceding the Six-Day War in 1967, demonstrated the depth of American Jewry's concern. True, in the 1950s and early 1960s, other concerns appeared to diminish the emotional identity with Israel that marked the years 1945 to 1948 and the years following 1967. Nevertheless, the transcendent place of the "destruction and renewal" theme in the group consciousness of American Jews was actually set in the formative decade beginning in 1945.

At the same time, American Jews were deepening and intensifying their identity as Americans. America's role in the defeat of Nazism and its emergence as leader of the free world—the one effective force blocking Soviet expansion—induced American Jews not only to participate in the civic and political life of postwar America but to do so with unprecedented vigor and effectiveness. The high percentage of Jewish participation in elections compared with the voting public as a whole, the prominence of Jewish contributors as financial backers for political candidates, and the increase in the number of Jewish elected officials were some of the outward indications. No less notable was the ease with which political figures of Jewish background began to move out from Jewish organizational life into the larger political world and then, with their enhanced stature, back again to the Jewish. Philip Klutznik is perhaps the most striking example. His Jewish leadership track took him through the ranks of B'nai B'rith to the presidency of the organization in 1953. In a parallel career in government, Klutznik moved from commissioner of Federal Public Housing under Franklin D. Roosevelt and Harry Truman, to U.S. representative to the United Nations at various times during the Eisenhower, Kennedy, and Johnson administrations, and then to a cabinet post during Jimmy Carter's presidency.

Most significant of all was the new departure of Jewish communal institutions in assuming an active role in American civic affairs. Community relations agencies, formerly almost exclusively concerned with discrimination against Jews, now entered the realm of social action in its broadest sense. They lobbied for legislation directed against racial discrimination, in favor of social welfare programs, against weakening trade unionism and for a foreign policy that stressed internationalism, aid to democratic governments, and a tempering of superpower confrontations. So, too, they joined in litigation against racial discrimination and for the strict interpretation of the constitutional principle of separation of church and state. In 1945, the American Jewish Congress created its Commission on Law and Social Action and committed itself to "working for a better world . . . whether or not the individual issues touch directly upon so-called Jewish interests." Soon after, the American Jewish Committee, in a more circumspect manner moved beyond its original purpose (as expressed in its charter) "to prevent the infringement of the civil and religious rights of Jews and to alleviate the consequences of persecution." It now declared its intention to "join with other groups in the protection of the civil rights of the members of all groups irrespective of race, religion, color or national origin."

The religious wings of Judaism followed suit. By the end of the Second World War, both the Reform and Conservative rabbinic associations had longstanding commitments to pursue the goals of social justice, and the Orthodox Rabbinical Council of America began taking a similar stand. In the 1930s, for example, Reform's Central Conference of American Rabbis had declared that the "individualistic, profit-oriented economy is in direct conflict with the ideals of religion." At the same time, the Conservative Rabbinical Assembly of America announced a program for world peace, declared for a thirty-hour work-week and proclaimed a goal of "a social order . . . based on human cooperation rather than competition inspired by greed." These resolutions, which undoubtedly reflected the social sensibilities of the rabbis, did not go beyond the ritual of affirmation by the annual conferences. But beginning in the mid-1940s, the Reform and Conservative movements as a whole, and not merely the rabbinate, placed both specific domestic issues and international policy matters on their lay agendas. They established commissions, organized local action groups, and collaborated with parallel Protestant and Catholic agencies on behalf of social justice issues. (In contrast, although the Orthodox Rabbinical Council began adopting annual resolutions on a number of welfare state issues such as price and rent controls and continuation of federal housing programs, social activism did not become an integral part of the Orthodox lay associations.) Thus, the militancy demonstrated by rabbinic leaders and Jewish organizations during the 1960s over civil rights, school integration, and the Vietnam War stemmed from the Jewish community's active stand on political issues that began in the 1940s.

In a broad sense, American Jewry's two public commitments—assuring Israel's security and striving for a liberal America (and, by extension, a liberal world order)—have constituted the basis for a "functional consensus" ever since the linkage between the two was forged in the aftermath of the defeat of Nazism and the establishment of the Jewish state. On the whole, the two elements have meshed well, and in fact have reinforced each other. American Jewish leaders have presented Israel as both a haven for the persecuted and a doughty democracy surrounded and threatened with destruction by totalitarian Arab regimes allied, until recently, with an expansive Soviet Union. This has been a theme repeated often when U.S. presidents address American Jews and when party platforms are formulated. As a consequence, the dual identity of American Jews has resulted in less anxiety than some would have anticipated. The fear that vigorous support of Israel would give rise to charges of divided allegiance and fan the fires of anti-Semitism has not been borne out. The patriotic fulminations of right-wing extremists, bearers of a fundamentalist anti-Semitism, and the revolutionary rhetoric of the radical Left that has equated Zionism with racism have of course been causes for concern, but they have not infected mainstream America. This is not to say that a latent disquiet has never been present, rising on occasion to the surface. For example, Jacob Blaustein, president of the American Jewish Committee, intervened with the government of Israel on a number of occasions until he obtained formal assurances from Prime Minister David Ben-Gurion in 1950 that the Jewish state held no claim on the political loyalties of American Jews, whose sole allegiance, it was stressed, was to the United States.

Nevertheless, American Jews intuitively sensed that the functional consensus based on supporting Israel and defending a liberal America was not sufficient. What was needed was a doctrinal or ideological core that, while identifying the group, would also justify the operative elements of the consensus. During the first postwar decade, American Jews almost unanimously viewed religion as that doctrinal core. It was the way Jews identified themselves. Sociologists studying the new Jewish communities documented its currency. They also noted the paradox of Jews defining themselves overwhelmingly by religion while at the same time showing indifference and apathy for actual religious practice. Contemporary observers explained this incongruity as a form of adjustment to an American society that recognized religious activity alone as justifying self-segregation. These were the years when Jewish communal leaders found so congenial the notion that a trifaith America—Protestant, Catholic, and Jewish, "the religions of democracy"—formed the underpinning of the "American Way of Life." This interpretation of American society placed Judaism and its bearers in the mainstream of the nation's cultural and spiritual tradition.

Since Judaism as interpreted by the American rabbi taught its followers to seek social justice, being Jewish in America meant fighting for open housing and fair employment practices, for social welfare and pro-union legislation—in short, for the New Deal, the Fair Deal, and their successors. Judaism also demanded fulfillment of the religious commandment that "all Israel are responsible for one another," hence the duty to rescue Jews and strengthen the Jewish state. As individuals, Jews identified themselves as belonging to a religious community. As a group, they acted like an ethnic minority.

It is important to remember that, for American Jews, Judaism and Jewishness became identical only during the decade beginning in 1945. Although such a religious self-definition long preceded the postwar years (it was the cornerstone of American Reform Judaism), the East European immigrants had earlier created an ethnic and secular reality that overran, without obliterating, the purely religious formulation of Jewishness of the older, established community. One need merely mention the variegated Jewish associational life the immigrants created and the flowering of Yiddish literature—the most impressive cultural creation in a foreign language by an American immigrant group—to indicate the range and depth of this Jewish ethnic world. In acculturated form, significant elements of this world carried over into the second generation. Obviously, Zionism and an aggressively secular Jewish radical tradition stand out. Yet the considerable numbers who were brought up in this milieu in the urban neighborhoods of the years before 1945 failed to seriously challenge or to qualify the religious identification of American Jewry that so quickly became universal in the post-1945 decade. Surely, the prevailing drive for conformity, which was in part a by-product of the Cold War and the accompanying fear of Communist influence at home, saw religion (*any* religion, to paraphrase Eisenhower) as the cornerstone of democratic society and an antitoxin against the Communist heresy. And quite possibly the political and financial aid being so prominently extended to the Jewish state was best explained to the nation as religiously motivated. Separation for religious purposes did conform, after all, with patriotic norms. In part, these factors hastened the trends toward consensus within the Jewish community.

On occasion Jewish secular thinkers gave explicit and anguished expression to this change. In 1951, the Labor Zionist Organization published an essay by C. Bezalel Sherman, "Israel and the American Jewish Community." The Labor Zionist movement, an amalgamation of socialist Zionist parties transplanted to the United States with the mass migration, was staunchly secularist. It had favored the formation of democratically elected Jewish communal politics and bilingual education in a manner similar to its European sister parties. Sherman himself was an ideologue of the organization's left wing. Nevertheless, in reappraising the future of the American Jewish community in the new era ushered in by the establishment of the Jewish state, he abandoned the position that American Jews should strive for the status of nationality. Now he wrote, "America, insensible to the existence of a Jewish nation, insisted on classing them [American Jews] with the religious communities," the only type of ethnic group recognized by "American constitutional life." Sherman continued:

> Jews thus have no other alternative but to constitute themselves as a community operating in a religious framework. . . . The irreligious Jew . . . will have to

> accept a religious designation for the group of which he wishes to be a member without sharing the tenets of its faith. This is the price a secularist Jew will have to pay for his voluntary sharing in a minority status.

Ten years later, in his study *The Jew Within American Society,* Sherman used this redefinition of Jewish identity to explain Jewish group survival in America. It was the key to understanding Jewish "ethnic individuality." On a note evoking Mordecai Kaplan's analysis of Jewish identity, Sherman concluded: "American Jews can no more conceive of the Jewish faith severed from the framework of Jewish peoplehood than they can conceive of a Jewish community removed from its religious base." Since Jewish peoplehood embraced Jews everywhere, concern for persecuted brethren abroad and the well-being of the State of Israel had increased the sense of "belongingness" among American Jews. "For this reason, they may be expected to continue as a distinct ethnic group—on the level of spiritual uniqueness, religious separateness, ethnic consolidation and communal solidarity, but not in a political sense."

In terms of the Jewish establishment (the synagogue movements, federations, defense agencies, and the Zionist organizations), American Jews had created by the early 1950s a consensus and a degree of equanimity they had not known before. They were meeting their dual responsibilities as Americans and Jews admirably. On domestic issues, they aligned with the liberal-centrist position and upheld America's role as defender of the free world. Within the Jewish community, the divisive issues of the interwar years—class differences, the intergenerational tensions between immigrant and native-born, conflicting notions of Jewish identity, the assimilationist-radical deprecation of Jewish life, and the strident polemics over Zionism—were vanishing or were gone altogether. Not surprisingly, then, the tercentenary planners proposed stressing not only communal harmony and achievement but also the beliefs and values Jews held in common with all Americans.

In December 1951, Ralph E. Samuel, the vice president of the American Jewish Committee, announced the formation of a committee to plan the three-hundredth anniversary of the establishment of the first permanent Jewish community in North America. Samuel emphasized the opportunity such celebrations would provide to pay homage to the "American heritage of religious and civil liberty." American Jews had built a "flourishing American Judaism," he declared, and at the same time they had taken part "in building the American democratic civilization that we have today." In his single reference to contemporary affairs, Samuel concluded his remarks with the note that the tercentenary celebration would demonstrate to the world "the strength of the American people's commitment to the principles of democracy in our struggle against communism and other forms of totalitarianism of our day."

This collective undertaking to popularize an American Jewish ideology proved to be an extraordinary enterprise in itself. It also raised a number of questions. Who indeed did the tercentenary organizers represent? How meaningful and tenable could a least-common-denominator ideology be? What were the constraints the planners faced in relating to the American-political and Jewish-political context? Were the provisional tenets Samuel set forth adequate for setting a course for postwar American Jewry?

In January 1952, when the committee on organization met to launch the tercentenary project, Samuel stressed that the American Jewish Committee saw its role as initiator rather than sponsor of the enterprise. In fact, it had been the American Jewish Historical Society that had first proposed the tercentenary celebration. Eager for the broadest communal participation, it had turned to the American Jewish Committee for organizational assistance; the success of the project depended on leaders whose eminence and integrity assured the nonpartisanship of the endeavor.

In addition to Samuel, who was chosen general chairman, two eminent members of the American Jewish Committee were appointed to key committees. Simon Rifkind, who had distinguished himself as a federal judge and special adviser on Jewish affairs to General Dwight D. Eisenhower in 1945 and 1946, headed the "Committee of 300," the policy-making body of the organization. Samuel Rosenman, also a judge, who had served as a principal adviser to Presidents Franklin D. Roosevelt and Harry Truman, chaired the program committee. Another important committee, that of research and publication, was headed by Salo W. Baron, professor of Jewish history at Columbia University.

The composition of the committee reflected nearly the entire spectrum of Jewish religious and communal life. Among the members of the steering committee were Samuel Belkin, president of Yeshiva University; Louis Finkelstein, president of the Jewish Theological Seminary; Israel Goldstein, president of the American Jewish Congress; Samuel Niger, the Yiddish journalist and critic; and Jacob S. Potofsky, president of the Amalgamated Clothing Workers Union.

In April 1953, after nearly a year of deliberations, the program committee, which, in addition to Rosenman, included Benjamin V. Cohen, Adolph Held, William S. Paley, and David Sarnoff, submitted its report on the "meaning of the anniversary" to a national meeting of the Committee of 300. Obviously the presence of Paley, the head of CBS, and Sarnoff, the head of NBC, indicated the direction and scale of the celebrations. The proposed theme of the celebration—"Man's Opportunities and Responsibilities Under Freedom"—was in fact suggested by Sarnoff and was approved at this meeting.

The major opening event, the National Tercentenary Dinner with President Eisenhower as guest of honor and keynote speaker, took place on October 20, 1954, at the Hotel Astor in New York. It was preceded and followed by forums, exhibitions, pageants, musical festivals, and public dinners organized by local committees in at least four hundred cities and towns. New York, for instance, was the venue of a coast-to-coast radio broadcast of the reconsecration of Congregation Shearith Israel (founded by the original settlers of New Amsterdam) in the presence of representatives of the Jewish and Christian congregations that had either aided or functioned alongside it in the eighteenth century. A special national committee supervised the preparation of a national historical exhibit on the theme "Under Freedom," which was shown at the Jewish Museum in New York and the Smithsonian Institution in Washington, D.C. The Chicago committee commissioned Ernst Toch to compose a symphonic suite for the occasion, while the national committee commissioned David Diamond to compose the tercentenary symphony *Ahavah,* which was given its premiere by the National Symphony on November 17, 1954, in Washington. (The other works on the program were Ernest Bloch's *Israel Symphony* and Leonard Bernstein's *The Age of Anxiety,* a thematically balanced program by Jewish composers.) In Atlanta, Georgia, the local committee presented the city with a portrait of Judah P. Benjamin, secretary of state of the Confederacy.

Television played a major role. The main events, such as Eisenhower's address, received national coverage. Leading commercial programs offered commemoration salutes. CBS broadcast a four-part teledrama, "A Precious Heritage," while NBC followed suit with a four-part series entitled "Frontiers of Faith." The tercentenary also generated a plethora of educational material—filmstrips, curricula, and guidebooks on American Jewish history—for use in schools and adult education circles that were sponsored and published by the national organizations. B'nai B'rith organized a nationwide search for historical source materials and provided programs and speakers for its lodges and Hillel foundations. The American Jewish Committee commissioned a series of studies that it published in the *American Jewish Year Book* and an *Inventory of American Jewish History* to further historical research. A volume of studies subsidized by the Workmen's Circle and other Jewish labor organizations gave special attention to the era of the East European Jewish migration.

This history-mindedness anteceded the tercentenary "revival." It was one expression of a self-assertiveness that stemmed from the new position of centrality that had been thrust upon the American Jewish community. And it paralleled the notion of the "American Century," the conviction that became popular during the war years that America had at last taken its "rightful" place as the leader of the free world and the guardian of world order. This national temper stimulated a reexamination of the American past.

Historians and political scientists elaborated the idea of an "American exceptionalism." Typical of their writing was Daniel Boorstin's book *The Genius of American Politics.* "I argue, in a word," Boorstin wrote, "that American democracy is unique. It possesses a 'genius' all of its own."

The new era that began in 1945 was, in a sense, also perceived as "the American Jewish Century." The conviction that American Jews were at last "making history" required recovering a "usable past" showing that Jews had indeed been "making history" for some time. One important expression of this sentiment was the Hebrew Union College's announcement, in the fall of 1947, of the establishment of the American Jewish Archives to document the historical record of American Jewry. The need for such an institution was explained in these words:

> American Jewry has become the "center" of world Jewish spiritual life. When the Jewish historian of the next generation reaches the year 1939, he will begin a new chapter in the history of his people, a chapter which must be called, "The American Jewish Center." This Jewish community has now become the pivotal and controlling factor in that historic development which began in the thirteenth pre-Christian century in Palestine.

There were more manifestations of a search for "American Jewish exceptionalism." In 1953, the Jewish Theological Seminary established the American Jewish History Center. Soon after, the center commissioned a series of communal studies and organized regional conferences to generate interest in the projects. The tercentenary accelerated this newfound interest in an American Jewish past. Jewish communities—Buffalo, Rochester, Milwaukee, Cleveland, and Los Angeles—allocated money for writing their communal histories. In September 1954, a revitalized American Jewish Historical Society convened the most impressive conference of historians ever held on the writing of American Jewish history. Thus the new self-consciousness American Jewry displayed after the conclusion of the war swelled under the impetus of the tercentenary. Pride and awareness of its preeminence in the Jewish world reverberated in the public and institutional interest in recording and interpreting the Jewish experience in America.

One interpretive history of Jewish life in America that appeared during the tercentenary year captured the tercentenary ideology faithfully. Oscar Handlin's *Adventure in Freedom* (1954) stressed the process of Jewish integration into a society that was distinguished by its "diversity, voluntarism, equality, freedom, and democracy." Handlin, who taught American social history at Harvard and who had won a Pulitzer Prize for his 1951 study on immigration in American life, *The Uprooted,* was perhaps the most influential writer on the American pluralist tradition. Handlin insisted that American Jews be viewed as one ethnic group among many in a pluralist America that neither impeded nor encouraged ethnic group maintenance. This was the open-ended, wholesome "adventure in freedom." Yet Handlin also struck an ominous note. Although the Jews of America were celebrating the year 1654, they could not forget "the stark facts of our present situation." Jews had not recovered "from the shock of the six million victims of the European catastrophe"; at the same time they shared in the "enormous burden upon American society," which was "locked in unremitting struggle" with "the forces of totalitarianism."

It was the tercentenary theme, "Man's Opportunities and Responsibilities Under Freedom," that required explication. When the program committee presented its recommendations after months of deliberations and after soliciting the opinions of scores of leaders from all fields and walks of life, it explained the criteria it had used in these words:

> The theme should express the outstanding fact of the past 300 years of our participation in America; that it should describe the significance of the present day for American Jews, and that it should express the hopes and aspirations and objectives of the future for ourselves and for all Americans—indeed, for all human beings throughout the world.

When the recommendations were published as a brochure—thirty thousand copies were distributed—no explicit reference was made to the Jewish community itself, or to the American Jew's "responsibility under freedom" to help other Jews, although the members of the committees in their other communal capacities were deeply involved in Jewish affairs. In a section entitled "All-Embracing Nature of Celebration," the committee warned that the tercentenary should not be made "a vehicle for propagation of any particular ideology in American Jewish life. . . . It should be neither Zionist, non-Zionist, nor anti-Zionist. It should not try to formulate or advance any particular definition of Jewishness."

The tercentenary committee defined the principal goal of the observance as a celebration of America's democratic ideals. Thus the American Jewish experience was significant in that it bore witness to the success of this free society. No less important was the emphasis placed on the congruence between Judaism and American democratic ideals. Indeed, the authors of the report declared, "The teachings of the Hebrew prophets have vitally affected the growth of freedom and the development of human dignity in America and throughout the world." In a summing-up statement at the conclusion of the year of festivities, David Bernstein, the tercentenary committee's executive director, justified the choice of the theme in these words:

> At a time when the Jewish community and its leaders felt that they were on display before the world, they chose to speak, first, in religious terms and, next,

> in terms of such political ideas as civic responsibility, strengthening democracy, protecting individual liberty, and expanding civil rights.

Was there perhaps, in the midst of the deserved self-congratulations, also a measure of anxiety and insecurity? What seemed implicit in Bernstein's statement and had been alluded to in Samuel's first announcement of a tercentennial committee four years earlier was stated explicitly in Handlin's measured words. Praising democracy and liberty at a time when the nation was locked in what it perceived to be a global struggle with an aggressive and ruthless totalitarianism was understandable enough. The "golden decade" for American Jews was also the decade of the Cold War, McCarthyism, and fear of Communist subversion.

Abroad, postwar America confronted an expansive Communist power that now possessed nuclear weapons. Not only had an "iron curtain descended across the continent," in Winston Churchill's words in his March 1946 address, but it was followed by the fall of China to the Communists and the invasion of South Korea by the North in 1950. At home, an alarmed government responded with drastic measures to curb and root out real and perceived instances of Communist infiltration. It began in 1947, when Harry Truman put into effect his loyalty program, and it ended, at least symbolically, in December 1954 when the United States Senate censured its member Joseph McCarthy—a time span nearly identical with the first years in the new American Jewish postwar era. Thus the years of optimism were also the years of the "Attorney General's list" of subversive organizations, the Alger Hiss case, the loyalty oaths and security clearances, the high-handed investigations of Senator Joseph McCarthy, and the congressional committees who went hunting for Communists and who blacklisted those they termed "Fifth Amendment Communists."

Here was the snake in the garden: the agony and trepidation caused by the conspicuous presence of Jews among those accused of disloyalty and even espionage, and the presence of a marginal but vocal radical Left within the organized Jewish community. Thus the arrest in 1950 of Julius and Ethel Rosenberg for handing atomic secrets to the Soviet Union, and their trial, conviction, and execution in 1953, jarred the self-confidence of American Jews. (The trial judge, prosecuting attorney, defense attorneys, and the principal witnesses who turned state's evidence were all Jewish.) Arnold Forster, general counsel of the Anti-Defamation League (ADL), recalled the period as a time when American Jewish leaders "came to fear the establishment of a link between being a Jew and being a 'communist traitor' in the popular mind." A bitter fight ensued within the Jewish community over aiding Jewish victims of the anti-Communist crusade. The most prominent instance was the campaign for clemency for the Rosenbergs in which Communist and left-wing groups were active.

The American Jewish Committee created a special committee to combat the "Jewish/Communist stereotype." It launched an educational program exposing the techniques and strategies used by the Communists to infiltrate Jewish organizations and called on the community to expel Jewish "Communist-front" organizations. During the height of the hysteria, the American Jewish Committee was less than forthright in its commitment to civil liberties. On this last score, in contrast, both the ADL and the American Jewish Congress maintained their aggressive stand in defense of civil liberties. In 1952, at the height of McCarthy's influence, the ADL chose to honor Senator Herbert Lehman at its annual convention because of his opposition to McCarthy. The American Jewish Congress, for its own part, waged an incessant battle against congressional and state legislation that required loyalty oaths, providing legal aid in appealing cases where there appeared to have been infringements of constitutional rights. To a considerable degree, the Red Scare hastened the political integration of American Jews. It greatly weakened Jewish radicalism, fortified the liberalism of "the vital center," and drew American Jews, as never before, into a whirl of "American" issues. In dealing with these issues, both civil libertarians and anti-Communist activists operated through Jewish agencies.

The official tercentenary ideology, orchestrated by a group of conservative and cautious leaders, aroused a spirited debate over the direction of American Jewish life. Jewish journals of opinion provided the platforms for a more reflective consideration of the issues. Robert Gordis, editor of *Judaism*, devoted an entire issue to the tercentenary in which contributors evaluated Jewish philosophy, culture, and communal life in America. Eugene Kohn gathered a dozen articles from *The Reconstructionist* on the communal and cultural life of American Jews and published them in a volume commemorating the tercentenary. The score of mass-circulation house organs published by B'nai B'rith, Hadassah, the American Jewish Congress, and others devoted whole issues to critical essays that examined American Jewish life. For the most part, the conclusions were laudatory and the prognosis for the future optimistic. Typical was Gordis's introduction to the tercentenary issue of *Judaism*. American Jewry, Gordis wrote, had not been "altogether without influence or creativity within the confines of Judaism." It had been innovative in the fields of religion, philanthropy, education, and group defense. Indeed. "the instruments for a renaissance of Judaism, in the days to come, are at hand."

There were also dissenting voices. Horace Kallen, the philosopher and ideologue of cultural pluralism, published a blistering piece in the *Congress Weekly* entitled "The Tercentenary, Yomtov or Yahrzeit." He accused the organizers of violating the essence of the "American Idea," that is, of his well-known notion of cultural pluralism. Kallen had interpreted American freedom as granting the right to any ethnic, religious, or racial group to preserve and diversify its communal culture. Nothing in the rhetoric of the tercentenary encouraged American Jews to do this, he argued; even the tercentenary emblem was assimilationist. Not a Hebrew word was on it, and above the menorah that dominated the face of the emblem was a star—but it was a five-pointed, American star rather than the six-pointed Magen David. For Kallen, the challenge of American freedom for the American Jewish community meant creating, first of all, a democratic communal polity. A community so organized would then be able to nurture—and here Kallen employed his famous metaphor of the orchestra—the specifically Jewish part in the total orchestrated production that was the pluralistic culture of the American people.

Mordecai Kaplan, the philosopher of Reconstructionism, criticized the planners for failing to confront one of the crucial questions in American Jewish life. "Why is no reference made in all the literature, speeches and lectures concerning the tercentenary to what it means from the standpoint of our survival as a people in dispersion? . . . This is the first time in the history of the Jewish people that it is jubilant over its sojourn in any land outside of Eretz Yisrael." What was the Jewish context of the celebration? What signposts for the future course of American Jewry had the tercentenary offered? The establishment of the State of Israel had raised the question of "the ultimate destiny of the Jewish People." Was Eretz Israel to be the ingathering of the exiles or merely the creative nucleus of the Jewish people? Building on his formulation of living in two civilizations (American and Jewish), Kaplan emphasized the permanence of Diaspora and rejected the Israel-Zionist claim that American Jews were in Galut (exile). For Kaplan, the influence of the American democratic tradition on the Jews and "the inexhaustible reservoir of Jewish creativity in Israel" promised a creative future for "the American sector of the Jewish people [that had] at last found a resting place for its feet." But these matters had to be debated, clarified, and decided upon.

Ben Halpern, the secularist Zionist thinker, began his study of the American Jewish community, *The American Jew, A Zionist Analysis*, by considering the conviction underlying the tercentenary that "America is different." Indeed it was different, Halpern agreed. In the shadow of Hitler's destruction of Europe's Jews and in the presence of Soviet totalitarianism and Stalin's anti-Semitism, Jews had special reasons for celebrating America's democratic tradition. However, American Jews had missed one crucial way in which America was different *for them*. As a historic entity, American Jews constituted one of the youngest Jewish centers of the Diaspora. In terms of "real history"—of grappling with the specific problems of their existence as a group—American Jewish history began at most with the rise of the first, authentic American Jewish creation, Reform Judaism, and the formation of native American Jewish institutions. Unlike European Jewry, Halpern argued, American Jews had never had to wrestle with the question of emancipation and self-emancipation; American Jewish history began long after the questions of equality and political rights were resolved. His analysis led him to conclude that the indigenous ideologies of American Jews, as programs intended to foster a creative Jewish group life, were failing. Neither the secular ideologies such as cultural pluralism and neo-Zionism nor an innovative religious movement such as Reconstructionism could prevent the erosion of Jewish life. Assimilation? Survival? Was America different from Europe? His answer was: "In Europe, the stick; in America, the carrot." Indeed, Halpern, the fundamentalist Zionist, was utterly pessimistic about American Jewish group survival.

Surely by the final years of the 1950s one could confidently point to a baseline that demarcated American Jewry from what had existed prior to 1945 and that would hold, for the most part, during the decades ahead. The searing recollections of the poverty of immigrant parents or the crushing collapse into destitution of the Great Depression years had been replaced with an affluence that opened new social opportunities. This affluence enabled the postwar generation to devote some of its time and wealth to societal needs. Establishing entirely new communities in the suburbs demanded an enormous collaborative effort. Building communities, expanding the institutions and agencies serving American Jewry as a whole, and meeting the needs of world Jewry also required politically sophisticated leaders, trained professionals, and efficient organization. An organizational ideology developed "of acts and tasks, of belonging and conforming, of *na'aseh venishma.*" "To be a Jew," one perceptive observer wrote, "is to belong to an organization. To manifest Jewish culture is to carry out . . . the program of an organization." Support for Israel as refuge and home—which more than it swept aside its opponents, co-opted them—became the overarching endeavor, the one that transcended the local and the particular. Hence it came to define the active community.

Purely *Jewish* concerns could also be linked to liberal politics through the argument that to support American liberal causes was in the "Jewish interest," or else group interests could be denied in favor of appealing to the universal teachings of Judaism. Whatever the justification, Jewish *communal* participation in American politics in the decade beginning in 1945 became widespread and was found acceptable. For postwar America commended communal ties that encouraged spiritual self-preservation and self-fulfillment. In the state of fluid pluralism then prevailing—of changing self-images and expectations of religious, ethnic, and racial groupings—any number of ways were possible for identifying oneself. Understandably, the Jews, eager to take their place in the more tolerant postwar society, defined their group identity to fit the reigning mood. Judaism as ethnic religion and Judaism as "peoplehood," as "religious civilization," and as one of the three "religions of democracy" were some of the terms that came into use. In the case of the tercentenary platform, Judaism became American democracy, reflecting a strand of insecurity that was present during the golden decade.

A number of ideologues were distressed by the assimilationist thrust of this formulation. They called on American Jews to instead confront the complexity of their dual identity, indeed to view it as the source of an American Jewish distinctiveness. Rabbis and theologians challenged the cult of organization and the emptiness of "religion as the American way." Yet ideologues and rabbis were also committed to a pluralist America. They collaborated in ways that were inconceivable during the prewar years, not only accepting but applauding the internal pluralism of Jewish group life. Precisely the give-and-take of contending movements and ideas within a communal consensus indicated a commitment to group survival. One could understand, for example, the much-criticized slogan, "Man's Opportunities and Responsibilities Under Freedom," as a shrewd strategy to maintain the community. (Rabbis used the phrase as the text for their sermons on the need for better Jewish education, support for Israel, and a richer synagogal life.) Unmistakably, whatever ideological issues were placed on the Jewish public agenda during the decade beginning in 1945—which have remained there to this day—no longer called into question the worth or desirability of Jewish survival. The issue henceforth would be the quality and character of Jewish group survival.

CHAPTER 20

In the mid-1930s, 71 percent of American Jews lived in the Northeast; 40.5 percent in New York City alone. Only 4.5 percent lived in the South and 4.3 percent in the West. By the mid-1990s, the percentage of Jews living in the Northeast had fallen to 47.9 percent (32.9 percent in the New York area) while the percentage living in the South and West had ballooned to 21 percent and 19.4 percent respectively. This massive internal migration paralleled general population movements within the United States, but impacted on Jews in special ways. The communities of Jews created by the migration introduced important changes into American Jewish life and identity.

Los Angeles and Miami, the two communities considered here by historian Deborah Dash Moore, absorbed more "Jews on the move" than any others in the immediate postwar decades and both quickly became major Jewish population centers, filled with men and women whose roots lay someplace else. Chain migration played an important role in the growth of both communities, newcomers urging their friends to come and join them, but economic opportunity and dreams of a good life proved even more important. Miami and Los Angeles became, for many Jews, the "golden cities" of America's golden land.

In New York in the 1950s, Jews enjoyed a high level of comfort, faced relatively little anti-Semitism, and experienced growing economic success. Instead of assimilating in the way that so many had predicted, they continued to express their Judaism (which they called "Jewishness") through their lifestyles and politics. As Moore wrote in an earlier work, entitled suggestively, At Home in America:

> *In the 1950s, second-generation Jews continued to nourish a world of unself-conscious Jewishness in their neighborhoods. They turned to their neighborhoods to translate what Jewishness meant into a livable reality and to their public institutions to give expression to the varied content of Jewish ethnicity. New York Jews experienced a sense of community in their neighborhoods. They felt at home where they lived. Through residential concentration, New York Jews often acquired a psychological attitude of a majority, in a country*

> *where they were a small minority. The clustering of thousands of Jews into city neighborhoods made Jewish living comfortable and natural.*

By contrast in Miami and Los Angeles, Moore shows, Jewishness became much more a matter of choice: it could not simply be absorbed like sunshine from the surrounding atmosphere. This resulted in changing forms of Jewish association, higher rates of disaffiliation, and new patterns of faith and identity—developments that in time, as the rush of internal migration continued, produced far-reaching consequences for the American Jewish community as a whole.

Jewish Migration in Postwar America: The Case of Miami and Los Angeles

Deborah Dash Moore

The Second World War and its aftermath ushered in a period of enormous changes for American Jews. The destruction of European Jewry shattered the familiar contours of the Jewish world and transformed American Jews into the largest, wealthiest, most stable and secure Jewish community in the Diaspora. American Jews' extensive participation in the war effort at home and abroad lifted them out of their urban neighborhoods into the mainstream of American life. In the postwar decades, internal migration carried Jews to new and distant parts of the United States. Occurring within the radically new parameters of the postwar world—the extermination of European Jewry, the establishment of the State of Israel, and the United States' achievement of unrivaled prominence on the world political scene—Jewish migration nonetheless represented a response to domestic pressures. These migrations gradually changed American Jews, influencing the character of their culture, the structure of their organizations, their pattern of kinship relations, the style and substance of their politics.

This essay offers a historical perspective on the migration process that created new American Jewish communities. It indicates some of the dimensions of internal Jewish migration, its sources, motivations, and consequences. By focusing on the extraordinary growth of two Jewish urban populations, the essay suggests some categories for analyzing the communal dynamic of postwar American Jewry. It also explores a number of parallels between immigration and the establishment of indigenous American Jewish communities. Given the historic dependence of the United States upon immigration for its social formation and the critical role of immigration in the growth of the American Jewish community, study of internal migration provides a useful framework to assess certain postwar changes. Specifically, *it encourages an emphasis upon the creation rather than the transformation of communities.* Observing the postwar migrations, Oscar Handlin, the eminent historian of immigration, noted that immigrants differed only in degree from native-born Americans who migrated within the United States. Where the newcomer came from was less important than that the migrant had turned his back upon home and family, abandoned the way he had earned a living, and deserted his community. Handlin's trenchant reflections not only linked immigration with internal migration, seeing them as a continuum, but made the problem of community central to both.

The mobilization of the war years drew young Jewish men out of the insular urban neighborhoods of their childhood and sent them to distant bases scattered throughout the South and West. Most of the Jewish servicemen, like their gentile peers, had not strayed far from their home towns during the difficult years of the Great Depression. Now, en route to the Pacific war theater, they discovered the West. Thousands of them passed through Los Angeles and were amazed by the apparently prosperous and easy way of life that they saw. Others who joined the Army Air Corps often found themselves stationed in one of the Miami Beach hotels requisitioned for the war. When their wives came down to visit, they, too, took in the beauty of the resort city. Smaller numbers went to bases near such Texas towns as Houston and Dallas. Even a small city such as Tucson, Arizona, attracted Jews who discovered it because of its base for training bombardiers and pilots. Often the opportunities these cities offered excited them. "You betcha, I loved it!" Leon Rabin recalled. "I wrote to my friends in Philadelphia and said there's no way for me to tell you what's going on down here and anything I'd tell you wouldn't make you come down here. But now that I'm here there's no way that I'll ever come back." Rabin was true to his word. He married a native Dallas Jew and spent the rest of his life building a Jewish community that reflected some of the values he had learned growing up in Philadelphia. He also understood how limited was the vision of most East Coast Jews and how reluctant they were to venture beyond the suburbs of their cities until propelled by the war. Once word spread of the opportunities available, however, especially in a large city such as Los Angeles, which had a substantial Jewish population even in 1940, the numbers of Jews who migrated quickly reached substantial proportions.

Jewish migration to these southern and western cities—ones that would subsequently be counted as part of an emerging Sunbelt—reflected a response shared by millions of other Americans to federal initiatives and policies. Not only did the war years lead the government to funnel enormous sums for economic development into southern and western states—California alone received 10 percent of all federal war monies—but these funds often went to provide the capitalization for defense-related industries. From airplane construction in Los Angeles to aluminum manufacturing in Miami to medical and communications research in Houston, entire industrial and postindustrial infrastructures were established. The subsequent eruption of the Cold War sustained the economic growth of these cities. The postwar socioeconomic changes produced regional convergence, with the outlying regions of the South and West growing more rapidly than the developed sections of the country. This rapid social change brought the South and West's economies, social patterns, and cultural styles closer to national norms. Federal postwar policies, especially the GI bill, with its low-cost mortgage provisions and college loans, also encouraged a generation to seek its fortunes far from home and family. These portable benefits loosened the ties that bound individuals to networks of kin and friends. No longer needing to rely upon relatives and neighbors to find work, to finance an education, or even to buy a house, Jews and other Americans were free to pursue their dreams of the good life. For many Jews particularly, the attractions of the apparently affluent and relaxed style of living of the Sunbelt cities proved irresistible.

The term *Sunbelt* is designed to link fundamentally different parts of the United States that share the characteristics of rapid social change and regional convergence. Nicholas Lemann, executive editor of *Texas Monthly*, argues persuasively that journalists invented the Sunbelt concept in order to speak about new political and economic trends. When the word first acquired popular usage in the mid-1970s, "millions of people were living in the Sunbelt without one of them realizing it," wrote Lemann. "They thought of themselves as Southerners or Texans or Los Angelenos." Of course, the particularisms Lemann mentions, the sense of identity derived from being rooted in a city, state, or region, had salience largely for old-timers, not for migrants. They just as often thought of themselves as ex-New Yorkers or former Philadelphians. "I am a refugee from Chicago of several years standing," announced Leonard Sperry, a wealthy migrant to Los Angeles. Sperry's self-definition after close to a decade of living in the City of Angels suggests the extent to which a migrant's identity derived from the home of his childhood. Similarly, the death notices of longtime Miami residents that announced burial in Detroit, or Chicago, or Rochester appear symptomatic of the unwillingness of Jews to identify Miami as "home." By linking a wide variety of locales, the notion of a Sunbelt helped to smooth away these differences in self-identification between the newcomers and the old-timers.

As the United States became a "nation of strangers," in the words of a popular journalist's account of one out of five Americans' propensity to move every year, Jews developed an ethnic variation on the American theme of internal migration. Federal policies drew Jews out of their old homes, but ethnic networks guided them to new ones. Not only did Jews come disproportionately from large cities where they previously had concentrated, most also settled in only a handful of southern and western cities. Ninety-six percent of Jews lived in urban places in 1957, compared with 64 percent of the total U.S. population—and 87 percent of American Jews lived in cities of

250,000 or more inhabitants. In other words, Jews not only lived in cities, they lived in big cities. Although Jews constituted only 3.5 percent of the American population, they made up 8 percent of the nation's urban residents. The high concentration in the New York City area, which held approximately 40 percent of American Jewry, contributed to the distinctive Jewish demographic profile. Aggregate data reveal the shift away from the Northeast and Midwest to the South and West, yet Jewish patterns of migration remained highly distinctive. Despite significant postwar migration, 75 percent of America's Jews lived in only five states in 1960, as they had prior to the Second World War. When these data are disaggregated, the particularities of Jewish migration appear. Enticed by the vision of easy living under perpetually sunny skies, Jews favored certain Sunbelt cities over others. In these cities the rate of Jewish population growth often exceeded that of the general white population. Above all, Jews went to two coastal cities: Miami in the East and Los Angeles in the West. These cities account for 80 percent and 70 percent, respectively, of the total postwar Jewish migration to the South and West. Thus they provide the best case study of the impact of the postwar Sunbelt migrations on American Jewish ethnic culture.

Miami and Los Angeles: Magnet Cities

The postwar Jewish migration put Los Angeles and Miami on the Jewish map of the United States. Miami and Los Angeles received new settlers in record numbers after the war. Both cities had grown during the war, but neither anticipated the postwar influx. In 1946, observers estimated that each month 16,000 newcomers were arriving in Los Angeles. Of these, slightly more than 2,000 were Jews. The new arrivals more than doubled the substantial Jewish population estimated at 100,000 before the war. By 1950, there were almost 300,000 Jews in the City of Angels. Seventh largest in Jewish population in 1940, Los Angeles displaced Chicago a decade later to rank second behind New York City. The number of Jews in Los Angeles continued to grow throughout the 1950s at an impressive rate of just under 50 percent. The rate of growth of the Jewish population exceeded that of the general population, such that the percentage of Jews in Los Angeles rose steadily. By the end of the decade, there were close to 400,000 Jews living in the City of Angels, roughly 18 percent of the total population. So many newcomers had arrived within such a short time period that only 8 percent of adult Jews living in the city in 1950 were native Angelenos and only 16 percent could be considered old-timers who had settled there before the Second World War. Continued migration in the 1960s and 1970s increased the city's Jewish population to more than half a million Jews, a Jewish city of enormous proportions.

Nowhere near Los Angeles initially in the size of its general or Jewish population, Miami grew at an even more rapid rate. Although the number of Jews doubled from 1940 to 1945, from a mere 8,000 to 16,000, the population increased more than threefold to 55,000 by 1950. This astonishing rate of increase far outstripped the 57 percent growth in the general Miami population. Five years later, the Jewish population doubled yet again to reach 100,000. Thus, within a decade after the war, Miami had zoomed from a small and insignificant concentration of 16,000 Jews to a major urban Jewish center of 100,000 Jews. Thereafter, the rate of growth slowed, but Jewish migration to Miami continued to outstrip general migration until the Jewish proportion of the population had increased to 15 percent. By 1970, Miami contained approximately the same number of Jews as Chicago's greater metropolitan area, roughly 250,000. Miami now ranked among the top five American cities in terms of its Jewish population. Even more than Los Angeles, it was a city of newcomers. A mere 4 percent of the Jewish population had been born in the city; virtually everyone had come from someplace else.

Those who chose to move to these cities charted a different path from the majority who made the more modest and popular move to the suburbs. "They came for several reasons," Bernard Goldstein explained,

> but all of them add up to economics. You had young people who were stationed in the army camps here. And they realized the opportunities—this was an open economic frontier. And as soon as the war was over, if they were single they just stayed here and if they had families they went back to New York or Chicago or wherever, packed their bags and came right back.

A move to the suburbs rarely involved the pursuit of economic opportunity, although it often reflected increased affluence and the pursuit of status. For Jews, moving to the suburbs meant choosing a residence within the city's expanding boundaries. For some, however, the suburbs were a "dress rehearsal" for the big move. "When you grow up in New York City—all the world is Jewish," explained Nathan Perlmutter. "When all the world is Jewish, nobody is Jewish, really." Perlmutter moved to Miami from New York City in 1956 to head the office of the Anti-Defamation League. "You've got to leave major metropolitan areas to fully understand what I mean about a sense of a Jewish community—of a 'we' and a 'they'—in New York, it's all 'we'." Miami and Los Angeles represented alternatives to suburbanization.

The growth of Jewish suburban areas stemmed from a different but related set of federal postwar policies that had promoted internal migration within the United States. The scarcity of adequate housing in the cities, the rapid building of modestly priced single-family houses, the extensive program of highway construction, and the easy availability of mortgages all encouraged young families to seek homes on the expanding peripheries of the nation's cities. Although energized by these policies, suburbanization represented a postwar continuation and extension of the movement out of older and poorer city neighborhoods into new and more affluent ones that had started as early as the First World War. Jews who moved to the suburbs did not lose touch with the city, its institutions and culture. Many returned daily to work and more visited on occasion. Nor did suburbanization disrupt the family network; it simply extended the reach of the intergenerational family. Similarly, although suburban Jews organized Jewish life anew, they also imported Jewish institutions. Synagogues frequently followed their more wealthy congregants to the suburbs. Such decisions provided suburban Jews with a significant measure of continuity and reaffirmed deference to established leaders. No changing of the guard took place, in contrast with internal migration, which shattered patterns of deference and disrupted structures of collective continuity.

Alongside the mass internal migration to Sunbelt cities of Jews seeking economic opportunity, one should also note a smaller but steady stream of migrants who moved specifically for occupational reasons. This pattern did not radically change the distribution of the Jewish population, although it did contribute a significant number of newcomers to many established Jewish communities. For example, in Toledo, Ohio, the expansion of the university and the centering of several large national retail chains in the city drew many aspiring Jewish academics and managers there. Toledo, however, experienced no overall growth in Jewish population because 45 to 60 percent of the young Jews raised there abandoned the city after college, seeking opportunity elsewhere. Similarly, Kansas City's relatively static Jewish population since the 1950s disguised both a substantial in-migration of Jewish professionals and managers—approximately 37 percent of Jewish household heads in 1976—and a sizable out-migration of adult children of Kansas City Jewish household heads. In the 1970s, fully half of those sons and daughters who grew up in Kansas City no longer lived there. The data on Omaha, Nebraska, reveal a similar pattern. Sidney Goldstein argues that migration of these young, ambitious Jewish professionals and managers indicates the strength of economic motives over the salience of kinship ties. It points to the predominance of the nuclear family among American Jews. It suggests that the residential clustering so characteristic of eastern and midwestern cities no longer appeals to these Jewish migrants, who have discarded an earlier preference for areas of high Jewish concentration. It reveals the extent to which Jews have come to resemble other Americans in social and cultural behavior, even as their distinctive occupational concentration propels them across the continent in search of jobs.

Given the urban choices, especially the rapid growth of such southwestern cities as Houston and such southern cities as Atlanta, it is worthwhile asking why so many more Jews migrated to Miami and Los Angeles. A different dynamic appears to be at work in the rapid emergence of these two cities in comparison with other patterns of migration, either to the suburbs or for occupational mobility. These two cities attracted Jewish newcomers not only through their climate and leisure style of life and their promise of economic abundance, but also through the substantial and visible Jewish presence in a major city industry. Although it would be unfair to compare the Los Angeles–based motion picture industry's enormous assets and glamour with the much smaller Miami Beach tourist trade, Jewish hoteliers in the latter city compensated in part by catering to Jews, advertising for their patronage, and encouraging them not only to visit but to settle in Miami. Such encouragement required Jewish efforts to change southern mores—specifically, to eliminate visible signs of anti-Semitic bias in Miami.

In 1945, as part of an effort by the Anti-Defamation League to remove discriminatory signs on the beach, seventeen ex-servicemen "paid quiet calls on managers of hotels and apartment houses displaying or advertising 'Gentiles only' policies," according to the historian Gladys Rosen. "The tactics and its timing proved effective," she concluded, because more than half of the signs disappeared. Jewish residents of Miami Beach, eager to attract Jewish visitors, then urged the local city council to outlaw anti-Semitic advertising. Although the Florida courts invalidated the council's 1947 law on the grounds that the municipality lacked jurisdiction, by 1949 the state legislature had enacted enabling legislation that granted the city council the power to prohibit discriminatory advertising. The Miami Beach Council then forbade "any advertisement, notice or sign which is discriminatory against persons of any religion, sect, creed, race or denomination in the enjoyment of privileges and facilities of places of public accommodation, amusement or resort." Given the widespread acceptance of legal segregation in Florida—as in the rest of the South—the modest action of the Miami Beach City Council reverberated as a loud rejection of discrimination. By passing the law, the council hung out a welcome sign for Jews, at least on Miami Beach. The law did not eliminate anti-Semitic discrimination and did not affect resorts outside of the council's jurisdiction, but it made Miami Beach's public milieu more accommodating to Jews and set an important precedent.

Despite their comparable attractions for Jewish migrants, Miami and Los Angeles appealed to slightly different Jews. Once they decided to move, Jewish migrants often allowed ethnic networks to influence their choices. These networks channeled postwar internal migration and sorted Jews. Miami drew a more geographically representative sample, including a sizable number of southern Jews, than did Los Angeles. In 1959 approximately 43 percent of Miami Jews came from New York City, a proportion that slightly exceeded the percentage of American Jews living in New York after the war. By contrast, only 24 percent of the migrants to Los Angeles in 1950 had left New York City. Los Angeles attracted a disproportionate number of Jews from the cities of the Midwest, especially Chicago. An estimated 17 percent of the newcomers hailed from Chicago (45 percent of all midwestern migrants to Los Angeles came from Chicago), although its Jewish population constituted less than 10 percent of American Jewry. Far more Jewish northeasterners moved to Los Angeles, however, than was true among the general white migrant population, which consisted largely of people arriving from states west of the Mississippi.

If Los Angeles attracted Jews disproportionately from the cities of the Midwest, it drew a representative selection of migrants in terms of age. Most Jewish newcomers were young people seeking work, although some came to the city for health reasons or to retire. Miami initially appealed to a similar age spectrum, but by the mid-1950s an ever-growing percentage of elderly retirees had settled in the city. The mass migration of elderly Jews to Miami Beach, which accelerated in the 1960s, received an impetus from the steady decay of the inner cities, accompanied by the rising rate of crime, the high cost of housing, and the arrival of new, poor immigrants. The portability of federal social security benefits and union pensions encouraged mobility among retirees in the way that the GI bill had aided a migration of young men after the Second World War. By 1959, the median age of Jews in Miami had risen to 46 from 33 years, while in Los Angeles it had dropped from 37 to 33 years.

The large number of elderly Jews migrating to Miami contributed to a third difference between the two cities. Most Jews moving to Los Angeles settled down and confined any subsequent moves to different sections of the city. Jews migrating to Miami, however, included in their ranks a sizable contingent of "snowbirds." These restless settlers resided in the city anywhere from one to eight months in the course of a year, spending the rest of their time back "home." Many eventually stayed year-round in Miami. Often the difference between an eight-month "snowbird" and a new resident was more a state of mind than a reflection of behavior.

Jewish migrants to Los Angeles and Miami also adopted different residential strategies. The large contingent of New Yorkers in Miami replicated the familiar pattern of dispersed concentration. The newcomers settled initially in two sections: in the South Beach section of Miami Beach and in the Shenandoah and Westchester areas of the city of Miami. By 1955, these two districts held 75 percent of the Jewish population. As more migrants continued to arrive, they drifted northward to North Miami and North Miami Beach. These patterns of concentration reflected in part a response to the restrictive housing covenants in several of the incorporated cities of Dade County that were part of metropolitan Miami. Jewish entrepreneurs in real estate and the hotel and building industry also influenced Miami Jewish residential patterns. The number of apartment houses constructed soared during the 1950s and on into the 1960s. Miami boosters noted that a new house or apartment was completed in Miami "every seven minutes of the working day for an annual average of more than 16,000 units." The migrants' decision to concentrate in certain sections of the city pointed as well to their immigrant and second-generation origins. The move to Miami represented less a decision to leave the familiar urban world of their past than an attempt to radically extend its boundaries. Jews dubbed Miami "the southern borscht belt" and joked that it had become a suburb of New York City. Their humor underscored the sense of connectedness that the newcomers felt with their old homes, which denied the radical character of their relocation.

In contrast, Jews moving to Los Angeles knew that they had left the old neighborhood behind; few sought to replicate the residential strategies of Chicago or New York. When the newcomers arrived in Los Angeles they settled in newly developing sections of the city, especially on the West Side and in the San Fernando Valley. Although significant concentrations of Jews appeared in the Wilshire-Fairfax, Beverly-Fairfax, Beverly Hills, and Westwood districts, these sections, with the possible exception of Fairfax, did not resemble eastern and midwestern urban neighborhoods. The intensity of public urban life characteristic of eastern and midwestern cities faded under the California sunshine. Yet an awareness of ethnicity persisted. Growing up in Beverly Hills, one knew that it wasn't 100 percent Jewish, "but it felt like it was," a resident recalled. The big ethnic distinctions were culinary. "All of my Jewish friends ate rye bread with mustard and there was one non-Jewish boy in the group that I went around with and he . . . used mayonnaise on white bread, and we used to call him 'mayo.'" The urban character of Los Angeles also muted distinctions between city and suburb, though residents recognized a difference in cultural style between city Jews and valley Jews. One resident who grew up in Los Angeles during the 1950s never understood what a suburb was until she traveled East to settle in Minneapolis. The migrants reversed the perception, thinking that all of Los Angeles was one big suburb.

A Community of Strangers

Despite their differences in age, motivation for leaving the familiar, and their diverse residential strategies, the migrants turned to peer group organization to forge the rudimentary bonds of community. Like the immigrants, they broke intergenerational family ties to reconstitute a voluntary community of peers. The new migrants similarly relied upon shared memories of the past or common values to unite them. Unlike the immigrants, the newcomers to Los Angeles and Miami did not convert their impulse to peer group solidarity into social welfare and mutual aid. The new *landsmannshaftn* remained essentially centers of secular ethnic sociability, anchoring their members in unfamiliar urban territory through nostalgic evocations of the well-known world that had been abandoned. By 1950, several dozen of these social clubs organized around city of origin flourished in Los Angeles, as did a smaller number in Miami. They held monthly meetings and hosted annual picnics. A few engaged in charitable endeavors. In 1947, the five hundred members of the Omaha Friendship Club of Los Angeles decided to raise money for a memorial to Henry Monsky, the recently deceased head of B'nai B'rith, who had lived in Omaha. But the clubs' main purpose was social. Most of the Los Angeles clubs limited membership to adults aged twenty-one to thirty-five. Those who didn't join could use the services of the many introduction clubs that sprang up, but often it was preferable to touch base with fellow *landslayt* whose identity with "home" was linked to the neighborhood of their youth. New York City Jews, for example, founded high school alumni associations in Miami and Los Angeles that encouraged contact between former classmates of the Thomas Jefferson or Abraham Lincoln high schools in Brooklyn, or of the DeWitt Clinton or Morris high schools in the Bronx.

The migrants also swelled the ranks of the handful of established American Jewish organizations. By the early 1950s, the one B'nai B'rith group of 1945 in Miami had multiplied into twenty other lodges with a membership exceeding twenty-five hundred. Labor Zionists, General Zionists, Hadassah, and the American Jewish Congress rapidly founded local chapters. Often, "even before a new apartment building is fully occupied," observed a Jewish communal worker, "there is already formed (with officers) a Men's Club, B'nai B'rith Lodge, Hadassah Chapter, etc." The newcomers' visible presence encouraged national organizations to refocus their activities. In 1952, the American Jewish Committee established a chapter in Miami and moved its southern headquarters from Atlanta to the new branch. Miami was rapidly becoming the Jews' new headquarters of the South. In Los Angeles, a similar process of recruitment added thousands to the membership rolls of national organizations already established in the city.

The burst of communal activity also affected religious life. In Miami, migrants joined the half-dozen established congregations—which offered special monthly or even weekly memberships to accommodate the "snowbirds"—while those who found the synagogues inconvenient, undesirable, or inaccessible initiated new congregations. By 1947, there were twenty-four congregations in Miami, nineteen of them with rabbis. Given the still modest size of the Jewish population, these figures represent significant communal ferment. Los Angeles, with ten times the Jewish population, supported only seventy-three synagogues, or three times the number in Miami. The newcomers found few precedents impeding their efforts to introduce a wide array of communal activities and organizations. Rabbis could, and did, build congregations that became personal fiefdoms unconstrained by an entrenched laity. These communities, a true frontier, were open to individual and collective entrepreneurship; both also contained significant numbers of exceptionally wealthy Jews.

The "snowbird" phenomenon, however, had a significant influence on Miami's communal development. Although it soon overshadowed Atlanta as the major Jewish city of the South, Miami attracted far fewer colonizers from New York than did Los Angeles. When local leaders tried to interest New York institutions in setting up branches in Miami, they more often encountered resistance. Irving Lehrman, rabbi of the Miami Beach Jewish Center (later Temple Emanu-El), grasped the high visibility potential of his synagogue for visitors and made arrangements to establish a branch of the Jewish Museum in the center as early as 1950. "It will not only bring prestige to, and raise the cultural level of the community, but will afford an opportunity to the thousands of residents, as well its visitors, to see the vast storehouse of Jewish artifacts and learn more about our cultural heritage," he explained. But Lehrman's vision was rarely shared by eastern leaders. Instead Miami Beach became the campaign capital for national Jewish fund-raising.

Despite its size and diversity, the Los Angeles Jewish community lacked entrenched interests and thus held enormous potential, especially for an elite of ideologically committed easterners. They came to the Southland after the war to establish branches of their institutions and solicit support among Hollywood's moguls. In a brief five-year period after the war, these committed individuals transplanted an institutional range of ideological diversity that had developed in the East. When the American Jewish Committee sent its field-worker for the West to Los Angeles to start a branch in 1945, he emphasized the unique committee ideology to overcome the reluctance of older residents to join the organization. Four years later, a young communal worker arrived in Los Angeles and dreamed "the vision of establishing a '92nd Street Y of the West'" in the new Westside Jewish Community Center. In 1946, Moshe Davis, a young professor of American Jewish history at the Jewish Theological Seminary, arrived in Los Angeles to recruit supporters for a new branch of the Seminary, the University of Judaism. As Simon Greenberg, the university's first president, recalled, "We had to overcome the feeling on the West Coast that here was a new community. Why did it have to import the divisions (Orthodox, Conservative, Reform) of the East Coast? Why can't we have one school for the Jews of the West Coast?" Eastern leaders' ability to colonize Los Angeles Jews successfully obviated the need to answer such questions. Of course, not all efforts to transplant ideological institutions succeeded. Los Angeles provided a receptive environment largely to a middle range of organizations in the immediate postwar decade. Their success established the foundation for subsequent colonizing efforts.

In the new urban milieu, Jewish self-perceptions gradually changed. "Jews are now free to be Jewish in a new way as an act of personal choice rather than imposition," writes the sociologist Neil Sandberg. The self-selection that lay behind migration reinforced the principle of personal choice of identity. As the Los Angeles lawyer and communal leader Howard Friedman explained, Jews felt able to innovate, experiment, indulge, in short, "to cultivate ourselves . . . in a context of complete freedom." However, according to Moses Rischin, a historian of Jewish immigrants in New York City, the Jewish way of life in Los Angeles was problematic. "Post-Judaic" and "post-secular," he wrote, the life-style was "remote even from an earlier subculture of Jewishness" and sustained neither by traditional religious patterns nor by a vigorous secular ethnicity. Others rejoiced in the absence of traditions. According to Charles Brown, the head of the Jewish Community Council in 1952, "here [in Los Angeles] there are no vested interests, here there are no sacred cows, here there is no cold hand of the past. There is an opportunity to develop new forms of Jewish communal living geared in a realistic fashion to the actual needs of the Jewish community." These new forms included such eclectic institutions as the Brandeis Camp Institute, pioneered by Shlomo Bardin. Constrained neither by traditions nor by vested interests, Bardin orchestrated moments of Jewish solidarity designed especially to appeal to a community of strangers, recruiting both old-timers and newcomers for weekend celebrations/explorations of the Sabbath that often inspired the participants to incorporate elements of Jewish study and observance in their lives. The heart of Bardin's program, however, was a month-long innovative leadership training program that raised the Jewish consciousness of the college youth who attended.

Outsiders to the dominant Protestant communities of Los Angeles and Miami, Jewish newcomers introduced additional ethnic diversity to their new homes. Rabbi Edgar Magnin, a fixture of the Los Angeles Jewish scene for decades as the leader of the Wilshire Boulevard Temple, the most prestigious Reform congregation in the city, deplored the new ethnicity introduced by the newcomers in an interview conducted in 1978. "This is a different ballgame today—you've got another Brooklyn here. When I came here, it was Los Angeles. Now it's a Brooklyn." Magnin exaggerated, of course, but other native-born Californian Jews also expressed unease at the changes introduced (mainly in the 1950s) by the newcomers. Often identifying themselves as white ethnics, despite the absence of other such comparable groups as Italians, some migrants used religious symbols to define their collective identity. Foremost among these symbols was Israel: Zion, homeland, state. The migrants' support for the establishment of the state and their subsequent identification with Israel as the vehicle of Jewish idealism helped to make sentimental Zionism the collective glue uniting American Jews. Their numbers overwhelmed the pockets of anti-Zionist commitment among the old-timers, while the attacks on Communists inspired by McCarthy undermined the organizational viability of the internationalist radicals.

Jewish migrants selected themselves to move to Sunbelt cities—to take advantage of the economic opportunities, to bask in the balmy weather, and to escape from the constraining intergenerational intimacies of parents and kinfolk. In the process they elevated the principle of self-selection that initially had guided them as migrants into the grounds for collective action. Thus they influenced the character of American Jewish life by creating new patterns of Jewish communal life that upheld the centrality of the consenting individual. Long before converts to Judaism adopted the label "Jews by choice," newcomers to the Sunbelt cities had transformed Jewishness into a matter of one's choosing. The migrants posited a Jewishness rooted in the future, in peer group sociability, in common values and in personal choice, all linked to powerful but distant surrogates—the old home that had disappeared and the Jewish State of Israel that rose like a phoenix on the ashes of the Holocaust. The newcomers created a loosely knit community that supported these possibilities, that allowed for eclectic Jewish styles and symbols of ethnicity, that provided fertile ground for individual entrepreneurship.

"In the past, Jewishness was absorbed by young people as they grew up in Jewish community and family environments," argues Sandberg. "No parental decision was involved in the creation of a sense of Jewish identification in the young person's growing identity and self-image. They were immersed in a culture where Jewish language, behavior, and symbolism developed as automatic responses. . . . Today," he concludes, referring specifically to Los Angeles, "most Jews have grown up without the support of such a community." Under the bright sunshine of Miami and Los Angeles, Jewishness gradually lost its ineluctability. If Jewishness was "not a matter of natural inheritance," then an individual Jew had to develop a number of interlocking networks to sustain a Jewish identity that meant more than self-definition. In Los Angeles, such networks emerged primarily within occupations and politics. In the postwar period, a majority of Los Angeles Jews shared their workplace largely with other Jews. Political lobbying for Israel also served to define the ethnic identity of Miami and Los Angeles Jews. Ironically, work and politics—the two public arenas that originally generated most intra-Jewish conflict—now provided a sense of shared Jewishness for the migrants. For decades Jewish workers had fought Jewish bosses over the conditions of the workplace, and the scars of the past's bitter political battles among Jews had only begun to heal. Yet in the new golden land, work and politics became sources of ethnic continuity helping to define the collective parameters of Jewishness.

In many ways, the Jewish worlds of Los Angeles and Miami and other Sunbelt cities can be seen as the offspring of the large urban Jewish settlements of New York, Chicago, Philadelphia, and Boston, and of the more modest communities of such cities as Omaha, Milwaukee, Cleveland, and Detroit. As Jewish New York, Chicago, and Philadelphia represent continuity with a European past because they were created by immigrants from the cities and towns of Eastern Europe, so Jewish Miami and Los Angeles are creations of the midwestern and northeastern cities, representing continuity with an American past. American Jews produced in the postwar era a second generation of cities, offspring of the first generation. It was, perhaps, a very American thing to send off the sons and daughters—and even the grandfathers and grandmothers—to colonize the new golden land, to build cities, to plant congregations, to forge symbolic bonds of ethnic identity. Borrowing from America's Puritan past, one might see these internal migrations as American Jews' own errand into the wilderness.

CHAPTER 21

Jews participated out of all proportion to their numbers in the great liberal causes that swept the nation in the 1960s. The civil rights campaign, the struggle to end the Vietnam War, and what was known at the time as the counterculture all engaged large numbers of Jews, particularly but not exclusively the "baby boomers" born after 1945. Already in the 1950s, as we have seen, liberalism and social activism had become characteristic features of American Jewish life, coupled with concern for Israel and consciousness of the Holocaust. All of these themes now found reinforcement in the tumultuous 1960s, exemplified by the establishment of the Social Action Center of Reform Judaism in 1961, the annual New York "Salute to Israel" parades, and the publication of a spate of Holocaust-related books, including Elie Wiesel's Night *(1960) and Arthur Morse's best-selling* While Six Million Died *(1967).*

The Six-Day War of June 1967 marked a turning point in the lives of many 1960s-era Jews. The paralyzing fear of a "second Holocaust" followed by tiny Israel's seemingly miraculous victory over the combined Arab armies arrayed to destroy it struck deep emotional chords among American Jews. Their financial support for Israel rose sharply in the war's wake, and more of them than ever before chose in those years to make Israel their permanent home. In addition, something of a spiritual revival washed over the American Jewish community after 1967. Many turned religiously inward, some were "born again" into Orthodoxy, and every movement in American Judaism witnessed new interest in traditional religious practices, heightened appreciation for mystical and spiritual sources, and an enhanced desire for Jewish learning.

In the chapter that follows, Jack Wertheimer, professor of history at the Jewish Theological Seminary of America, looks back at the upheavals of the 1960s and places them within a comparative religious context. He argues that the events of the 1960s "transformed the contours of Jewish religious life" and mounted challenges that affected all Jewish religious institutions. These challenges, in turn, paved the way for polarizing debates that in subsequent decades would transform American Jews into what Wertheimer calls "a people divided."

Two movements with far-reaching significance for American Jews emerged during this period, both of them influenced by the domestic struggle for civil rights. One was the movement to save Soviet Jews who were denied under the Communist regime basic religious and human rights, forbidden to emigrate, and in some cases imprisoned for crimes like teaching Hebrew and promoting Zionism. Using political skills well-honed by the antiwar movement, American Jewish activists, in concert with Israel and with memories of the Holocaust fresh in their minds, waged a relentless "let my people go" campaign that ultimately proved successful; hundreds of thousands of Soviet Jews emigrated to Israel and the United States in the 1970s and 1980s.

The other movement that emerged in the 1960s was Jewish feminism, which advocated gender equality and promoted increased roles for women in all arenas of Jewish life, including the synagogue. The ordination of women rabbis, beginning in 1972, the burgeoning Jewish educational opportunities opened to women, the development of women's rituals and prayer services, and the emergence of women in many positions of communal responsibility once open only to men all attest to the revolution wrought by Jewish feminism, and to the impact of the 1960s on subsequent decades of Jewish life.

The Turbulent Sixties

Jack Wertheimer

The decade of "sober serenity," as one historian dubbed the 1950s, gave way to the turbulent 1960s. And just as Jewish religious institutions enjoyed a boom period during the American religious expansion of the postwar era, they were buffeted by the upheaval that shook American society during the tumultuous 1960s. The historian Sydney Ahlstrom has described the latter decade as a time when "the foundations of national confidence, patriotic idealism, moral traditionalism, and even of historical Judeo-Christian theism, were awash. Presuppositions that had held firm for centuries—even millennia—were being widely questioned." Despite the postwar expansion of religious institutions, Ahlstrom concluded, "Jews like other Americans, would discover that the religious revival had provided very feeble preparation for the social and spiritual tumult of the 1960s." Arising from a range of circumstances both endemic to the Jewish condition and generic to the American and even international mood at the end of the twentieth century, new movements reshaped the agenda of religious institutions and individual Jews. The convulsions of the 1960s transformed the mid-century contours of Jewish religious life.

The Impact of Protest Movements

The most visible symptoms of social dislocation in the 1960s were new movements of protest—the civil rights struggle, the antiwar movement, the battle for women's equality, and the so-called counterculture. Each profoundly challenged American society at large and religious institutions in particular. In criticizing the status quo in the name of idealism and morality, these movements trod on turf properly considered the domain of religious communities. Churches and synagogues became staging grounds for pitched battles, as civil rights and antiwar activists recruited supporters for their causes. From within sanctuary pews, advocates of women's rights and countercultural values issued demands for reform. And religious leaders such as the Reverend Martin Luther King, Jr., Father Daniel Berrigan, and Rabbi Abraham Joshua Heschel led tens of thousands of marchers in protest demonstrations, thereby thrusting religion into the maelstrom of the American social upheaval.

The emerging prominence of religious institutions in the public arena was first displayed in late November 1963, during the national outpouring of grief for the fallen president, John F. Kennedy. Via the relatively new medium of television, the entire nation attended a Catholic funeral mass. For many Americans this was the first sustained exposure to Catholic religious ritual. It served to educate them about Catholicism and opened American society to greater tolerance of religious expression outside of mainline Protestantism—a process already advanced by the election of the first Roman Catholic president. It also made manifest the intertwined relationship of organized religion and American politics.

With the assassination occurring on a Friday afternoon, stunned Jews flooded into their synagogues in search of solace at Sabbath services. A contemporary observer estimated that more Jews attended services that weekend than during the High Holidays a few weeks earlier. An estimated six thousand worshippers attended services at New York City's Temple Emanu-El; and in White Plains, N.Y., the same number of Jews attended synagogues, comprising half the Jewish community in that suburban city. Those mournful days foreshadowed the heightened involvement of synagogues and other religious institutions in the social upheaval of the 1960s.

As the civil rights and antiwar movements spread, some Jewish religious leaders jumped into the fray. At the forefront of Jewish activists were the official leaders of the Reform movement, who defined social justice as central to their agenda. Under Rabbi Maurice Eisendrath, the Religious Action Center and the Union of American Hebrew Congregations moved far more boldly to the left on social issues. In southern cities individual Reform rabbis, such as Jacob Rothschild of Atlanta, threw their energies into the civil rights movement. And to the dismay of many Jews in the South, rabbis from the North proudly traveled south to march in civil rights demonstrations. It was, of course, the local Jews who paid the price for their virtuous coreligionists: southern synagogues were fire-bombed and Jews in the South were held accountable for the deeds of Jewish visitors from the North.

Reform rabbis were also in the vanguard of Jewish antiwar activities. Addressing the General Assembly of the Union of American Hebrew Congregations in 1965, Eisendrath declared: "We transgress every tenet of our faith when we fight on another's soil, scorch the earth of another's beloved homeland, slay multitudes of innocent villagers." The assembly passed a resolution urging a cease-fire and negotiated peace in Vietnam, a position that in 1965 was not yet popular with either the American public or American Jewry. Even the Reform movement, however, was not spared the divisiveness that characterized American life during the Vietnam War. When Eisendrath published an open letter to President Lyndon B. Johnson in 1967 comparing the president to Antiochus Epiphanes, the tyrant of the Chanukah account, twenty-five Reform congregations joined with New York's Temple Emanu-El to secede from the UAHC for more than a year in protest over Eisendrath's extreme position.

The protest movements over civil rights and the war in Vietnam brought religious leaders unprecedented public exposure. For the first time since the establishment of the State of Israel, rabbis had fighting causes to galvanize the laity of the staid synagogue precincts. A Reform rabbi in Boston confessed that his congregants took him more seriously since his arrest in antiwar demonstrations: "My actions, more than all the sermons I had preached, got my point across." Rabbis across the religious spectrum threw themselves into the new social activism. To cite two examples: the Massachusetts Board of Rabbis declared California grapes not kosher because they were picked by oppressed laborers. Their counterparts in Philadelphia voted to provide draft counseling in some of their synagogues. Jewish religious leaders, along with their Christian counterparts, would eventually recognize, however, that social protest might energize the laity in the short term, but over time it would also blur the boundaries between society and congregation—to the detriment of the latter.

The Challenge of Feminism and the Counterculture

Even as public attention was focused mainly on civil rights and antiwar activists, more subtle and profound challenges to religious institutions were mounted by other, newly emerging movements. By virtue of their unusually high levels of educational attainment, Jews were particularly receptive to the new movements promoted by feminists and the counterculture. To be sure, Jews initially drawn to these movements were generally indifferent to religious life and did not expect to introduce their revolutionary agendas into Judaism. But by the late 1960s, more committed Jews took the first steps toward bridging the worlds of Judaism and of feminism and the counterculture.

The so-called second wave of American feminism is generally traced to the publication in 1963 of *The Feminine Mystique* by Betty Friedan. Arguing that this mystique kept women trapped in a life of emptiness and frustration, tied to their suburban homes, and dependent upon men for financial support, Friedan also accused religious institutions of restricting women and imposing a male worldview upon women's religious expression. Friedan's book inspired American women to reconsider their lives and spawned a vast literature of feminist protest, much of it written by women of Jewish background. With the incorporation of the National Organization for Women (NOW) in October 1966 and the emergence of a women's liberation movement out of the New Left in 1967, a new phase of American feminism had begun.

Influenced by these new movements, Jewish women concerned about inequality in Jewish life began to organize and speak out. Initially, their goals were meliorative: they sought equal opportunities for women in the synagogue service and as religious leaders—as rabbis, cantors, educators, and synagogue board members; they fought stereotypes of women and girls in Jewish educational materials; and they demanded due recognition by the Jewish community for the critical role women played as volunteers who sustained synagogues and communal institutions. Gradually, in the early 1970s, some knowledgeable Jewish women also questioned whether women's sensibilities were given adequate attention and influence in the shaping of liturgy, rituals, and other forms of religious expression. Two particularly influential essays posed these challenges directly: Trude Weiss-Rosmarin's "The Unfreedom of Jewish Women" denounced "the unfairness of Jewish marriage laws to divorced and abandoned women"; and Rachel Adler's "The Jew Who Wasn't There" "contrasted male and female models of traditional Jewish piety" and called for greater sensitivity to the religious experience of females.

In September 1971 a group composed mainly of Conservative Jewish women in Manhattan founded Ezrat Nashim to discuss the status of women in Judaism. The following March they held a "countersession" at the national convention of the Conservative rabbinate and issued a series of demands for the full acceptance of women as the religious equals of men. One year later the first National Jewish Women's Conference drew an audience of five hundred.

All the movements of American Judaism were challenged by the new Jewish women's movement, and all began to search for ways of bridging the gap between their conception of Judaism and the demands of Jewish women. It was symptomatic of the heightened awareness of women's protest that in 1969 Rabbi Aaron Soloveitchik addressed the Union of Orthodox Jewish Congregations on the "Attitude of Judaism toward the Woman." In early 1974 the Young Israel movement, another Orthodox synagogue body, held a conference to consider the status of Jewish women. By 1972 the (Reform) Hebrew Union College Ordained Sally Priesand as the first woman rabbi. And the following year, the Conservative movement's Committee on Law and Standards issued a *takkanah* (legislative enactment) empowering each pulpit rabbi to decide whether women might be counted as part of a prayer quorum (minyan) of his synagogue. Although most of the major strides of women in the religious sphere took place in the 1970s, profound changes in outlook were already occurring in the 1960s, during the early years of the feminist revolution.

Virtually simultaneously, a Jewish offshoot of the American counterculture emerged among college and graduate students. As products of the "youth movement," the self-proclaimed "new Jews" espoused the political ideology of the time. They adopted the rhetoric of the New Left and supported the general critique of American society and especially of the Vietnam War. But what distinguished this group from so many other young American Jews was their involvement with Jewish concerns. For even as they criticized established Jewish institutions, they were engaged in the process of remaking Jewish life, rather than rejecting it wholesale. Alan L. Mintz, the first editor of *Response,* the most prominent journal of the Jewish counterculture, wrote: "A most startling discovery has been made that Judaism does not have to be identical to the scheme of middle-class values. . . . A new consciousness of the past has brought us to believe that a more fundamental and nourishing Judaism existed, was discussed, and did not need a middle-class life style and its constellation of values." Some set out to reform existing Jewish institutions, while others formed alternative Jewish communities.

Although a few prominent gurus were drawn from the older generation, the Jewish counterculture was primarily created by and for Jewish baby boomers who came of age in the 1960s. Many were third-generation Americans whose parents had participated in the exodus to suburbia after World War II. Now they openly rebelled against their parents' style of living, the tedium and complacency of suburbia, and the desiccated Judaism practiced in suburban synagogues. As Hillel Levine, a prominent activist, wrote: "We woke up from the American dream and tried to discover who we really were. For many of us this now means turning our concerns inward into the Jewish community because we are disenchanted with the crass materialism of the larger society. Yet where can we find inspiration in the multimillion dollar Jewish presence of suburbia?"

The Jewish counterculture scorned Jewish organizational life and criticized in particular the misguided priorities of the Jewish community. The youthful critics could find nothing worthwhile in suburban synagogues that touted the values of "success, wealth, and rote religious performance" above all else. Suburban Judaism, wrote one activist, was "a spiritual Hiroshima which had been the setting for the transformation of the Hebrew spirit into an increasingly dispensable appendage of middle-class culture." Nor could the family offer Jewish meaning. The young activists bitterly denounced the Jewish family as yet another institution fostering Americanization and assimilation. In place of the middle-class family, they called for "real community" and "real intimacy."

And so they appropriated the ancient rabbinic *havurah* (fellowship) for radically new ends. In the fall of 1968 Havurat Shalom, "the first countercultural Jewish community," was founded in Somerville, Massachusetts. Begun as an alternative seminary, it was soon transformed into an experimental community that encouraged ritual innovation and sought to avoid having a single authority or rabbi. Within a short time the New York Havurah was formed, and not long afterward, young Jews formed the Farbrangen in Washington and a minyan in Germantown, Philadelphia. By the early 1970s new groups proliferated at major universities. For the most part, these early havurot were closed to nonmembers. They were run democratically and generally included some program of communal study, as well as regular communal meals and occasional weekend retreats.

The havurah was intended as an alternative to suburban Judaism. According to one of the founders, members "wanted to create a participant community rather than to be in a large impersonal institution in which culture or religion was dished out to us. We didn't want to be an audience, we wanted to be the *kahal* (community)." If the large suburban synagogue was a gargantuan, impersonal creation, the havurah would offer a "Judaism of scale," where Jews could pray and study in intimate fellowship. The havurah model appealed because it offered its members the opportunity to form small intimate fellowships for study, prayer, and friendship that seemed impossible in the large, decorous, bureaucratized synagogues of their youth. It allowed individual participation and spontaneity, whereas established synagogues were dominated by professionals who "led" formal services. The founders of Havurah Judaism sought a religious community that would alter "the relationship between the individual and society, between making and consuming, between membership and community, and between instrumentality and authenticity."

The goal, however, was not only to alter the setting of religious interaction but also to construct a different type of Judaism. Although they appropriated traditional forms and even fancied themselves neo-*hasidim,* adherents of Havurah Judaism fundamentally rejected a normative approach to Judaism and sought instead to experiment and improvise. The anthropologist Riv-Ellen Prell notes astutely: "The countercultural aesthetic that shaped the *havurah* depended on expressive individualism that featured the activism of all participants. Expressive individualism in turn was the product of the American culture that gave rise to American Judaism and promoted Jewish secularism." Despite their superficial adherence to traditional forms of behavior, the early havurot created a framework that was not normative.

Although they felt alienated from the official Jewish community and regarded themselves as outsiders, the new havurot were nevertheless taken seriously by the Jewish religious establishment virtually from the start. True, some scorned the innovations of Havurah Judaism, but they never ignored the movement; it was impossible to avoid the challenges posed by the havurot, particularly because members constituted the vanguard of committed

Jewish youth. Writing in the house organ of the Conservative rabbinate, Stephen Lerner declared in early 1970, just a year and a half after the founding of Havurat Shalom:

> If the *havurah* does nothing else, it should remind Jewish leaders that . . . religious creativity, fervor, and a sense of community have not passed from this earth. . . . Rabbis will have to surmount their own inertia, the resistance of synagogue boards and ritual committees, and get youth involved in every aspect of synagogue life. They must make sure that services provide at least some modicum of informality, youthful participation and creative study.

Within a decade some aspects of Havurah Judaism were adopted by many synagogues and in time havurah members assumed positions of influence in the Jewish community. But the outlook of Havurah Judaism was broadcast widely even earlier, with the appearance of the first *Jewish Catalog* in 1973. The catalog and its successors became Jewish best-sellers, further testament to the growing influence of this movement. Originating in the American counterculture of the 1960s, Havurah Judaism and its sometime ally, the Jewish feminist movement, challenged the established institutions and movements of American Judaism to rethink their priorities and reshape their religious programs in the concluding quarter of the twentieth century.

Changes in American Religious Life

Judaism in America was also affected by the general turmoil in American religious life during the 1960s. Like their Christian counterparts, Jewish religious groups were both inspired and confused by the protest movements. The antiwar movement, for example, provoked mixed feelings, particularly after the Six-Day War of 1967, when concerns arose that a weakened military in America would be unable to provide the Israeli army with effective weaponry. Whereas in the past religious institutions had routinely supported the troops and conferred their blessings on American policies, some religious groups now rethought their relationship to the American government and its policies—but not without much turmoil and soul-searching. Similarly, religious leaders were forced to respond to the growing influence of the provocative sexual and interpersonal mores promoted by the counterculture. Not only did religious institutions confront the programs of these movements, but they also had to assess the consequences of taking any position. How would support for the antiwar movement affect congregational or denominational unity? And how would taking any stance on public policy redefine the mission of a religious institution? The 1960s, in short, pushed religious leaders to rethink the role of religion in society.

This mood of self-doubt was stimulated as well by new patterns within American society that profoundly affected the fate of religious institutions more generally. Although the impact of these changes on Jewish religious life became clear only in the mid-1970s, the process of restructuring had already begun in the 1960s.

Perhaps the most troubling new pattern was the declining involvement of young people, the baby boomers, in religious life. Beginning in the mid-1960s, liberal Protestant churches began to hemorrhage—with the oldest and hardiest Protestant denominations losing the most members: in the decade after 1965 Episcopalians, Methodists, Presbyterians, and other so-called mainline groups sustained a drop of over 10 percent in membership. Among Catholics, there was a perceptible decline in mass attendance by the well-educated young. And in the Jewish community similar declines were noted in synagogue membership. This was confirmed in a 1971 national survey, which indicated that less than half the Jewish population was affiliated with a synagogue.

The crisis within Protestant mainline churches was sufficiently clear by the late 1960s to prompt the publication of a book by Dean M. Kelley, *Why Conservative Churches Are Growing,* the first in a series of studies examining the failure of liberal churches and the resurgence of conservative forms of religion. Kelley contended that religious groups most identified with mainstream American culture were declining, while those that challenged the prevailing American way were growing. The historian Martin E. Marty explained this phenomenon by noting that established, mainline churches flourish when "the official culture is secure and expansive . . . [but suffer] in times of cultural crisis and disintegration, when they receive blame for what goes wrong in society. . . . So they looked as good in the 1950s as they looked bad by the 1970s." Kelley went further, however, and traced the problem not to Zeitgeist but to ideology: the more a denomination blurred its boundaries with the surrounding society and the more it deferred to ecumenism and denied the particularity of its outlook, the greater the chances it would fail to retain members. Although the circumstances would differ within American Judaism due to peculiarly Jewish concerns, liberal forms of Judaism suffered similar declines, while more traditional versions held their own.

The sociologist Robert Wuthnow has argued persuasively that rising levels of educational attainment were the critical factor in the declining rates of religious participation. An expanding proportion of young Americans attended college in the postwar era. In the decade of the 1960s, alone, the proportion of eligible young people who actually attended college rose from 22.3 percent to 35.2 percent. Survey research at the time indicated the profound impact of higher education upon the attitudes of young people regarding sexual mores, divorce, the status of women, and government support for social programs. Concomitantly, attendance at religious services declined among the better educated. According to Wurthnow, church attendance among the college educated fell by 6 percent between 1969 and 1970 alone, but levels remained constant among those without college education. When asked whether religion could answer all or most of society's problems, 26 percent fewer people who had some college education answered affirmatively in 1974 as compared with 1957. Jews, a population with a disproportionately high level of educational attainment, followed these patterns as well, with consequences we shall yet examine.

The expansion of higher education was a central factor in the increasing levels of tolerance in American society that also marked the 1960s. The civil rights movement, the new ethnic consciousness that grew out of the black power movement, the election of a Catholic president, and the enormous respect and goodwill accorded to Pope John XXIII, as well as many other factors, opened American society to heterogeneity. Americans learned to tolerate diversity and the offbeat, such as new hair styles, innovative dress, experimental musical and artistic expression—and unconventional religious behavior. Eastern religions made inroads, as did religious cults and experimentation with forms of mysticism. Due to the activism of black religious leaders, African-American churches and their distinctive religious services came to public attention. Similarly, Catholic liturgy and rituals became more accessible to the American public during the Kennedy presidency. Whereas the dominant liberal churches of Protestantism had once defined proper religious decorum and self-presentation, the decline of an official American religion and the loosening of cultural norms opened a vast new space for traditional religious groups. This opening of American society enabled more traditional versions of religion—including varieties of Jewish Orthodoxy—to flourish. It was symptomatic that in this era, as never before, observant Jewish males were comfortable wearing a yarmulke in public rather than going bareheaded or wearing a hat.

Paradoxically, greater toleration for nonconventional groups also created new lines of religious division, for as traditional rivalries and animosities between Protestants and Catholics and between Christians and Jews gave way, new polarities formed. As one observer put it: "Increasingly, Fundamentalist, Evangelical, and Conservative Christians realized that the real enemy was not the Roman Catholic or Jew but the smiling, flexible, civil Protestant modernist who wrote them off as 'religious fanatics' unwilling to take the rough edges off their beliefs and practices and glide along smoothly with others in the prosperity of post-war America." As new rivalries developed in the 1960s, the stage was set for heightened religious polarization within each religious tradition.

The Jewish Preoccupation with Survivalism

Although affected profoundly by broader trends in American society and religion, American Judaism reoriented itself in the 1960s for reasons internal to Jewish life as well. A palpable shift in the outlook of Jews affected communal priorities and morale. The social scientists Steven M. Cohen and Leonard J. Fein characterized the reorientation as a move from a preoccupation with accommodation to survivalism: "Jewish survival—that is, the survival of Jews as a distinct ethnic/religious group—has become a major priority of at least equal, and perhaps greater, concern to many Jews and, more particularly, to the agencies and institutions that determine the collective agenda of the Jewish community."

The communal agenda shifted in the late 1960s from universalistic concerns to a preoccupation with Jewish particularism and threats to Jews, as fears for the physical safety of the Jewish people surfaced after lying dormant for almost a generation. The trauma of the Holocaust, buried in the American Jewish psyche since 1945, erupted into public consciousness. First came the rediscovery of the murdered six million with the Israeli abduction and trial of Adolf Eichmann. The capture of Eichmann had been intended to serve a pedagogic purpose: "We want the nations of the world to know," declared Israel's prime minister, David Ben-Gurion. Even he, however, could not have anticipated the educational impact of the trial on Jewish consciousness in Israel and throughout the world. In short order new books on the Holocaust appeared—Raul Hilberg's *The Destruction of the European Jews* in 1961, Hannah Arendt's provocative assessment of the Eichmann trial, *Eichmann in Jerusalem,* in 1963, and one year later Rolf Hochhuth's *The Deputy,* a scathing indictment of Pope Pious XII for his indifference and moral failure during the Holocaust. Then in 1967 Arthur Morse published *While Six Million Died,* a controversial work of journalism that brought the Holocaust home to the American Jewish community through its critical evaluation of Franklin Roosevelt, the hero of most American Jews. Symptomatic of the new personalized involvement with the Holocaust was the self-critical question posed in a review of the Morse book: "The indifference and insensitivity of those non-Jews who stood by *While Six Million Died* doing nothing when 'They Could Have Been Saved' has been exposed and documented. But what did American Jews do in the years of the holocaust?" That question haunted American Jews and inspired a new commitment to Jewish survival, succinctly expressed in the newly coined Jewish credo—"Never Again!"

In the spring of 1967 American Jewish fears were rekindled by Arab threats to the State of Israel. Describing those frightening days, Abraham Joshua Heschel linked the trauma of the recent past with fears for the future:

"Terror and dread fell upon Jews everywhere. Will God permit our people to perish? Will there be another Auschwitz, another Dachau, another Treblinka? The darkness of Auschwitz is still upon us, its memory is a torment forever. In the midst of that thick darkness there is one gleam of light: the return of our people to Zion. Will He permit this gleam to be smothered?" Despite their relative safety during the Holocaust years, American Jewry came to identify with the collective insecurity of Jewish victims. All over the country Jews turned to their synagogues in record numbers, with attendance on the Sabbaths before and after the Six-Day War approaching that on Yom Kippur. "Before the war, Jews went to pray for the survival of Israel, and afterwards, to give thanks."

The war also converted American Jewry to Zionism. Whereas American Jews had demonstrated sympathy in the past, Israel now was incorporated into the very structure of American Jewish identity. As the fighting raged, surveys found that "ninety-nine out of every hundred Jews expressed their strong sympathy with Israel." For many the newfound identification with Israel was a conversionary experience. As one Jewish woman wrote in the left-wing *Village Voice:* "Two weeks ago, Israel was they; now Israel is we. . . . I will not intellectualize it; I am Jewish; it is a Jewish we. Something happened. I will never again be able to talk about how Judaism is only a religion, and isn't it too bad that there has to be such a thing as a Jewish state. Roots count."

The war transformed religious institutions as well. At the Jewish Theological Seminary of America, which in 1948 had banned the playing of "Hatikvah" (the Israeli national anthem) at its commencement, Professor Saul Lieberman, the rector and most influential faculty member, issued a statement on June 5, 1967, to

> all Jews in the world and, in particular, the members of the Rabbinical Assembly and the congregations of the United Synagogue: the people of Israel have the privilege to give their lives to preserve the very existence of the nation. The best we Jews in America can do is to support them with our money. This day is our great opportunity, one that may never repeat itself, to save *Klal Yisrael* [the Jewish people].

The Six-Day War also signaled the virtual dismantling of the Reform offshoot, the American Council for Judaism, a Jewish anti-Zionist organization. Its leading spokesmen broke ranks and contributed to the Israel Emergency Fund, while other members resigned.

The intense identification with Israel transformed Jewish religious education in America. Since 1967 it has become more common for Jewish adolescents to spend summers in Israel, sometimes at the expense of local federations of Jewish philanthropy. Israel figures prominently in the curriculum at Jewish schools. And it has now become almost universal at all but Orthodox synagogues and schools to use the Sephardic pronunciation of Hebrew, as is popular in Israel. To cite a minor but symptomatic change, the traditional Ashkenazic Sabbath greeting *gut shabbos* has given way to the Israeli *shabbat shalom.*

The war also inspired a greater political activism in behalf of Jewish causes. Most notably this translated into lobbying activity in support of Israel and the freeing of Soviet Jews. In addition, as we shall see, religious groups within American Judaism felt freer to lobby for their own agendas. The new activism energized congregations and other religious institutions, but it also diverted attention from more narrowly religious concerns, such as ritual practice, prayer, and observance of the commandments, a development captured by the quip that American Jews were "reverse Marranos"—Jews in the streets but not in their homes.

The turn to more parochial Jewish interests was promoted not only by self-confidence engendered by the Israeli victory and a commitment to Jewish survival but also by alienation from former allies in the struggle for a better society. In the weeks prior to the Six-Day War, Jews who had nurtured interfaith ties were shocked at the indifference to Israel displayed by their partners in religious dialogue. For the most part, Christian clergy could not fathom the attachment Jews felt to Israel. Many Christian leaders remained neutral as Arab armies arrayed themselves against Israel. Even more disturbing, liberal clergy criticized Israel for its handling of the war. Perhaps the most savage attack came from the former president of the Union Theological Seminary, a leading seminary of liberal Protestantism. In a letter to the *New York Times,* Henry P. Van Dusen wrote:

> All persons who seek to view the Middle East problem with honesty and objectivity stand aghast at Israel's onslaught, the most violent, ruthless (and successful) aggression since Hitler's blitzkrieg across Western Europe in the summer of 1940, aiming not at victory but at annihilation—the very objective proclaimed by Nasser and his allies which had drawn support to Israel.

Samuel Sandmel, a professor at the Hebrew Union College and frequent participant in interfaith dialogue, voiced the disappointment of Jews:

> We Jews and you Christians had co-operated on the national level in many enterprises, such as civil rights [and] many Jews assumed that the same outpouring of sympathy for the beleaguered Jews that animated next-door Christian neighbors would be reflected in the organized Christian Bodies. . . . To the consternation of these Jews, such support was not forthcoming. . . . In the dismay at the Christian neutrality, some Jews felt completely abandoned by precisely those Christians with whom they had so much affirmative cooperation.

Indeed, some Jewish leaders active in the ecumenical movement considered the dialogue silenced, if not dead. David Polish, a Reform rabbi, wrote in the *Christian Century* that in light of the Christian "moral failure, the much-touted Christian-Jewish dialogue is revealed as fragile and superficial."

Jews also felt rebuffed by the separatist and anti-Israel positions adopted by the black power movement. Jewish religious groups that had been active in the civil rights movement noticed a dampening of interest among their members, a state of affairs lamented by Maurice Eisendrath in the early 1970s: "Wounded by anti-Semitic public statements of some lunatic-fringe blacks; bruised by the apparent indifference of non-Jews to the 1967 war in Israel; hurt by those blacks who . . . turned sour on interracial amity and cooperation, a considerable number of Jews have withdrawn from all such outstretch of hand and heart." Eisendrath tried to convince his group to continue programs of social action that had worked earlier in the decade; he even called for a major campaign similar to the United Jewish Appeal in order for the Jewish community to pay its share of reparations to American blacks. But the UAHC refused to support him.

As they recoiled from the hostility or indifference of former allies, American Jewish groups also confronted an emerging threat to Jewish survival from within—the rising rate of intermarriage. The mid-1960s brought unmistakable evidence of a significant increase in the number of Jews taking non-Jewish spouses.

Item: As early as 1960 a leading sociologist engaged in research on intermarriage cited findings of the U.S. Bureau of the Census indicating a national intermarriage rate for Jews of 7.2 percent in 1957 and compared it with surveys in Iowa and the San Francisco area, which indicated rates ranging from 17–32 percent. Erich Rosenthal warned:

> If we accept the findings of the [Federal census] and if, at the same time, we assume that the statistics for Iowa and San Francisco are merely regional variations of the overall rate, we can probably be justified in defending the current survival formula as adequate for the preservation of the Jewish group. If we assume, however, that the findings for Iowa and San Francisco are the first indications of the future over-all rate of intermarriage, then the efficacy of the survival formula must be seriously doubted.

Item: A survey published in the *National Review* in 1963 found that perhaps as many as one-third of Jewish collegians declared themselves as not opposed to intermarriage.

Item: By 1970 Marshall Sklare, the dean of American Jewish sociologists, sounded the tocsin: "If by 1965 one in five young Jewish couples in Boston constituted a case of intermarriage, we can safely assume that the figure is now approaching one in four. And if that is true in so conservative a city as Boston, it must mean that intermarriage has reached large-scale proportions throughout the country as a whole." Based on admittedly sketchy evidence, Arthur Hertzberg placed the intermarriage rate in the mid-1960s at 15 percent, a figure borne out by the National Jewish Population Study of 1971.

Fears of increased intermarriage were further fueled by new evidence that the American Jewish population was no longer growing. Survey research conducted in the early 1970s confirmed what Jewish institutions—especially synagogues and religious schools—had encountered already in the mid-1960s: the end of the baby boom. A survey conducted under the auspices of the Council of Jewish Federations in the early 1970s indicated that American Jewry had entered an era of demographic stagnation: Jews were having fewer children relative to the American population; immigration had virtually ceased; and rates of intermarriage had been spiraling since the mid-1960s. Demographers of American Jewry vied with one another to issue gloomy prognostications, with one author contending that by the year 2076, American Jewry could shrink to one-fifth its size or even less if current rates continued. Demographic stagnation coupled with rising levels of intermarriage demoralized community leaders and affected the tone of Jewish public discourse about the future of American Judaism. The new pessimism was captured in a feature essay published by *Look* magazine entitled "The Vanishing American Jew." Little wonder, then, that Jewish survival at home and abroad became the new preoccupation, as self-absorption and doubt replaced the buoyant mood of the 1950s.

The Malaise in Organized Jewish Religious Life

The organized movements of American Judaism were particularly hard hit. Whereas Jewish philanthropic federations experienced a resurgence because of their close involvement with fund-raising for Israel, and Jewish communal agencies threw their energies into lobbying in behalf of beleaguered Jews at home and abroad, synagogues lost their luster. Oriented toward programming for youth, they suffered as the numbers of young Jews dwindled. But the malaise in organized Judaism also reflected a loss of bearing about the proper role of synagogues in Jewish life and a loss of faith in the ability of organized Judaism to respond to the new world created by the 1960s.

Much as in the Christian world, liberal religious movements suffered the most. As the standard-bearer of American Judaism at mid-century, Conservative Judaism was especially hard hit by the upheaval of the 1960s. In contrast to the earlier, frenetic pace of synagogue growth, not one new Conservative synagogue was founded between 1965 and 1971. Congregational membership began to decline as many Conservative families left their synagogue once the youngest child had celebrated a Bar or Bat Mitzvah. A 1965 survey by the United Synagogue found that during the previous three years the primary reason members left a congregation other than death or geographic relocation was that a "son had completed Bar Mitzvah or Hebrew School." Now that their children had completed their studies, some parents no longer felt any need to retain their membership. Congregational schools suffered a consequent decline in enrollments and were forced to cut back or eliminate their programs. By the 1970s, numerous Conservative congregations were forced to merge their schools and even synagogues because their membership bases could no longer sustain programs.

The Conservative movement also suffered the loss of its left wing in the 1960s, when the Reconstructionists broke away to form their own movement. Since the 1920s Rabbi Mordecai M. Kaplan had led proponents of change within the movement by preaching the need for a new "Copernican revolution" that would substitute the Jewish people for God as the center of the Jewish universe. "Torah," wrote Kaplan, "exists for the sake of the Jewish people." Kaplan understood Judaism as a "religious civilization" encompassing "language, folkways, patterns of social organization, social habits and standards, spiritual ideals, which give individuality to a people and distinguish it from other peoples." The radical import of Kaplan's revolution was to dethrone God as a being above nature and deprive the Jewish people of its "chosenness," for Kaplan believed that all people regard themselves as chosen. Kaplan was a radical within Conservative Judaism, because he viewed Jewish laws as folkways that could be altered by the will of the people, just as they had been created by the will of the people.

Kaplan and his disciples had preached the ideology of Reconstructionism since the appearance of his most important work, *Judaism as a Civilization,* in 1934, but they had taken few steps to create a fourth religious movement. On the contrary, Kaplan believed that Reconstructionism would eventually become the dominant religious movement of American Jews. He steadfastly refused the entreaties of his followers to institutionalize his movement and focused instead on disseminating his views through a journal of opinion, *The Reconstructionist,* and a synagogue in New York, the Society for the Advancement of Judaism. Kaplan remained firmly within the Conservative camp, presenting his viewpoint to generations of rabbinical students at the Jewish Theological Seminary and arguing for change before his colleagues in the Rabbinical Assembly.

In 1963, at the age of eighty-two, Kaplan retired from the Jewish Theological Seminary. This freed him to support his followers' desire to expand Reconstructionism from an ideological movement to a distinct denomination within Judaism. Plans were made to establish the Reconstructionist Rabbinical College, which opened in 1968. And even before that, a federation of Reconstructionist congregations was founded to unify like-minded synagogues, as well as to bring more groups into the fold. Although the movement was poised for growth by the late 1960s, it was still only a fringe phenomenon of a few thousand adherents, overshadowed by Reform, Conservative, and Orthodox Judaism. The secession by Reconstructionists, however, created the need for an internal realignment within the Conservative movement, a restructuring that threw the movement into turmoil for more than fifteen years.

All the uncertainty and self-doubt in the Conservative movement surfaced in the early 1970s, with the publication of a critical article by Marshall Sklare. Updating his classic study of the Conservative movement, Sklare "offered a thesis that the Conservative movement at the zenith of its influence, has sustained a loss of morale," attributable to "the emergence of Orthodoxy, the problem of Conservative observance, and the widespread alienation among Conservative young people." According to Sklare, the festering crisis of morale in the movement had been brought on by the defection of young people who left the movement in order to join the nascent havurot, coupled with the perception of rabbis that they had failed to persuade the laity to live as observant Jews. In the journals of the Conservative movement and at national gatherings of its leaders, rabbis vented their frustration: "We are touching only the periphery of Jewish life. We are failing in those areas that concern us most," lamented Rabbi William Lebeau. Others voiced their concern that the movement "had become less identifiable" and was in danger of "los[ing] its force and becom[ing] of less and less consequence on the American Jewish scene." The Conservative mood was aptly captured by one rabbi who remarked to his colleagues that "self-flagellation appears to be the order of the day for the leadership of Conservative Jewry."

Reform Judaism fared no better. Summing up the shocks of the 1960s, the increasingly influential Reform theologian Eugene Borowitz wrote: "The crisis in American society, the peril to the state of Israel, the new appreciation of ethnicity all seemed to call for a reexamination of Reform Jewish principles. . . . The style of synagogue life which seemed so fresh a few years previous, seemed somewhat stale and in need of invigoration." Unlike the other movements of Judaism, Reform undertook two major surveys in this period to take the pulse of rabbis and lay people. The findings were hardly encouraging.

Based on research conducted at a dozen representative congregations, the authors of *Reform Is a Verb* found that members of Reform temples were thoroughly alienated from temple life: the majority of respondents, both young and old, saw the temple as peripheral to their concerns. Youth were even more indifferent to their Judaism than their elders and found nothing wrong with intermarrying. A second study conducted by Theodore Lenn confirmed these bleak findings. According to Lenn, "The vast majority of Reform congregants *do not consider themselves religious.*" Moreover, "on every issue of Jewish identity on which they were queried, Reform youth seem to be more detached from Judaism and Jewishness than their parents." Rabbis in particular expressed their concern: over 50 percent of rabbis and congregants surveyed felt that "Reform Judaism was in the midst of a crisis—a situation that will become worse, many felt, before it becomes better."

The Lenn study highlighted the confusion of Reform rabbis: they believed they had lost their aura of authority and felt unappreciated as orators. Moreover, Reform rabbis were under intense pressure to officiate at mixed marriages. The Lenn study found that more than one in three congregants aged twenty to twenty-four was married to a spouse who was born non-Jewish. One in four of this age group was married to a spouse who had not converted. By the early 1970s, 41 percent of rabbis in the sample officiated at mixed marriages with no prior conversion; and of those who did not, half referred couples to such rabbis. Indeed, by 1969 a list of colleagues who officiated at mixed marriages was circulated to all members of the CCAR. Simultaneously, and in a seemingly contradictory fashion, 43 percent of the same rabbis wished to incorporate more traditional beliefs and practices into Reform Judaism. Reform was in serious need of reorientation after the crises of the 1960s, as articulated by Rabbi Richard N. Levy:

> The American Reform synagogue is in trouble. It has generally defaulted on all three of its traditional functions. . . . There are few Reform synagogues where prayer is a regular and significant event for the majority of members; even fewer where there is a serious study of Jewish literature and ideas . . . ; and as Reform congregations grow in size, meetings in any sense beyond occasional social affairs where few members know each other, have become equally rare.

As by far the smallest of the wings of Judaism in the postwar era, Orthodoxy had been written off as a vestige of the immigrant past. With no more than 11 percent of American Jews identifying themselves as Orthodox as compared with 33 percent for Reform and 42 percent for Conservative Judaism, Orthodoxy seemed peripheral. Moreover, there was little reason to anticipate anything other than further decline in their numbers, since studies of local communities found Orthodox Jews to be the oldest segment of the Jewish population with the highest percentage of foreign born. Remarkably, however, in the 1960s Orthodoxy showed itself to have unanticipated staying power. Writing in 1965, Charles Liebman argued the need for a second look: "The only remaining vestige of Jewish passion in America resides in the Orthodox community," he declared. "There is a recognition and admiration for Orthodoxy as the only group which today contains within it a strength and will to live that may yet nourish all the Jewish world." Liebman also noted the growing isolation of Orthodox Jews from the rest of the community and the rising power of sectarian Orthodoxy over modern elements, patterns that would accelerate in the coming decades. Thus, despite their continuing numerical decline, Orthodox Jews did not experience the same malaise as did other movements in American Judaism during the 1960s.

The growing importance of Israel in American Jewish consciousness by late in the decade increased the self-confidence of Orthodoxy. In Israel, after all, Orthodox leaders helped govern the country and monopolized Jewish religious expression. As ties between American and Israeli Jews strengthened, Orthodoxy acquired a new legitimacy in the American Jewish community, as well. By contrast, as non-Orthodox groups increased their involvement with Israel, they encountered a religious establishment intolerant of all except Orthodox versions of Judaism. An incident in 1968 was symptomatic of the problem. The World Union of Progressive Judaism (Reform) held its international convention in Jerusalem to express its solidarity with the people of Israel and announced plans to conduct a prayer service at the Western Wall with men and women seated together. The announcement set off a vitriolic debate on the floor of the Knesset, Israel's parliament. Describing Reform Jews as "traitors to their people, their land, and their God," the newspaper of one religious party, Agudat Yisrael, suggested they "build a wall near one of their temples and go pray there with their wives and mistresses." By virtue of their monopoly on Jewish religious expression, Orthodox groups in Israel felt no compunctions about giving full vent to their animosity toward non-Orthodox forms of Judaism.

This kind of rhetoric spilled over into the American Jewish community, where tensions had anyway been building for a while over a range of issues. At a private meeting designed to thrash out differences, rabbis from the three major movements could not reach a consensus. They could agree only on support for the civil rights movement and the war on poverty; they were deeply divided over internal Jewish matters, especially the issue of Jewish-Christian dialogue. With Israel now assuming a central role in American Jewish consciousness, with growing concerns over intermarriage, and with new pressures on all of the movements to respond to new social and religious developments, American Judaism was poised for changes that would intensify religious polarization.

CHAPTER 22

The waning days of the twentieth century found the American Jewish community at a crossroads in its history. The great issues of the past—free immigration, Zionism, church–state separation, the battle against anti-Semitism at home and abroad—all seemed largely settled. They neither inspired nor united Jews as once they had. The new rallying cry, born of a survey that showed more Jews marrying out of their faith than within it, was "continuity." To ensure that the Jewish community did not assimilate and disappear like so many American minority groups before it became American Jewry's new challenge.

To be sure, part of the problem that American Jewry faced stemmed from good news: anti-Semitism was on the decline, more Jews than ever before had achieved positions of prominence in government or corporate boardrooms, and Jews and Christians interacted freely in numerous social settings. Jews could also take heart from a religious awakening that brought many young Jews back to their faith, and from a growing demand for Jewish education at all levels, including day schools, university-based Jewish Studies programs, and adult Jewish education. But many saw the declining absolute number of American Jews, the drop in the percentage of the general population that identified as Jewish, the rising number of intermarrieds, and the growing ideological divisions within the Jewish community (highlighted by the burgeoning number of converts and children of intermarrieds whose very status as Jews some deemed questionable) as more likely indicators of future trends. Gnawing tensions between some segments of the American Jewish community and Israel only added to the crisis of confidence that overtook the community as the twentieth century wound down.

In the article that follows, Arthur Hertzberg, an historian, rabbi, and longtime critic of Jewish life, examines both positive and negative trends on the American Jewish scene. Religion, particularly the study of Jewish texts and the Hebrew language, seems to him to offer the best hope of maintaining the American Jewish community in the years to come, but he concedes that "the unforeseen can happen, as it often has, in the history of the Jews, and seemingly reasonable calculations will become widely wrong." Appropriately, his article ends with a question mark.

Other questions also suggest themselves. Will conversions to Judaism mitigate future losses from intermarriage? Will the American Jewish community decline when (as now seems likely) Israel succeeds America as the largest Jewish community in the world and Islam overtakes Judaism as America's largest non-Christian faith? Will religion replace peoplehood as the glue that holds the Jewish community together? Will assimilation take its inexorable toll, reducing American Jewry's numbers and status in the twenty-first century? The past offers many answers concerning these questions, but no sure single one. As for the future, it will depend upon those with the fortitude to shape it.

United States Jewry—A Look Forward

Arthur Hertzberg

In a famous dictum, the Talmud declared that after the end of biblical prophecy, only children or fools would attempt to predict the future. The unforeseen can happen, as it often has, in the history of the Jews, and seemingly reasonable calculations will become widely wrong. Here too, the Talmud comes to our help. It declared, in another famous passage, "do not depend on miracles." Those who invoke the unexpected are generally people who hope that the unexpected will bail us out from an unhappy near future. The only meaningful function of trying to predict the future is not to be right in 30 or 50 years; it is to define present trends while there is still some possibility of constructive action. The best kind of prophecy consists in words of warning which are heeded—and thus, the very prophecy acts to disprove itself.

The mainstream of American Jewish life is today the third and fourth generation of the mass migration which came from Eastern Europe between 1881 and 1924—and they numbered more than two million. At least three-fourths of the American Jewish community today consists of their descendants. By every sociological index, the Jewishness of this mainstream is weakening. Contrary to some hopeful noises that were being made a few years ago about the stabilization of the rate of intermarriage, it is now approaching 50 percent among the fourth generation, the young, who are being married. To be sure, there is less serious anti-Semitism in America than ever before, so that being known as a Jew brings with it few public or private disadvantages—but this means that the communal and social barriers between Jews and Gentiles as individuals are lower than ever.

The American Jewish community has been living for at least a century on social activism. The immigrants of the 1830s and those who came to join them later fought for better conditions in the working place. Their children were boxed in by anti-Semitism, as they attempted to enter the mainstream of the American economy. Their grandchildren, who were born after the end of World War II, have made glorying in and supporting Israel, remembering the Holocaust, and fighting for the liberation of Soviet Jews into their shared Jewish agenda.

The great-grandchildren are now in the opening stages of their careers. Few of them have ever had any serious personal encounters with anti-Semitism, for quotas against Jews are very nearly a thing of the past. The immigrant memories of their great-grandparents have faded, along with the memories of their grandparents and parents of exclusion and economic depression. In recent years, even Israel has come into question. Every recent study of this youngest generation shows that there is already a majority among them for public dissent from Israel's policies, when these young people find themselves in disagreement with the dominant line of Jerusalem.

On the other hand, this is a generation which is quite comfortable with public affirmation of its Jewishness. The identity is not hidden in job interviews, and Jewish observances and activities on campus are felt to be a very normal part of the scene. It is, however, possible to exaggerate these affirmatives. A recent, as yet unpublished, study of the Jewish students at one of the Ivy League schools found that about half of the students were willing to reply to the questionnaire; the other half refused, despite repeated telephone calls, stating they wanted to be left alone on campus, to disappear as individuals into the large scene. But there is some reason to believe, from the occasional attendance at religious services and Hillel functions of some of those who refused to answer the questionnaire, that the other half of the Jewish students is not totally lost to assimilation. Some, perhaps even many, are simply "taking off" during their college years from being bothered with any aspect of the organized Jewish community. But, even among the identified half, nine out of ten dated across religious lines, without giving the matter a single thought, and seven out of ten said that their parents would not be at all upset if they intermarried.

The great-grandchildren reflect their family origins. The Jews who came to America, from the very beginning of the settlement, did not take the journey across the Atlantic because they were lacking synagogues in Russia or Poland. The inner religious and social lives of Jews were, in fact, the only aspect of their existence which was relatively free. Haym Salomon attested, in a letter to his family in Posen in the 1780s, that there was "*wenig Yiddishkeit*"—"little Judaism"—in America, even as he agreed that there was economic opportunity.

Jews came to the New World to succeed, to be better off than they had been in Europe. This has been true of almost all other immigrants. Jews have needed more room in America than an often anti-Semitic society provided. Thus, Jews were in the forefront, upon arrival, of the forces which were trying to remake American society toward greater freedom and equality for all. American life as a whole—and Jewish life with it—has thus been marked for generations by an ongoing tension between social activism and materialism. When social activism wanes in America, its place is taken, all too often, by materialism. There are many signs that we are living through such a moment. Therefore, the American Jewish community is in the midst of a crisis of faith and morale. American Jewish life has been based on togetherness—on group feeling, on fighting for social reform and on resisting our enemies—but that togetherness is clearly weakening.

It is clear that Jewish identity still exists, and statistics can even be adduced to suggest that it is as pervasive as ever, but the Jewishness of the third and fourth generations has become more porous. American Jewishness is beginning to resemble American Irishness and American Italianness. But, if Jewishness is ethnicity, it will almost inevitably have the same destiny in America as all other ethnicities. The lives of American Irish are not centered in pride in Ireland, or on the continuing pain of their cousins in Belfast. Italian Americans do not run Sunday Schools to teach their children the importance of Venice and Florence in the history of the West, nor do Italian Americans maintain afternoon schools in the hope that the Italian language will not be entirely foreign to their children and grandchildren.

There is, of course, one dimension of Jewish ethnic experience which is unique: anti-Semitism. Every American minority has been under some attack, but the Jews are different. They have been, until almost yesterday, the only non-Christians in an overwhelmingly Christian society. Jews are the bearers of a tradition which has been the object of calumny for three millennia. The battle against anti-Semitism has been at the core of American Jewish ethnicity. Indeed, for the last two centuries of Jewish history, as the Jewish community has become ever more plural and divided, it has asserted its unity because the anti-Semites make no distinction between Jewish believers in all their varieties and Jews who would prefer to disappear. It is an open secret that the battle against anti-Semitism often continues to be the last Jewish act of those who would rather cease being Jews. They reason that, if only anti-Semitism could be made to disappear, they and their children would at last become unlabeled individuals, free of any responsibility toward the group into which they were born.

Anti-Semitism continues to exist, even in America, at a time when Jews are freer and more equal than they have ever been anywhere in the Diaspora. Nonetheless, opposing anti-Semitism cannot remain the basis of Jewish continuity. On the contrary, some Jews will be tempted—if anti-Semitism is their only concern—to abandon their Jewishness altogether. No less a figure than Theodor Herzl played with the idea of mass conversion of Jews to Christianity, to evade anti-Semitism as an alternative to creating a Zionist state. My own research on college students has shown that those of the young whose Jewishness is primarily a fear of anti-Semitism are significantly more likely to want to intermarry—to live permanently among the anti-Semites! What explains this paradox is that such young people really want to "pass" into a society in which there is neither Jew nor Gentile. Nor does the memory of the Holocaust act decisively to keep all Jews from assimilating. On the contrary, from the day that the death camps were opened, some of the very survivors (there is no way of estimating their number), simply disappeared as Jews. Younger students of today ask: If being Jewish means that I remain, uniquely, a candidate for the gas chambers, why should I live in that danger? Should I not strive to save my descendants from such a destiny by making an end of this dangerous identity? Anti-Semitism may drive many Jews toward their Jewishness; it has given some others who have no other reason for caring, the impetus to leave. Anti-Semitism needs to be fought, but it is not the tie that binds Jews together.

Inevitably, therefore, one turns to religion—but the situation of Judaism in our century, like that of Christianity, and even of Islam, is one of increasing fragmentation. The wars of religion are becoming sharper within each of these communities, not least our own. More fundamentally, American Jews have been socialized by American culture as a whole to express their being by solving problems rather than by looking inward to their soul or outward toward the meaning and purpose of creation. The commandments of the "civil religion" of American Jews express togetherness; they leave the soul alone—and lonely—in the universe, with only activism to light the way.

One revealing piece of evidence, from the very circles of Jewish activist leadership, suggests that the ultimate source of Jewish continuity is not in activism but in the religious tradition. A few years ago, some of the leaders of the fund-raising bodies were asked whether they believed in the chosenness of Israel. Seventy percent said they did. These were not Orthodox believers; they were overwhelmingly the kind of people to whom the rhetoric of cultural pluralism is almost second nature. The answer one would expect from this circle is that Jews are, in America, one ethnic group among the many. But those who were surveyed knew better than such surface rhetoric. They knew that the irreducible premise on which Jewish continuity rests is the faith that it makes a profound and transcendent difference whether Jews exist as a distinct and affirming community. Those surveyed were willing, as liberals, to grant Italians and Irish in America the right to disappear quietly in an open society, but they regarded it as a tragedy if Jews followed suit and opted out en masse. Indeed, it is the paradoxical function of Jewish leadership to work for an American society in which everyone can choose without any fear or coercion to abandon his past and be who he wants to be—and to convince Jews that abandoning their Jewishness is profoundly wrong.

Ethnicity is not forever; anti-Semitism can, at least in logic, chase Jews out of their Judaism rather than make them rally together, and our deepest held religious convictions are ill defined and splintered. So how can American Jews survive?

The only realm to which they are the heirs, together, are Jewish texts and the Hebrew language. They can no longer agree to study the Mishnah or the writings of Maimonides from the same perspective, and they are even less likely to find common ground on the question of how obedient they are to the injunctions in these texts, but the Mishnah and Maimonides, and all the texts of the classic tradition which belong with them, are the heritage of the Jews in a way in which they do not belong even to the most learned scholars among the non-Jews.

The essential crisis of the American Jewish community, which is now coming into view, is that it has essentially defined its Jewish experience without classic texts. American Jewish life has been constructed out of immigrant memory and achievement, with few roots in the Jewish literature of all the centuries before. Since immigrant momentum almost inevitably runs down, even among Jews, in three or four generations, this experience will at best be an aroma for a community that might remain for a generation or two loosely associated with its Jewish identity.

There are, however, counter-tendencies, which are much more assertive. Most immediate and tangible, Jewish activism has kept finding new causes, or permutations of older ones, with which to identify. The contemporary Jewish community has, in fact, become a smorgasbord of such causes: Soviet Jews, Ethiopian Jews, services in the Third World in the name of Jewish idealism, the tracking of Nazis, and, of course, all of the preexisting causes, such as the political and economic defense of Israel and the battle against anti-Semitism in all its forms. Even as activism is declining, the labor for these causes will continue to provide a kind of secular religion for some.

It is more significant that a religious revival has appeared among a minority of third- and fourth-generation American Jews. This is not an unprecedented event. In Central Europe, such figures as Franz Rosenzweig and Gershom Scholem, in the early years of the twentieth century, represented a comparable phenomenon, the return to Judaism of children and grandchildren of already assimilated Jews. Now in America, as before in Europe, some younger people find not enough meaning in ethnic pride, or ethnic hurts, and want to find their way to the accumulated content of Judaism, to the tradition.

The young, who are now beginning to be not so young, in the *havurot*, or who have turned fiercely Orthodox, indicate that some Jews will prefer the journey that Rosenzweig once described as "from the periphery to the center." That journey is being repeated right now on many university campuses, as some students feel deprived by their lack of Jewish knowledge. This "return" is not likely to become a mass movement, but it will certainly continue to capture a minority.

Most tangibly, the American Jewish community now houses an unprecedented Orthodox element, those who came after the end of World War II.

For the first time, after the Holocaust, Jews who never had any intention of moving to America were forced to come, because there was nothing left in Europe. Hasidic courts, such as those of Satmar and Lubavich, and what remained of the great European *yeshivot,* were transplanted to America. These communities arrived not in order to succeed in America, in material terms, but to use America as a haven for the kind of life that they had always lived and which they now, perforce, had to reconstruct and defend even in an open and relativist America.

These groups have pulled Orthodox Judaism in America, and many non-Orthodox elements with them, in the direction of Jewish separatism, for the sake of religious authenticity. There is, no doubt, even in these communities, some scaling of the self-imposed walls by young people who run off into the American open society. However, Monsey, Borough Park, and Lakewood are not the old East Side; they are confident bastions of an alternate Jewish community; one that is constructed on different principles from those on which the existing life of the Jewish majority is based. That these communities will continue to reproduce themselves in generations to come, in much the form in which they have defined themselves, is more than likely. Thus, not the "moderate Orthodoxy" but the much less liberal new immigrant Orthodoxy is the likely wave of the future, in those circles.

The imponderable, the unexpected which "prophets" cannot estimate, is the question of will and choice. The American Jewish community is capable of deciding to create a network of elite boarding schools and day schools which would educate many more, perhaps even most, of the American Jewish young. It is at least conceivable that American Jews might decide that activism and togetherness are running down as forces of cohesion and as sources of meaning. It is conceivable that American Jews might decide that they cannot be the only Jewish community in all of history in which Jewish learning is not a prerequisite for Jewish belonging and Jewish leadership. American Jewry might become the great, final experiment in the whole history of the Diaspora: Is it possible to keep a Jewish community alive and robust in a truly free and open society? When Jews are not under attack, and they have free choice, will Jewish learning persuade them of the importance of being Jewish? Such a classical program seems to be working now on a minority—but what of the rest?

FOR FURTHER READING

The postwar period of American Jewish life has been surveyed by historian Edward Shapiro in *A Time for Healing: American Jewry Since World War II* (1992), and by two sociologists: Chaim Waxman in *America's Jews in Transition* (1983), and Samuel Heilman in *Portrait of American Jews: The Last Half of the Twentieth Century* (1995). See also the final chapters in Howard M. Sachar, *History of the Jews in America* (1992), and Arthur Hertzberg, *The Jews in America: Four Centuries of an Uneasy Encounter* (1989). Jack Wertheimer has authored two significant articles in the *American Jewish Year Book,* "Recent Trends in American Judaism," 89 (1989), pp. 63–162; and "Jewish Organizational Life in the United States Since 1945," 95 (1995), pp. 3–98. See also his *A People Divided: Judaism in Contemporary America* (1993). Arnold Eisen in *American Jewish Year Book* 91 (1991), pp. 3–33, summarizes recent developments in American Jewish theology. Significant articles on postwar American Judaism may also be found in *Studies in Contemporary Jewry* 8 (1992), pp. 3–149; in Bernard Martin, *Movements and Issues in American Judaism* (1978); and in the ten-volume collection of articles edited by Jacob Neusner, *Judaism in Cold War America 1945–1990* (1993).

The gnawing problem of America and the Holocaust has attracted a wide range of scholars since Arthur Morse penned his indictment of American policy in *While Six Million Died* (1967). Book-length studies include Henry L. Feingold, *The Politics of Rescue* (1970) and *Bearing Witness: The Holocaust, America and the Jews* (1995); David S. Wyman, *Paper Walls: America and the Refugee Crisis 1938–1941* (1971); Richard Breitman and Alan M. Kraut, *American Refugee Policy and European Jewry, 1933–1945* (1988); Yehuda Bauer, *American Jewry and the Holocaust* (1981); Monty N. Penkower, *The Jews Were Expendable* (1983); and the best of them all, Wyman's *The Abandonment of the Jews* (1984). Sander A. Diamond, *The Nazi Movement in the United States* (1974), and Moshe R. Gottlieb, *American Anti-Nazi Resistance* (1982), cover pro- and anti-Nazi activities in the United States before Pearl Harbor. Deborah E. Lipstadt, *Beyond Belief: The American Press and the Coming of the Holocaust, 1933–1945* (1986), and Robert W. Ross, *So It Was True* (1980), chronicle press reactions to Nazi persecutions. Leonard Dinnerstein, *America and the Survivors of the Holocaust* (1982), moves beyond World War II and analyzes postwar attitudes toward

Jewish refugees. Lipstadt's *Denying the Holocaust* (1993) looks at the more recent phenomenon of Holocaust denial. Finally, Leon A. Jick, "The Holocaust: Its Use and Abuse Within the American Public," *Yad Vashem Studies* 14 (1981), pp. 303–318, and Stephen J. Whitfield's "American Jewish Intellectuals and Totalitarianism" and "The Holocaust in the American Jewish Mind" reprinted in his *Voices of Jacob, Hands of Esau* (1984) trace the impact of the Holocaust over subsequent decades.

Marshall Sklare, the pioneering American Jewish sociologist, took the pulse of the American Jewish community during the 1950s and 1960s. See especially his *Conservative Judaism* (1955), *The Jews* (1958), and with Joseph Greenbaum, *Jewish Identity on the Suburban Frontier* (1967). Perceptive articles by contemporaries can also be found in Oscar I. Janowsky (ed.), *The American Jew: A Reappraisal* (1964); Peter I. Rose (ed.), *The Ghetto and Beyond* (1969); David Sidorsky (ed.), *The Future of the Jewish Community in America* (1973); Marshall Sklare (ed.), *The Jewish Community in America* (1974) and *The Jew in American Society* (1974), and Jack Nusan Porter and Peter Dreier (eds.), *Jewish Radicalism: A Selected Anthology* (1973). See also Yosef Gorni's *The State of Israel in Jewish Public Thought* (1994), which analyzes many aspects of American Jewish thought during this period, as well as Daniel Elazar's pathbreaking political analysis of the American Jewish community, entitled *Community and Polity* (1976, 2nd ed., 1995).

Deborah Dash Moore expands on the themes of her essay in her book, *To The Golden Cities: Pursuing the American Dream in Miami and LA* (1994). For another perspective on postwar migrations, see Sidney Goldstein, *Jews on the Move* (1996). More broadly, southern Jewry has been examined in, among other works, Nathan M. Kaganoff and Melvin I. Urofsky, *Turn to the South* (1979), while western Jewry has been the subject of Moses Rischin and John Livingston, *Jews of the American West* (1991).

No full-scale analysis of the transformation of American Jewish life in the late 1960s and 1970s has yet appeared. Sylvia B. Fishman has probed the impact of feminism in "The Impact of Feminism on American Jewish Life," *American Jewish Year Book* 89 (1989), pp. 3–62, and in her book, *A Breath of Life: Feminism in the American Jewish Community* (1993); see also Deborah E. Lipstadt, "The Impact of the Women's Movement on American Jewish Life: An Overview After Twenty Years," *Studies in Contemporary Jewry* 11 (1995), pp. 86–100. Murray Friedman has critically evaluated some of the era's other leading themes in *The Utopian Dilemma: New Political Directions for American Jews* (1985) and in his *What Went Wrong? The Creation and Collapse of the Black-Jewish Alliance* (1995). Paul Ritterband and Harold Wechsler chronicle the development of university-based Jewish studies in *Jewish Learning in American Universities* (1994). Charles Liebman, *The Ambivalent American Jew* (1973), and Jacob Neusner, *Stranger At Home* (1981) comment on broader and sometimes contradictory patterns found in Jewish identities and belief structures. And Riv-Ellen Prell, *Prayer and Community: The Havurah in America* (1989) provides an anthropological analysis of a prayer community, using it as a springboard to shed light on Jews' changing religious identities; see also Lynn Davidman, *Tradition in a Rootless World: Women Turn to Orthodox Judaism* (1991).

The impact of the Six-Day War on American Jews was described a year later by Marshall Sklare, "Lakeville and Israel: The Six-Day War and Its Aftermath," *Midstream* 14 (October 1968); and is viewed in the context of subsequent events in Moshe Davis (ed.), *The Yom Kippur War, Israel, and the Jewish People* (1974). For its impact on American Jewish settlement in Israel, see Gerald Engel, "North American Settlers in Israel," *American Jewish Year Book* 71 (1970), pp. 161–187 and Chaim I. Waxman, *American Aliya* (1989). Other studies are listed in Haim Avni and Jeffrey Mandl, *The Six Day War and Communal Dynamics in the Diaspora* (1994). For the larger relationship between Israel, American Jewry, and the United States government, see David Schoenbaum, *The United States and the State of Israel* (1993) and Eliezer Don Yehiya, *Israel and Diaspora Jewry* (1991).

The immigration of Russian Jews to the United States since the Six-Day War forms the subject of Steven J. Gold, "Soviet Jews in the United States," *American Jewish Year Book* 94 (1994), pp. 3–57, and Fran Markowitz, *A Community in Spite of Itself: Soviet Jewish Emigres in New York* (1993). William W. Orbach, *The American Movement to Aid Soviet Jews* (1979), analyzes the movement from the point of view of its meaning for American Jews; see also Yaakov Ro'i, *The Struggle for Soviet Jewish Emigration 1948–1967* (1991).

The 1990 National Jewish Population Survey first became known to the wider community through the publication of its widely publicized pamphlet of *Highlights* (1992), followed by a more substantial communal profile by Sidney Goldstein, published in the *American Jewish Year Book* 92 (1992), pp. 1–24. A wide range of responses ensued, as well as countless analyses in Jewish periodicals. Seymour Martin Lipset and Earl Raab, *Jews and the New American Scene* (1995), takes account of some of these developments. Others may be followed in the annual volumes of the *American Jewish Year Book*.

APPENDIX 1

THE GROWTH OF THE AMERICAN JEWISH POPULATION

	Estimated totals (low–high)	*Percentage of total population*
1660	50	—
1700	200–300	—
1776	1,000–2,500	.04–.10
1790	1,300–3,000	.03–.08
1800	2,500	.04
1820	2,650–3,000	.03
1830	4,000–6,000	.03–.05
1840	15,000	.09
1850	50,000	.22
1860	125,000–200,000	.40–.63
1880	230,000–300,000	.46–.60
1890	400,000–475,000	.64–.75
1900	938,000–1,058,000	1.23–1.39
1910	1,508,000–2,044,000	1.63–2.22
1920	3,300,000–3,600,000	3.12–3.41
1930	4,228,000–4,400,000	3.44–3.58
1940	4,771,000–4,831,000	3.63–3.68
1950	4,500,000–5,000,000	2.98–3.31
1960	5,367,000–5,531,000	2.99–3.08
1970	5,370,000–6,000,000	2.64–2.95
1980	5,500,000–5,921,000	2.42–2.61
1990	5,515,000–5,981,000	2.24–2.43

Source: Jacob R. Marcus, *To Count a People: American Jewish Population Data, 1585–1984* (1990), pp. 237–240; Jack J. Diamond, "A Reader in Demography," *American Jewish Year Book* 77 (1977), pp. 251–319; *American Jewish Year Book* 91 (1991), p. 209; 92 (1992), p. 143.

APPENDIX 2

A CENTURY OF JEWISH IMMIGRATION TO THE UNITED STATES

	Total Jewish	Annual average	Jews as percentage of total
1881–1889	204,300	22,700	4.3
1890–1898	366,600	40,700	10.8
1899–1902	214,000	53,500	11.3
1903–1907	615,200	123,000	12.1
1908–1914	656,500	93,800	9.8
1881–1914	2,056,600	60,488	9.4
1915–1919	65,700	13,140	5.6
1920–1924	286,500	57,300	10.3
1925–1929	56,200	11,240	3.7
1930–1934	26,500	5,300	6.2
1935–1939	85,800	17,160	31.5
1940–1944	78,400	15,680	38.4
1945–1949	105,100	21,020	16.1
1950–1954	48,400	9,680	4.4
1955–1959	36,000	7,200	2.6
1960–1964	43,000	8,600	3.0
1965–1969	39,000	7,800	2.2
1970–1974	34,700	6,940	1.8
1975–1979	89,239	17,848	3.9
1980–1984	55,351	11,070	2.0
1985–1989	88,039	17,608	2.5

Source: Simon Kuznets, "Immigration of Russian Jews to the United States: Background and Structure," *Perspectives in American History* 9 (1975), pp. 35–124; *American Jewish Year Book* 77 (1977), p. 319. Figures since 1975 estimated from HIAS *Annual Report* (1992), pp. 14–15, corrected to exclude assisted non-Jewish immigrants, and to include approximately 5,600 non-assisted immigrants annually.

REFERENCE SOURCES IN AMERICAN JEWISH HISTORY

Bibliographical Guides

William W. Brickman, *The Jewish Community in America: An Annotated and Classified Bibliographical Guide* (1977)
Jeffrey Gurock, *American Jewish History: A Bibliographical Guide* (1983)
Nathan M. Kaganoff, *Judaica Americana: An Annotated Bibliography of Publications from 1960 to 1990* (1995)
Sharad Karkhanis, *Jewish Heritage in America: An Annotated Bibliography* (1988)
Moses Rischin, *An Inventory of American Jewish History* (1954)
Robert Singerman, *Judaica Americana: A Bibliography of Publications to 1900* (1990)

Encyclopedias and Dictionaries

The Concise Dictionary of American Jewish Biography (1994)
Encyclopaedia Judaica (1971–72)
Jewish-American History and Culture: An Encyclopedia (1992)
The Jewish Encyclopedia (1906)
Universal Jewish Encyclopedia (1939–43)

Leading Periodicals

American Jewish Archives (1948–) [Index to vols. 1–24 (1979)]
American Jewish History (1978–); formerly *Publications of the American Jewish Historical Society* (1892–1961); and *American Jewish Historical Quarterly* (1961–1968) [Index to vols. 1–80]
American Jewish Year Book (1899–) [Index to vols. 1–50 (1967)]
Jewish Journal of Sociology (1959–)
Jewish Social Studies (1939–) [Index to vols. 1–25 (1967)]
Leo Baeck Institute Yearbook (1958–) [Index to vols. 1–20 (1982)]
Modern Judaism (1981–)
Rhode Island Jewish Historical Notes (1954–) [Index to vols. 1–7 (1984)]
Studies in Contemporary Jewry (1984–)
Western States Jewish Historical Quarterly (1968–) [Index to vols. 1–12 (1981)]
YIVO Annual of Jewish Social Science (1946–)

Indexes

Index to Jewish Periodicals (1969–)

The Jewish Experience in America (1983) [Abstracts of articles in scholarly journals, 1973–1979]

Jacob R. Marcus, *An Index to Scientific Articles on American Jewish History* (1971) [Indexes major articles 1888–1968]

Selected Subject Bibliographies and Guides

John M. Cohn, "Demographic Studies of Jewish Communities in the United States: A Bibliographic Introduction and Survey," *American Jewish Archives* 32 (April 1980), pp. 35–51.

Lenwood G. Davis, *Black-Jewish Relations in the United States 1752–1984: A Selected Bibliography* (1984)

Michael N. Dobkowski, *Jewish American Voluntary Organizations* (1986)

Daniel Elazar, "Jewish Community Studies: A Selected Bibliography," *Community and Polity* (1995), pp. 452–460.

Rudolf Glanz, *The German Jew in America: An Annotated Bibliography* (1969)

Alexandra S. Korros and Jonathan D. Sarna, *American Synagogue History: A Bibliography and State-of-the-Field Survey* (1988)

Ezekiel Lifschutz, *Bibliography of American and Canadian Jewish Memoirs and Autobiographies* (1970)

Jacob R. Marcus, *To Count a People: American Jewish Population Data 1585–1984* (1990)

Ira Nadel, *Jewish Writers of North America: A Guide to Information Sources* (1981)

Pamela S. Nadell, *Conservative Judaism in America: A Biographical Dictionary and Sourcebook* (1988)

Kerry M. Olitzky et al., *Reform Judaism in America: A Biographical Dictionary and Sourcebook* (1993)

Jonathan D. Sarna and Janet S. Liss, *American Jewry: An Annotated Bibliography of Publications in Hebrew* (1991)

Ann R. Shapiro et al., eds., *American Women Writers: A Bio-Bibliographical and Critical Sourcebook* (1994)

Moshe D. Sherman, *Orthodox Judaism in America: A Biographical Dictionary and Sourcebook* (1996)

Robert Singerman, *Antisemitic Propaganda: An Annotated Bibliography and Research Guide* (1982)

Herbert A. Strauss, *Jewish Immigrants of the Nazi Period in the U.S.A.* (1978–1987)

Gary P. Zola, *The American Rabbinate, 1906–1986: A Bibliographic Essay* (1988)

David S. Zubatsky, *Jewish Autobiographies and Biographies* (1989)

Textbooks and Surveys

Henry L. Feingold (ed.), *The Jewish People in America* (five vols., 1992)
Henry L. Feingold, *Zion in America* (1982)
Nathan Glazer, *American Judaism* (1972)
Arthur A. Goren, *The American Jews* (1982)
Arthur Hertzberg, *The Jews in America: Four Centuries of an Uneasy Encounter* (1990)
Abraham J. Karp, *Haven and Home* (1985)
Rufus Learsi [Israel Goldberg], *The Jews in America* (1972)
Jacob R. Marcus, *The Colonial American* Jew (three vols., 1970); *United States Jewry, 1776–1985* (four vols., 1989)
Howard M. Sachar, *A History of the Jews in America* (1992)

SOURCES

The American Colonial Jew: A Study in Acculturation
Reprinted with permission of Jacob R. Marcus from *The American Colonial Jew;* the B. G. Rudolph Lectures in Judaic Studies, Syracuse University, copyright © 1967 by Jacob R. Marcus.

The Impact of the American Revolution on American Jews
Reprinted with minor revisions and without accompanying footnotes from *Modern Judaism* 1 (1981), pp. 149–160, copyright © 1981 by Jonathan D. Sarna and Johns Hopkins University Press; by permission of *Modern Judaism.*

The 1820s: American Jewry Comes of Age
Reprinted with minor revisions and without accompanying footnotes from *A Bicentennial Festschrift for Jacob Rader Marcus,* edited by Bertram Wallace Korn (New York: KTAV Publishing House, 1976), pp. 539–549, copyright © 1976 by KTAV Publishing House, Inc.; by permission of KTAV Publishing House.

From Württemberg to America: A Nineteenth-Century German-Jewish Village on Its Way to the New World
Reprinted with permission and without accompanying footnotes and appendix from *American Jewish Archives* 41 (Fall/Winter 1989), pp. 143–161, copyright © 1989 by the American Jewish Archives.

America: The Reform Movement's Land of Promise
Reprinted without accompanying footnotes by permission of the author from Michael A. Meyer, *Response to Modernity: A History of the Reform Movement in Judaism* (New York: Oxford University Press, 1988; reprint Detroit: Wayne State University Press, 1995). Copyright © 1988 by Michael A. Meyer.

The Christian Agenda
Reprinted without accompanying footnotes from Naomi W. Cohen, *Jews in Christian America: The Pursuit of Religious Equality* (New York: Oxford University Press, 1992). Copyright © 1992 by Oxford University Press; reprinted by permission of Oxford University Press and Naomi W. Cohen.

A Business Elite: German-Jewish Financiers in Nineteenth-Century New York
Reprinted in somewhat abridged form and without accompanying footnotes from *Business History Review* 31 (Summer 1957), pp. 143–178, copyright © 1957 by the President and Fellows of Harvard College; by permission of *Business History Review* and Barry E. Supple.

Immigrant Jews on the Lower East Side of New York: 1880–1914
Reprinted without accompanying footnotes and charts from "Health Conditions of Immigrant Jews on the Lower East Side of New York: 1800–1914," *Medical History* 25 (1981), pp. 1–18, copyright © 1981 by the Wellcome Institute for the History of Medicine; by permission of the Wellcome Institute and Deborah Dwork.

Germans versus Russians
Reprinted by permission and without accompanying footnotes from Moses Rischin, *The Promised City* (Cambridge, MA: Harvard University Press, 1962), copyright © 1962 by the President and Fellows of Harvard College.

Immigrant Women and Consumer Protest: The New York City Kosher Meat Boycott of 1902
Reprinted by permission and without accompanying footnotes from *American Jewish History* 70 (September 1980), pp. 91–105, copyright © 1980 by the American Jewish Historical Society.

Adapting to Abundance: Luxuries, Holidays, and Jewish Identity
Reprinted without accompanying footnotes from Andrew R. Heinze, *Adapting to Abundance: Jewish Immigrants, Mass Consumption, and the Search for American Identity* (New York: Columbia University Press, 1990). Copyright © 1990 by Columbia University Press. Reprinted with permission of the publisher.

The Jewishness of the Jewish Labor Movement in the United States
Reprinted by permission from *A Bicentennial Festschrift for Jacob Rader Marcus*, edited by Bertram Wallace Korn (New York: KTAV Publishing House, 1976), pp. 121–130, copyright © 1976 by KTAV Publishing House, Inc.

***Henry Ford and* The International Jew**
Reprinted in abridged form and without accompanying footnotes from *American Jewish History* 69 (June 1980), pp. 437–477, copyright © 1980 by the American Jewish Historical Society; by permission of the American Jewish Historical Society and Leo P. Ribuffo.

The Emergence of the American Synagogue
Reprinted by permission and without accompanying footnotes from Jeffrey S. Gurock, *When Harlem Was Jewish* (New York: Columbia University Press, 1979), copyright © 1979 by Columbia University Press.

The Jewish Home Beautiful
Reprinted without accompanying footnotes from *Getting Comfortable in New York: The American Jewish Home, 1880–1950*, ed. Susan L. Braunstein and Jenna Weissman Joselit (New York: The Jewish Museum, 1990). Copyright © 1990 by The Jewish Museum. Reprinted with permission of the publisher.

Zionism: An American Experience
Reprinted by permission and without accompanying footnotes from *American Jewish Historical Quarterly* 63 (March 1974), pp. 261–282, copyright © 1974 by the American Jewish Historical Society.

The Midpassage of American Jewry
Reprinted by permission and without accompanying footnotes from *The Midpassage of American Jewry, 1929–1945*, The Fifth Annual Feinberg Memorial Lecture (May 13, 1982), copyright © 1982 by the Judaic Studies Program, University of Cincinnati.

Who Shall Bear Guilt for the Holocaust? The Human Dilemma
Reprinted by permission and without accompanying footnotes from *American Jewish History* 68 (March 1979), pp. 261–282, copyright © 1979 by the American Jewish Historical Society.

A "Golden Decade" for American Jews: 1945–1955

Reprinted without accompanying footnotes from *Studies In Contemporary Jewry; An Annual: Vol. VIII: A New Jewry? America Since the Second World War,* ed. Peter Y. Medding (New York: Oxford University Press, 1993).

Jewish Migration in Postwar America: The Case of Miami and Los Angeles

Reprinted without accompanying footnotes from *Studies In Contemporary Jewry; An Annual: Vol. VIII: A New Jewry? America Since the Second World War,* ed. Peter Y. Medding (New York: Oxford University Press, 1993).

The Turbulent Sixties

Reprinted without accompanying footnotes from Jack Wertheimer, *A People Divided: Judaism in Contemporary America* (New York: BasicBooks, 1993).

United States Jewry—A Look Forward

Reprinted from *Encyclopaedia Judaica Yearbook, 1900–1991* (Jerusalem: Keter Publishing House, 1992).

INDEX

About the Editor

After teaching at Hebrew Union College, where he also directed its Center for the Study of the Jewish Experience, Jonathan D. Sarna joined the faculty of Brandeis University as the Joseph H. & Belle R. Braun Professor of American Jewish History. He has authored or edited thirteen books, including *Jacksonian Jew* (1981), a biography of Mordecai Noah that was nominated for the National Jewish Book Award; *People Walk on Their Heads* (1982); *The Jews of Boston* (co-editor with Ellen Smith, 1995); *Religion and State in the American Jewish Experience* (co-author with David G. Dalin, 1997); and *Minority Faiths and the American Protestant Mainstream* (editor, 1997). Sarna holds a Ph.D. from Yale University and is a recipient of fellowships from the American Council of Learned Societies and the National Endowment for the Humanities.